*Problems in Social and
Political Thought*

A PHILOSOPHICAL INTRODUCTION

Problems in Social and Political Thought

A PHILOSOPHICAL INTRODUCTION

Whitaker T. Deininger
San Jose State College

THE MACMILLAN COMPANY, NEW YORK
COLLIER–MACMILLAN LIMITED, LONDON

Preface

A recent English political philosopher, Professor T. D. Weldon, emphasized the peculiar relation of abstract concern for politics and society to the intellectual traditions of university life. What struck him is the fact that while in ordinary social life most political questions reveal a fact-oriented side ("How can we improve the committee structure in the state legislature?"; "What criteria shall we establish for selecting a new college president?"; "What measures can we take to reduce urban racial tensions?"; and the like), in university life the discussions of political and social matters are often more general in nature, often related to what men sometimes call "theorizing."

It is obvious that intellectuals seem to enjoy kinds of talk about politics and society which are not immediately relevant to specific issues. Given the intellectual setting of university life, questions which in practical life may seem pointless can sometimes make all the difference in the world. Historically, many men who came later to exercise political power received their educations at universities, suggesting that at least a contingent and indirect relation between university life and practical public affairs has existed through the actions of educated men and women among the official and unofficial leadership in society. Moreover, in modern university life, the advancement of the social sciences has increased rather than decreased interest in philosophical aspects of social and political issues. Finally, in governments which permit some exercise of rights and political action by the citizens it stands as a commonsense conviction that broad philosophical attitudes have an influence on the course of public affairs in the long run.

This book about social and political philosophy seeks to introduce academic readers to some perennially troubling topics, presenting what are judged as important types of argument and analysis. Its aim is not to produce a final synthesis between differing views, nor does it seek to prove that there must be one true way of philosophizing about social and political issues, although it is highly probable that teachers and students will want to disagree with some of the judgments in fact rendered in one or another chapter. Such disagreements are welcome. If the book expresses a viewpoint or a philosophical bias, it is probably the view that piecemeal treatment of philosophical topics is preferable to broad philosophical generalizations or syntheses. This need not mean that such comprehensive syntheses are unimportant but that, in the author's judgment, they should follow analysis rather than precede it, if they are to be attempted at all. The great philosophical "visions" so central to the history of Western philosophizing did not emerge quickly or without historical roots in specific cultures.

This book has three major aims. The *first* is to focus attention on a number of topics which have preoccupied philosophical minds through the centuries by presenting brief versions of important classical as well as contemporary treatments of these topics in a functional rather than a chronological manner. The *second* aim is to introduce readers to ways in which contemporary philosophers are discussing topics in social and political thought. Contemporary concern with language by some philosophers in England and the United States has produced some novel treatments of very ancient philosophical issues. The *third* aim is to present interpretations of some broad philosophical movements which have acquired importance in this century and have influenced thought about politics and society.

Of course, the embracing aim of the book is to stimulate independent analyses of selected topics in a classroom context so that, whatever methods a teacher may want to employ, a degree of intellectual clarification will result. Doubtless many teachers will want to supplement this book with readings in original works. To give just a few examples of how this might be done, selections from Machiavelli's *The Prince,* Hobbes's *Leviathan,* or J. S. Mill's *The Second Treatise of Government* could be assigned along with Chapter 7 ("The Sovereign State"); T. D. Weldon's *The Vocabulary of Politics* with Chapter 15 ("Language Analysis and Politics"); readings from Plato, Aristotle, Kant, or J. S. Mill with Chapter 2 ("Ethics and Political Thought"); and selections from Marx's conveniently available writings might be assigned with Chapters 12 ("Historicism") or 14 ("Ideology").

I am indebted to so many colleagues and former students for encouragement and criticism in writing this book that I cannot possibly name them all. Obviously, they share no responsibility for any mistakes I may have made here. Nonetheless I want to express my gratitude to a number of helpful friends and colleagues. I want to thank Professors Frank Ebersole; Robert Larsen; George Jones—without whose extensive personal library I would have been lost; and my close friend Herman Shapiro. Other colleagues have served as admirable models, among them: Sidney Zink, whose early death on Memorial Day, 1963, caused a genuine loss to philosophy; Philip Davis; Ved Sharma; Edward Madden; and Murray Kiteley. I owe much to the helpful guidance of John D. Moore who, in the capacity of critical but friendly editor, sometimes had faith when I did not. To Miss Elizabeth Epps I give thanks for the cheerful and competent manner in which she typed the manuscript.

Finally, I dedicate this book to my parents.

WHITAKER T. DEININGER

Table of Contents

PART I

Preliminary Considerations

CHAPTER ONE

What Is Social and Political Philosophy?

What are the boundaries of this subject? When intelligent and naturally curious persons first look into a new subject matter, they want an intellectual map by which to orient themselves, much as any foreign traveller often needs a map—even before entering a new country—in order to decide where to go, what routes to follow, and which purposes to fulfill. Also, a traveller may want to choose between visiting Country X or Country Z, perhaps thinking: "If Country X has many lakes and mountains, I shall go there rather than to Country Z, which according to the map is rather flat."

Similarly, many persons curious about problems in social and political thought and events may tend to think they want to study social and political philosophy, but want first to see a "map" of the subject. Thus, a potential reader of any book which is an introduction to social and political philosophy may believe he wants to read its contents and yet, after a cursory examination of some of its chapter headings, feel uncertain what the author includes in the subject-matter. Such a prospective reader might, quite understandably, want to ask the author to supply a brief but clear definition of the book's subject matter.

The Definitional Problem

The trouble with asking how philosophers have defined social and political philosophy stems from the notorious fact that philosophers have seldom fully agreed on any one definition of a subject matter to the exclusion of others. The history of philosophizing is marked by important differences of viewpoint about the aims and methods of philosophizing itself. Nonetheless, philosophers have tended toward one or the other of two extreme positions which may be named "system-building" and "criticism." Many philosophers have looked on philosophizing as an intellectual effort to produce a broad, systematic, general *vision* of reality (restrictedly, of social and political reality, keeping our immediate subject matter in mind). Such a quest after a comprehensive knowledge has often, in classical times, been known as the practice of *metaphysics*—a "science" (as defined by Aristotle) which seeks to lay bare the most pervasive traits of reality. The systematic philosophers often write as if they are "describing" a genuine reality which is accessible only to "philosophical" knowers. In contrast, the critical and analytically inclined philosophers often go about raising troublesome questions about the results of the philosophical inquiries undertaken by the systematic thinkers.

Fortunately, social and political philosophers can point with substantial agreement to a list of books devoted to the kinds of topics they most like to discuss and analyze. Scholars who hold to a variety of interpretations of the meaning of these books nonetheless tend to agree about their value as classics in the history of social and political thought—just as students of the drama, say, will always include the works of Shakespeare in their subject matter even if they happen to disagree about the relative merits of *this* or *that* Shakespearean play. Of course, on such a list of classical books some titles appear that an occasional scholar may question. For example, should *The Communist Manifesto* appear on the list—since Professor X may feel this is more a propagandistic than a scholarly work? Many arguments will probably occur if an exhaustive and exclusive list of titles is sought, but if different social and political thinkers the world over were asked to submit lists (containing, say, a limited number of titles) certain famous books would appear on a number of these lists and some, probably, on all. Even lists containing titles of different books would probably be found to include books whose contents concerned some fairly central social and political issues. Thus most lists would contain at least a few books concerned about political liberalism, radicalism, and conservatism, even if the specific books listed were different on each list.

What are some of the books which could be expected to appear on the lists of scholars concerned with social and political thought? Such lists would contain Plato's *Republic* and *Laws* (as well as other dialogues written by Plato), Aristotle's *Politics* and *Ethics,* Cicero's political letters and dialogues (like *De Finibus*), Augustine's *City of God,* Aquinas' political treatises (like the *Treatise on Law*), Machiavelli's *The Prince,* Hobbes's *Leviathan,* the second of Locke's *Two Treatises of Civil Government,* Hegel's *Philosophy of Right,* Kant's *Science of Right,* Bentham's *A Fragment on Government* and *An Introduction to the Principles of Morals and Legislation,* Austin's *Lectures on Jurisprudence,* Marx's *The Communist Manifesto* (and other writings), Lenin's *State and Revolution,* Dewey's *The Public and Its Problems,* and Weldon's *The Vocabulary of Politics.* This is simply a brief and illustrative list which omits many important books. The point is that any one of these books can profitably be read by a person who wants to know what social and political philosophy is about. The more comprehensive a knowledge he desired, the more he would need to read a number of these books. On the other hand, he might read a historical work in which the leading ideas treated in these books are described and perhaps analyzed in chronological order.[1]

Most persons curious about social and political philosophy do not aim to become comprehensive scholars in the field. Thus, presented with a list of famous titles, they may well feel a bit confused. Which one or two of the books listed might *most* profitably be read? Can a person learn more from Plato's *Republic* than by reading Weldon's *The Vocabulary of Politics?* Are some of Marx's writings more basic than others? Can a general reader choose among the listed books so as to avoid reading the poorer book if he has time in which to read only one book? Does any one book on the list contain more *truth* about politics and social life than do the others? It is doubtful that a person

[1] For example, Chester C. Maxey, *Political Philosophies* (New York: Macmillan, 1950), revised edition.

could find an absolute authority accepted as such by all philosophers, from whom wisdom of an unquestionable kind could be obtained in answer to such questions. The questioner would have to ask a specific scholar these questions and then decide whether to follow the scholar's advice. Were he to question several scholars, he might find that different advice would be given. Nonetheless, the questioner might very well discover that all advised him to read Plato's *Republic* if he has time to read only one book.

One might still wonder what, if anything, these different books possess in common. He might not be satisfied by being told about some of the books important in the history of social and political thought in what is loosely termed "the Western intellectual tradition" as usually studied in colleges and universities. Thus he might still insist on a general definition of the subject matter to which these books are said to make a contribution.

Now, philosophers have defined the subject matter of social and political philosophy in different ways. Some of these definitions are broader than others; some are "characterizations" of a field rather than definitions. Some of the definitions may be said to overlap. Among the available definitions the following may be said to be a representative sampling. Social and political philosophy may be defined variously as

- a quest after the most general, most pervasive human wisdom in social and political affairs.

- the analysis, clarification and criticism of what thinkers have said, and are saying today, about the nature and functions of society and politics.

- the creation of ideal standards and utopian schemes against which, as it were, to "measure" existing social and political institutions and values.

- that special branch of moral philosophy concerned with showing what ought to be the goals sought by men in their social and political affairs.

- the linguistic "camouflage" beneath which raw and predatory class, religious, social, etc., interests hide their ruthless lust for power.

- a critique of a legal order in the light of universal moral standards.

- any reflective concern about social and political affairs such that immediate practicality is not the major emphasis.

- the attempt to discover and to make precise the fundamental nature of Justice (Right, State, Equality, Authority, etc.).

- the attempt to use human reasoning to separate what is fleeting and transient from what is permanent and lasting in human affairs.

Any one of these definitions may in a general way help to orient a beginning student. On the other hand, any one of these definitions may lead him to ask for further clarification, especially if he happens to possess a critical intelligence. What is meant by "wisdom" (first definition), or "analysis" (second definition), or "standards" (third definition)? Indeed, in a number of these definitions what is meant by the phrase "social and political affairs"? Given any definition, a person may go on to ask for clarification (indeed, for a definition) of one or more of the terms which occur in the predicate of that definition. Here, two possibilities may be said to exist: either the quest for an adequate definition will end at some point or the process may in some sense be infinitely continuous. Some philosophers have debated just this issue through the centuries, asking if there are "real" (final) definitions which can be shown to be conclusively binding for all rational beings. However, since what is wanted here is an *initial* definition of social and political philosophy, to engage in a thorough philosophical analysis of the problem of definition is inappropriate. Many thinkers try to avoid the problem of definition by talking about the *kinds* of topics, or problems, to which a substantial number of thinkers in social and political philosophy have in fact addressed themselves.

Some Topics in Social and Political Philosophy

The books and essays written by social and political philosophers usually express something of the individuality of their authors, yet they address a finite range of topics considered important by these authors. Thus these books are, at least partially, subject to a topical ordering. Of course, any topical classification may distort the uniqueness of a specific book, just as we may want to say of a certain favorite girl (named Harriet, say): "Harriet's all girl—but in her own distinctive way, you understand!" This means that students should not expect from classifications more precision than their proper use allows. Take the instance of political classifications. If we are asked whether a friend of ours is, say, a Democrat, we may reply: "Well, he's a Democrat in the voting booth, a Republican when he handles his checking account, a Fascist in his relations with his wife and children, and a Communist with other men's wives." A topical classification of the inquiries of social and political philosophers can tell something about the subject matter. However, such a classification emphasizes a common intellectual concern shared by a number of thinkers in a field and tells nothing, in itself, about how these thinkers may differ in crucial ways.

Among the topics pursued by social and political philosophers, though not with universal steadfastness, are the following:

- What is meant by "justice"? Is this question philosophically meaningful?

- How, if at all, are legal and moral rules (laws) related?

- Is there a distinctive kind of political freedom, distinguishable, say, from social and religious freedoms?

- What are the ways by which to "justify" the fact of punishment?

- Does a political state require the existence of an indivisible sovereign power? If so, in what respects?

- Are there any universal human "rights"?

- Are notions like "freedom," "equality," and "fraternity" (so central to the slogan-writers during the French Revolution) logically compatible?

- Is the political state best viewed as a means to certain "ends" otherwise unobtainable, or is it an end-in-itself—perhaps more like an organism than like a machine or an association?

- Can social and political philosophy guide men in their daily decision making, or does this question reflect a mistaken notion of what philosophizing is about?

- What is the relation, if any, between the social sciences and philosophy?

- Do ideological movements—like democracy, communism and fascism—rest on differing *philosophical* "foundations"?

- Does the notion of a "social contract" (central in the thought of men like John Locke, Thomas Hobbes and Jean Jacques Rousseau) make any sense?

These sample topics read almost like the table of contents of a topically oriented book in social and political philosophy. This is as it should be. Either the list of topics temporarily satisfies a beginning inquirer, or it does not. So be it! If the list does satisfy, then an inquirer will (perhaps) want to know in greater detail how one, or several, of these topics has been treated by leading social and political philosophers. Reading a restaurant menu is like that, too, since the list of available fare is never to be confused with a meal itself. To learn how a specific chef manages to "translate" this or that item on the menu into a meal, a person must sit through all the courses and "do the eating" for himself. Similarly, a person intrigued by any of the topics central to social and political philosophizing must learn the kinds of arguments and reasoning which have been directed to them.

The Contemporary Intellectual Mood

Any inquirer lives in a specific intellectual "climate of opinion," including the reader of this book. What the inquirer finds important and challenging is, in part, a function of how seriously he is looking for "answers" and the manner in which he chooses to do his "looking." Probably an inquirer wants to formulate as comprehensible a "picture" of a subject matter as he can, hoping that when he has completed his studies the separate parts will "fall together" into a more orderly pattern than there seemed to exist at the start of his labors. Although he may not necessarily discover or create a completely finished system, the inquirer may legitimately hope that initially distinct topics in social and political philosophy will eventually "hang together" more readily than his first impression indicated they would. His knowledge of the subject matter may grow more *systematic,* even if it may not be said to fall into *one* system. This perennial search after a greater degree of comprehension remains a force in contemporary thought.

Nonetheless, a contemporary student lives in an age made somewhat cautious—perhaps almost dogmatically sceptical—about the possibility of satisfactory philosophical systematization. Western philosophers, both European and American, see leading philosophical movements like language analysis (Chapter 15) and existentialism (Chapter 16) as reflecting their proponents' deep doubt about the possibility of comprehensive philosophical knowledge. Some of the factors feeding this doubt are *external* to philosophizing; others are internal to the philosophical tradition. The latter includes the usual argument that, after long centuries of dispute, few if any philosophical views are universally accepted—indicating that tests usually applied in science and ordinary life to men's knowledge-claims are useless when philosophers disagree—that philosophical disputes, puzzles, doubts aren't *really* about matters of fact in any ordinary way; and the insistence by some thinkers that philosophy seeks to confront men with their human condition, giving them a problem rather than a solution or set of "answers." As a result, the great classical interest in system-building and synthesizing is, in some important philosophical quarters, at least temporarily on the defensive.

The loss of a rational faith in the very possibility of reliable philosophical descriptions of "reality" has resulted, also, from a number of happenings, both intellectual and political, which stand as landmarks in the history of the past one hundred years. These are known to most of us, but bear frequent repetition. (1) Relativity theories in physics (Einstein) and evolutionary postulates in biology have led to a host of scientific inquiries which are difficult to state in nonmathematical terms. Some scientists doubt that a commonsense "picture" of the universe is possible on the basis of the scientists' discoveries. (2) Psychology in both its behavioral (experimental) and Freudian (therapeutic) forms tends often to suggest either (a) that men's views of reality are the results of their social and psychological conditioning or (b) that these views are "projections" into *something-supposedly-out-there* of unconscious and often irrational wishes. (3) Twentieth-century wars, revolutions, and some severe economic dislocations managed to produce social consequences leading to (a) loss of faith in the powers of human intelligence to solve basic human problems without a resort to force or (b) dogmatic assertion of the truthfulness of specific ideologies backed by powerfully organized groups which often sharpen, rather than compromise, the situations of human conflict. (4) Some thinkers insist there is a fundamental logical distinction between factual statements, like: "The book is on the table," and value judgments, like: "The book on the table is worth reading." This suggests that, ultimately, any attempt to justify value judgments simply by an appeal to facts can break down, that value judgments are not literally true or false but rather tend to be "emotive" expressions. (5) Contemporary scholars are sophisticatedly aware of the fact that language has different functions. Some philosophers among them have become concerned about the possibility that philosophers abuse language. (6) Finally, the growth of scientific knowledge and the accompanying need of scientific specialization has helped to produce a lack of interest in philosophical system-building, chiefly because the knowledge now available about the world is too vast to be absorbed by an individual philosopher.

Consequently, today's social and political philosopher (like his interested students) must pursue his studies and researches in an era marked by cool scepticism and a philosophical "loss of nerve." The philosopher wants to generalize on the basis of the most authoritatively established knowledge available from the sciences and common sense as well as to relate his generalizations to real problems in the social, legal, and political orders of human experience. The question is whether in doing these things, a philosopher can remain a philosopher and not become, say, a social scientist or a "plain" man in the street. Can a social philosophy get beyond ideology? Most social and political philosophers, including those who never create a system, will be found trying to say something important about three general topics:

- *First,* the problem of what kinds of actions and events can be described and explained in the social and political spheres (thus, *description*).

- *Second,* the question how to establish legal and moral criteria for deciding between the possible uses of available knowledge in the light of better and worse "ends" or aims of human effort (thus, *norm formation*).

- *Third,* the attempt to comprehend and prepare for inevitable kinds of human defeat and frustration which may occur even in the best social and political circumstances (thus, *therapy*).

Conclusion

Social and political philosophizing serves other than purely practical aims. These great old problems over which thinkers have "broken their heads" for many centuries often attract one by their apparent obdurateness. Like a mountain climber, sometimes we want to "climb" them simply because they are there. Perhaps we hope to obtain a broader view than we can get while, daily, we are encamped on the dusty plains of routine, beset by immediate needs. Individual philosophers tend to be rooted in this or that tradition, in one or another nation or class, and often write as men who possess serious personal convictions about some of the issues they try distinterestedly to analyze. This is a side to social and political philosophy—its "bounce," so to speak—which must be learned from a fairly long and steady acquaintance with individual men and arguments. As the English thinker J. M. Cameron has written about this aspect of social philosophy, not lightly to be overlooked:

> The systems of the political philosophers achieve their effects in so far as they displace our customary centre of vision and substitute for it a centre from which everything looks new and strange. Who can view tradition in the same way after reading Burke? or the justifica-

tion of a regime after reading Marx? or imagery in political speech after reading Sorel? [2]

It is possible the reader who has read this far will still have misgivings about the subject matter. Such a person might feel he knows more about the subject matter than when he began the chapter, yet be convinced he should know even more than he does. Perhaps the author would, in this imagined case, be subject to the criticism that he has failed to make the subject matter as clear as a more gifted or differently oriented writer could make it. On the other hand, a troubled reader might think that he is at fault—that the author's introductory explanations were perfectly adequate, but the reader's ability to "grasp" them was inadequate. A third possibility might exist: namely, that perhaps no clear-cut subject matter of social and political philosophy exists either for the author or his readers. Given this last possibility, the reader may find consolation in the words of Ludwig Wittgenstein, a recent philosopher who worried greatly about what philosophizing is about and who wrote in a context where he pondered the exactness of concepts:

> One might say that the concept "game" is a concept with blurred edges.—"But is a blurred concept a concept at all?"—Is an indistinct photograph a picture of a person at all? Is it even always an advantage to replace an indistinct picture by a sharp one? Isn't the indistinct one often exactly what we need? [3]

An introductory chapter to a book such as this, which functions as a map of an intellectual domain, can succeed only in marking points of interest—calling attention to prominent features which in the author's judgment deserve a careful scrutiny. The creator of such a map cannot arbitrarily alter the "terrain" which the actual "traveller" will find if he undertakes a journey. What the map maker hopes, if he is mapping his favorite territory, is that no traveller will want to say at journey's end, "I'm sorry I ever took that route!"

---

[2] "The Justification of Political Attitudes," *Proceedings of the Aristotelian Society,* Suppl. Vol. XXIX (London, 1955), p. 100.

[3] Ludwig Wittgenstein, *Philosophical Investigations,* trans. G. E. M. Anscombe (New York: Macmillan, 1953), p. 34.

Some Questions and Problems

1. Persons who enroll in a specific academic course generally possess at least a vague notion as to what the subject matter will, or should, involve. Can you give a definition of social and political philosophy which reflects some of your own expectations about what a course in this subject matter should cover? Do you believe an initial definition of a subject matter is important? If so, how important?

2. Suppose you should overhear a philosophy professor say the following: "Perhaps none of the great political philosophers has presented a view which can be called literally true. Nonetheless, some important things are to be learned by a reading of their writings." Would you tend to think about such a statement that

   - it represents an intellectual confusion?
   - it is sheer nonsense?
   - it reflects the "death" of genuine philosophizing about politics?
   - it may be an irresponsible statement?

3. Imagine that you are asked to write out the six English words you consider the most important words for persons concerned about social and political matters. Which six English words would you list? For what reasons?

4. Do you believe a political philosopher should seek to present a "true account of political reality" or, rather, simply to clarify and to analyze the meanings of what other thinkers have said, or are saying, about politics and society? More simply stated, should a political philosopher seek to present a comprehensive "vision" or concentrate on critical analyses of existing views?

5. Can you mention some ways in which sociologists are sometimes involved in philosophical activity? What about historians? Political scientists? Economists?

6. Can any thoughtful person really avoid raising philosophical questions about notions like freedom, law, equality, justice, etc.? Discuss.

7. Should voters attempt to inform themselves about the political philosophies of the candidates who seek office? If so, in what ways and for which purposes? If not, why not?

8. Did you find the preceding chapter a defensible introduction to social and political philosophy? Be prepared to explain your position.

9. Imagine that you have just received a grant with which to invite professors from four different disciplines to a conference on the topic: What is political philosophy? What academic disciplines would you

most want represented? Why? Which renowned scholars would you want to invite? Can you anticipate how one or more of your invited guests might handle the assigned topic? Are there professors on your own campus whom you would like to hear on this topic? If so, why not attempt to arrange a panel?

10. Would you expect to learn some significant things about social and political philosophy by talking with persons who have had wide practical experience in politics? If so, who are some of the persons you would like to hear? Which deceased political leaders do you think you would like to have heard discuss the topic?

Some Suggested Readings

Berlin, I. "Does Political Theory Still Exist?" *Philosophy, Politics and Society,* Second Series, eds. P. Laslett and W. G. Runciman. Oxford: Blackwell, 1962.

Bogardus, E. S. *The Development of Social Thought.* New York: Longmans, Green, 1940.

Cowling, M. *The Nature and Limits of Social Science.* London: Cambridge University Press, 1963.

Mabbott, J. D. *The State and the Citizen.* London: Hutchinson, 1948.

Murray, A. R. M. *An Introduction to Political Philosophy.* New York: Philosophical Library, 1953.

Olafson, F. A. (ed.) "General Introduction" in *Society, Law, and Morality.* Englewood Cliffs, N. J.: Prentice-Hall, 1961.

Runciman, W. G. *Social Science and Political Theory.* London: Cambridge University Press, 1963.

Sabine, G. *A History of Political Theory.* New York: Holt, 1950.

Strauss, L. *What Is Political Philosophy? And Other Studies.* Glencoe, Ill.: Free Press, 1959.

Weldon, T. D. *The Vocabulary of Politics,* Chaps. I and II. Hammondsworth, Eng.: Penguin, 1953.

White, M. *Social Thought in America: The Revolt Against Formalism,* rev. ed. Boston: Beacon, 1957.

Winch, P. *The Idea of a Social Science.* London: Routledge & Kegan Paul, 1958.

CHAPTER TWO

Ethics and Political Thought

Men's political concerns usually reflect urgent needs and practical interests. Whatever may be its goal, life *is* real and life is earnest—a fact which comes as no surprise or important bit of new knowledge to anyone who has lived a few years, facing the cares and responsibilities entailed by living. *That* men do hold others responsible to act in certain ways, and are so held by others, is as much a social fact as are the basic needs of men for food, shelter, and protection from harm. Children must be reared and educated, bills paid, contracts made and met, conflicts resolved, emergencies faced and sometimes overcome in the workaday world of human activities.

Most men accept as natural that they have some duties and obligations at the same time that they possess some rights. To know what these duties and rights are, as well as to learn how to realize them, men living in modern societies need an enormous amount of factual information, some of which is gained informally, a part also through formalized education. To know how to solve many social and political problems involves learning "how to do" many routines—from entertaining one's employer graciously to getting a permit to build a house or knowing how to construct a budget for an entire state or nation. To solve most social and political problems involves finding out the relevant facts or knowing whom to consult as an authority on the facts. The study of law and legal institutions, history and the social sciences, and business and engineering and other subject matters aims often at the discovery of factual knowledge essential to the continuation of a meaningful social existence.

Yet, important as factual knowledge is, it has never been men's sole intellectual concern. Men have sought also to raise questions, such that if they should be asked about them: "Are the questions you here raise clearly factual ones?", they would sometimes have to admit they are not certain they are. There are kinds of questioning in which doubt or uncertainty about the meanings of the questions themselves may play an intrinsically important role in the quest for answers. If, as Socrates does in *The Republic,* someone asks: "What is justice?", part of the intellectual interest may reside in wondering just what, after all, is being asked in such a question. "Getting clear" about what is being asked may be a good part, if not all, of one's concern to unearth an "answer."

In the long history of Western intellectual inquiry, some men have asked general questions whose nature turns out to be troubling as questions—yet about which they act like men who judge the questions significant. When stated in general form, many philosophical questions look like straightforward ones, yet on analysis often turn out to be far from clear. Some of these general questions look like requests for definitions of terms or concepts, yet involve terms for which many philosophers are unwilling to accept a standard dictionary definition. When reading Plato's account of how Socrates worries about the nature of justice, a philosopher does not seek quickly to resolve the problem by running to consult, say, an English dictionary. The philosopher can always appeal to the English philosopher and mathematician Alfred North Whitehead's argument that in philosophical matters there is no perfect dictionary as a sourcebook for solutions to our philosophical inquiries. Philosophers have raised a number of questions which, if it should turn out that they are peculiar, the philosophers themselves treated as if they were nonetheless genuine questions. In this respect, social and political philosophers seem to have asked what appear to them to be significant questions. They have also indicated a common interest in a limited range of intellectual problems, even when they handled these problems differently. To some of these questions and problems this book aims to serve as an introduction in which some questions important philosophers have asked and answered are made clear and, also, what some critics have said about the philosophical questioning and answering receives rather thorough consideration.

Philosophical literature contains fairly detailed treatments of a number of general questions. Men who disagree about the answers, or who sometimes even doubt the ultimate meaningfulness of the questions, write like men possessing a common subject matter. Take away this central material—the central problems that have concerned a number of differently tempered philosophers—and one would find it difficult to get started as a social and political philosopher. The questions that have perplexed some philosophical minds include: What is justice? How free are men, actually or potentially? How, if at all, can men develop a rational justification of punishment? What are rules, and how if at all are legal and moral rules related? What is sovereignty? Is there a basic social contract which binds men together? Are there any natural rights? How are rights and obligations related? Do philosophers *really* understand what they are asking in raising such questions as the foregoing? Even a contemporary sceptical writer, convinced of the literal meaninglessness of such questions, must analyze their treatments by traditional philosophers in order to point out what is wrong with these treatments. Thus, an important twentieth-century political philosopher says about the traditional questions in social and political philosophy that "they possess some very puzzling features." [1] Other philosophers insist that the questions are perfectly acceptable—as questions which are sensible in their own terms and not properly to be treated as scientific questions. In any event, university life has often revolved about the asking of such questions whose practical import is often not clear and social and political philosophizing has played its role in the development of liberal minds prepared to try to follow wherever the arguments may lead.

Political Philosophy and Ethical Thought

Central to the great traditions in philosophy since the cultural achievements of the ancient Greeks are questions about the nature

[1] The philosopher was T. D. Weldon, whose *The Vocabulary of Politics* has exerted great influence in some philosophical quarters. (Hammondsworth, Eng.: Penguin, 1953).

and aims of the moral life. How thinkers go about answering the broad question, On what basis can men reasonably decide what makes acts good or right?, has tended to influence some of the things they say about politics and social life. Political and social philosophers usually tend to favor one of the major ethical theories when they seek to justify their views. Usually, they also write with specific historical conditions in mind, hoping to persuade their hearers to "see" the political landscape as they do, or to adopt their own judgments about it. Yet, like ethical theorists, their judgments often presuppose some general principles. Even their concerns about specific human problems (like particular revolutions or wars or social reforms) result in writings often thought to have elements of universal significance. Like some outstanding cultural historians, great social and political philosophers give reasons in support of their views. In writing about concrete events they make claims to the validity of their interpretations for epochs other than those in which they are writing. Such thinkers stand, so to speak, with one foot rooted in the concrete trials of their own times and the other grounded in principles said to apply universally to men's understanding of political life. They tend to make judgments about better and worse and, thus, to reflect the justificatory beliefs of one or another ethical theory.

Because what moral philosophers have written has influenced the ways in which political and social thinkers address themselves to their problems, it is important for a person to possess at least a summary knowledge of the leading traditions in moral philosophy. There are at least three such traditions which attempt to give constructive answers to the question, What (if any) is the moral criterion for determining the goodness or rightness of human acts? These traditions are known in philosophical circles by the names "teleological," "formalist," and "utilitarian." These traditions need not be considered mutually exclusive. For teleologists and utilitarians in ethics the most important words are "good" and "happiness." The formalist in ethics, on the other hand, is most prone to emphasize words like "right" and "duty." Teleologists and utilitarians want to know what is the good, while the formalist is concerned to analyze the notion of obligation, concentrating on the moral uses of the word "ought." While these three great ethical traditions do not necessarily exclude or contradict one another, nonetheless they do represent a number of differing emphases in ethical thought.

There are other ethical positions, of course; but these require no treatment in a work devoted primarily to social and political thought. Perhaps a number of these other positions can, for our purposes, be named "scepticism," though this word may mislead. These positions are called sceptical in that their defenders often argue that ethical judgments are not the products of reason, nor fully justifiable in terms of reason. One contemporary form of this sceptical position in ethical theory is known as *emotivism:* the doctrine that ethical judgments express the feelings of a speaker, who thereby hopes to influence the emotions of others. If such judgments are descriptive at all, they describe only the emotions and attitudes of their speaker—not an objective property of the things called "good" or "right." The sceptical position tends to argue either that one can't *know* that his ethical judgments are true or false, or that whatever truth or falsity such judgments may possess is psychological or sociological—true or false reporting on what individuals or groups judge worthwhile.

Teleological Justification

Probably the oldest of the great ethical traditions is the teleological. An influential spokesman for this position is the ancient Greek philosopher Aristotle (384–322 B.C.), who viewed politics as a crucial expression of man's basic nature. His two great books concerned with ethical and political analysis—*The Nichomachean Ethics* and *The Politics*—may be taken as arguing in support of a common thesis. The thesis is that ethics and politics are inescapably related. Man is seen as a political animal whose ethical capacities can reach fullest development only in regulated social contexts. The political state is necessary for the maintenance of ordered cultural conditions and the achievement of means by which to distribute those external goods without which an individual cannot realize his full moral development. In addition, the state functions as the means by which to establish proper relations between citizens by standards of justice. Justice is a social concept, thus inseparable from politics. There are two main kinds of justice: a concern for what is lawful (customary and criminal rules) and a care for what in particular cases is fair and equal (distribution of honor and wealth plus remedial justice between one man and another). The aim of politics is, thus, to make it possible for individuals to live in situations permitting their achievement of virtue through the exercise of their human capacities.

Aristotle's position is a teleological one in that it seeks to provide an understanding of the *purposeful* nature of political action. Action is viewed as inherently purposive, aimed at achievement: the doing of acts which "fall together" into a pattern with regard to some "end," goal or result. Aristotle does not mean that, for any one action to qualify as purposeful, the human agent must always self-consciously possess awareness of its purpose. What he does mean is that *in principle* any rational man, reflecting about his own or other persons' actions, can discern patterns which unite many otherwise separate, discrete acts into unities leading to the results to which those acts are appropriate. Suppose we take as an example of this position the action of a football player in kicking a point after a touchdown. Here, the context of the whole action involves innumerable acts which, if viewed outside of a teleological context, would reduce to such things as arm and leg movements. What makes the arm and leg movements components of an action is the fact that, if one asks the kicker *why* he is performing those movements, he can reply: "(In order to) (try to) kick the goal between the posts!"—although what in fact he will say is something like: "To kick the ball between the posts." To decide whether a kicker performs the action badly or well, we need to know what the aim is (namely, kicking the extra point) as well as many things about the most appropriate ways in which to realize the aim. Thus, we may say the kicker performed the action well even if, occasionally, the ball fails to clear the crossbar between the posts. He may have performed the appropriate movements well but failed to make the extra point. ("How so?" a perplexed reader may want to ask; to which the reply might well be: "Well, just as the ball left his toe, a sudden gust of wind blew it wide of the mark. There wasn't time for him to adjust his movements to the unexpected wind.")

Also, about an action which leads to success (say, kicking the extra point), we may sometimes want to say that an agent has performed badly though successfully. ("How so?" our perplexed inquirer may ask; to which the reply might be: "He was lucky. Nine times out of ten a kicker who performs as sloppily as he just did will fail to make the extra point.")

The notion that action is purposeful—directed to some end—need not entail that the performer is self-consciously aware that he seeks the end, for habit often makes such awareness needless. The point is that *if* the agent is asked why he does certain things, he (or someone who has the adequate knowledge) can reply by stating a purpose for the acts. In this sense there can be teleological explanations of human actions, as illustrated by a situation in which someone asks a person why he has just crossed a street and receives the reply: "To get to the other side." Teleological explanations answer the question "Why?", asked of any action, by giving the agent's purpose.

Similarly, for teleologists in political philosophy, the institutions which make up the state are to be evaluated as means toward the full realization of human capacities. To know whether political practices are sound means to know something about human nature as well as about the conditions which favor its fullest development in individual lives. In this respect, the teleological position in ethics and politics seeks to measure human actions and social institutions in terms of their contribution to individuals' self-realization. Since men are social animals having to regulate much of their conduct in accordance with rules and public procedures, politics becomes the organized expression of a cooperative human effort to build, as well as to perpetuate, those social environments in which human potentialities can become actualities. While Aristotle thought any state is logically prior to the individual, he nonetheless thought it needs to be judged in relation to its citizens' needs and full moral development.

This conception of politics and human action presupposes existence, in some sense, of what may be termed a basic human nature. That is, men are thought to possess some common characteristics which, in any social setting, lead to demands and needs requiring satisfaction *if a political system is to be healthy*. Contemporary social scientists who emphasize the permanence of basic human needs in a variety of cultural settings call attention, in modern terms, to what the classical teleologists meant when they insisted that all men seek self-fulfillment. Aristotle and others believed that men display a natural tendency to seek after happiness—even though the cultural means by which they do this can vary widely from time to time and place to place. By happiness Aristotle meant a continuing *activity,* ceasing only at death, rather than a finished state once and for all achieved—a state which could be dated and thus located like other biographical events. This activity involves the full use of all human powers, including men's ethical capacities. Without ethical development no meaningful happiness is possible, according to the famous Greek philosopher. Rather than seeing the practical moral life as an achievement of rare saints and eccentric persons, Aristotle thought it the potentially available goal of all men—men, that is, possessing average physical and mental endowments and not disturbed by overwhelming external calamities. Ethical self-realization therefore represents an achievement, yet one never completely finalized so long as breath remains.

The ethical life centers around the pursuit of virtuous activities. For Aristotle, the moral virtues were viewed as capacities or *dispositions*—tendencies to act in given ways. A man's character was made up of his dispositions. To say that a man is brave, or honest, or liberal means, thus, to say something important about his character and about his tendencies to act in expected ways in specific situations. The moral virtues are thus concerned with conduct. These virtues are acquired by long training and discipline. A man learns to be virtuous (brave, honest, liberal) by doing brave, honest, and liberal acts. Moral training is thus aimed at the creation and maintenance of stable habits. The ends of moral action are fixed, in some sense "given" or known. How to achieve those ends results from deliberation. That is, a man can use his intelligence to determine what means best fit a specific situation. The fully developed man is one who enjoys opportunities to act, among them those which permit him to exercise his prudential capacities for making decisions which fit varying occasions.

Coupled with the moral virtues are what Aristotle calls the intellectual virtues. The fully developed man learns how to use his intellect, seeking knowledge for its own sake. Perhaps a misleading but none-theless helpful way of putting this is to say that for Aristotle, as for the American jurist Oliver Wendell Holmes, life should involve both thought and action in some balanced way. This means that the con-templative life, as the highest or most valuable form of life, has great moral significance for Aristotle. What makes this conception of man a necessary aspect of Aristotle's thought is the view that any healthy man is *potentially* in quest of happiness, thus capable of a self-realization which involves both action and reflection. The moral life is thus viewed as an achievement made possible by the human tendency to engage in those activities whose culmination is the pro-duction of happiness. Aristotle was the Greek aristocrat in thinking very few persons capable of the truly contemplative life, while he had a more democratic view of men's abilities to realize a goodly share of the practical moral virtues. Nonetheless, his actual opinions in his own time—probably borrowed from his culture—fell far short of his ethical philosophy, for Aristotle believed in the *natural* necessity of human slavery.

Such a view of man and of human ethical activity has obvious sig-nificance for an understanding of politics treated teleologically. Politi-cal activity becomes the social means by which to create those minimal conditions for a community without which individuals cannot hope to realize their basic potentialities. Thus, the state is seen as a necessary means to the individual's fullest development—in this way is itself inescapably connected with ethics. The creation and the direction of states (of which there can be different forms, as Aristotle knew) is in part a human function. The reason is that some things exist *by nature,* others *by art.* Those things exist by nature whose immediate causes do not include human deliberation or choice—things like trees and the growth of the plants and the actions of the planets in their orbits. Those things existing by art are in some sense the results of human causes in that they could not exist were it not for an initiating human agency. Human decisions inevitably help to shape existing political arrangements. Inevitably there will be states, but *what* these states will be like is determined in great measure by the purposes and decisions of men. What men themselves do, or decide to do, plays a crucial role in the establishment of the economic, social, and political conditions which make up the specific environments in which human moral and intellectual effort can take place. From a teleological view of politics, *how* any state is established and managed affects the possible limits to men's moral development. No final separation between ethics and politics can exist. The individual always operates in a social situation such that pursuit of his private interests eventuates in actions having public consequences. The nature of the institutions in a man's society shapes his possibilities of moral development, especially insofar as those institutions provide him with an education of one kind or another. Therefore, ethical and political questions go hand in hand. Like individuals, states are subject to evaluation according as they do, or do not, encourage the full moral expression of their citizens' capacities. So enduring is this classical, teleological conception of politics that contemporary theorists can even argue that legal rules are subject to judgment in terms of their tendency to produce desired ends.

Aristotle's basic humanism is a moral one. Yet, as a realist, Aristotle knew that the standards by which reasonable men judge existing institutions (rules, procedures, habits) need not always be dominant in a given community. The standards may themselves experience modification and alteration. The life of reason itself requires nourishment, much as the body needs a proper diet and constant exercise if its potentialities are to be realized. As a background to his political realism, Aristotle holds to the humanistic conviction that, in all times and places, a basic human nature makes possible a reasoned criticism or defense of some of the more fundamental standards which in fact may happen to exist. His ethical and political views reflect what is sometimes called the *consequentialist* position: the conviction that the good is determined by the result of what men do, by what eventuates from their numerous acts. The function of ethical discourse is not simply to make possible talk about how to behave but an actual learning of how to behave. Education obviously must play an important role in aiding men to learn how to behave morally.

The teleological conception of ethics so briefly sketched here has enlivened the intellectual life of men in countless ways, through many centuries. It has played a stubborn role in disputes about the nature and aim of political activity. More than this, such a conception has—especially during times of trouble and threatened chaos—kept alive the view that, within limits, political affairs can be subjected to intelligent direction and criticism and that men are responsible for at least some of the conditions which either encourage or frustrate their natural tendency to seek self-fulfillment. The teleological position finds perennially meaningful the questions: "What are existing social and political institutions supposed to produce? What purposes are they intended to realize?" The questions themselves indicate the basic faith, though a reasoned one, that even politics is to some extent within men's powers to control.

The Formalist Tradition

A second influential ethical tradition is that which makes duty the central concern. Known often as the *formalist* position in ethics, and sometimes as the *deontological,* this tradition includes thinkers who worry about the problem of human obligation. They are thinkers for whom the word "ought" (rather than words like "good" or "happiness") holds a prominent place in the vocabulary used to discuss ethical issues. The formalist tradition does not so much openly contradict the views of the teleologists (indeed, there are at least formalist elements in Aristotle's ethics) as it gives a different emphasis to the inquiry into the nature of the moral life. Nonetheless, this tradition does contain thinkers who would sometimes argue that the right action may at times be one which need not lead to the individual's (or even to a society's) immediate happiness. In its most extreme form, formalism is a position in ethics which stresses the importance of an intention behind an act more than it emphasizes the significance of the act's consequences. Thus, the aim of the ethical man is seen as the doing of whatever is right. Such a view implies, though not strictly, that the ethical man will perhaps perform acts which it is his obligation to do in spite of some inconveniences to his own happiness. As regards this view, ethical analysis should pay attention to the question: "What ought a man to do?" It should do this in such a way that some acts may be obligatory even if they are not happiness-producing.

Against this extreme type of formalism some critics argue that *as a matter of fact* it can never be the case that doing one's duty can, in the long run, lead to an actual decrease in happiness. But this issue is not particularly crucial in this context. In any event, there is at least one famous philosopher, Immanuel Kant (1724–1804),[2] who has sometimes been interpreted as arguing that the intention alone makes an action morally right or wrong. This interpretation suggests that a man should do his duty "come hell or high water"—regardless of the consequences. ("Right is right, after all!" someone may be heard to exclaim, illustrating this position. "What?" a listener may ask. "Do you mean that it would be right to do an act which produces endless misery for men?") So there can begin an argument between those who think that intention alone makes an act moral and those who believe that the results of an act are what really count. Since the formalist position has been a long and important one, Immanuel Kant's views will here be used—though quite schematically—as one example of its expression of ethical and political convictions.

What the formalist takes seriously is that the rightness of some acts follows from principle rather than from circumstance. The ethical life involves subordination, perhaps even devotion, to moral principles. If someone argues that to every principle there's an exception ("The exception proves the rule, you know!"), the formalist can reply: "Perhaps so. But a principle which has too many exceptions to it will soon cease to function as a principle." Even if one allows exceptions to a principle, thus arguing: "Always obey Principle Y except in circumstances a, b, c," he implies that there will come a point at which no exception is allowable. At that point, the formalist will insist, what makes an act right is that the doer conforms to the principle. Especially is this the case with promise-making, even according to some thinkers who are critical of the formalist position

[2] The classical works in which Kant presents his major arguments on morality are his *Fundamental Principles of the Metaphysic of Morals* (1785) and *Critique of Practical Reason* (1788). Convenient selections from these works can be found in T. M. Greene (ed.), *Kant Selections* (New York: Scribner, 1929), pp. 268–374.

in ethics. A man who constantly breaks his promises, excusing himself on grounds that to have kept them would prove in many instances to have been inconvenient, will soon come to be viewed as unprincipled or, at least, as unreliable. If someone argues that a principle often is right but the times are not propitious for putting it into effect, then where will one propose to draw the line? It is to this side of the moral life that a formalist like Kant wants to draw our attention. To do so, Kant even uses arguments which suggest that morality has absolutely nothing to do with action but only with what men intend. In an important work Kant has argued: "Nothing in the world—indeed nothing even beyond the world—can possibly be conceived which could be called good without qualification except a *good will*." [3]

The psychological facts which the formalist in ethics wants to emphasize are quite easily recognized. They include the usual feelings of doubt and self-questioning which occur in situations marked by, first, a person's knowledge of what he ought to do and, second, a clearly recognized desire not to do the right. These are cases involving a clear conflict between one's desires and the obvious demands of obligation. Probably any person who is not completely lacking in feelings can supply numerous examples of such instances of tension between duty and desire. "Darling, I *want* to take you to the dance tonight," a conscientious student may be imagined to say to his beloved, "but I promised old Professor Killjoy that I'd finish my theme by tomorrow. I have an obligation to the Professor." Thus, formalists use psychological materials to argue that these indirectly illustrate how a central fact of the moral life involves dedicated pursuit of principle, sometimes at great cost and perhaps even for its own sake.

A difficulty attending such use of psychological materials illustrating tensions between duty and desire is that a teleologist can always recognize it and yet continue to argue that a principle itself often requires justification. Thus, even Aristotle realized that men can know the good without always doing it. In fact, Aristotle rejected Plato's argument that men do injustice only out of ignorance—a position

[3] T. M. Greene (ed.), *op. cit.,* p. 270; and A. I. Melden (ed.), *Ethical Theories* (2d ed.; Englewood Cliffs, N.J.: Prentice-Hall, 1955), p. 295. Melden uses the translation from Lewis White Beck, *Critique of Practical Reason and Other Writings in Moral Philosophy* (Chicago: University of Chicago Press, 1949).

which he thought contradicted our basic moral experience. Aristotle would want to insist that there will be times when men will have to say: "I knew it was wrong to do what I did, but nonetheless I did it." Aristotle will not accept the view that every moral transgression can be excused by someone's saying: "By the fact that I did it, I couldn't have known what I was doing." For Aristotle, the burden of proof would rest with those thinkers who, ignoring the common man's knowledge in this matter, insist that persons who know what is good will always do it. Thus, to emphasize the tension between duty and human desire (as formalist writers sometimes do) is not sufficient to show that what makes an act right is the principle behind it—or the intent of the moral agent to act in conformity with principle. Where, then, if at all, does the difference occur between formalist and teleological treatments of ethics?

According to Kant, the core of the worthwhile or ethical life involves action based on a pure respect for law. This suggests a rigorist conception of the ethical life, a puritanical model of human conduct. Some critics "see" in Kant's ethical formalism a reflection of his own Protestant background. Philosophically, however, the problem is much more difficult than such a summary interpretation would indicate. Suppose that what Kant was seeking to illuminate was not how extensive the ethical life is (or should be) but, rather, the question of *what makes ethical life possible* wherever there happens to occur an instance of it. Often, the Puritan is one who wants to transform all phases of human existence into ethical ones—a seeker after an elaborately and consistently developed set of rules, a moral code marked by its extensiveness. To say with critical intent: "Oh, that Harry Prune is a Puritan!" may mean, in one context, not that Harry has principles (scruples) but that he has principles where none are required. A sympathetic reader of Kant's ethical writings can argue that Kant does not tell the reader how extensive (or how limited) the ethical life is. Rather, Kant wants to show what—given any example of the ethical life—is a *necessary* feature of that life. That feature is the existence of moral principle. For the formalist, the ethical man acts in conformity with principle (law) because it is principle. In this sense, there can be no final purpose beyond the agent's acting because the principle of the action is right. To a critic who might say: "Yes, but to act in accordance with a right principle may sometimes bring disaster!" a formalist could reply: "Well, in that event if someone chooses not to honor the principle, all I want to say is that he chooses not to act morally."

A formalist like Kant seeks to make a meaningful distinction between what is prudent and what is moral—admitting at the same time that an act may be both. Kant seems to think that a teleological position in ethics can make sense out of prudential acts but not out of genuinely moral ones. Any act is prudent if it serves some purpose held by a human agent, if it does in fact tend to produce a desired state of affairs for that agent. A prudent man is one who, knowing what he wants, knows also how to go about getting what he wants (that is, understands how to realize his own purposes). Kant makes an important distinction between two kinds of judgments, one of which he calls "hypothetical," the other "categorical." The hypothetical judgment often expresses prudential considerations and has the form: "If you want (expect, desire, hope for) X, then (you ought to) do Y." The doing of Y is thus contingent upon what the agent happens to desire. Moreover, the doing of Y must be a reasonable means by which to realize X. The command (imperative) portion of hypothetical judgments is sound only if it is based on an understanding of those means which can actually lead to a desired result. If a person wants to act prudently, then he must know what he desires and also know how to achieve a portion of what is desired. Thus, the statement "A prudent man wouldn't spend all his money on present luxuries if he is planning a future trip to Europe" makes the obvious point that saving one's money is a necessary means to making a future European trip.

Yet, on one possible interpretation, Kant's ethical views suggest that no universal rule exists to the effect that one ought always be prudent. Indeed, one might argue that Kant asserts something to the effect that, if a man wants to be genuinely moral, then he ought not always to act prudently. There will be times when the demands of morality are incompatible with the requirements of what at least is ordinarily understood as prudential action. For example, a moral man adrift with thieves will "get it in the neck" for doing what is morally right. In such a situation, a man may confront the choice of acting morally or not. But Kant would probably argue that a moral man will never decide whether to act morally solely on the grounds of prudence, for he will "see" that sometimes the demands of obligation are clear and inescapable. Kant's ethical rigorism need not obscure the logical force of his central ethical point: namely, that the demands of the moral life can be stated in categorical rather than in hypothetical form. A categorical judgment has the form: "Do Y!" This is the basis of Kant's formulation of the famous Categorical Imperative, one version of which reads: "Act only according to the maxim by which you can at the same time will that it should become a universal law."

Reading Kant's ethical philosophy raises many difficult problems of interpretation. Formalists exist who, liking Kant's emphasis on the categorical nature of moral demands, want to reject his own apparent *absolutist* position that moral rules are unconditional—that is, are not necessarily relevant to the agent's natural purposes. But to argue that moral rules are categorical need not require that they be inviolable. The crucial point for our immediate purposes is that Kant thinks ethical life involves action in accordance with moral principles which are not principles solely because a human agent happens to want certain things. Such a view has important implications for social and political thought which touch closely on discussions of responsibility, moral freedom, and the justification of punishment. Operating as a broad background to Kant's ethical views is a set of basic convictions which have played influential roles in Western thought. Included among these is the notion that men are morally autonomous, free to live according to what ought to be done rather than according to what one selfishly may prefer; and a rough "picture" of reality which "sees" an inevitable gap existing between the objective requirements of a moral life and the available extent of the knowledge needed to realize it. Kant seems to think that historical men, men of bone and blood, can to a degree perfect their moral existence but never, this side of Paradise, realize it so fully as to bring the demands of obligation into complete harmony with the requirements of human happiness. Nonetheless, on this point, similar to Aristotle, Kant recognizes men's *natural* tendency to seek happiness.

Utilitarianism

A third impressive ethical tradition is known as utilitarianism. This is a doctrine which had its historical roots in fairly recent times, chiefly the nineteenth century, yet which bears some striking similarities to aspects of the teleological position in ethics. The utilitarians argue that happiness is the end of human action, but they show an obvious disquietude over how to establish the criteria by which men are to judge acts as genuinely happiness-producing. To the question, "What is happiness?", a number of answers might be given, no one of which would necessarily prove universally convincing. It is as if a man might say in puzzlement: "I agree that I want happiness, but how do I know *exactly* what it is and how to go about getting it?" To such a query, philosophers have sometimes replied that one simply "sees" or "knows"—and that's the end of the matter. To this query, utilitarians think they have a sounder response. Their answer is that happiness is a life in which there is an abundance of pleasure over pain. In the psychological fact that men tend to seek pleasure and to avoid pain, the utilitarians think they have found a basis on which to erect an objective, even something like a measurable ethical doctrine. They argue that men ought to do those acts which produce pleasure, both individually and socially. The early defenders of this doctrine were chiefly Englishmen: Jeremy Bentham (1748–1832), James Mill (1773–1836), and John Stuart Mill (1806–1873). The latter's views will here be used as an illustration of some basic arguments associated with ethical utilitarianism.

Utilitarianism arose, historically, as an intended solution of the legislative problem of how fairly to formulate rules to guide human conduct within a parliamentary political system. In making rules, the ruling body can refuse to justify its acts, saying simply that the rules follow from the power of that group which holds authority. Thus, a ruler (or a representative body) can command that certain requirements are in effect, stated in terms of laws. But logically men can ask of any command: "Why should that particular command exist?" If the rule makers show concern for fairness, its members will want to give reasons for the established rules. Utilitarianism functions as a system by which to justify the actions of legislators and, in its classical version, even judges. Acts are good and reasonable (as are rules) insofar as they produce happiness for the citizens making up a community. Since conflicts of interest will occur in any relatively free community, those rules will be good which, on the whole, tend to produce the happiness of the greater number. This may be interpreted to mean either that there occurs a greater total amount of happiness or that a larger number of people are made happy if a given rule is obeyed. Utilitarianism usually functions as a social ethic, since the justification of acts often involves a person in consideration of others' interests. There is thus an altruistic stance to the utilitarian doctrine, which can be used both to determine if a specific act is good or if a rule or a practice is so.

Utilitarianism is therefore an ethic of consequences. Good intentions do not constitute the core of morality. The reason is that one can imagine a well-intentioned "fumbler" who, though meaning well, acts frequently in such a way as to damage the happiness of his fellows. "That Charlie means well," an imagined person may say, "but he's like a bull in a china shop. Though he means to do well, he brings misery to almost every person and every cause he chooses to support." The utilitarian therefore insists that one must always look to the consequences in judging whether acts are good or bad. Ethics has to do with human action. Justice results from a concern for those actions which bear an inescapable relation to an individual's security. John Stuart Mill argued that ". . . the moralities which protect every individual from being harmed by others, either directly or by being hindered in his freedom of pursuing his own good, are at once those which he himself has most at heart and those which he has the strongest interest in publishing and enforcing by word and deed." [4] The sources of the sanctions of the utilitarian principle—that men

---

[4] From chapter 5, "On the Connection Between Justice and Utility," from J. S. Mill, *Utilitarianism* in *Utilitarianism, Liberty and Representative Government* (New York: Everyman's Library, 1910), p. 56.

should so act as to produce the greatest happiness for the greatest number—are conscience (the pain which results from one's knowledge that he has violated the principle) and fear of external punishment and, in political contexts, the social feelings of mankind. Thus, the tendency of men to avoid pain functions as a basis for providing a sanction for the principle.

Mill stated a problem which any half-thoughtful person can reconize. The problem is that innumerable kinds of pleasure exist which in fact radically differ. There are pleasures of the body and pleasures of the intellect. Probably most healthy persons want and need a balanced diet of both types. Still, reading a good book and enjoying a hearty meal are very much unalike. Similarly, some acts produce immediate pleasures which are intense, as is the case with most sensual delights.

> My candle burns at both ends;
> It will not last the night;
> But ah, my foes, and oh, my friends—
> It gives a lovely light.[5]

Other acts function as means to the realization of future pleasures, some of which may be long lasting. It also often happens that certain possible pleasures require a preparation for their achievement—as the pleasure of playing a certain game well may require discipline and training. If the standard of ethical conduct is pleasure (pleasure, that is, insofar as it can produce happiness), will not the lowest denominator triumph in a democratic society? Will not the tastes of the mass of men strangle those of the aristocrat and the experienced man? Jeremy Bentham tried to develop a calculus of the pleasures, by which pleasures might be rated according to their intensity, duration, certainty or uncertainty, nearness or remoteness, fecundity, purity, and extent.[6] He seemed to want a purely *quantitative* standard of judgment when what his critics realized is that often there may be a

[5] From *Collected Poems* (New York: Harper, Copyright 1922, 1958 by Edna St. Vincent Millay.) Permission of Norma Millay Ellis.

[6] By "fecundity" Bentham meant a pleasure's chance of being followed by similar sensations; and by "purity" he meant the chance of a pleasure's *not* being followed by "sensations of an opposite kind." *An Introduction to the Principles of Morals and Legislation,* reprinted in E. A. Burtt, *The English Philosophers from Bacon to Mill* (New York: Modern Library, 1939).

qualitative problem. The obvious point here is that two very different inquiries are covered by the questions: What will produce the greatest *amount* of pleasure? and What will produce the *highest* type of pleasure? To argue that something is worthwhile means to make a judgment about a pleasure-producing state of affairs, a fact which John Stuart Mill made no effort to conceal.

It is as if Mill wanted to argue that some classes of pleasure will, in fact, produce the greatest happiness of the greatest number. This position entails the view that pleasures can be discriminated. To answer the question, How can pleasures be so discriminated?, Mill suggests that knowledge of many kinds of pleasure produces an experienced judge who can tell which of several available (competing) pleasures is the better. He emphasizes the qualitative issue by stating a dictum: "It is better to be a Socrates dissatisfied than a pig satisfied." By so doing, he makes a *graded* pleasure the criterion of right and good acts. Consequently, some critics "see" that Mill reopened the whole question which Bentham's strictly quantitative criterion sought to answer once and for all. Now the social and political problem becomes that of getting experienced men into the legislature and the judicial chamber, who *know* which pleasures are *genuinely* happiness-producing. The political problem is now that of determining who is competent to apply the utilitarian view to practical affairs. Since in a democratic community any man may, in principle, be elected to a legislature whether or not he has the requisite experience and knowledge, in such a community the legislator may make mistakes in grading and comparing available pleasures. The quantity-quality distinction introduced into utilitarian thought by Mill weakens the scientific intent which motivated Bentham, who sought an objective and public criterion of human conduct. What Mill clearly understood was that, from the ethical point of view, the sentence "Frank Frolic gets pleasure from what he's doing" need not be inconsistent with the sentence "Yes, but Frank Frolic ought to stop doing what he's doing!"

Mill's democratic sympathies show in his argument that only something actually desired (by someone) can be of interest to ethical theorists. His aristocratic side appears when he admits that not all pleasures (or desires) are equally worthwhile. Yet, in one place, he makes the somewhat peculiar argument that the sole evidence a thing is desirable is that someone actually desires it. *That* something is desired gives us evidence that it may be (ethically) desirable, many a critic wants to point out; while the judgment that what is desired is desirable suggests that the ethical problem connected with the fact of human desiring is one of estimating the relative worths of different desires for various objects. Critics often insist that one's desires may represent a *claim* for ethical attention without necessitating the judgment that the claim is a justified one.

The social criterion ("the greatest good of the greatest number") dominated Mill's version of utilitarianism. If the interests of individuals should come into conflict, only those interests which further a community's general happiness deserve a legislative recognition. Mill insisted that the utility principle is as sound a guide for ethical decision making as any others which have been proposed in the long, indecisive historical debate about ethical justification. Unless an individual is viewed as possessing a right to protection from harm-producing acts—thus, obligating others in a social community to guard him in his right—men cannot picture a society marked by the minimal conditions needed for happiness. On this basis, Mill insisted that to seek for the community's general good can never result in a chaotic, egotistical scramble for pleasures without regard to the social consequences. Like Bentham, however, he thought that ethics (practically, rules and decisions) must be based on the objective fact that the human organism seeks pleasure over pain.

One aspect of utilitarianism that has bothered many otherwise sympathetic persons is the attendant view that, if the general welfare should be the consequence for deciding about the rightness or wrongness of acts or rules, then utilitarianism would justify acts of punishing directed at innocent persons—a charge to be considered in a later chapter. One could argue that innocents may be punished if the community will benefit—for example, by placing blame on "scapegoats." Critics wonder about the extent to which a society which would so punish innocent persons could be a just one. This is admittedly a difficult issue for utilitarians. Historically, utilitarianism has actually tended to produce an opposite result—the removal from existing penal codes of rules which are shown to possess no social utility. Thus, utilitarianism has functioned to "soften" the strictness of criminal codes, showing that a too severe view of guilt often leads to punishments which do not in fact produce a betterment in the society. There is no need to punish even guilty persons if such punishment fails to improve the amount of happiness of the members of a community. Still, this leaves the logical question unanswered whether utilitarianism permits the punishment of the innocent under certain conditions. One example often given, in some form, involves the (hypothetical) judge who—alone aware that a man brought before him is innocent—yet *knowingly* condemns him because he thinks the condemnation will avert a panic or disaster in the community. The example is used to show how a knowing punishment of an innocent person seems to run counter to our basic notion of human justice. A crucial question to be asked about this example is whether it makes sense—whether, if we fill in the details in a sufficient degree, we shall ever picture a case which will lead us to think the judge ought to punish an innocent man to make a community happier.

The social criterion of utilitarianism has kept alive the quest for an objective, impartial yardstick by which to measure the worth of a community's rules and to judge the actions of men in novel situations. Along with the teleological and the formalist traditions in ethics, utilitarianism has influenced what social and political thinkers say about topics near and dear to their hearts. The doctrine has sought to weaken outrightly metaphysical treatments of social and political issues and to turn men's attention to psychological, social, and legal facts as a basis for understanding human happiness.

Conclusion

Social and political philosophers often make use (knowingly or unknowingly) of one or another of the great traditions in ethical thought. They do this when seeking to justify some of their statements about the nature of the state, legal and moral rules, human rights and obligations, the nature of an ideal political system, and related topics.

In this sense, no complete separation can be made between ethical and political thought and analysis. Even thinkers who openly hold to a sceptical position—arguing that value judgments are neither true nor false but rather efforts to persuade others to a certain way of seeing things political—show concern for these ethical traditions, if only to argue against them. For this reason, any person who wants to participate in the philosophical discussion of social and political topics needs at least a summary knowledge of a few of these traditions—such as the *teleological,* the *formalist,* and the *utilitarian.* This summary knowledge should prove helpful for the later understanding of the arguments connected with topics which the bulk of this book will describe and analyze. One recurrent and fundamental general question joining ethical and political thinkers is: What (if any) is the necessary relation of ethics and politics? How this is so will become clearer in the following chapters devoted to more restricted subjects in the domain of social and political philosophy.

First, however, one major inquiry remains. The thinkers who favor one or another of the great ethical traditions often write as if they are giving *answers* to clear and important general questions. Assuming that the question, What is good? is a meaningful one, they answer in various ways, among them (as we have seen) that the good is an ultimate natural purpose sought by all men (teleology), the doing of one's objective duty (formalism), or the search for the greatest good of the greatest number (utilitarianism). Yet, for some philosophers, none of the available answers has proved absolutely convincing, or even satisfying. The reason is that some philosophers are uncertain whether philosophical questions as such are really genuine ones. Their position is that unless we can "get clear" about the nature of our philosophical questions, we cannot know that we have arrived at significant answers. For such thinkers, the philosopher's primary function is not so much the getting of adequate answers as the attempt to clarify the nature of certain (presumably) philosophical *questions.* Here operative is the view that perhaps answer and question are "all of a piece" in genuine philosophizing—that, in some sense, to know what the question is means to have solved or answered it already. Once one has found out the nature of the philosophical question, then he may on this view be said to have done all he can to give a philosophical treatment of it.

At the very heart of the philosophical tradition this issue received brilliant treatment. The famous Greek philosopher Plato wrote a number of dialogues in which Socrates, the central participant, may be seen as illustrating the philosopher's task by the methods he used in discussion. Socrates is pictured as trying to get answers to philosophical questions by giving attention to language and definitions. He seeks to illuminate what is being asked when men raise questions of the sort: What is justice? What is virtue? His method has influenced social and political philosophers down through the centuries. Let us now turn to a consideration of the Socratic method in philosophy as illustrated in Plato's *Republic,* paying close attention to its application to central perennial concerns of the social and political philosopher.

Some Questions and Problems

1. Do you think an Aristotelian, a Utilitarian, and a Kantian in moral philosophy will *necessarily* come to differing conclusions about specific social and political issues? Why or why not? How might a proponent of any one of these ethical positions reason about any, or all, of the following questions?

   a. Should a President of the United States enforce Supreme Court decisions which arouse exceptionally strong popular resistance?
   b. Would it be wise for this country voluntarily to dismantle its nuclear military capacities even without similar action by other countries?
   c. Is it fair to tax citizens' incomes on a sliding-scale?
   d. Should public employees—teachers, policemen, firemen, and civil servants—be allowed to form unions? Should they be permitted to strike for higher wages?
   e. Should the United States ever send military forces into a minor Latin American country in order to try to upset an existing political regime?
   f. Should genuinely controversial issues openly be taught and discussed in the public schools? Would you impose any limits?
   g. Is the government obligated to pursue policies to care for persons thrown out of work by the spread of automation?

    h. Would Presbyterians, Catholics, Quakers, Baptists, etc., necessarily act morally in political life? Would they differ as to what is meant by "morality"? Does religion make much of a difference in politics?

2. Assume that two powerful countries possess nuclear rockets aimed at each other. Would it make a difference whether their leaders were Kantians, Aristotelians, or utilitarians if a crisis-situation should arise? Would the ethical views of the soldiers actually manning the "buttons" perhaps make a difference?

3. Is it always possible for political leaders to act prudently without sacrificing principles? Can you locate some examples to use as a basis for your consideration of this question?

4. Choose several classmates in order to dramatize the following topic in a debate: *Resolved,* That the whole effort to make political life fit the demands of morality is a useless one foredoomed to inevitable failure. Make sure that as many persons argue against the resolution as for it.

5. Should persons who seek to guide their political actions by moral considerations try to deal morally with those who openly deny any relation between politics and morality? Will your answer vary with the political issues?

6. What would you say to a person who asserted that, in politics, belief in ethical principles is a mark of immaturity?

7. What might a President of the United States have meant when, referring to racial difficulties in this country, he asserted that American citizens faced a moral crisis? Are all political crises essentially moral ones? Can all moral crises be handled in political terms?

8. Discuss the assertion: "The greatest realist in politics is that person or party who brings moral principles to bear on the issues of the day and age."

9. Can you think of any political principles which are universal? Are they also moral principles?

10. Suppose you were appointed to determine a policy for constructing bomb shelters against nuclear attack. What policies would you pursue, and for what reasons? How would you determine whom to save by shelters if you were unable to provide shelters for all?

Some Suggested Readings

Aristotle. *The Nichomachean Ethics,* trans. J. E. C. Welldon. London: Macmillan, 1934.

Baumgardt, D. *Bentham and the Ethics of Today*. Princeton, N.J.: Princeton University Press, 1952.

Broad, C. D. *Five Types of Ethical Theory*. London: Routledge & Kegan Paul, 1930.

Hare, R. M. *The Language of Morals*. Oxford: Clarendon Press, 1952.

Bentham, J. *An Introduction to the Principles of Morals and Legislation*, reprinted in the *The English Philosophers from Bacon to Mill*, ed. E. A. Burtt. New York: Modern Library, 1939.

Girvetz, H. K. (ed.) *Contemporary Moral Issues*. Belmont, Calif.: Wadsworth, 1963.

Kroner, R. *Kant's Weltanschauung*, trans. J. E. Smith, Chicago: University of Chicago Press, 1957.

Mill, J. S. *Utilitarianism, Liberty and Representative Government*. New York: Everyman's Library, 1910.

Milne, A. J. M. *The Social Philosophy of English Idealism*. London: Allen & Unwin, 1962.

Moore, G. E. *Ethics*. London: Oxford University Press, 1958.

Mothershead, J. L., Jr. *Ethics: Modern Conceptions of the Principles of Right*. New York: Holt, 1955.

Randall, J. H., Jr. *Aristotle*. New York: Columbia University Press, 1960.

Sidgwick, H. *Outlines of the History of Ethics*. London: Macmillan, 1960.

Singer, M. *Generalization in Ethics*. New York: Knopf, 1961.

Toulmin, S. E. *An Examination of the Place of Reason in Ethics*. London: Cambridge University Press, 1950.

CHAPTER THREE

Socrates, Plato, and
Philosophic Method

To a question such as: What is political philosophy?, suppose a questioner received the reply: "I'm not certain I can give you a meaningful definition, but perhaps I can *show* you." The *showing* what political philosophy is would involve something like a pointing to an activity, much as a baseball enthusiast might introduce a novice to the game by pointing at some players engaged in baseball and saying: "See those rascals over there? They're playing baseball!"

To answer a request for a definition by pointing or showing means to give what is called an *ostensive* definition. ("What do I mean by 'rabbit'? Look, see that animal over there? That long-eared, bushy-tailed thing is a rabbit.") But how can a person give an ostensive definition of an intellectual procedure? At what would a person be able to point, except perhaps a philosopher seated in a chair, *perhaps* thinking? How can one point out ideas and thoughts, which aren't quite like men throwing baseballs? If philosophy is an intellectual pursuit, dependent on the uses of words and ideas; and if—unlike rabbits, ducks and baseballs—ideas aren't the kinds of things which can be pointed out—how is a person to satisfy a philosophical inquirer by pointing? The answer must be that political philosophers use words and ideas in patterns known as *arguments,* and that they tend to talk about fairly standard kinds of topics—perhaps even to show a common interest in a selected body of apparently meaningful questions. To give an ostensive definition of political philosophy would mean, then, to give *examples* of the kinds of questions political philosophers ask and try to answer. It would also involve the implicit argument that men cannot hope to understand some kinds of activity, including that of philosophizing, without actually taking part in them. This would seem to entail the peculiar argument that, at least in some sense, to understand a game and to play that game are identical functions.

"That's surely strange!" a serious listener might exclaim at this juncture. "Certainly, to define an activity and to participate in it are two separable functions. I can understand *what* baseball is without ever having to play it, can't I? Similarly, can't I understand what political philosophy is without actually doing political philosophy?"

Such questions from our philosophical novice are not patently absurd or nonsensical. Yet, some philosophers would want to insist an argument can be made that some types of activity are subject only to ostensive definition. For example, it is possible to argue that a person cannot understand what love is without actually loving nor what pain is like without ever experiencing pain. This might mean that verbal definitions can be uttered by a person who nonetheless fails to understand their meaning—a meaning to be understood only by direct experience. "Oh, words are often so inadequate!" we sometimes want to say when, trying to explain features of our experience to a very young person, we realize how inadequately our effort is proceeding. It is not so much that definitions cannot be given as that, in many cases, they are unhelpful. Why should a person be interested in defining baseball unless he wants actually to play the game, to hold a place on an official baseball rules committee, or to watch some games being played? Who ever wants a definition of philosophy who, at the same time, is unconcerned about doing some philosophizing? Thus, some thinkers prefer to introduce individuals to the *doing* of philosophy which, for them, may encompass the whole purpose of the activity.

In a number of famous dialogues the Greek philosopher Plato has left to the intellectual world a portrait of his teacher, Socrates, who is shown as having perfected a method by which to philosophize. Socrates pursues a method of analyzing philosophical topics, including political issues such as: What is justice? What would the ideal state be like? How are knowing and ruling related, if at all? This Socratic method, as it came to be called, involves the cooperative effort of several persons to render tentative "answers" to a specific philosophical question such that a give-and-take discussion occurs. In the discussion, presumably something gets learned even if no universally accepted solution to the original question emerges. It is as if a person might say about the dialogue method, used by Socrates, that there may be no final correct answer to some philosophical questions and, yet, one may still discover that some suggested answers simply will not do. More than this, however, Socrates sometimes emerges from the discussions looking like a man who has shown that some answers are better than others, even when at times they appear to go against our common sense judgments. For Socrates, philosophy involves argumentation such that, if a person gives assent to a specific statement, he must, if he is to be consistent, give assent to some other statement which is said to follow from it. The method he employed seeks to make men follow an argument to its conclusion, even if that conclusion should prove inhospitable to some of their most cherished beliefs. One substantial value of the Socratic method is its capacity to reveal consequences of beliefs which, in the normal course of life, otherwise intelligent men often fail to discern. The method often reveals how, given a specific definition of a term or concept, the definition involves consequences which lead men to reject or to modify it.

The Question of Justice

Take the question, What is justice? and supply an interested group of intelligent persons anxious to listen to anyone who thinks he can say what the definition (or answer) should be. By so doing, we have the ingredients which form the basis of Plato's *Republic,* a perennially influential book in which this central question gets raised informally at an Athenian social gathering and results in a prolonged conversation of which Socrates is the master. This conversation pursues many twists and turnings, yet always proves relevant to the central theme. Finally, in an effort to make clearer sense out of the original question, Socrates constructs an ideal state, hoping that men who "see" justice exemplified in a social setting will better understand what it is like in an individual man.

The discussion of the nature of justice proceeds in such a manner that a reader of the *Republic* is led to suspect there *must* be a position which is final and authoritative. Socrates shows how the question of justice cannot be settled simply by an appeal to conventional or customary definitions of the word "justice." What Socrates seems to look for is a universally satisfactory definition—a definition which is not subject to the specific conditions of *this* or *that* culture or historical situation. It is as if a participant in the discussion cannot legitimately answer the *philosophical* question by saying something like: "Here in Athens, Greece, we mean by justice such-and-such!" One reason is that custom or convention may be in error, according to Socrates— that there must be some more adequate standard for measuring instances of just behavior than some conventional "ruler" actually in existence. If no existing state seems to be wholly just, then perhaps by building up an imaginary state men can produce an ideal against which to mirror their own imperfect achievements. Socrates works diligently to avoid a resigned relativism of a kind which would permit numerous definitions of justice, each "justified" by the culture which produced it and whose members live by it. Socrates considers a number of definitions advanced by participants in the discussion. Yet, he does this in such a way that each participant is supposed to discover some inadequacy in his definition as a result of reasoning rather than of emotive persuasion or coercion. Only after a number of definitions have been found wanting does Socrates advance his own developed views about the nature of justice. Thus, a goodly part of the philosophical method used by Socrates consists in finding out what is wrong with specific arguments.

A pattern develops early in the discussion. When a specific definition is discarded, more adequate ones are sought and, in their turn, also found inadequate. The inadequacy follows from the inability of a participant to make the definition apply universally, without exception. In one place or another justice is defined as

- telling the truth, and paying back anything we may have received. . . .
- to render every man his due. . . .
- doing good to friends and harm to enemies. . . .
- doing good to friends who are good, and harm to enemies who are wicked. . . .
- what is to the interest of the stronger party. . . .

With each of these definitions Socrates has reasons for discontent. The basis of his dissatisfaction is that he knows the speakers cannot literally mean what they say—that they are making a mistake such that, once it is pointed out, they will want to "take back" their definitions. One's head begin to swim as he reads on, wondering: "When *will* I come upon the correct definition?" Often, the reader finds himself wondering "what the game is," puzzled by what Socrates is trying to prove, if anything. What can the point be to all this verbal wrangling? Why doesn't Socrates step in to clear up on the spot the confusions caused by other persons' definitions? Is Socrates able to present an adequate definition? Is anyone so able? Such troubling questions come to mind as the reader seeks to understand what is taking place in the developing pattern of philosophical discussion.

A reflective reader comes to "see" how Socrates makes one important "move" in several crucial places. For example, when a participant in the discussion defines justice as the harming of enemies and the helping of friends, Socrates wants to know if we should harm those we *think* are our enemies or only those who *in fact* are our enemies. Socrates introduces the problem of knowledge into the discussion. Since we may wrongly take someone to be an enemy, we may actually harm a friend if justice means to harm those who actually are our enemies. Would this constitute a just action? The answer must be in the negative *if* justice is defined as harming those who really are our enemies. We can wrongly believe that something

is the case—thus, can wrongly harm someone we believe to be our
enemy, who, in fact, is not so. The point is that a relation exists between knowing and doing what is just.

"Hold on a moment," a listener may want to interrupt. "Can't one
do what is just *accidentally?*" Apparently not, if Socrates' insistence
on knowledge is taken seriously. In any event, the point about knowledge made by Socrates means that someone would have to know
what is just about any instance of action. Even if persons may be said
to do just acts out of habit (an assertion Socrates probably would
have wanted to question), someone must be in a position to make
the judgment: "Those acts done by Sam, Sally, and Dagbert are
instances of just actions!" Given any speaker who renders such a
judgment, another person can ask: "Why do you say so? Do you
know they are just actions or only believe so?" The crucial point is
that men are simply giving opinions or expressing preferences—
unless knowledge is involved in the judgments. And if it should turn
out that Socrates has no convincing argument of his own about the
nature of justice, and that judgments about what is just are matters
of personal opinion, then there can be no point to the philosophical
discussion except that of piling up a wide list of such opinions. Also,
to show that any specific definition of justice is inadequate would
mean to show that someone else, for personal reasons, desires to
define it differently.

From the philosophical discussion in the early portion of the
Republic the reader gains a deeper awareness of the problem of universal definition of a concept. What had seemed possible comes to
look, if not impossible, at least extremely difficult. Philosophic
method works to turn what had seemed a clear and direct question,
subject to an unambiguous answer, into a troubling issue. Of every
definition rendered, Socrates asks "why," as if a speaker who knows
what he is talking about should be able to supply final and convincing
reasons for his definition. Yet, the discussion also produces anger,
especially in the dialogue when Thrasymachus—previously a silent
observer—bursts forth in irritation at the way Socrates seems to lead
other discussants by the nose. Thrasymachus thinks he knows what
justice is—thinks, too, that others know what it is until Socrates man-

ages to embarrass them by intellectual maneuvers. Thrasymachus also has the courage of his convictions. The passionate outburst made by Thrasymachus reflects many an ordinary person's sense that something important is being discussed as well as his suspicion that the method used by Socrates leads men to conclusions they do not really hold. Plato writes that Thrasymachus frightened the persons in the discussion when "gathering himself up like a wild beast he sprang at us as if he would tear us in pieces." The section of the *Republic* in which this event occurs is a dramatically important one.

> What is the matter with you two, Socrates? Why do you go on in this imbecile way, politely deferring to each other's nonsense? If you really want to know what justice means, stop asking questions and scoring off the answers you get. You know very well it is easier to ask questions than to answer them. Answer yourself, and tell us what you think justice means. I won't have you telling us it is the same as what is obligatory or useful or advantageous or profitable or expedient; I want a clear and precise statement; I won't put up with that sort of verbiage.[1]

What Thrasymachus does by this outburst is to imply that (1) either Socrates knows what justice is or does not know and (2) in either case, his continuation of the discussion is peculiar. If Socrates knows what justice is, he should tell his audience and put an end to the matter. If Socrates does not know what justice is, he is probably playing a meaningless game with the members of the audience. A characteristic Socratic response to the second possibility is that Socrates makes no claim to know but does want to find out from those who do. The purpose of the method used by Socrates, therefore, is to attempt to find an answer to a question which, at some point, the confident person claiming to know the answer actually lacked. Therefore, Socrates listens to those who think they know what justice is; and whenever he displays dissatisfaction with their views, he seeks by questioning to discover the source of this dissatisfaction. Yet, Socrates operates in such a manner as to help the claimant to knowledge to "see" that his claim is somehow unjustified—that he has not

[1] F. M. Cornford, trans. *The Republic of Plato* (Oxford: Clarendon Press, 1945), pp. 15, 16.

actually answered the original question. Even the irritated Thrasymachus makes a knowledge-claim, which is then subjected to Socratic analysis.

The knowledge-claim made by Thrasymachus occurs in the following way:

> *Thrasymachus*: What I say is that "just" or "right" means nothing but what is to the interest of the stronger party. Well, where is your applause? You don't mean to give it to me.

> *Socrates*: I will, as soon as I understand. I don't see yet what you mean by right being the interest of the stronger party. For instance, Polydamas, the athlete, is stronger than we are, and it is to his interest to eat beef for the sake of his muscles; but surely you don't mean that the same diet would be good for weaker men and therefore be right for us?

> *Thrasymachus*: You are trying to be funny, Socrates. It's a low trick to take my words in the sense you think will be most damaging.[2]

In such a way does Socrates, in the *Republic,* require a person making a claim to know what justice is to give his reasons and to participate in an analysis of his views.

Thrasymachus comes to grief in his position when Socrates shows how rulers can mistake their interests. Unless someone argues that rulers can make no mistakes, he is confronted with the possibility that mistaken interests will be pursued—some goal seems to be to the interests of the rulers when in fact it is not. Such situations frequently occur in human affairs, leading wise persons to want to make some such remark as: "I thought it was to my interest to take that job, but now I see how I was mistaken." Therefore, rulers must know what their interests are in the sense of being able, without exception, to separate presumed from genuine interests. This means that Thrasymachus must define justice as what *in fact* is to the interests of the stronger party. Yet, since Thrasymachus actually denies that rulers can be infallible, it then turns out rulers can do acts which go counter to their interests. The fact that acts are done by rulers, then, does not alone determine whether those acts are just. Thus, knowledge of

[2] F. M. Cornford (trans.), *op. cit.,* p. 18.

genuine interests is needed for rulers to do just acts. What is this knowledge and how can it be acquired? How can rulers know *that* they possess this knowledge such that, on a later date, they would not find they had been mistaken about their interests? Such questions are important not only for the position which Thrasymachus seeks to defend but for any view which makes a distinction (whether relative or absolute) between knowledge and opinion.

The Question of Knowledge

It is one thing to point out how a specific definition (or characterization) of justice contains deficiencies, another thing to present a more adequate definition (or characterization) of one's own. A contemporary writer has emphasized this fact by reminding men they do not score a goal simply by keeping another team from scoring. Thus, even if Socrates is judged to have succeeded in his criticisms of differing definitions of justice, he can be accused of having failed to win a positive or constructive philosophical victory. "Look, if I ask you how to get from San Francisco to New York City," someone may want to argue in illustration of this point, "how do you help me if you tell me a number of ways *how not* to get there?" To such a plea we may reply: "We have at least kept you from getting lost needlessly. Indeed, you may even decide to stay in San Francisco!" The difficulty is that, in the matter of asking what justice means, many persons will judge a position inadequate which sometimes seems to imply that no one really knows. Readers of the *Republic* (as of some other dialogues written by Plato) often suspect that Socrates cannot be in earnest when he portrays himself as ignorant, seeking merely to find out what others claim to know when, for instance, they bring forth definitions of justice. Yet in the *Republic* Socrates eventually tries to characterize, if not to define, the nature of justice. He does this by sketching his vision of an ideal state—one in which three major social classes, each possessing a distinctive function, operate to produce a harmonious whole.

The argument is that, in the individual soul, elements analogous to the social functions exist which, when properly functioning, produce an integrated personality—a human person whose rational, emotive, and appetitive capacities do not war with each other. Socrates' purpose seems to be to indicate what justice is by considering social and political life and organization. An ideally ordered state could then serve as a model by which to measure the relative degrees of justice found in actual, nonideal states as well as, by analogy, in individual persons. Justice in states and in individuals turns out as a peculiarly appropriate relation between distinctive parts or functions. The implication is that to know what justice is like, one must know what functions social classes ideally should possess and how the major functions of the human soul can most fully be realized in an individual life. Justice becomes, then, a kind of harmony, balance, proportion of the distinctive parts.

Socrates makes a crucial distinction between believing and knowing—that is, between believing that something is the case and knowing that something is the case. Either men can know what justice is, or they cannot. Unless they can *know*—as contrasted with guessing, hoping they know, or believing—their conception of justice can always be challenged by that conception held by someone else. What Socrates seems to want is an absolute knowledge which, used as a standard for judgment, can be applied with confidence in different times and places. According to this view, to know that something is the case means to possess certainty of a very special kind—a certainty based on unchanging properties of things and relations objectively in existence, discovered by, but independent of, the mind. Unless men can know with certainty what justice is, Socrates fears they must continue to wallow in the possibly chaotic and surely relativistic realm of opinion.

Contemporary writers, many if not most of whom would reject the notion that men can possess absolute knowledge, point out a significant difference in the logic of the phrases "I know that something is the case" and "I believe that something is the case." If a person says "I believe the book is on the table" only to find out, later, he has been mistaken, he will then say: "I was mistaken, but still I *believed* (then) the book was on the table." On the other hand, if a person says "I know the book is on the table" and learns he has made a mistake, he will *not* (then) say: "I made a mistake, but nonetheless I *knew* the book was there." Of course, it may be the case that knowledge is merely a certain order of belief—that men have nothing but beliefs and should substitute "I believe . . . (firmly, weakly, fairly confidently, etc.)" for the phrase "I know." But for Socrates this would not constitute knowledge, since he sometimes leads men to agree they believe something to be the case which turns out to be erroneous. Yet Socrates is portrayed by Plato as thinking it possible for men to come to know what justice is. In the *Republic* Socrates argues that an ideal state can become actualized only when, or if, a philosopher becomes the ruler. What qualifies a philosopher-king to rule is his possession of a unique knowledge of the good. To know what justice is a person must become a philosopher. The mark of being a philosopher is not something external (determined by holding a learned degree, say) but the actual possession of knowledge lacking to most men. Socrates introduces the notion of the good to illustrate why the earlier quest for definitions failed. The men who rendered the definitions lacked the proper knowledge. They had notions of what justice is, but they did not have knowledge. Perhaps an imaginative dialogue between two persons centering on the question "What is justice?" will summarize what has been written to this point as well as dramatize how Socrates seeks for a special *kind* of definition.

Puzzled: What is justice?

Friend: I can't answer your question until I know better what you're asking, if anything. Can you clear up for me what you're asking?

Puzzled: I'm not sure. If I were, I wouldn't ask.

Friend: You know the word "justice," of course. Isn't that so?

Puzzled: Yes, but I want to know what it means.

Friend: Look it up in the dictionary and stop all this stewing about over nothing!

Puzzled: No, no. That's not what I want. I want to know what justice *really* means. I'm not interested just in the dictionary.

Friend: Is there something wrong with the dictionary and its definitions?

Puzzled: Not for its purposes. But suppose the dictionary is wrong!

Friend: How so?

Puzzled: Suppose the people who made up the dictionary, or those whose uses of the word "justice" form the basis for the dictionary definitions, are in error?

Friend: You mean, how are we to judge the dictionary . . . or among different dictionaries? How can we find out whether the dictionary definitions are correct?

Puzzled: Something like that, yes. The dictionary contains meanings of words used by people in a specific culture. These meanings can even change, though slowly.

Friend: Now I understand! You want to know the *real* meaning of justice, not just what English-speaking people, say, happen to mean by it at a given time.

Puzzled: Yes. Something like that is what I have in mind. What *is* justice? That's what I want to know.

Against Socrates, in the *Republic,* one could say that a questioner who had absolutely *no* idea what justice is would never be able to get started. ("Do you mean you have no idea at all, really? Where were you raised?") Because Socrates is portrayed as a man unable finally to produce an adequate definition of justice need not lead readers to believe he had no moral convictions. From numerous textual contexts we know that he had. He is convinced, for example, that it is better to suffer than to cause suffering—that some men *know* moral truths more adequately than others—that an "inner voice" (his *daemon*) tells him what not to do even when often he does not know exactly what to do (not doing something may even be a peculiar form of "doing" if the temptation is to do what one judges to be wrong)—that knowing what justice is can never be just like knowing ordinary facts (like knowing what and where tables and chairs are). Rather, Socrates is a man who has a peculiar *intellectual* problem. He wants proof, demonstration, definition of a special kind. When he fails to obtain these, does he thus fail to know what justice is? Isn't it possible that he knows but can't demonstrate? Socrates uses a method which judges the intellectual justifications of men's beliefs. The method shows how difficult it is to give adequate definitions of important concepts, yet Socrates himself indicates that men can know the good even if *what* is so known is not subject to adequate definition. To read the *Republic* as solely a criticism of men's claims to knowledge, especially moral knowledge, would mean to read it as arguing for the view that men cannot in any sense know what they are unable to define or demonstrate. It is possible that Socrates thinks men do know what justice is in some cases, but are nonetheless in possession of a kind of knowledge which is not amenable to real definition.

This question about when, and under what circumstances, men can be said to have knowledge has troubled philosophers over long centuries. The question is not only *whether* men possess genuine knowledge but, if they do, whether they can *show* why it is that what they possess *is* knowledge. It is always possible to argue that one knows but can't prove; and certainly, in the *Republic,* what the philosopher-king knows in knowing the good can't be proved to those who aren't themselves philosopher-kings. Thus, the philosophical problem is one of *justification* of claims to knowledge. Are we to believe that men cannot know at all, or that they cannot know *unless* they can always demonstrate how it is that they know something to be the case? Some philosophers have argued, among other doctrines, that men cannot (really) know an external world exists. How is this to be taken? Are such philosophers denying that an external world exists or that they can prove it exists? Or, on the contrary, are such philosophers pointing out how something independently known (namely, that an external world exists) is not the kind of knowledge which can be demonstrated? Similarly, to conclude that men cannot know what justice is because each and every definition of it carries difficulties would mean to disregard that portion of Plato's *Republic* in which philosopher-kings are portrayed as knowing the good.

Many readers of the *Republic* agree that Socrates attributes a unique kind of knowledge to the philosopher-king. Apparently, the philosopher-king is not simply a man who knows, say, how to win elections or how to manage the practical details of running a government. Rather, what he knows are the ends most worthy of pursuit. This is a knowledge of what *ought* to be done—thus, a knowledge about ideals and values. It is, as one will discover on a single reading of the *Republic,* the surest kind of knowledge—absolute, certain, even eternal. Knowing what justice is, then, is knowing what the good is—a kind of knowing which cannot be reduced to adequate definition.

"Where does the philosopher-king learn this knowledge—and from whom?" any perceptive reader will now want to ask. "How can one little human head hold such amazing knowledge?"

The Philosopher-King

Having political knowledge usually means knowing how to organize and manage practical affairs. A goodly portion of such knowledge is concerned with how to get things done. The "getting things done" can refer to an enormously diversified set of practical operations. Much of it concerns what may be termed "administrative functions"—specialized knowledge of a type which can be learned in academic institutions or through "on-the-job" training. Practical politicians in modern times put to sound use wide ranges of knowledge—psychological, economic, sociological, military, scientific, and the like. Yet, this is not the kind of knowledge to which Socrates refers when he talks about that which could make a man into a philosopher-king. In fact, Socrates finds great difficulty in trying to characterize philosophical knowledge. He is driven to the use of analogies in showing features of the philosopher's political knowledge or wisdom. In the *Republic* Socrates uses a number of political analogies in an effort to make understandable what cannot, on one view, adequately be defined.

According to Socrates, the philosopher-king's knowledge is *like* the kinds of knowing possessed by practitioners of technical arts and crafts.[3] Socrates gives numerous examples, among them some taken from navigation, others from medicine, mathematics, and music. Thus,

[3] A contemporary English philosopher, now lecturing at Cambridge University, has written a suggestive essay on this topic: Renford Bambrough, "Plato's Political Analogies," in Peter Laslett, ed., *Philosophy, Politics and Society* (First Series; New York: Macmillan, 1956).

a ship's captain is one who knows how to run a ship well; a musician how to produce harmonious sounds (melodies); a doctor how to heal the sick (to bring a sick body to a state of health); a shepherd how to tend his flock; a mathematician how to order arithmetical relations. Analogously, a philosopher-king is said to know how to rule *well*—that is, he is said to know how to direct political affairs much as craftsmen know how to produce the proper results of their crafts. Like craftsmen, then, the philosopher-king brings about a desired state of affairs by virtue of a special knowledge. Here, of course, the analogy between ordinary crafts and ruling breaks down, since what the philosopher-king knows is *what is worthwhile*. Nonetheless, he is seen as ruling well because of something he knows which other men do not know.

Plato's portrayal of Socrates as a man who argues for a specialized political wisdom in the philosopher-king has led many sensitive readers to note an essentially undemocratic consequence of his political philosophy. The craftsman works on available materials to bring a certain form out of them. More than this, the materials (ships, sheep, bodies, sounds, arithmetical symbols) are unable to resist—to answer back, so to speak. Analogously, if the philosopher-king is viewed as a superior kind of (political) craftsman, he must work on human materials which *should not* answer back. Lacking knowledge, they are not qualified to speak. If the philosopher-king knows what is politically required—knows, in other words, the genuine interests of his political subjects—he should direct politics to the proper ends even if, mistakenly (because they lack his knowledge), the subjects think their interests are other than what the philosopher knows them to be. The philosopher-king does not achieve his political knowledge by asking subjects what their interests are. He already possesses this knowledge, by virtue of which he directs his subjects to the proper ends. A philosopher-king must, then, at times resist the mistakenly conceived interests—as seen by his subjects—for their own better welfare. To the extent political rule involves knowledge of what should be done—that is, of what is required—there is little point in asking citizens to vote on the issues. Only those who possess the requisite knowledge *could* know the grounds on which, if politics is exclusively a matter of knowledge, a vote ought to be cast. Similarly, the knowledge of the philosopher-king obligates him to resist the pressures exerted by those human elements in a community which confuse their own immediate desires with what, objectively, is good for the situation.

The political analogies used by Plato, in the *Republic,* do tend to illuminate the sense in which politics need not be simply an arbitrary power struggle, composed of unreasoned and even unreasoning demands and decisions. They dramatize the sense in which ruling well is an art that requires men to make judgments of better and worse, of what ought to be the case rather than simply of what is the case. Yet, Socrates is pictured as believing that the knowledge required for wise political rule is quite distinct from ordinary knowledge. It is a knowledge hard to come by, apparently knowable by a very few. Socrates says that political affairs tend to influence a philosopher to want to hide himself behind a wall—a circumstance which suggests that past and present political affairs leave much to be desired. Such affairs will be improved only when, and if, a philosopher-king actually gains the power to rule—a possibility Socrates never predicts *will* occur. As a result, the political analogies in the *Republic* are ultimately unhelpful to someone who takes seriously the argument that there is a knowable object, called the good. Apparently a person already has to possess knowledge of the good to qualify as a philosopher—meaning that a person who lacks such knowledge has no way of separating the genuine philosophers from the frauds who come forward claiming to have this knowledge. The average man must, then, simply accept the claims of the philosopher-king (assuming his existence) and can never, on his own, understand those claims unless he, too, becomes a philosopher.

At this point a wary student may want to remark something to the effect: "I've known a number of philosophers—persons who teach subjects like logic, ethics, and metaphysics. Some of these are kind and even good men. Others, however . . . well, I'm not so sure about them. But, most of the philosophers I've known seem very far removed from knowing much about active politics. Some of them don't seem practical enough to get their hair cut on time. If they appear knowledgeable about politics, it's because they also know some history, business practices, economics, and the like. As a matter of fact, their philosophical interests seem to disqualify them for ruling. Much of the time they're lost in philosophical researches in an Ivory Tower!"

In the *Republic* the problem of knowledge of the good is a serious one. Someone who possesses this commands a knowledge which is self-authenticating. That means that the philosopher not only knows but *knows that* he knows, even if he finds himself alone or in a small minority. In no usual manner can he communicate his knowledge to the uninformed. He has the knowledge and that's all there is to it, even if—when asked to prove that he has it—he cannot submit himself to a standard battery of tests, objective or otherwise. What he knows, apparently, is not simply how his or other states are actually governed (a matter for factual inquiry) but, rather, how they ought to be governed. And this does not simply reduce to philosophical opinion, according to Socrates. Rather, it is a certain knowledge without which any ruler must continue to "muddle about" in his attempts to manage human affairs. This muddling about done by competent, practical, run-of-the-mill politicians fills Socrates with deep anxiety. *Their* muddling prompts him to seek for a better means by which to conduct political affairs. Perhaps in modern terms Socrates is seeking for the distinction between the politician and the statesman, in a context in which it is assumed the statesman functions by virtue of a special competency or knowledge.

The trouble is that though statesmen may be said to know more about politics than the politician—also perhaps to have a more exalted view of men and events—nonetheless someone may argue that we cannot train statesmen in any certain way. We can feel gratitude if some exist without knowing how to prepare them in advance. On the other hand, if a person knows some branch of economics, say, he can be examined; and if repeatedly he gets poor scores, he can be told that he lacks the knowledge he has perhaps claimed to possess. Similarly for men who claim to know something about subjects like mathematics, the biological or physical sciences, history, home cookery, or public administration. We can test them by using experts—persons who have achieved their status by acquiring public kinds of knowledge which can be taught to others. Their knowledge is based on something normally called evidence and logic. But who can test Plato's philosopher-king except another philosopher-king, and how can those who lack the knowledge recognize the philosopher-king? The kind of knowledge a philosopher-king would possess must lack all ordinary marks of what men *normally* call knowledge. It is certain and incommunicable. Such a ruler can tell us how we ought to act—can even make us so act if he holds power—but he cannot explain to nonphilosophers how he knows if, in a sceptical vein, we ask for the credentials of his knowledge. "I have 'seen' the object, the good," he can tell us; and we can accept his word. But that does not mean we can understand what it is he has seen.

A contemporary writer has found Plato's political analogies illuminating but vague. In the instance of the ship's navigator, in which the philosopher-king is said to know how to direct well the ship of state as the captain manages a sailing vessel, no distinction is made between the technical competency to run the ship and the deeper problem of deciding its destination. A democratically oriented thinker can argue that only the people should determine *where* the state should seek to end (what goals and policies it should pursue) and, having done so, delegate power to officials to see that it seeks the end. Professor Renford Bambrough has written:

> The point can be put in the familiar terms of ends and means. Plato represents a question about what is to be done (as an end) as if it were very like a question about what is to be done (as a means) in order to achieve some given or agreed end. He obscures the fact that, in politics as well as at sea, the theoretical knowledge and the practical ability of the navigator do not come into play until the destination has been decided upon; and although navigators may have their own preferences for particular destinations, these preferences have no special status, and are neither better nor worse than those of their masters. It follows that the democrat can state his anti-Platonic case in terms of Plato's analogy.[4]

Yet, Plato's main point was that the philosopher-king should be likened to a navigator who knows *where* to direct the ship. And it is

[4] Renford Bambrough, *op. cit.*, p. 105.

this knowledge which seems to disqualify customers (citizens) from choosing the destination and *then* picking a navigator to get them where they want to go.

So, given the fact of an existing philosopher-king, the ruler will know what is best. This will be the case even if others cannot know *that* he knows. This is one reason why Socrates is portrayed as doubting that a philosopher will ever become a ruler, although he does not say this is an absolute impossibility. In a state ruled by a philosopher-king, in Socrates' view, "Our institutions would be the best, if they could be realized, and to realize them, though hard, is not impossible." Nonetheless Socrates is pessimistic, for of those who might under proper conditions become philosophers he writes:

> One who has joined this small company and tasted the happiness that is their portion; who has watched the frenzy of the multitude and seen that there is no soundness in the conduct of public life, nowhere an ally at whose side a champion of justice could hope to escape destruction; but that, like a man fallen among wild beasts, if he should refuse to take part in their misdeeds and could not hold out alone against the fury of all, he would be destined, before he could be of any service to his country or his friends, to perish, having done no good to himself or to anyone else—one who has weighed all this keeps quiet and goes his own way, like the traveller who takes shelter under a wall from a driving storm of dust and hail; and seeing lawlessness spreading on all sides, is content, if he can keep his hands clean from iniquity while this life lasts, and when the end comes take his departure, with good hopes, in serenity and peace.[5]

If Socrates is too pessimistic, and if a philosopher-king should in fact become a ruler, we need to understand that he will rule by decision rather than by laws. For every conceivable situation his knowledge of the good will qualify him to know what is best. His decisions can be conveyed by language to his subjects or citizens, who in turn can obey them if they accept his authority. The philosopher-king can use his knowledge and power to tell, to command, to persuade, to direct the state to its proper ends. Such a philosopher-king, if he issues rules, will have to alter them *if* a situation alters and a new solution is required to the problems originally covered by his rules.

[5] F. M. Cornford (trans.), *op. cit.,* p. 204.

Beyond all existing rules and human decisions stands the good, in terms of which any political decision must be judged. And this object, the good, is not itself subject to definition but is either known or not known. In the *Laws*—a later dialogue—Plato advocated what he called a second-best state which would, in our terms, be a state governed by laws rather than by men.

In the *Republic,* Socrates sketches a just state in which three social classes (rulers, guardians, and artisans) perform their functions without disturbing the harmony of the whole order. He also indicates that the individual *psyche* or soul harmonizes three functions—reasoning, desiring objects in a way which is in principle amenable to reason, and nonrational passions or "drives." The virtuous is he who manages to achieve a harmonious integration of these functions, while the just person is he who senses his proper social function. But the reader is left with something like a paradox. The just state creates the conditions in which individuals can perform their proper functions; and the just state cannot exist without individuals who are integrated or virtuous. The problem of the individual and the social seems to be "solved," in Plato's *Republic,* by erasing any meaningful distinction between the two. It is as if Plato were to argue (through the mouth of Socrates) that one will not get virtuous individuals until he gets a just social order, and that a just social order presupposes virtuous individuals. The model of politics seems, in the end, to be an organic one, in which the parts—individuals—can be understood only as functions within an operative social and political whole.

Conclusion

The Socratic method does appear to teach something. What is taught is a unique method of finding a type of self-understanding which cannot be arrived at in any other way. Perhaps the foregoing sentences should be rewritten to read: The Socratic method does facilitate a certain kind of *learning*. In the process of philosophical discussion, a person can come to learn something he had not known before. The person knows he has learned something, yet is still embarrassed if asked to state exactly *what*. What he has learned cannot neatly be summarized and communicated in an authoritatively final set of definitions, answers to questions, or propositions. The learning is more like illumination—"coming to see" details in a new way, in a significantly new context. "Something is going on," a student once said after a series of discussions about some of Plato's views, "but I can't seem to say exactly what. I *know* I'm learning something of what it is to be intellectually alive even though, in the *Republic,* I don't seem to be learning the one true definition of justice!" Perhaps what is learned is that whatever answer we give to a question such as "What is justice?" we give the answer in a context which need not be universal, as we find out if we try completely to analyze it into its component parts. Asking such a question is not quite like asking similarly structured questions such as: What is uranium? What is football? What is the sum of two plus two? More restrictedly, in attempting to answer we are led to learn more about inadequate answers than we could normally learn if we did not use the Socratic method. At the very least, we learn about the limits of language and human reasoning.

Perhaps the method permits us to "see" how politics can become more than a matter-of-fact business of rules and procedures. It can be in part an extension of ourselves. The method can dramatize how, in an inescapable way, social and political life may be more than routine in its consequences, though it is always that too. Instead of feeling ourselves as atoms adrift in an always partly unknown sea of circumstances, we may come to understand a bit about the mysterious boundaries of that sea which seems to operate upon us. The sea may even become strangely *ours* in a new way, for good or ill—though partly unknown, nonetheless ours. Sometimes we may even glimpse—or think we glimpse?—the possibility, hardly taken seriously in practical life, that we may inhabit a universe far richer than we had ever previously imagined. This glimpse may move and even disturb us. We can, at such times, at least identify ourselves with the (perhaps mistaken?) spirit of James Joyce's fictional character, Stephen Dedalus, who writes in the front of his school geography book:

> Stephen Dedalus
> Class of Elements
> Clongowes Wood College

Sallins
County Kildare
Ireland
Europe
The World
The Universe [6]

In any event, many students of Plato have insisted, against their critics, that reading Plato produces a kind of knowledge very different from the ordinary.

Some Questions and Problems

1. Keeping in mind Plato's uses of political analogies, do you think democratic governing is compatible with the view that only qualified experts should rule?
2. What, if any, are the differences between having political knowledge and possessing political opinion?
3. Is there any difference between a politician and a statesman? If not, why not? If so, what accounts for the difference?
4. Should legislators, executives, and judges possess the same kinds of fundamental knowledge about politics? Do they rather need to possess different kinds of knowledge? How, if at all, are their functions similar? How, if at all, do their functions differ?
5. Write a brief essay in which you attempt to make clear the essentials of political justice.
6. Assume that you belong to a constitutional committee empowered to create a constitution for a new government. What would you seek to include in your constitution?
7. Do you believe that philosophers, or other "intellectuals," make especially competent political leaders? Why or why not? Do you believe that social scientists should have an active role in governing a nation in today's world, even if they fail to be elected at the polls?
8. In choosing political leaders, do you think the voters should consider a candidate's personal morality in addition to how he "stands" on current issues? Give supporting reasons if you can.
9. Do you think Plato's version of a philosopher-king makes any political sense at all?
10. Is democracy (defined here as government by consent of a people)

[6] *A Portrait of the Artist as a Young Man* (New York: Viking, 1961), p. 16. Used by permission of The Viking Press, Inc.

necessarily superior to other forms of government? Is dictatorship ever morally justified? Are there ways in which democracy is inferior to other forms of government?

11. Discuss the topic of the relation of philosophical and scientific methods. Are they alike in some important ways? Are they fundamentally unalike?

Some Suggested Readings

Bambrough, R. "Plato's Political Analogies," *Philosophy, Politics, and Society,* First Series, ed. P. Laslett. New York: Macmillan, 1956.

Cornford, F. M. *Before and After Socrates.* London: Cambridge University Press, 1950.

Grube, G. M. A. *Plato's Thought.* London: Methuen, 1935.

Hamilton, E., and Cairns, H. (eds.) *Plato: The Collected Dialogues.* New York: Bollingen Foundation, 1961.

Macdonald, M. "The Philosopher's Use of Analogy," *Logic and Language,* First Series, ed. A. Flew. Oxford: Blackwell, 1951.

Nettleship, R. L. *Lectures on the Republic of Plato,* 2d ed. New York: St Martin's, 1961.

Stace, W. T. *A Critical History of Greek Philosophy.* London: Macmillan, 1920.

Taylor, A. E. *Socrates.* Boston: Beacon, 1951.

————. *Plato: The Man and His Works.* London: Methuen, 1952.

————. *The Mind of Plato.* Ann Arbor: The University of Michigan Press, 1960.

PART II

Some Perennial Topics

CHAPTER FOUR
Legal and Moral Rules

The notion of regularity is not hard to come by. Quite ordinary persons acquire it fairly early in their lives, if in crude ways. Familiar expressions reflect the pervasiveness of regularity in human experience: "Sam's a dependable man—as regular as clockwork in attending to his duties"; "The Colonel lives by the regulations"; "As a rule, Harry jerks his head to one side when emphasizing a point in an argument"; "Regularly, at nine o'clock, Mrs. O'Felix puts the cat out each night."

It is difficult to understand how men could have acquired the notion of regularity were experience itself not so obviously marked by instances of orderliness and connectedness. The notion itself is not hard to account for, but its sophisticated application to ever-widening spheres of subject matter and experience requires serious thought. Men become able to consider the possibility that extensive features of experience and existence are subject to regularity in ways which are not readily apparent—meaning that the regularities have to be searched out and stated. In the social and moral realms, men can face puzzling situations with the thought that more order and regularity *ought* to exist in human affairs than, in fact, does exist at a specific time. Men can then work to achieve such social and moral regularity. To say that events or experiences occur regularly allows one, on reflection, also to say that such events and experiences happen in a lawlike fashion.

To say a sentence like "Mr. Orderly is a law-abiding citizen" means to assert that careful observation will show that Mr. Orderly *regularly* will be found acting in accordance with existing rules. Someone who is law-abiding is a person who has acquired a habit of giving obedience in action to a body, or set, of rules (unless we are asked to imagine a strange society in which there is only one existing rule, say). The phrase "law-abiding" is what philosophers call a *dispositional* one— one which describes a tendency of character, a settled disposition to perform in a calculable way. As such, the phrase is like a number of other dispositional terms such as "honest," "reliable," "hard-working," "conscientious," and the like. About a person who *consistently* obeyed traffic rules but disobeyed rules governing the payment of income taxes, we would not say (assuming we had knowledge of the situation) that he is a law-abiding citizen. This does not mean that a person who "breaks" a single legal or moral rule is not a law-abiding citizen. It does mean such a person has made a mistake or fallen short in one instance. Thus, the telling of one lie never makes a man a liar; nor does the doing of a single honest deed provide adequate grounds for calling a man honest. Dispositional terms refer to tendencies—in social matters, to human capacities to perform in expected and knowable ways. We have commonsense reasons for expecting honest persons to behave honestly in the future, though in this we may sometimes turn out to have been mistaken in a given instance ("Well, Charlie Forthright *was* honest with the firm's accounts until he met up with that office redhead!").

In the social sphere, of course, to act in a lawlike manner means to act not only in conformity with rules but, in some sense, *because* of rules. Men consider the existing rules (or what they think should morally be the rules) before they perform some of their actions. Or men judge the actions of others in terms of legal or moral rules (written or assumed). The moral man is one who attempts to appropriate the rules—to make them an influential aspect in the determination of some of his actions. There are lawlike forms of behavior which seem to occur independently of human volitions. In a lawlike manner we can describe instances of bodies falling from one height to another because bodies move according to ascertainable laws. On the other hand, the lawlike behavior of citizens acting because of rules usually involves kinds of action which, in some sense, might be other than they are. Legal and moral rules can be broken or disregarded in a way in which the rules (laws) governing falling bodies cannot. Moral praise and blame require that the behavior of human beings be viewed as if the agents performing the actions could, under certain circumstances, perform other actions. Thus, legal and moral rules are stated in order to try to influence persons to act in given ways. It is because men sometimes *do* murder that societies establish rules forbidding murder, threatening punishments to those who murder and are detected. The sanctions of legal and moral rules are usually the results of what men decide to impose, while the sanctions of nonhuman laws do not immediately depend on human decisions.

For example, if a man falls from a flying airplane, he will usually suffer painful injury, probably death (unless he wears a parachute which opens). In regular, lawlike ways certain actions result in painful consequences. As a result, an airline company may post a rule saying: "All passengers are to stay away from the plane's door while in flight." The company may create a sanction against those who disobey such a rule—perhaps fining the passenger a certain amount of money or refusing, in the future, to permit him to make flights. Many legal and moral rules are made—in a relatively sane social system—that aim at protecting individuals from dangerous types of behavior which often can be the forerunners of painful consequences.

A contemporary political philosopher has sought to distinguish legal and moral rules from simple commands on the ground that commands can sometimes be disobeyed. Of course, so too can legal and moral as opposed, say, to physical laws. But the philosopher's point is an important one. What he wants to emphasize is a difference between humanly created legal and moral rules (aimed at influencing human behavior) and scientific rules or laws (aimed at describing forms of behavior, nonhuman and human, which occur independently of human choices or decisions). Professor T. D. Weldon has argued for the noncommand aspect of rules in the following way:

> While it is true that we cannot logically contradict "Put out your cigarette!" it is significant, though sometimes unwise, to ask for a reason for doing so. Hence we may have A. "Put out your cigarette!" B. "Why?" A. Either "There is a rule prohibiting smoking in

this room," *or* "There is an escape of gas and if anyone smokes we shall be blown up." Thus a command, unless it is simply of the type mentioned in the last Section "The Boss says so" needs to be backed by a reason, and the reason may be either a rule or a law.[1]

The same author makes the major point when he later writes: "Rules of conduct are made, not discovered." Of course, a person may also ask for a justification of (legal and moral) rules; and in some instances the justification of such a rule may be stated in terms of a (physical) law. Thus, the reason for the rule "No smoking in this compartment" *might* be the statement of a fact plus a probability: namely, "Escaping gas exists which might cause an explosion if passengers smoke." Also, the sanctions which back up legal and moral rules may often not happen to someone who breaks such rules, as when a court decides not to punish an offender. This means that many of the sanctions backing up legal and moral rules occur only if the authorities charged with enforcing such rules decide to apply them to specific offenders' conduct. For example, more men consistently are painfully injured by falling from great heights than are thieves consistently put in jail because of violating rules made by men.

Moral Approval and Disapproval

Legal and moral rules can be sanctioned in other than physical ways. How men praise and blame one another can act as sanctions, since most men prefer to be praised rather than to be blamed. Sometimes we can influence another person's behavior by giving or refusing to give praise and blame. If we see someone light a cigarette in a room containing a sign "Smoking is prohibited," we may influence the person not to do so again by frowning or saying something such as: "That's an irresponsible action!" Of course, if the person unlawfully smoking is not deterred by such disapproving comment, we may then call an official and threaten him with legal punishment. A callous person may not alter his behavior until he is put in jail for his antisocial behavior. Thus, men often support legal rules with moral expressions

[1] T. D. Weldon, *The Vocabulary of Politics* (Hammondsworth, Eng.: Penguin, 1953), p. 64.

of approval or disapproval, hoping to influence others to abide by the legal rules. On the other hand, men can also appeal to legal rules to support their moral notions. If a community operates by an unwritten moral notion (rule) that men ought not to tell lies about their neighbors, they may pass legal ordinances specifying certain penalties for specific kinds of lies told. In this way legal and moral rules, though not always identical, may be said to overlap and, in many situations, to reinforce one another.

In most cases, if Mr. A says that Mr. B is "law-abiding," the statement carries with it a note of moral approval. But not in all. If we enjoy football games, say, we take the coach to be complimenting a player of whom he says that the training rules are faithfully obeyed. Of course, we also assume there are good reasons for the kinds of training rules which are in effect. Given a set of rules which we judge needless or foolish or perhaps even wickedly wrong, we will not morally approve of the persons who abide by them in all circumstances. If we dislike criminal groups, we will not think favorably of a person about whom the syndicate "boss" says that he never goes back on the rules of the group. The Greek philosopher Aristotle had this type of situation in mind when he asked whether a "good" citizen can ever be a "bad" man. If we judge Nazi totalitarianism to have been vicious, then we will also probably judge law-abiding Nazi citizens to have been morally derelict persons. To know whether the statement "Mr. Orderly is a law-abiding citizen" is to be taken as a favorable judgment by us, we need to know, *first,* of what social or other group he is a member and, *second,* what the rules are which govern the actions of members of that group.

Once a person has learned the rules of a game, as well as something about the kinds of action to which they are applicable, he often lives according to them without self-conscious awareness that he is doing so. In baseball, a batter is beaten to the base by a fielder's throw of the ball and retires to the bench ("You're out!" shouts the umpire, in cases where one is present). The player may be abiding by a rule in a handbook covering baseball without thinking about the rule at all. On the other hand, a person who does not understand the game may wonder why the batter is not on base, since he *did* in this instance at least hit the ball. Here, to explain the game (thus, to make it understandable) means to tell the person about the rules. The game analogy probably proves misleading if pressed too hard—perhaps like all analogies that are so pressed. The reason is that if someone happens not to like the rules, he is not required to play baseball except, perhaps, in a physical education class. It is not so apparent that a person may be said to choose to "play the game of life" (meaning: to participate in political and moral affairs). Of course, a person can sometimes escape the legal and moral rules of a social group by emigrating, becoming a hermit, or commiting suicide. Also, many games are purposely competitive two-team affairs whose outcomes are normally marked by a victory of one team over the other. Being a good citizen by obeying political and other rules need not lead to an outcome analogous to a team victory. Morally, the aim of social education might better be a victory in which, in principle, each and every person can participate.

Consistency in Rules

Given any existing set of rules, there arises a question whether the individual members of the set are consistent with one another. For this reason, in developed political systems official bodies of persons usually possess special functions concerned with maintaining and implementing existing rules—judicial bodies to clarify rules and legislative bodies to create new rules. Clearly, a body of rules some of whose members are inconsistent with one another will be, to that extent, a weakened body if, when shown the inconsistencies, its supporters make no effort to remove them. This need not mean that the ideal of a completely consistent *finished* body of rules is necessarily a realizeable one. It does mean that inconsistent rules in a body of such regulations strike normal persons as morally and legally indefensible *once they are discovered*. Perhaps an imaginary example will help to make this fact clearer.

Imagine an existing set of club rules, Y, a single rule t of which states: "All members whose dues are not paid by the first of January of each year must be refused use of the clubhouse facilities"; and another rule z of which states: "No person who has ever been a past dues-paying member of this club may *for any reasons* be denied use of the clubhouse facilities." These two rules are clearly incompatible, since no conscientious officer of the club can consistently apply them if confronted by a past dues-paying member who fails to pay his current dues. A club officer would have to decide which of the two rules to apply to relevant cases; but unless that decision became the basis for a new rule (thus, led to an alteration of the present rules), each new club officer would be able to decide relevant cases differently. This would soon mean that questions of fairness of treatment of relevant cases would arise, unless the club members were ignorant, morally insensitive, or mentally unbalanced.

The foregoing example of an inconsistency among rules in a body of regulations differs from another example in which, given only rule t, say, a club president decides not to apply the rule against Mr. Sam Mortgaged because the latter has promised to pay later and has overwhelmingly excusing reasons for having failed to pay by the first of January. This means that inconsistency among rules differs from making exceptions to a given rule or from an officer's inconsistency in the application of a rule. In the first case, the fault lies with the rules, since it is they which cause the inconsistency. In the second case, the rule may be sound but in need of some exceptions. In the third case, if there is a fault it lies with the lack of judgment or fairness in the club officer. Even if a body of rules contains no obviously inconsistent members, a club officer may in exceptional circumstances decide not to apply one or another of them. In this event, the grounds on which an exception is made *should* become grounds for excepting others in similar circumstances. Thus, rule t in our imaginary set of regulations might be amended to read: ". . . except when a club member becomes unemployed, is seriously ill, or is declared an exception by a vote of the members." The reasons for declaring an exception to a rule, in a given case, must be public and applicable to others in the club. Otherwise, the club's rules function only when, by his decision, a club officer decides to apply them. The authority in such an event would shift from the rules to the whims of the officer.

The just application of existing rules requires that presiding or judicial officials treat similar cases similarly. Often a vaguely stated rule becomes clarified by careful enumeration of excepting circumstances. Men living in sane social situations will criticize a leader who makes exceptions to existing rules for purely personal reasons, excusing his friends and applying the rules to his more distant acquaintances or enemies. In an orderly society rules are general in form, and their application to cases is such that officials behave predictably and fairly. It is difficult to understand how any person could make sense of a body of rules without adopting the moral principle that he should act fairly in applying the rules to others or in judging their performance in the light of the rules. A society possessing a fine set of rules is not thereby a just one if its officials disregard them or, in applying them, fail to treat similar cases in a like manner. This does not mean that any official who happens to treat similar cases differently has necessarily meant to be unfair. He may simply have made a mistake. The point is, however, that if the mistake is made known to him, and if he seeks to be fair, he will want to remedy it in some way.

An illustration in the form of a dialogue will make clear the important difference between an official who makes a mistake and one who is unfair. Consider the following:

> *Professor Favoritism:* A student named Lament came to my office yesterday and complained about a grade I put on his objective examination.
>
> *Professor Fairness:* Yes, that often happens. Why did he complain?
>
> *Professor Favoritism:* Well, he said that he got a C for a paper containing the same number of mistakes as Miss Vivacious, who got a B.
>
> *Professor Fairness:* That happened to me last year. I went to the registrar's office and made sure that both students received the same grade. Is that what you did?
>
> *Professor Favoritism:* Goodness, no! I was quite honest with the boy. I told him I liked Miss Vivacious better. She's a very attractive girl. I told him not to make a mountain out of a molehill, since girls should be treated a bit more delicately than boys in such matters. They're such delicious little creatures!

This imagined dialogue between two professors shows how, while it is not necessarily unfair for a person to like some individual more than others, it is unfair in rule-bound situations to apply a rule only to actions of those whom one does not particularly like. One major reason for the creation of rules concerns the need to protect persons from the introduction of just such very human but irrelevant considerations into judgments made about cases falling under the rules. Who could feel secure living in a community whose judges freed all those murderers happening to have blue eyes? Surely, not the potential blue-eyed victims of such murderers!

There is a difference between acting in accordance with rules and telling someone that he *ought* either to follow the rules or, if he is a judge, to apply them fairly. It is the difference between an activity which can be described and an activity which, though describable, is also subject to moral or legal justification. If someone asks whether a person is obeying a rule, his question can be answered (in most cases) by observing the person's behavior and then looking up the rule. But if someone asks whether a person ought to obey a rule, or a set of rules, he is asking that reasons justifying the rule or set of rules be given. To say that something *ought* to be the case is not identical with saying that it *is* the case. Often we observe behavior of which we disapprove and say something like: "Look at old Vitamin Irresponsible there! He's using that big stick to beat that poor old horse! Why, he oughtn't to be doing that!" Also, there are times when we say that something ought to be taking place which, in fact, is not taking place, as in the case of someone's saying: "Harry ought to be doing his homework, but he's not doing it."

In pluralistic societies permitting some freedom of judgment about which organizations to join persons often find themselves attempting to live by incompatible rules of different organizations. What is at stake here is the degree to which a person can consistently give loyal allegiance to all the social groups of which he is a member. Sometimes one's church advocates rules or principles which conflict with those of other groups. Perhaps one's church forbids the taking of oaths as a means to join secret organizations and one's fraternity requires the taking of just such an oath. A decision is required here. Such conflict situations can prove deeply disturbing to conscientious persons wanting to retain their allegiances and, at the same time, to seek to obey the rules if possible. Perhaps a person's belief in the rule that men ought never to kill conflicts with the rule that citizens are expected to become fighting men during periods of war. A morally serious person *tries* to act consistently with his principles and to avoid radically incompatible allegiances. Still, to live in a pluralistic society made up of numerous groups means to become involved in such conflicts.

Conflicts between rules or allegiance to incompatible authorities raises the question whether such conflicts can be resolved by appeal to higher principles. Sometimes the argument is made that men have a right, or are even obligated, to disobey rules which violate their moral principles. In this way a distinction is made between moral and legal rules. In turn, this can lead to the question whether one's moral principles can be shown to be just or are merely preferences. In less dramatic form, many persons often have to weigh the *importance* of different rules which usually govern their actions. They have to order their behavior in accordance with some scheme which makes some rules more significant than others. Emergencies may occur in which it is impossible to abide by the rules normally binding a person. In such emergencies a person must follow those rules which are taken as most important, much as a captain of a storm-tossed vessel must jettison machines before throwing overboard needed supplies of food or medicine.

Many philosophers have asked whether some rules are not basic to human life in a very peculiar way. Are there some principles without which other rules cannot themselves be justified? More than this, are some principles deeply moral—reflections of the order of things rather than conventional formulations by legislators or judges? Does the argument that legal and other rules may at times be judged in the light of fundamental moral rules make sense? Can it be justified? Such broad questions presuppose that serious persons are concerned to order their behavior as responsible agents. As a contemporary thinker has expressed this fact,

If 'having' moral principles means anything at all, it means acting in accordance with them. But to act in accordance with moral principles is to be moral. When we say of someone that he has no moral principles, we mean that he is immoral, that he does not act in accordance with moral principles.[2]

But the same author insists that to be asked to prove that a person ought to be moral is to be asked a strange question, and he concludes:

Therefore the real meaning of the sentence, "A man who has no principles that he is prepared to apply impartially has no moral principles," is "A man who is not impartial in his treatment of others, who treats others unfairly, is not acting in accordance with moral principles, is violating the principle of justice, and is thus acting immorally." Any other meaning that might be given to the phrase "having moral principles" is irrelevant in this context.[3]

But to say that men ought to have moral principles does not state what those principles are. How does someone go about finding out the content of such principles? Indeed, are there any moral principles which apply to all persons? The pages of political and social philosophy books are marked by men's attempts to answer such questions. There are those who argue that moral principles can be discovered by the use of human reason, others who insist that they are simply the agreed-on ways by which a specific culture or group subjects its members' behavior to rules. The discussion about this great issue now requires some consideration.

Natural Law and Its Critics

To the question "What makes a law (rule) *genuinely* a law?", the defenders of what is called the "natural law" position want to argue, usually, that the proper answer cannot simply be: "It is the fact that the law is written down in a proper manual, which is put out by official persons in a society." Not *who* writes down the laws but *what* the content of the laws is, determines their genuine status as law. On this view, authorities charged with the function of promulgating

[2] Marcus G. Singer, *Generalization in Ethics* (New York: Knopf, 1961), p. 50.
[3] *Ibid.*

laws can make mistakes and even, at times, promulgate immoral or vicious laws. Natural law thinkers want to resist the view that, if asked to justify an existing law, a philosopher has behaved adequately if he simply names the officials who made it.

Even thinkers who disagree with the natural law position can understand some of the reasons why, historically, its tenets came to be formulated. One reason is that even in the ancient world there existed different bodies of rules whose contents often conflicted with one another. This became a problem in the practical life of men when empires arose—usually as the result of military conquest—confronting the conquerors with the task of attempting to maintain some kind of order in the newly conquered areas. How was a person in authority to overcome such conflicts in an intellectually satisfying manner? For example: How were the Romans to treat the legal and other rules of the different conquered peoples? One possible way was to replace the rules of the conquered by those of the conquerors—simply to change the rules and then to enforce them by military power. Certainly this sometimes happened, since a domineering conqueror could justify his own commands by making some such declaration as: "Do things as we say or take the sad consequences!"

Yet sometimes even a conqueror may find some rules among the conquered peoples which seem to "make sense." A conqueror may then adopt some of the foreigners' rules, even perhaps make them part of his own basic system. A person can sometimes learn from his enemies in this way. Given this kind of experience, a reflective person among the conquerors might ask: "What is the significance of this? What makes one rule superior to another?" Perhaps this can be a meaningful question if it is not taken to be open to a single straightforward answer. The natural law position partly developed out of such experiences of attempting to give justificatory reasons for the superiority of one rule or principle to another. The justification "went" to the effect that one was more reasonable. A rule was considered more reasonable in the light of its justness, fairness, relevancy—not because it happened to agree with a group's narrowly selfish interests or preferences. More than this, such a rule was thought "natural," meaning that any reasonable person should be able to understand its status as, in some manner, grounded in the very nature of things. Thus, a natural rule (law) was thought to take precedence over other existing rules which conflicted with it. Like a measuring instrument, a natural law functioned to test other rules. In this way the distinction between moral and legal rules arose—moral rules being those which had greater "weight" than the customary and legal rules of a people which were to be judged by the former.

Of course, men can make moral judgments about any existing rule. Existing rules are facts in the social landscape. But men can use words like "good," "right," and "wrong" to evaluate facts, including rules. Men can say: "That's a bad rule" or "Rule X is a good rule." Men can argue that an existing rule is not morally justified as well as that an appropriate rule exists which is moral. A legal rule is one which is announced by properly designated authorities. But such authorities may be judged as having made mistakes. In this way the question about the relation of legal rules to morality can arise. If by legal rules we mean any regulations made by duly elected or designated judicial officials, operating in a given social context, or the interpretation of existing bodies of rules by such officials, then it is possible for us sometimes to recognize the *legality* of such rules while wanting to criticize them for moral reasons. During the Second World War, in Germany a law permitted a woman to testify against her husband about his political beliefs—a practice which most persons would want to condemn both on legal and moral grounds. Yet, in the Nazi system, this was a law. About this example Professor Fuller has argued cogently that "if the wife's act in informing on her husband made his remarks 'public,' there is no such thing as a private utterance under this statute." To say "A practice is legal" need not mean the same as to say "A practice is moral" unless one wants to argue there can be no meaningful distinction between legal and moral rules.

Suppose a society to exist whose promulgated legal code permits the killing of all babies that weigh more than ten and less than seven pounds. Probably all of us would condemn a rule of this kind—yet, if it were a part of a legal code, we could not consistently deny its legal status. Apparently, some natural law thinkers want to argue against this view by insisting that a rule which is blatantly vicious or immoral is, thereby, somehow *not really* a law. Their point is that it ought not to be regarded as a law for moral reasons; and yet they must make the point against something which exists, namely, the rule that babies of a certain weight are to be killed. Natural law thinkers often want to restrict the meaning of the word "law" to those rules which do not conflict with what they take to be basic moral principles. Their problem concerns what to do with regulations they consider immoral which, nonetheless, exist in a given society and influence for good or evil the lives of living persons. Seeing this difficulty, a modern school of thinkers—often known as legal positivists—argue in reply that even a bad rule (law) remains a rule. Legal positivists attempt, therefore, to construct an understanding of what makes a law genuinely a law by rejecting the notion men can find out by introducing moral views into the discussion. It is not so much that legal positivists want to deny that moral considerations ought to influence the making of rules but that, as a matter of fact, they need not. St. Thomas Aquinas recognized what contemporary legal positivists emphasize, for he insisted that some rules can be morally indifferent —in the sense that a number of adequately phrased rules can sometimes be justified, though only one can be stated. Of course, St. Thomas thought such neutral rules made up a philosophically unimportant aspect of a system of laws. Thus the issue between natural law thinkers and their critics rests heavily on the question of the relation of legal and moral rules.

Natural law thinkers insist that genuine laws cannot be set aside by human agreement (whether by legislators or judges). True, they admit, men can go counter to such laws or even fail to recognize them; but if men do so, they go counter to the very heart of law and morality. The body of such laws can change. Conservative natural law thinkers agree they can change only by addition, never by subtraction—meaning that a natural law, once discovered, remains true for all future occasions. Many more liberal natural law thinkers take a more contextualistic stance, arguing they can change even by subtraction—that a law for situation X, say, may not apply to situation Y. These natural laws are the principles without which no rational justification of laws can be obtained. They are simply "there" in some nonspatial sense of "thereness"—genuinely objective and enduring features of the universe of men. In this sense, law and morality are inseparable. It is impossible to define the nature and province of law except by recourse to these natural principles. The principles themselves are discovered by reasoning—"seen" to be what they are by intellects capable of understanding the conditions of lawlike human existence in a universe which has common factual and moral properties binding all men. Natural law thinkers need not insist they know all of these principles, only that those they do know are universally applicable to specific situations.

This view that there are natural laws, discoverable by human reason and applicable to human affairs, carries an impressive historical record with it. This view is expressed in some Greek philosophical works; played a central role in the great Stoic tradition; influenced the development of the body of Roman law and critical reflection on that law; found a positive statement in the medieval synthesis, as in the writings of St. Thomas; and received widespread support during major revolutionary crises in the seventeenth and eighteenth centuries. One English political thinker who is critical of the philosophical arguments for natural law has nonetheless written: "It later seems probable that the Communist Manifesto owed much of its success not to its 'scientific' analysis of capitalist society, but to its denouncement of wage slavery degrading to human nature and its appeal to all workers to assert their equal brotherhood." [4] The natural law position has often functioned as an intellectual justification of rebellion against otherwise legally established authorities. The appeal to Nature as a standard is an appeal to something "outside" already existing historical and social conditions. The American Declaration of Independence made such an appeal, for its authors sought the goodwill of mankind by resisting a legal British authority in the name of principles "according to the laws of Nature and of nature's God."

The fact that men have believed there are natural laws is not proof that such laws exist. More weakly, even if such laws exist, men may

[4] Margaret Macdonald, "Natural Rights" in Peter Laslett, ed., *op. cit.,* p. 36. This article originally appeared in *Proceedings of the Aristotelian Society* (London, 1947–48).

be unable to know them—or at least be in a difficult position to prove
that those laws they think natural are in fact so. To critics who are
sceptical about claims for natural law, its defenders can reply: "You
just haven't come to understand what law is. You're in ignorance!"
Critics can insist that passionate belief in any position tends to gain
success for the believers. Moreover, a distinction can be made between legal and moral rules which does not presuppose that moral
rules are apprehended by reason. Some writers have argued that
moral rules are simply the more general principles by which existing
societies happen to regulate many forms of their behavior—that many
such rules never get written into official legal codes because they are
efficacious without this.

Not the reasonableness of a law makes it law, according to some
legal positivists, but the *source*. On this view a law is intimately related to the power of a ruler, a sovereign possessing the power effectively to command. A legal order presupposes an existing political
sovereign capable of supporting his commands by applying sanctions
against disobedient citizens. If a rule is "on the books" and is consistently enforced by political machinery (including the legal), then
it is a law even if it violates some persons' conceptions of morality.
Sometimes in frustration persons are heard to say something like:
"What's the use of resisting the weight of The System by mouthing
moral principles? If the judges and police do not agree with our
moral principles, then we'll end up in jail!" A consideration of this
kind has led careful thinkers to put forward a command theory of the
law. Among them must be numbered a nineteenth-century Englishman, John Austin—whose writings deeply influenced contemporary
legal positivism—and a very much living writer, H. L. A. Hart,[5]
Professor of Jurisprudence in the University of Oxford. Men such
as these have raised searching questions about arguments for the

[5] Two stimulating essays in a 1958 issue of the *Harvard Law Review* discuss
many of the issues associated with positivism and natural law traditions. Here
and elsewhere in this chapter references are made to these essays: namely,
H. L. A. Hart's *Positivism and the Separation of Law and Morals* and Lon
Fuller's *Positivism and Fidelity to Law—A Reply to Professor Hart*. These
essays are conveniently reprinted in Frederick A. Olafson, ed., *Society, Law
and Morality* (Englewood Cliffs, N.J.: Prentice-Hall, 1961), pp. 439–505.

natural law position, though Professor Hart has been quite willing to modify the simple command view of law. Their aim has been to show that distinctions between the legal and the moral which seek to evade the independent force of legal rules give a misleading picture of what makes law what it is.

Professor Hart admits that the unqualified "command theory" of the legal order fails adequately to account for significant features of law. He suggests that this theory too restrictedly reflects only a most important characteristic of the criminal law, which is far from constituting the whole domain of law. Elsewhere, in his book *The Concept of Law* (Oxford: Clarendon, 1961), though he defends the positivist view of the relation of legal and moral rules against one version of the natural law position, Professor Hart shows a willingness to consider, as more or less empirically acceptable, a few generalizations which might be identifiable with a natural law view. These "simple truisms," which in Hart's view express the sensible aspect of natural law doctrine, concern men's common human vulnerability, approximate equality, limited altruism, limited resources to meet needs, and limited understanding and strength of will. This fact is mentioned here to avoid giving the erroneous impression that Professor Hart denies *any* lasting insights to the natural law tradition.

If the natural law theorist argues that moral considerations ought to get written into the legal rules, the positivist can reply that, until they do, they remain *legally* inoperative. The legal rules of a society need not be as extensive as are the moral rules; and the moral rules can work without legal sanctions to the extent a community enforces them in other ways. All kinds of individuals and groups hold power to enforce rules, where the power is not that of a legal sovereign. A primitive society may even enforce its moral rules (sometimes called *mores*) by direct action, exercising an immediate social sovereignty. In practical terms, appeals to natural law often are made by groups who are resisting a legally existing situation. For example, a state may exist in which the legal system recognizes the right of physicians to perform stipulated types of abortion, though in that state there may be groups which view such abortions as immoral. The significant point here is that groups having moral objections cannot take legal action against those physicians who perform the permitted abortions. They can, of course, work to alter the legal rules and also educate their own members to abide by their version of moral rules. On moral grounds, members of a group can choose not to recognize an existing legal rule as law (perhaps even becoming revolutionaries); but they must nonetheless suffer the legal consequences resulting from such a choice.

Still, a natural law theorist can ask: "What happens in the situation involving a judge's need to decide about the relevancy of legal rules to a given case? Is this an arbitrary matter? Doesn't reasoning enter into this procedure?" What the natural law theorist seeks to emphasize here is the manner in which a judge, even in making an exception to a rule, must try to understand the purpose behind the rule—the rule's reason for being, as it were. The making of exceptions itself involves often the giving of justifications. To this question a legal positivist might say: "Ultimately, how the judge *decides* is what makes up the law." To which again the natural law thinker might respond by emphasizing a distinction between a reasonable judge *who knows how he is proceeding* in reaching a decision and an irrational judge who does not.

A contemporary lawyer, Professor Lon Fuller of Harvard University, has argued that a judge is morally obligated to disregard what he knows to be insupportable legal rulings. He mentions a case (one which is most puzzling) involving a judge who, sitting on the bench of a lower court, knows that the decisions in commercial law of a higher court are based on inadequate knowledge. According to the thesis of Professor Fuller, such a judge should ignore the decisions of the higher court. But if he acts in accordance with this view the judge —who is in our society expected to apply existing legal rules—becomes in such a case almost a judicially robed subversive. The judge substitutes his own view of what is good law for what the courts have decreed. Suppose every judge in such a situation should so proceed? Would not the result be judicial chaos? Professor Fuller fails, in other words, to distinguish the judge's obligations qua judge (to apply existing rules) from his obligations as a citizen (to come off the bench and work to change the rules). In the name of morality, Professor Fuller's judge may very well disrupt a large segment of a legal system.

For this reason many thinkers have argued it is better to obey even a bad rule than, on one's own, to act as if the self were the legislator or judge in the matter. Of course, the judge in such a situation could resign his position to dramatize his unhappiness over what he knows to be bad decisions by yet higher courts.

Professor Fuller touches on a more vital aspect of the debate between natural law theorists and legal positivists when he discusses features of the Nazi legal system which, following the recent war, had to be reformed. He argues that a newly formed judiciary in Germany had the right (even the obligation) to declare that established Nazi legal rules were not in fact laws at all. They so blatantly went counter to established morality that it would have been wrong to consider them as law. Yet, though not disagreeing with Professor Fuller's moral judgment here, H. L. A. Hart pointed out that they were laws within the Nazi system. The *legal* question how to handle them in a reformed legal system had to be separated from the moral issue, since a legal system has a status in its own right. In the end, both men agree that—in the case of this specific legal statute—the thing to have done was to enact a retroactive statute.

The natural law theorists keep alive the moral sense of men concerned about the law. The legal positivist emphasizes the ways in which even bad legal systems are nonetheless *legal.* The former insist that no absolute separation between the *law as it is* and the *law as it ought to be* can be consistently maintained. The latter argue that it must be maintained if men are to understand law as a system. Significantly, both a natural law theorist and a positivist can agree on moral judgments in specific cases (though there is no logical necessity behind this for the positivist). What, then, is really behind the apparent disagreement between them? The disagreement apparently concerns what is most important (if a decision here has to be made)—understanding law as a system or understanding law as a moral phenomenon. What happens is that the positivist emphasizes the importance of the former, while the natural law theorist—rooted in a humanistic and rationalistic ethical tradition—stresses the deep moral significance of all phases of law. Adherents of the two positions do not so much disagree about factual matters as about the significance of the law as a phenomenon calling for moral analysis. The legal positivist appears often to write more for lawyers and specialists in the law, while the natural law theorist seems to emphasize broad human problems which —even for his severest critics—most frequently have concerned philosophers.

Legal Rules and Obedience

Legal rules constitute one device by which to influence the behavior of men. They bear a crucial relationship to other types of devices used to direct and control human conduct in that they presuppose the possibility of enforcement. Their aim is, in a practical context, to encourage a habit of steady obedience to their contents. Thus, legal rules are closely bound to a functioning political system which provides the source of power needed to carry them into effect against unwilling members of the community. The nature of political authority will receive attention in a later chapter; but some aspects of the problem of obedience to existing legal rules deserve a brief treatment here. This is so because, though legal rules are not self-enforcing, they do possess their own kind of authority in a functioning political system. As the English thinker Professor W. J. Rees has written: "Legal authority, therefore, is one species of authority, and, when exercised, may be defined as the determination of a person's actions in certain intended ways by means of a law, law being defined as an unwritten convention or a written regulation, enforceable either directly by the exercise of a supreme coercive power, or indirectly by a serious threat of the exercise of such power." [6]

If a person asks of any specific legal rule, "Why should I obey *that* rule?", he can be given a number of reasonable answers, among them statements such as: "Because it's the wise thing to do"; "You'll have to pay a fine or go to jail if you don't"; "It's better to obey rules than to disobey them"; "The rule was democratically instituted, and you say you believe in democracy"; "You can't do anything at the moment to change the rule"; "Because you tend to be a law-abiding citi-

[6] From W. J. Rees, "The Theory of Sovereignty Restated" in Peter Laslett, ed., *op. cit.*, p. 69.

zen"; "Only a fool flies in the face of authority"; "It's a good rule"; and any number of similar statements. Of course, practically minded persons usually justify obedience to a rule by considering the consequences—to themselves and others—of disregard for the rule. Now, if the rule is one seldom enforced, it may turn out that a person ought not to obey the rule if the only reason for obeying rules is the fear of their being enforced. If a person stops his car at a sign saying "Stop!" only because he sees a policeman on the corner, he can be expected to disobey the sign when the policeman is absent. Clearly, however, among the reasons for obeying rules is the argument that laws usually deserve respect. Most persons who ask why they should obey a specific rule are either seeking advice and information about the consequences of disregard for the rule, or reinforcement to their sagging habits of obedience. There is nothing specifically philosophical in such asking.

Suppose, in some imagined context, a member of a social group asks: "Why should I obey any of the laws of our group?" Some philosophers believe this to be a specifically philosophical question (if it can be said to be a genuine question at all). Considered as a meaningful question, the inquiry is subject to several kinds of reply. One might simply answer by reminding the questioner that members of the group happen to live by the rules—that the rules make up an important part of their whole "way of life"—and that's that. A philosophically inclined citizen, seeking still further reasons, might be told something about the undesirable consequences of attempting to live a completely lawless existence. These undesirable consequences might follow from a person's being caught disobeying rules (leading to punishments externally applied) or from the manner in which the questioner, raised in the society, has already appropriated the rules. The latter instance would be one involving internalized conscience. The breaker of the group's rules might be reminded that serious guilt feelings will probably result if he ignores the rules he has been taught to honor since childhood.

Reasoning of the kinds mentioned tries to point to consequences of disregard for the rules. "Look, before you decide to live as if laws don't exist," this general reasoning goes, "consider what your life, and the lives of those individuals close to you, will be like within a brief time!" Still, a philosophically obdurate questioner might say something like: "Do you mean I should obey laws only to avoid unhappy consequences of disobeying them? Isn't this a reason for obeying bad laws as well as good?" Such questions appear to seek a justification of obedience (in our immediate context, obedience to legal rules) in terms of properties or characteristics of the rules themselves (their "goodness" or "badness"). The questioner may want to discover the reasons for the rules' existence, implying that some rules may be unreasonable—even though it may be true that unfortunate consequences can follow from disobedience to unreasonable rules.

Such "answers" seem, however, to reject the original question, which did not ask whether a person should obey bad laws but whether he should obey *any laws at all*. To a person giving any of the previous replies, the original questioner can say: "But I didn't ask if I should obey bad laws. I asked rather why I should obey any laws at all!" The problem is to discover what, if anything intelligible, the questioner is attempting to ask. Perhaps an example will serve to make the problem clear. Suppose that Mr. Rebel asks: "Why should I obey the street sign there which says 'No Parking from 8 to 5 Daily'?" He receives the reply that, if he disobeys the sign, he'll receive a traffic ticket and suffer the inconvenience of reporting to court. "But I knew that already," Mr. Rebel replies. "I still don't see the sense of the sign's being where it is! It serves no obvious traffic function, since there's little 'through' traffic here. Yet, shopping centers are nearby and, by permitting people to park here, the glut of traffic on the main parking areas would be eased. By disobeying the rule I shall produce more public good than I can by obeying it." But in this speech Mr. Rebel is saying he finds no good reason *for this particular rule*. In asking: "Why should I obey the rule?", he is not unfamiliar with the possible penalties connected with disobedience; he is making a rhetorical demand for a justification for the rule (sign) which, he thinks, really cannot be given. Only by asking such questions can persons know enough to seek to change what they consider unjustifiable laws.

But we are still left with the original philosophical question about why persons should obey any rules whatever. Does the philosophical questioner make a demand which he thinks cannot be met? Is he dramatizing a philosophical conviction that *only* practical (as opposed to philosophical) reasons for obeying rules can be given? If so, does he think this a significant point to dramatize? A philosopher who so asks seems to want a general justification of authority without regard to the context and the circumstances. If, on the other hand, he is really asking: "Why should we have rules in the first place?", it is hard to know how he should be answered. Presumably we must simply point out that human existence involves the kinds of relations between persons from which, inevitably, rules eventuate. To a questioner who would look puzzled by such an answer we would then have to say: "Your question is unintelligible. You do not understand what it is you are asking!"

Conclusion

Legal and moral rules function to introduce and maintain kinds of regularity in social life which probably would not exist in their absence. Ideally, men who are thoughtful prefer to create legal codes which clearly reflect the needs of the times and the moral notions basic to the society. In any society, to find out the differences between legal and moral rules means to discover how, by whom, and under what circumstances the rules governing human behavior are made and enforced. Many moral rules are enforced by a social group—by persons who can apply and enforce sanctions. Thus, they are first learned within a family setting and, later, through a continuing contact with associates in a number of primary associations. A moral rule sometimes becomes a legal rule when the complexity of group life makes informal enforcement of the rule increasingly difficult. A specific authority is established, within the larger social group, which is charged with the *special* task of making and applying the rules. Often an elaborate institutional arrangement is needed to watch over the rules as well as to modify and to enforce them. Legal rules are those members of a much larger body of rules which designated members of the community are required to make public and to protect.

Legalized rules need to be systematized to avoid needless confusion in a society. Inconsistencies must be discovered and, if possible, removed from the body of legal rules. Legal institutions become the specialized channels through which the community applies its moral notions directly, with political backing, to its various members. Clearly defined procedures, applied rigorously and uniformly, are essential to a coherent legal system. Such procedures are needed if citizens of a community are to avoid the mistakes of "quick" justice—justice of the kind sometimes provided in the old communities of the American frontier when, lacking a paid police force or available army, the citizens were often at the mercy of bandits and other lawbreakers able to terrorize them. The private citizens who sometimes tried to cope with such emergency situations—the *vigilantes*—had to take the law into their own hands. Sometimes they meted out the most rigorous penalties for rather minor crimes, often giving the death penalty. They also had to work in secrecy, with the result that different groups of citizens had no uniform code of procedures or penalties which could be made public. Thus arose the need to institute public and official bodies whose function is to apply legal rules to relevant situations in as uniform a manner as possible.

Legal rules are not self-enforcing. They need officials to apply them. In established political systems the judges hold special responsibilities for interpreting the rules and for applying them to individual cases, while legislators in a democratic republic function to create general rules (statutes) as the need for them becomes clear. A consistent body of legal rules enforced by no one would be ineffective. There is a clear relationship between legal rules, a legal system, and the political power of a community. A later chapter will consider the question of political sovereignty. Now, to supplement this discussion of legal and moral rules, attention must be turned to the nature of human rights. Many thinkers argue that legal rules impose obligations on persons and, correspondingly, rights on others. How a legal system operates crucially influences the rights and obligations which citizens of a community may be said to possess. Our next task is to learn how and why this is the case.

Some Questions and Problems

1. Imagine you are a judge required to apply some laws you think immoral. Should you refuse to obey these laws? If so, under what conditions? Are there other alternatives available to you? What might they be?
2. Should a judge ever act like a legislator? If so, in what kind of situation?
3. What considerations should a judge keep in mind whenever he is tempted to declare an instance as an exception to an existing rule?
4. Are there any universal moral rules? If so, can you name some? Can there be universal moral rules to which exceptions can sometimes be made?
5. Can courts enforce morality? Either discuss or debate this question at some length in class.
6. Is every instance of passive resistance to an existing rule an instance of revolutionary activity?
7. Imagine that the United States lacked a Supreme Court and Congress alone had power to determine the general rules of the society. What important consequences might follow in this country from such a situation? What problems might now remain unsolved? What problems now unsolved might not be problems still?
8. Can an atheistic society produce adequate legal and moral rules binding its members? Discuss at some length.
9. Consider the assertion that no human court can put aside the eternally binding natural laws.
10. How should a citizen go about trying to alter rules he thinks immoral or unjustified? Will such a citizen ever have a right to revolt? Can a right to revolt ever become a legal right?

Some Suggested Readings

Cahn, E. *The Moral Decision*. Bloomington, Ind.: Indiana University Press, 1955.

Cairns, H. *Legal Philosophy from Plato to Hegel*. Baltimore: Johns Hopkins press, 1949.

Cohen, M. R. *Reason and Law: Studies in Juristic Philosophy*. Glencoe, Ill.: Free Press, 1950.

d'Entreves, A. P. *Natural Law: An Introduction to Legal Philosophy*. London: Hutchinson, 1951.

Friedrich, C. J. *The Philosophy of Law in Historical Perspective.* Chicago: Chicago University Press, 1958.

Gierke, O. *Natural Law and the Theory of Society 1500 to 1800,* trans. E. Barker. Boston: Beacon, 1957.

Ginsberg, M. "The Concepts of Juridical and Scientific Law," *Reason and Unreason in Society.* New York: Macmillan, 1960.

Guest, A. G. (ed.) *Oxford Essays in Jurisprudence,* 2nd ed. London: Oxford University Press, 1961.

Hart, H. L. A. *The Concept of Law.* Oxford: Clarendon Press, 1961.

————, and Honore, A. M. *Causation in the Law.* Oxford: Clarendon Press, 1959.

Konefsky, S. J. *The Legacy of Holmes and Brandeis.* New York: Macmillan, 1956.

Paton, G. W. *A Textbook of Jurisprudence,* 2nd ed. Oxford: Clarendon Press, 1951.

Weldon, T. D. "Political Principles," *Philosophy, Politics and Society,* First Series, ed. P. Laslett. New York: Macmillan, 1956.

Williams, G. "The Controversy Concerning the Word 'Law,'" *Philosophy, Politics and Society,* First Series, ed. P. Laslett. New York: Macmillan, 1956.

CHAPTER FIVE

Rights and Obligations

Most men living under fairly stable social and political conditions act as if they assume that they possess some rights and are also under some obligations to other persons. They learn to use words like "right," "ought," and "duty" as they learn the other words in their vocabulary—in specific contexts which, then, often become precedents for extending use of the words to yet other, similar situations. A parent may say to a child: "You have no right to that toy. It belongs to your brother!", thus introducing the child to an instance of a property right. Or, perhaps the parent may sometimes say something such as: "It wouldn't be right for you to go to the football game, since you promised that you'd mow the lawn today." Such a statement would be a reminder that a specific person has made a promise, thus has an obligation to do a certain act which, until that act is done (or, if not done, is shown to be outside the power of the person to do), nullifies the rightness of other possible acts which would be permissible in other circumstances. Sometimes men's duties and obligations require the (perhaps temporary) setting aside of other rights. For example, a person's right to a modicum of leisure may be set aside during a community emergency in which the public welfare requires an exceptional immediate effort by all citizens if a disaster is to be averted. The dutiful man is one who, consistently, performs those functions which his status requires and his talents make realizable. As the philosopher Immanuel Kant argued, quite ordinary persons do not equate the doing of one's duty with doing always what one wants or prefers to do. Rights and obligations exist always in a social setting. They are rights to do (or to have done or to refrain from doing) certain acts; and obligations to act (or to refrain from acting) in specific ways in stated contexts.

Some philosophers like to distinguish the meanings of words like "duty," "obligation" and "being obliged." Duties are said to be requirements of social action (or refraining from action) which follow from a person's social and professional status (such as policeman, fireman, doctor, father, mother, teacher). Such duties are treated as defined by the roles which persons holding a specific status are expected to fulfill. The status *is,* in some sense, exactly those duties. Obligations are seen as a special *class* of requirements following from a person's having made promises. These promises may be either explicitly or implicitly made. Obligations follow from a person's having said, or having placed himself in a position to be interpreted as having meant, something like "I promise to do X" or "I will do X" or some similar assertion. To know a man's obligations is to know, according to this view, what he has promised or agreed to. The important point here is that someone can enter into obligatory relationships by virtue of some special act he performs—like the *making* of an agreement—which often may fall outside the functions of his particular status situation. (Whether he promises or not, a policeman has the duty to perform those acts defined by the nature of his job; he has an obligation to his wife, say, if he has said: "I promise to pick you up at the store at five o'clock!")

In contrast to duties and obligations, according to H. L. A. Hart— a contemporary legal philosopher mentioned in the previous chapter —being obliged may entail *neither* an obligation nor a duty, as illustrated by the instance of someone's saying: "Sam was obliged to hand his money to the thief, who had a gun pointed smack at his head!" Here, "being obliged" means something like "having to perform an act, unwillingly" because one is coerced by a situation in which at least one alternative action is open ("Give me your money or get shot!" the thief may say to his victim, coercing a restricted choice from the latter). On this interpretation, the two sentences: "Sam was obliged to hand over the money" and "Sam could have refused to hand over the money and been shot, instead" are not inconsistent with each other. These distinctions in the meanings of terms are often helpful in specific philosophical contexts, but for our purposes having duties and owing obligations will be treated as meaning roughly the same thing.

There are many ways in which to talk about rights. Men can *confer* rights and *claim* rights ("I give you the right to vote for me at tonight's meeting of the PTA" and "I have a right to criticize the government if I want"). Men can also be said to *have* rights and to *use* rights. Often, we possess rights which we do not exercise—as when citizens having the right to vote in specified elections fail to go to the polls. We exercise our rights constantly, often without being aware that we are doing so—yet in such a way that, if challenged for doing some act, we can say that it is our right ("How come that Harry Goodfellow got a box at the baseball game?" "Oh, he's president of the Student Morale Boosters and, as such, has a right to a box seat!"). More than this, men can *acquire* rights (legitimately or by fraud or usurpation) by meeting conditions set as essential to the having of those rights. ("You want to know why Sally Bookreader didn't take the final examination? I can tell you why. She didn't have to take the exam. She had a right to miss it because Professor Subtle said any student with an A average up to the exam could choose not to take it, and Sally had a solid A.") In addition, men can *lose* rights as well as *give up* rights voluntarily. ("All the coeds had the right to three late evenings a week until those crazy Party Pu girls got caught cheating and Dean Meansbusiness changed the rules!"). There are all kinds of instances where persons give up genuine rights, as when a father with many children says to the mother trying to save a final pork chop for him ("I know they've all had their share, but let them divide the remaining pork chop—it's mine, but I don't want it."). Legal rights—in contrast to other kinds of rights—are those which men confer, obtain, use, or give up in accordance with the decisions authoritatively rendered by an existing legal system. To find out whether someone has a legal right, if a dispute arises, means to take a case to the courts. This is why claiming rights is never the same as actually having them, since persons may claim what, in fact, is not theirs.

Only a shallow egotist never forced by circumstances to come to terms with the pressing needs of other persons can fail, on reflection, to understand that human rights and obligations are crucially related. Talk about human rights also entails talk about human obligations. Most reasonable persons realize that to claim rights for themselves means to saddle others with obligations. If I say, "My neighbor and I have a right to be protected from vandalism," I must be willing to continue by saying something like: "The police department, as well as my fellow citizens, are obligated to see that our right is protected." A social world in which persons claimed rights but admitted no obligations would make no sense, for there would be no one to whom to talk about those claims and no one to make them possible of realization. Normally, to say that a person has a legal right means to say (imply) that someone else has an obligation with regard to that right. For example, if Mr. Conservative has a legal right to the use of his own driveway, then his neighbors have a legal obligation to keep their cars from blocking that driveway. In the case of a violation of a legal right, a person can appeal to some public authority to back up his claim to that right (thus, Mr. Conservative can call the local police department and have a neighbor's car removed from his driveway). A sane social and legal system is one in which legal and other rights are achieved even if, at times, the use of coercion or even force is required.

Even a claim to an unsupportable right may sometimes illuminate the issue of human obligation. An example will help to make this clear. Suppose a person says: "I have a right to play with the school football team, since I've never missed a single practice." Asked to justify my *claim* to this particular right, I may add something like: "You should recognize my right—that is, you're obligated to do so!" A friend may try to challenge my claim by getting me to "see" that the coach and members of the team are not genuinely obligated to me in the way I have claimed. Such a friend must attempt to influence me to understand the difference between claiming and possessing a right. In this imagined case, suppose my friend says to me (perhaps putting an arm about my shoulder as he does so): "Mr. Arrogant, you don't actually have a right to play on the team, although you may have a claim which the proper authorities should hear. Possibly a mistake has been made in your case. In other words, perhaps the coach and other team members are obligated to reconsider your case. But this doesn't mean they'll have to grant you the right you claim!" The point here is that the criteria on which a person qualifies to play on a football team need not include the sole fact that a person has been present at all practice sessions.

Because conflicting claims often arise in life, as in games, intelligent persons work to create institutions which can render authoritative decisions. Thus, a football coach is granted the right to decide (in cases of claims to play on the team by competing students who attend the practice sessions) whether a candidate for the team is acceptable. Similarly, legal systems are developed whose function it is, in part, to decide whether—in a given case—a person has the legal right he claims. In some court cases, we cannot answer the question, Which of the claimants to the right *legally* has the right? until we know the court's verdict. We can disagree with the umpire's decision in a baseball game, but under the rules we cannot question his right to render the decision. To do so would mean to question the nature of the baseball game itself. The umpire *is* the source of binding decisions according to the baseball rules.

Natural Rights

Some philosophers have argued on behalf of the view that men possess "natural rights" while others have argued, just as strenuously, that no such rights exist. The natural rights position reflects a moral stance of a particular kind: its claim is that some rights belong to men as essential properties of their humanity, neither delegated nor determined by human fiat or legislation. Many men have believed in the truthfulness of the natural rights position. This is an historical fact. But what is at issue, philosophically, concerns the extent to which— if at all—the belief is one which can be supported by sound argument and something called convincing evidence. On driving through a hot desert country, a person may say: "There's a body of cool water ahead!", only to find, on examination, that he has experienced a mirage. Similarly, a person may believe that there are natural rights when, in fact, his belief is mistaken.

Advocates of a natural rights view often belong to the teleological strand of philosophizing—persons who believe in an objective, basic human nature capable (provided the proper conditions are supplied) of achieving certain ends which are potential to that nature. Thus to say that men have natural rights may mean that *potentially* they exist. To be a man is in some sense to achieve that potential integration which occurs only when social and political conditions permit its full realization. It is as if the natural rights advocates want to argue that men can sometimes be born without an arm or a leg *and still be men,* but they cannot be said to be born without essential rights if they are (in some sense) to be men. On this basis, men have fought against strong odds to limit what they considered to be an illegitimate power of princes over their daily lives. Even slaves—disenfranchised by an existing legal order—have resisted established authorities, claiming as their natural right what, in fact, those authorities denied to them by their actions. The first ten amendments to the Constitution of the United States, known as the Bill of Rights, reflect a crude but popular eighteenth-century view of this doctrine—granting to citizens inalienable rights, as if to place these rights outside the proper jurisdiction of elected or appointed officials. The natural rights doctrine has worked in different times and places as a moral force directed against the crushing weight of established power. It has even functioned as a moral justification of revolution, often in a religious form in which the rights are seen as granted by God.

Even critics of the doctrine, discontented on philosophical grounds, often willingly admit its long and stubborn historical influence. For example, a late English philosopher says about the doctrine:

> Punctured by the cool scepticism of Hume; routed by the contempt of Bentham for 'nonsense upon stilts'; submerged by idealist and Marxist philosophers in the destiny of the totalitarian state; the claim to 'natural rights' has never been quite defeated. It tends in some form to be renewed in every crisis in human affairs, when the plain citizen tries to make, or expect his leaders to make, articulate his obscure, but firmly held, conviction that he is not a mere pawn in any political game, nor the property of any government or ruler,

but the living and protesting individual for whose sake all political games are played and all governments instituted.[1]

Nonetheless, men have also stubbornly held to beliefs in ghosts and demons, even in a scientific age. A philosopher must insist that the length of a belief's history is not good evidence for its truth.

To say that men have natural rights can be interpreted as saying that men *ought* to be treated as if they are genuine moral agents. Governments ought to recognize the essential nature of man as including a moral dimension—a capacity to be free and to achieve happiness if artificial obstructions are not placed in the path of human achievement. The capacity is *there,* needing only recognition and encouragement—and no ruler has the right, though he may for a time possess the power, to impede human self-realization. Natural rights are "written in the stars," so to speak. For men to claim natural rights means to assert something important about their source. It means for them to claim that human authorities can never be the source of certain rights, though such authorities may hinder or hamper their actualization in individual and group life.

An imagined discussion between two persons—one a believer in the doctrine of natural rights, the other a sceptic—may help to clarify both what the former is trying to assert and why the latter remains puzzled or unconvinced.

> *Believer:* I mean to argue that certain rights inherently belong to a man as a man. No one can legitimately take these rights away, nor can they confer them. To define man's nature means to claim that he possesses natural rights.

> *Sceptic:* I've heard this argument many times. It has many puzzling features. Even you say that no one can *legitimately* deny these rights, implying, I take it, that men can illegitimately deny them. Thus, men can in some sense keep these rights from being realized?

> *Believer:* Men—especially tyrannical rulers—can choose to be unreasonable, just as they can refuse to accept the truth of

[1] Margaret Macdonald, "Natural Rights," in Peter Laslett, ed., *Philosophy, Politics and Society* (First Series; New York: Macmillan, 1956), p. 35. This article originally appeared in *Proceedings of the Aristotelian Society* (London, 1947–48).

theorems in geometry. Similarly, thieves can steal property which, legally, is owned by another. In doing so, they go against the natural order of things. I mean to assert that men cannot reasonably deny the natural rights doctrine— nothing more, nothing less!

Sceptic:　Suppose a person said to you the two following sentences: "Mr. Biggs owns a Cadillac" and "Mr. Biggs ought to own a Cadillac." Would you take these two sentences as saying the same thing?

Believer:　In ordinary situations, no. One sentence describes what is factual (if it is a true sentence), while the other asserts that something ought to be the case (when in fact it may not be so).

Sceptic:　Aren't defenders of a natural rights view saying sentences like these two I have presented? Isn't there a difference in saying that men do possess natural rights and that they ought to possess them?

Believer:　I see the force of your questions. You think I claim that men actually possess what, in some sense, they do not possess. Thus, to be consistent, I must argue that a slave possesses natural rights even if he lives in abject slavery.

Sceptic:　Yes, you're right. You see what I'm getting at. But you don't seem to be worried! Why not?

Believer:　Because it's obvious I can't be saying what you want me to appear to say. Like you, I realize that ordinarily either we possess something or we don't possess it. Yet the power of the natural rights view rests on the argument that men can possess rights which, at a given historical moment, they are unable to exercise.

Sceptic:　Why should so peculiar an argument be powerful?

Believer:　It is powerful because it rests on a firm conviction about man's nature. What he possesses are *rights,* which are not quite like arms, legs, and noses. One cannot both have and not have a nose, say. But a man can have rights which he is unable, because of unreasonable men, to put into effect. They are his by virtue of his being a man. The natural rights position is a moral one which claims to describe a moral state of affairs. To be moral, a man must admit that natural rights exist.

Sceptic: But who or what makes a ruler act morally?

Believer: If anything can, it must be his reason. Reason tells him that the rights I talk about exist potentially. It is their potentiality which he can never destroy.

Sceptic: We have come full circle. You simply refuse to understand the force of my criticism!

Many modern thinkers—including some who share the social and political ideals of natural rights philosophers—tend to side with the sceptic's arguments. A conservative like Edmund Burke, a famous English parliamentarian who rejected the excesses of the French revolutionaries, insisted that human rights arise always from a community's practices and are rooted only in custom. Rights are acquired, he thought, and must be protected by an enlightened citizenry's refusal quickly to tamper with established social practices. Innovation is possible. Yet, Burke insisted that innovators always threaten to disrupt the patiently developed fabric of rights and privileges without which a sane social life would be impossible. Therefore, he felt that the burden of argument must rest on the shoulders of persons wanting to bring about social or political reforms. Similarly, David Hume's political thought tended toward a conservatism based on the respect for custom and the fear that too radical a disruption of accustomed ways will destroy the springs of social *sentiment,* needed always as the condition of continued social development.

The most influential criticisms of the natural rights view probably came from nineteenth-century utilitarians, who distrusted metaphysical conceptions of man and wanted a standard for deciding right from wrong in the light of social utility. They believed the political problem concerns a fair distribution of available pleasures, producing maximum happiness within a state. Bentham thought the notions of natural law and natural rights were so much empty nonsense, while a legal philosopher like John Austin argued that some defenders of natural rights and civil liberties acted like "ignorant and bawling fanatics who stun you with their pother about liberty." [2] Utilitarianism

---

[2] John Austin, "Lectures on Jurisprudence," in Frederick A. Olafson, ed., *Society, Law, and Morality* (Englewood Cliffs, N.J.: Prentice-Hall, 1961), pp. 414–415. Also cf. Austin's *Lectures on Jurisprudence,* fifth edition, 1885.

functioned *historically* to buttress liberal aspirations in England, but *philosophically* it is a position which argues men must assign human rights situationally, according as their assignment furthers the public welfare. This means that no rights are *in principle* lasting, since a situation may arise in which their exercise will destroy the general welfare.

Austin's rejection of an unqualified natural rights position also reflected his own strict conception of the nature of a legal system. According to Austin, legal rules alone make up the body of genuine law—"law properly so-called"—in that they rest on the commands of a sovereign capable of harming subjects who disobey. Thus, what is called "the positive law" is confined to the body of legal rules. This means that, for Austin, moral rules and moral rights can be enforced, if at all, only by a broad community. If they are enforced by a sovereign, they become legal rules—consequently, enforced by the power of a human ruler. According to this view, a sovereign may show wisdom in submitting to the moral notions of the community he rules, but he is not bound to do so. Thus, legal rights are granted by a sovereign and may be revoked by him.

Austin's extreme command theory of genuine law also involves the argument that a sovereign is never legally bound by his own commands (a matter which will receive fuller attention in the chapter on sovereignty). Although in fact Austin believed a sovereign *ought* to seek the community's welfare, his command theory of law entails the view that the sovereign cannot legally be made to do so. The reason is that the source of command is independent of legal restriction. Human legal rights eventuate from the edicts of a sovereign and achieve their legal status by that fact alone. Although "the rights which a government confers, and the duties which it lays on its subjects, ought to be conferred and imposed for the advancement of the common weal, or with a view to the aggregate happiness of all the members of the society," [3] there is no legal way in which to guarantee the sovereign must adhere to the principle of general utility. Therefore, Austin gives the name "positive morality" to all rights and obligations which have no public legal status and are, at the same

[3] *Ibid.*

time, not supposed to be laws of God. Laws of God, he thinks, are themselves actually only those rules which conform to whatever produces utility.

A natural rights advocate—on learning that Austin meant by laws of God those rules which in social fact produce the most general happiness of a community—might want to say: "Aha, Mr. Austin! Then you, too, believe in natural rights. We can say that they are those rights which actually do, or would if recognized, produce the greatest community happiness!" This means that one version of natural rights could be made to rest on the utilitarian view of how acts are morally to be justified. Some natural rights philosophers would be wary here. They would want to know *how* the greatest happiness of the community is to be established. Is it to be determined simply by asking people what they want? Will it involve distinguishing peoples' apparent interests from their genuine interests? The classical natural rights position has often followed from the conviction that men can be mistaken about their interests. Thus, to satisfy this classical version of the position, a person would have to make utilitarianism compatible with the older metaphysical views of teleology—the doctrines which insist there is an essential nature possessed by all men which, if real happiness is to result, must have the environmental cooperation of objectively adequate moral rules and rights. As regards this view, God's laws might turn out to be quite different from what men in a specific community judge to be the laws most conducive to their happiness.

Suppose that in the fictional community of Togetherness the citizens are told that God's law forbids sexual activities between men and women after the age of thirty. Suppose also that a number of citizens in Togetherness regret this law, asserting that they are made miserable by its existence. "Change God's law!" the citizens say to the government (or, if they pray, to their God). "Change the law and make us happier!" In such a situation, a natural rights advocate could argue either (1) that God's law must be obeyed if one wants to be moral (whether this obedience makes one happy or miserable) or (2) that this is God's law, but at the same time God's laws alone *in the long run* make human happiness possible (meaning either that the citizens mistake their condition or, if they are temporarily miserable, will be more so if they disobey the law). "Live by this law long enough," the advocate of natural law and natural rights could say, "and you will experience a deeper happiness than you can now imagine." Only the natural rights advocate who also argued that such rights are compatible with happiness need show concern for the complaints of the citizens in Togetherness. The reason is that a version of the position which rested solely on the view that one is obligated to obey God's laws (commands) regardless of the consequences would make obedience itself the norm.

A natural rights doctrine is, in one of its versions, safe from effective criticism. Anyone who questions whether there are natural rights can be told he has not lived long enough to understand what is at stake. A person who denies that a specific right is a natural right can be told that, if he holds to his position long enough, he will see social and political consequences *inevitably* develop which he would want to escape. The persuasive force of the doctrine stems from a prophetic stance. Disregard the view there are natural rights, the doctrine seems to run, and in time come to see the destruction of a human social order. It is as if the natural rights advocate thinks a society has about as much chance of enduring if it rejects natural rights as an automobile has to continue operating without grease and oil. Still, he is left in the position of having to admit existence of rights which, admittedly, numerous persons whose possessions they are said to be live without the ability to exercise. This *is* a strange doctrine, as many critics hasten to point out. Yet there are natural rights advocates perennially ready to do battle for their convictions in spite of the critics' puzzlement.

Perhaps the long philosophical controversy between those who believe in natural rights and persons critical of the doctrine reflects a basic disagreement about the relation of legal and moral rules and rights. This disagreement may, in turn, reflect a difference of perspective. Perhaps the natural rights advocate approaches the discussion with the perspective of the citizen, while the critic chooses to view the individual as a subject of sovereign powers capable of helping or harming him. The former expresses the concern of the free citizen that political power may engulf him, making him helpless. The latter may want to make sense of the fact that, in any functioning political system, there is as much a need for legal restraint of action as a need for protecting the individual's rights. This important difference in perspective occurs in political theorizing—for government has as much a function to rule (meaning to use its legitimate powers) as to refrain from ruling for fear of hurting certain persons' rights. Political theorists thus "see" two functions of governing which seem sometimes incompatible—the governmental processes exist to get things done, thus require order and obedience; but such processes need to be limited, too, so that they may not arbitrarily invade the lives of private citizens in need of protection against coercive power.

The philosophical world contains many persons who, though often *personally* committed to the defense of certain basic human rights, show deep uncertainty whether such rights can be shown to have anything like "natural" (or, perhaps, metaphysical) foundations. There are understandable historical grounds for their scepticism. Many social and political communities have existed for long periods without recognizing many of the rights now claimed by liberally minded persons. Also, contemporary thinkers are not as naive about the language of rights and obligations as were some earlier thinkers, some of whom assumed that statements about rights and obligations are descriptions of states of affairs. Their problem has been to make clear what it is that value assertions describe. It has turned out, actually, that many contemporary moral and political philosophers now understand that value assertions are not simple descriptions of properties or qualities of things, but are in some sense prescriptions. To say "The book is a good one" is not just like saying "The book contains 245 pages." Prescriptive statements usually contain a descriptive element plus an expression of personal attitude. To learn a natural language (in our cases, to learn the English language) involves learning how to use words like "right," "ought," "good," "wrong," in many social and political situations. The moral uses of the words belong to the language—are embedded *in* the language, as it were—such that any attempt to imagine a developed social community lacking such words is (for the English-speaking person) to attempt the impossible. If *we* can meaningfully use such terms, then the question: "Are there any moral rights and rules?" requires that even the philosopher give as an emphatic answer: "Of course there are! Don't you know English?" An influential contemporary philosopher has argued that, even in philosophical analysis, an appeal to how words are used in the language is always the first word though not necessarily the last.

So long as persons speak the English language, and that language allows the formulation of the interrogative sentence "Are there any moral rights?", it would appear that words like "moral" and "rights" have uses in that language. The scepticism of those who deny there are *necessary* rights seems to rest on the view that a given language may change (along with the "way of life" it expresses), thus that the contents (facts) which the moral terms express may also alter. A person may feel compelled to say: "Yes, there are basic moral rights!", in a context in which he cannot commit himself to the position that any *specific* or *concrete* right need be lasting. But this means simply to assert that the human social universe is such that human beings alone are able to talk about rights—moral or otherwise.

This does not cover the whole problem. What worries some defenders of the view there are moral, perhaps even "natural," rights is that the *content* of some sentences employing words like "moral" and "right" cannot change without limitation. If people may be said to have (restricted) rights to freedom of speech, say, this means to say that—in some important sense—there are conceivable situations in which no one can *rightfully* deny that freedom. This does not mean that freedom to speak out openly need be considered a right in each and every situation, nor that such a right may not rightfully be curtailed in dangerous social and political situations. It *does* mean that our conception of social and political reality is such that, if the right is imagined as subject to *total* curtailment, it ceases to function meaningfully as a right. That is, even exceptions to the rule that men possess a right to free expression must, morally, be made within a social and political framework based on the perpetuation of conditions which allow persons actually to exercise it. Believers in the doctrine that fundamental moral rights exist must, therefore, strive to create a society in which unrestricted curtailments of the right are impossible.

Some Legal Considerations

No hard-and-fast distinction can be drawn between legal and moral rights. Historically, many of the legal rights upheld by a specific legal system existed earlier—perhaps in less carefully defined ways—as parts of a community's style of social and political life. The legal system often clarifies rights, in a public and formal way, which are more informally rooted in the practices and beliefs of a people sharing common aspirations and traditions. Legal rights are maintained, and their violations punished, by specifically legal means; while there may be many moral rights which, if they are to be preserved or sanctioned, rest on the actions of persons done independently of the legal system. To say that moral rights exist means to say that, if they are to be exercised, a community has some special justification for restraining classes of action even by use of coercive measures. Professor Hart argues this point as follows:

> It is not merely that as a matter of fact men speak of their moral rights mainly when advocating their incorporation in a legal system, but that the concept of right belongs to that branch of morality which is specifically concerned to determine when one person's freedom may be limited by another's and so to determine what actions may appropriately be made the subject of coercive legal rules.[4]

There remain many areas, of course, in which rights can be protected by forms of coercion other than legal.

To say that some person has a particular legal or moral right usually means to say the person should be permitted to exercise the right. This in turn means that others are obligated to protect him in its exercise. In the case of legal rights, the administrative weight of the legal order can legitimately coerce relevant actions even by limiting our liberty. In the fifth chapter of his *Utilitarianism,* J. S. Mill sought to divide obligations into two broad classes—those thought to

[4] H. L. A. Hart, "Are There Any Natural Rights?" originally appeared in *The Philosophical Review,* Vol. LXIV (1955) and is reprinted from Frederick A. Olafson, ed., *op. cit.,* p. 175.

be binding on all members of the moral community and others which, though worthy of recognition, do not appear to justify the use of coercion against persons who fail to meet them. Mill termed those obligations which must be met to guard existing rights "duties of perfect obligation." The obligations which men ought to seek to perform, but which do not seem to involve a correlative right for someone else, he called "duties of imperfect obligation." The latter duties remain obligatory, according to Mill, but the time and circumstances of their performance can be determined by the person. Mill thought that men are obligated to be charitable and beneficent but not, apparently, that others have a necessary right to such treatment. On this view, justice is that part of morality concerned with duties of perfect obligation—close to that province in which, for Professor Hart, legal and moral obligations coincide.

Mill's distinction between the two classes of obligation makes good sense, yet there are situations to which it seems not to apply. The following account—based on a report to the author by a close friend —will illustrate a possible instance in which moral considerations not written into a legal system seem to point to something like a perfect obligation nonetheless.

> Sally X is a child, aged four, left under the brief care of a neighbor woman while her own mother takes a baby sister of Sally's to have a physical examination. While the mother is gone, Sally gashes her right wrist in a serious way while playing with a bottle which breaks. She is bleeding profusely. The neighbor woman, upset, telephones a local hospital asking that she be allowed to bring Sally to the Emergency Treatment section for immediate care. The hospital official asks if the child's mother will sign a form permitting a hospital physician to perform surgery if it is needed. Told that the child will not be admitted without the mother's signature, the neighbor woman explains why she cannot get hold of the mother. The result is that the bleeding child cannot be treated at the hospital. Fortunately, the mother returns in time to take the child there and to agree to allow many stitches to be taken to the serious wound.

Assuming that the author's friend got the facts straight (which may be questionable), this account raises the question whether, given certain legal rules, a person's sense of obligation will not sometimes be shocked by these rules. Suppose a hospital (or the physicians working in it) should be subject to serious liability suits for doing what, in the light of medical knowledge, appears to be required if a patient is seriously wounded. Our sense of justice demands that seriously wounded children receive proper and immediate medical treatment. Yet, legally, it may be possible for this treatment to be denied if the existing rules are that a parent's signature is required. If the parent cannot be found, is a child to be put in the position of perhaps bleeding to death? Is a hospital, or its physicians, morally obligated to perform an act for which the consequence may be severe legal application of penalties? Morally, the child has the right to such treatment; but it is not clear that a *legal* order need say that a hospital, or its physicians, has a correlative obligation to provide it under certain circumstances. Yet, it seems clear most persons would feel they do have such a moral obligation. Apparently, if such a situation existed, the liability rules should—on moral grounds—be altered. On this assumption, there can be duties of perfect obligation which do not necessarily find statement in the legal system.

Cases occur, in the legal field, in which persons have rights that do not entail correlative moral obligations on the part of others. This is uniquely what occurs in competitive situations, not all of which need be legally coerced. Candidates may have a right to compete for an important position in a business organization. Yet, this does not place others in the organization under any special obligation to permit them to win the position. Competitive situations and games happen to involve fairly strict notions of winning, and the prizes usually go to a very few who possess the special talents and dedication to make victory possible. Thus, to say that a number of persons (whether a large or a small number) possess a right to compete for specific rewards in a defined situation does seem to imply that others are obligated to recognize that right. But their right to compete does not obligate others to see that each one wins a prize. Similarly, those who compete for the rewards in competitive situations are not obligated to permit others to win, though they are obligated perhaps to recognize certain rules of procedure regarding their relations with the other competitors.

Cases sometimes occur which, in a significant way, show that questions about rights and obligations may require a judicial decision. Until the decision is rendered, it is not possible to answer the question, "Who has the right in this situation?" Thus, there are situations in a complex social system possessing a legal machinery for legal decision making, in which questions about rights and obligations are temporarily unanswered and unanswerable. Justice Holmes is sometimes criticized for his assertion that law, from the lawyer's viewpoint, is an effort to predict how the courts will decide. Yet, in one respect, this is so. Disputes about legal rights and obligations mean that only the courts can decide by the rules of the social and political community. Only the legal machinery can *legally* determine the nature of legal rights and obligations in a community, though many may say of some of those decisions that they are unwise or even, perhaps, immoral. In the latter cases, men may experience the disquietude associated with deciding whether to obey the legal decisions. They may even sometimes decide to resist, or even to rebel. What they rebel against, in such situations, is someone's legal right or obligation as decided by the courts. Social communities whose members are fairly evenly divided about the wisdom or moral fittingness of some legal decisions affecting men's legal rights and obligations are communities faced with serious problems of authority and obedience.

Historically, legal rights and obligations emerge into explicit statement from a less defined background of general moral agreement among influential segments of a social and political order. This results simply from the need to differentiate functions—to endow specific groups with the duties of attending to legal questions. A community often recognizes rights and obligations to exist before establishing specialized departments of government for overseeing them. These are said to become legal rights only when they are written out and made public by an authorized agency. Prior to such time, they are said to have customary status. Some thinkers look upon legal rights as conventions and natural rights as more enduring facts. But this can be most misleading, as argued by T. D. Weldon in his account of the normal historical relation between legal and moral rights:

> It does not matter whether we say that in the earlier stage everybody had a right$_1$ to act in such and such a way and that a right$_2$ came into existence only with the new regulations, or whether we say that in the first stage there was only custom and in the second for the first time rights. What is mistaken is to suppose that either stage is more natural or fundamental than the other. Historically rights$_2$ are normally later than rights$_1$, but this is not inevitable. We can invent a new game which nobody has ever played and then rules come before customs. In this sense only can rights be invented, but the situation is not one which occurs in political development. There I think it is safe to say that rights$_2$ as a matter of fact always follow rights$_1$ and do not precede them.[5]

Courts may often hold individuals legally responsible for actions for which judges, or other members of a community, would not consider these same individuals morally blameworthy. Men's legal liability for certain classes of action need not coincide with their moral judgeability. In a society containing many automobiles and heavy city traffic, accidents can be expected to occur. The legal order may establish fairly strict rules of financial liability, such that some person involved in an accident shall be held legally and financially accountable. Obviously, however, only a small number of automobile accidents will be put at the doorstep of individual drivers' moral turpitude. In his *The Concept of Law,* Professor H. L. A. Hart maintains that strict liability often permits a legal requirement that compensation be paid which, in specific cases, need not be considered morally just. Strict liability may be defended in a broad manner by arguing that, in spite of individual hardships caused, it tends to promote society's general welfare.

A case in which possible legal liability need not necessarily entail moral judgeability, chosen from among numerous possibilities, might be that in which an almost blind person named Joseph living in Pennsylvania injured himself by falling into an open trench. The

---

[5] T. D. Weldon, *The Vocabulary of Politics* (Hammondsworth, Eng.: Penguin, 1953), p. 60.

ditch had been dug across the sidewalk by a Peter Sn——, who was making a sewer line from street to house. On one side of the trench a protective barricade had been built, but on the other—the side from which Joseph came upon it—only a pile of dirt had been erected. Almost blind, walking by looking at the line of housetops and trees, Joseph slipped on the dirt and fell into the trench. He sued Peter Sn——, at one point winning a small sum. (This first verdict, holding Peter Sn—— liable, was later put aside on the grounds that a nearly blind man could be expected to have used precautions, like a cane or a trained dog.) [6] The point here is that, even if Peter Sn—— had been held liable for Joseph's accident, many persons would wish to say he had exercised reasonable care in protecting the trench; or, that if they thought he had not, his failure to do so was not really a moral one since blind persons, say, might be thought obligated not to walk about public streets without a source of proper guidance. Thus not all legal rights need be considered moral ones—since some successful persons in liability cases often feel that they get a settlement by virtue of the liability rules alone—rules which on strictly moral grounds sometimes seem questionable.

A Contemporary Analysis

Many contemporary thinkers have displayed an obvious discontent over the manner in which philosophers discuss rights. The grammatical form of a sentence like: "Harry has some rights" is very much like that of: "Harry has the measles." Yet, it is far from clear how a critic can locate Harry's rights quite in the way he can expect a competent doctor to diagnose his case of measles. To locate Harry's rights, a person must often take his attention from Harry to study legal documents. Similarly, causal questions about rights are often more complicated than causal questions about some specific disease. Perhaps Harry acquired some of his financial rights from a will by which he was bequeathed money, and to "check up" on such rights may require the services of a lawyer. Perhaps

[6] This is just one of the cases discussed by Edmond Cahn in his *The Moral Decision* (Bloomington: Indiana University Press, 1955), pp. 215–216.

some of Harry's rights derive from practices which are not written into law but which are, nevertheless, supported by the moral beliefs prevalent in his community. Perhaps some claims to rights by Harry need be supported by action in the courts such that some of his claims will prove to have been mistaken.

The language of rights sometimes suggests that rights are possessions to be described in the ways in which other property may be described. Yet, rights are not quite like tables and chairs and gold coins. They are rather like tickets to a play or a concert, available for use if the possessor wants to make use of them. They are permissions for a person to act in given ways in specific situations such that of two men performing the same act we can often say that one has a right, while the other lacks the right, to perform that action. Of two men taking money from a bank, we can often say that one has a right ("It's his money, you know!") while the other is a thief ("He's stealing the money!").

As a prominent contemporary contributor to the literature on law and morals, Professor H. L. A. Hart, has sought to discuss the quite old topic of rights in a fresh and suggestive manner. Sensitive to the actual ways in which the English language is used, as well as suspicious about efforts to treat rights as phenomena which can be described like other objects, he has argued that rights—as well as responsibilities—are *ascribed* rather than described. The reason is that the objects of description, where rights are concerned, are often sentences used in situations in which rights are granted or denied. Professor Hart thinks his notion here can prove helpful to philosophers seeking to avoid confusions about rights and responsibilities.

The ascriptive theory of rights is a contextual one. To know whether rights are being granted or denied, a person needs to have certain facts at his disposal—knowledge about features of concrete situations in which persons either say relevant words or perform specific actions, like signing official papers from which (legal) rights or responsibilities may be said to eventuate. Professor Hart's ascriptive theory has something in common with Professor John Austin's notion of "performatives"—statements which are the actions when uttered in certain contexts. Thus, the minister who utters certain words at a wedding actually "marries" the couple standing (or kneeling) in front of him just as the college president, by uttering specific phrases, may be said to grant an advanced degree to some honored visitor. Similarly, speech or writing performed in some contexts brings rights into existence or withdraws rights formerly granted (as an official divorce document withdraws marital rights granted earlier in an official marriage ceremony). Thus, the saying or writing of certain words *in some situations* conveys or withdraws rights. The words in themselves are not enough, of course, since not every person who says "I now pronounce you man and wife" is in an official position to do so. Similarly, a person on his sickbed may say "I give you all my fortune" only to have a court, after his death, decide that in the absence of a will much of the man's fortune must go to someone else.

Professor Hart argues that sentences like "This is mine (his) (yours)", "You have a right to this," etc., are used to ascribe rights and responsibilities. They are not descriptions in any ordinary sense and, like other claims, are subject to defeat in court if presented with certain kinds of challenge. Claimants to rights must, if challenged, show in court that there has been no fraud, innocent misrepresentation, failure to disclose important facts, duress, undue influence, making of immoral contracts, contract to restrain free trade, contracts perverting the course of justice, intoxication, lunacy, unexpected events like war or revolution to interfere with meeting a contract, any extraordinary lapse of time in a contractual arrangement. That is, claims to rights are such that unless they can be "defeated" (the notion of *defeasibility* operates here) the claims may be said to stand. The result is that the language of rights can be illuminated by studying features of legal procedures, for as Professor Hart has argued:

> The position is, of course, that a very common good reason for recognizing that a person has some rights to the possession of a thing is that he is observed physically in the possession of it; and it is, of course, correct in such circumstances to ascribe such rights with the sentence "This is yours" in the absence of any claim or special circumstances which may defeat them. But as individuals we are not in the position of a judge; our decision is not final, and when we have notice of new circumstances or new claims we have to decide in the light of them again. But in other respects the function of sentences

of this simple and non-technical sort resembles that of judicial decisions. The concepts involved are defeasible concepts like those of
the law and similarly related to supporting facts.[7]

Of course, it may be argued that checking up on claims to rights
involves something like a description of existing legal rules. To find
out whether someone who claims certain rights actually has them
means to look up the legal record. Yet, it is the power of Hart's view
that it emphasizes how, standing behind that official record subject
to later description, there are authoritative spoken or written sentences which convey the rights. Thus we may check the records of a
specific college in order to learn when, if at all, a certain person
received an honorary degree. That is the record to be described, in
other words. Nonetheless, what conveyed the degree, if anything, were
certain words spoken at a past commencement as well as certain
words put on an official document. The giving or withdrawing of
rights, then, involve ascriptions rather than simple descriptions. The
ascriptive theory of rights thus may save philosophers from asking the
wrong kinds of questions about rights, as if to a question such as
"Where did his rights come from?" there must be some profound
metaphysical reply at hand.

Professor Hart has also made a suggestive contribution to the literature on natural rights. He has asserted that possession of a right
involves the justified interference in the lives of others seeking to
deny or abuse that right. Consequently, Hart insists that "if there are
any moral rights at all, it follows that there is at least one natural
right, the equal right of all men to be free." [8] The reasons are that all
persons morally able to make choices can expect that others will refrain from coercion or restraint against them unless they are coercing
or restraining others and that they are free to perform those actions
which do not restrain or coerce others, or seek to injure them.

There are general rights as contrasted with special rights, according

[7] H. L. A. Hart, "The Ascription of Responsibility and Rights," in Anthony
Flew, ed., *Logic and Language* (First Series; Oxford: Basil Blackwell, 1962),
p. 159. Reprinted by permission of the author.
[8] H. L. A. Hart, "Are There Any Natural Rights?" originally appeared in
The Philosophical Review, Vol. LXIV (1955) and is reprinted in Frederick A.
Olafson, ed., *op. ci* p. 173.

to Professor Hart's analysis. Special rights reside in a specific person, eventuating from promises, authorizations to others to act for us, mutuality of restrictions, special relationships (like parent and child), and the granting of special liberties. Under mutuality of restrictions, all persons who have obeyed rules under a political superior have a right to expect others to obey them when, and if, they acquire the legitimate political authority to apply the rules. Contrasted with such special rights, general rights belong to all men who are capable of choice outside the areas already marked off by special rights. Moreover, general rights do not come into existence out of special transactions among men (as do special rights), nor can they rightfully be claimed for some men and not for others. General rights are clearly related to the notion of morality, for

> to assert a general right is to claim in relation to some particular action the equal right of all men to be free in the absence of any of those special conditions which constitute a special right to limit another's freedom; to assert a special right is to assert in relation to some particular action a right constituted by such special conditions to limit another's freedom.[9]

It is Hart's contention that to assert a general right means directly to invoke the principle that all men have an equal right to be free, while to assert a special right invokes this notion only indirectly.

Conclusion

Talk about human rights occurs in numerous contexts. The philosophical problem is concerned with what may be said to be conveyed when rights are granted, or withdrawn when rights are retracted, or refused when rights are denied. The natural rights advocates insist that moral rights are a necessary condition for any meaningful legal rights, but they find it difficult to give literal meaning to their views. Rather, they seem to be arguing for a specific view of the human situation and the human being, apparently wanting to make the possession of rights part of their definition of "man." Nonetheless, the

[9] *Ibid.,* p. 183.

natural rights doctrine—though a modern one—has played a crucial historical role in men's quest after equality and fair treatment in some political contexts.

Some contemporary thinkers deny that claims about rights can be treated in a *philosophically* meaningful fashion if these claims are supposed to point to special properties of men or human actions. Professor Hart has emphasized the language in which rights are talked about, suggesting an ascriptive as opposed to a descriptive theory of rights. Like others, he has turned to the legal order to discover parallels to ordinary talk about moral rights. Contemporary philosophers have sought "to save the appearances," as it were, hoping to make a defense of natural rights on some nonliteral basis. It is clear that these thinkers believe that talk about rights involves a number of philosophical issues, no one of which is subject to neat and easy resolution. The philosophical concern about talk of rights reflects the difficulties faced by philosophers aware of the logical distinction between statements of fact and statements of value. It is questionable that, in our day and age, a strong case can be made for the older metaphysical defenses of philosophical claims. Thus philosophical talk about rights will probably continue to rest on analysis of legal and historical examples.

Some Questions and Problems

1. Confining your attention to domestic affairs in this country, try to list some ways in which claims to the possession of rights by different groups may produce political conflicts. Can you think of ways in which such conflicts may be resolved or compromised?
2. Does the notion of rights necessarily entail the notion of obligations? Discuss.
3. Imagine that you are an important political figure, holding a high office. Imagine also that a minority seeks to achieve a widened exercise of personal and civil rights. Should you either tolerate or encourage the members of this minority in peaceful demonstrations and marches? Why or why not?
4. Should the Bill of Rights be treated as exceptionless?
5. Can legal rights conflict with moral rights? If so, how is that possible? Are there any legal rights which might be said to be morally neutral?

6. Discuss the following assertion: "Civil rights will sometimes come into conflict with basic property rights. In that event, a free people must choose to protect property rights at all costs."

7. Think of some rights you possess which, in certain situations, you might not claim. Should a person always claim his existing rights? Why or why not?

8. Under what situations might you want to restrict the following rights?

   - freedom of speech

   - freedom of religion

   - freedom of press

   - freedom of assembly

   - freedom to petition for redress of grievances

   - freedom of personal movement

9. How do you stand on the question of whether natural rights exist? Can you make some kind of case for the doctrine?

10. Discuss the following assertion: "All human rights exist only in so far as organized political power is available to protect persons in the exercise of them." Be prepared to express your views in class.

Some Suggested Readings

Becker, C. *Heavenly City of the Eighteenth-Century Philosophers.* New Haven: Yale University Press, 1932.

———. *Modern Democracy.* New Haven: Yale University Press, 1941.

———. *Declaration of Independence.* New York: Knopf, 1945.

Brown, S. M. "Inalienable Rights," *The Philosophical Review,* Vol. XLIV, 1955.

Cahn, E. *The Moral Decision.* Bloomington: Indiana University Press, 1955.

———. (ed.) *The Great Rights.* New York: Macmillan, 1963.

Dilliard, I. (ed.). *One Man's Stand for Freedom: Mr. Justice Black and the Bill of Rights.* New York: Knopf, 1963.

Frankena, W. K. "Natural and Inalienable Rights," *The Philosophical Review,* Vol. XLIV, 1955.

Hart, H. L. A. "Are There Any Natural Rights?," *The Philosophical Review,* Vol. XLIV, 1955.

Macdonald, M. "Natural Rights," *Proceedings of the Aristotelian Society,* 1947–8. Reprinted in *Philosophy, Politics and Society,* First Series, ed. P. Laslett. New York: Macmillan, 1956.

Ritchie, D. G. *Natural Rights.* London: Macmillan, 1903.

Strauss, L. *Natural Rights and History.* Chicago: University of Chicago Press, 1953.

UNESCO: *Human Rights: A Symposium.* New York: Columbia University Press, 1949.

Weldon, T. D. *The Vocabulary of Politics.* Hammondsworth, Eng.: Penguin, 1953.

CHAPTER SIX

Authority

In the long tradition of philosophical reflection and analysis, covering several thousand turbulent years of historical development, political thinkers have bequeathed to harried librarians an enormous body of writings about authority and sovereignty. These thinkers have argued in different ways for diverse views about the nature and function of political authority. Some managed a greater disinterestedness than others. A few even succeeded in altering men's attitudes, even as they sometimes wrote as passionate propagandists for their political views.

For example, John Locke's political writings justified the compromise known in England as the Glorious Revolution of 1688 and served as influential sources when American Revolutionists, a full century later, wrote in defense of their principles. Certainly, the writings of Karl Marx, a dedicated revolutionary, have influenced the political opinions of most contemporary thinkers by confronting them with a new way of "seeing" the relationship between economic and political events and processes. During the Middle Ages, the body of St. Augustine's writings—especially his *City of God*—helped to shape European men's conceptions of the relation of church and state as well as of politics and history. Political thinkers often argued for what they judged the *proper* or *best* political system, revealing how even philosophers are not immune to the temptations of self-interest or religious and national favoritism. A few great classics on political authority reveal that, under certain circumstances, a thinker may seek to justify a particular political outlook and yet write a classic which, though rooted in its genesis and subject matter to a specific

historical period, expresses political principles which remain suggestive and important to later thinkers often laboring in quite different
political climates or seeking goals quite distinct from those of the
classical writer.

Great political classics—Plato's *Republic,* Augustine's *City of God,*
Machiavelli's *The Prince,* Hobbes's *Leviathan,* Locke's *Treatises on
Civil Government,* Marx's *The German Ideology,* Mill's *Essay on
Liberty,* Lenin's *State and Revolution,* Dewey's *The Public and Its
Problems,* to mention only a few of the works central to any history
of political thought—contain all sorts of important arguments and
perspectives which each new generation needs, for very practical purposes, to reconsider and to judge. There is a perennial greatness about
works such as these. They make politics, so often seeming like dry-
as-dust practicality, assume an aura of importance, reminding men
who, happily, may live in fairly settled political times, that perhaps no
political argument is eternally settled and that no functioning political
system was not, in some sense, a human achievement.

What the political classics make clear is how, in different times
and circumstances, thoughtful men treated a number of enduring
problems, not the least among these the problem of political authority.
Because political authority is a cooperative affair, requiring the
efforts of numerous individuals and some organization of these efforts
toward achievement of common social ends, all societies which
emerge from simple agrarian styles of life tend to develop fairly
complex habitual ways of ordering some of the relations between
individuals and groups of individuals. The basic choice men confront
as political animals is not one between freedom and authority, order
or lack of order; rather the choice is one between kinds of freedom
and authority, types and degrees of organization, kinds of social goals
and techniques for realizing them. Men can never live socially without
some kinds of authority and organized systems of behavior. Driven
as they are by basic needs and even possessing a positive delight in
some forms of social participation, men soon find that they must plan
to meet those needs in a relatively stable, orderly manner if their
communal living is to avoid perpetual crises and the disastrous consequences of hurried, even emotional responses to these crises. Thus,

the argument has seldom been about *whether* men shall order their relations with one another but, rather, *how* they shall (or ought to) do so, and for what ends as well as to how great an extent. Most political classics, at the very least, remind average persons how inescapably they are members of political communities—like it or not—and how certain towering political issues dog their careers as social creatures.

The chief institutional means—symbolic as well as organizational—by which men have responded to common needs of order and effort has usually, in modern times, been known as the state. For this reason, concern about authority in modern political writers, from Thomas Hobbes to John Dewey, say, has emphasized the role of the state; and political discussions of a theoretical nature have reflected men's worries about the relations of state (as a special power) and individuals (who are weak and naked before the state's organized power). Thus, many discussions about authority and sovereignty have centered on the concept of the state. Differences among political philosophers have often reflected disagreements about the nature and functions of state power, differences often influenced by specific conditions prominent in a given historical period. Behind the differences among the philosophers, even if unexpressed, exists a state-of-affairs which may be called the perennial problem of human politics—the problem faced by men in any age. A perceptive thinker has expressed awareness of this perennial problem in the following way:

> Now, experience informs us that there exist some apparently lasting *relationships* between man and nature. They express themselves as "natural wants," and can be met variously; but if they are not met, man cannot survive. He needs food and other necessaries of life; he must produce. He is mortal; he must reproduce. He has enemies; he must defend himself. The conditions dictated by nature to men as a species carry over to society; any lasting grouping of men must provide sustenance for its members, as well as reproduce and defend itself. And in this sense, it is natural to visualize society as a sequence of human events arranging themselves in patterns to meet these primary *social functions*.[1]

[1] John Lindberg, *Foundations of Social Survival* (New York: Columbia University Press, 1953), pp. 3–4. Used by permission of Columbia University Press.

Power and Authority

Of course, there are numerous authorities which any person must acknowledge in the course of a lifetime, some of which are in no direct way always related to a political state. Parents exercise authority over children; older brothers and sisters over younger ones; scholarly critics over the contents of the learned journals they supervise; schoolyard "bullies" over the behavior of more timid school children whom they often terrorize. The political thinker usually attempts to present a justification of authority as *legitimate, proper,* or *natural* as opposed to pretenders to the title. While those persons said to possess authority are usually in possession of certain powers of action and decision, they need not be the strongest; for even losers in political conflicts can distinguish between a present state-of-affairs (the authority of an existing situation, so to speak) and *ultimate* authority, indicating that the notion of authority need not be synonymous with an actual successful exercise of power. Although authority usually rests on some existing power (or claim to power), needed to "back up" authority in troubled circumstances, there seems to be a difference between such power and true authority, since power (force) can be used *against* existing authority as well as in its behalf. Thus, philosophical discussions of authority are often peculiar admixtures of description (accounts of how specific authorities came into existence and how they function) and value appraisal (efforts to prove that a certain authority ought to operate as it does or, if it doesn't, how it should). There are, of course, thinkers who insist that all questions about authority are ultimately questions about power— a view to be considered. However, their view seems one not easily supported if one appeals to how English-speaking persons use words like "power" and "authority." Authoritative power sometimes means power *legitimately* used, or power emanating from some *approved* source as opposed to power usurped.

Decidedly, the question of the relation between authority and power is a troubling one in the history of thought. The "hardheaded" thinkers, suspicious of men's tendencies to rationalize power displays by reliance on a moral vocabulary, raise a quizzical eyebrow whenever ethical writers argue that matters of fact are never in themselves sufficient to establish what *ought* to be the case in human political affairs. Yet English usage indicates that men have made distinctions between authority and power—that the logic of the two English words is not the same. T. D. Weldon has pointed out the following consideration:

> Thus it is misleading to suppose that the possession of authority adds something to the exercise of power or the employment of force. It is rather the case that force exercised or capable of being exercised with the general approval of those concerned is what is normally meant by "authority." It is therefore too simple to identify "authority" with "force rightly or justly applied." The proper use of force is always authoritative, but authorities can be wicked and remain authoritative if most of their followers want wickedness. The career of Hitler is instructive on this point.[2]

To understand why some philosophers refuse to treat the concepts of power and authority as identical, consider the following imaginary cases:

1. You come upon a huge, angry-looking man who is dragging a small child by one arm. The child seems to be in pain, but his kicking and crying fail to slow down his tormentor. You ask the man why he is treating the child so roughly. He replies: "I'm bigger than he is, that's why!" You object to his behavior, only to be told in forceful language: "If you stick your nose into this affair, you'll find I'm big enough to handle you, too!"

2. After a football game, a scuffle breaks out between partisan fans, one of whom deliberately hits another over the head with a cane. A burly man dressed in tweeds grabs the offender and steers him through the crowd. Someone says: "You've no right to interfere in this affair!", and the burly man replies: "I'm a plainclothes detective."

3. A riot breaks out in a prison. The warden agrees to speak privately with the prisoner leading the riot, knowing that he risks some

---

[2] *The Vocabulary of Politics* (Hammondsworth, England: Penguin, 1953), p. 56.

danger by so acting. The discussions prove fruitless. When he seeks to return to his office, the prisoners pin his arms to his sides and forcibly detain him. The warden says: "I order you to release me at once. You have no right to detain me." Nonetheless, the prisoners refuse to act in terms of his spoken order. One prisoner says, laughingly: "What can you do about it, Warden?"

These three imagined situations raise questions about someone's right to perform certain kinds of acts even in instances when they appear strong enough to "get away with it" (at least temporarily). In the first case, a request for a justification of rough treatment of a child receives, as answer, an open appeal to power. In the second case, the justification comes in the form of an appeal to authority, since detectives often have legal authority to apprehend offenders. In the third case, an appeal to authority is made in a situation in which authority is powerless to enforce its order. All these cases also illustrate how power is crucially relevant to human actions as well as how important questions about authority arise in situations involving the use of force. The first case is an example of a "might makes right" argument, as is the third—but the third is more immediately social, since the whole enforcement operation in a prison can work against the rioting prisoners even if, with the particular warden, they manage to destroy the man who gives them an order. For the prisoners to succeed in defying the warden's order, they must escape and lead a successful revolution one of whose results will be the kinds of prison reforms they want. Otherwise, to achieve their ends (say, prison reforms) they must work *with* existing authorities (using persuasion) rather than *against* them. As a last resort, of course, a man or group of men can choose to defy authority and be destroyed or, in extreme cases, destroy themselves by committing suicide.

Clearly, most persons live fairly obedient lives within the framework of rules and procedures operating in their societies. If this were not so, particular societies would experience perpetual revolutions— and no habits of obedience would develop in any society, however democratically instituted its rules, for men could decide after leaving a meeting to ignore whatever rules they had just instituted. Again, if most persons set about breaking the rules whenever an authority was not on the corner—or if the authorities themselves constantly broke the rules—social existence would become a continuous terror, lacking the least degree of security and predictability. Thus, it could be argued on factual grounds that most persons, most of the time, are inclined to obey existing authorities, not because they fear them (although this can at times be the case) but because they approve of them and fear, rather, the consequences which would follow on their removal. Still, a "realist" in political thought can argue that obedience to authority in the absence of its personal representatives rests on a fear of what might happen *if* breaches of authority should be detected—that what, say, gives a rule its authoritative status in a society is the fear on the part of a citizen that, should he break certain rules, he will face the concrete situation in which a law-enforcement agent knocks on his door eventually and says something like: "Come with me peacefully or be dragged to court!" Such a person "sees" all instances of authority as resting, ultimately, on naked repressive force. Analogously, the state can be viewed as an ultimate, more or less omnipotent repressive force which backs up legal authorities by threat of sanctions against offenders. Such a view tends to lead to the position, not that authority often requires enforcement, but that authority *is* actual or threatened enforcement of sanctions.

The absolute identification of authority with power is unable to account for certain facts of social and political life. One is that a person or political group may meaningfully be said to have lost authority without actually losing power. There is an obvious difference between two powerful political states, one of whose citizens obey simply out of fear while hating the authorities, the other of whose members obey willingly by giving their consent to the decisions of the rulers. In the first state, if the example is not a meaningless one, in some sense the rulers in power have lost their authority although they may be able by terror and cruelty to operate successfully over a long period. Another problem for the cynical view stems from the way in which, though political administrations may change (sometimes even by virtue of a radical revolution), the legal system of a state usually continues to operate providing a continuity between the generations. A third problem of the "realistic" or cynical view is that a person or group may sometimes lose power while retaining authority—as when, say, in the prison riot case, the warden may be said still to be an authority although (temporarily) unable to make his captors release him by giving a verbal command.

If power and authority are synonymous concepts, then, apparently the sentences "So-and-so has the power" and "So-and-so has the authority" should have always the same meaning, thus be interchangeable. Yet, this is not the case. About a person in an official administrative position, we can sometimes say, "He has the authority to call Smith 'on the carpet,' but he lacks the power!", perhaps meaning that he is weak-willed or lacks sufficient "willpower," thus is in a sense unable to assert the rights of his authorized office. Similarly, a policeman has the authority (meaning that he is officially authorized) to arrest certain classes of offenders, but there would be nothing misleading if during a lynching someone should say: "Sheriff Harpie has the authority but not the power to halt this lynching." Also, to show the other side of the coin, we might say about a physically aggressive gangster, "Boss Tomlin has the power but not the authority to steal goods from peaceful citizens."

Part of the basis for the making of a distinction between having power and exercising authority rests on the notion that authority entails *authorized* as opposed to *unauthorized* use of power. Often, in political situations, the powers of an office are "seen" as belonging to the office—as an authoritative link in a hierarchical or administrative chain—rather than to the person happening to hold the office. G. W. F. Hegel stated this view as well as any writer by saying, in his *Philosophy of Right:* "The particular activities and agencies of the state are its essential moments and therefore are proper to *it*. The individual functionaries and agents are attached to their office not on the strength of their immediate personality, but only on the strength of their universal and objective qualities. Hence it is in an external and contingent way that these offices are linked with particular persons, and therefore the functions and powers of the state cannot be private property." Sometimes people complain about political leaders who seem slow to act by asking: "Why doesn't he exercise his authority? Why's he afraid to use the powers of his office?" By so doing, they are calling attention to what they consider character faults of an officeholder rather than raising any question about an authoritative office. Men therefore tend to characterize leaders as *weak* or *strong* authorities, *decisive* or *indecisive* officeholders.

Sometimes men want to distinguish the "authority" of an office or a position from the manner in which a specific individual carries out his functions while possessing that office. We can speak of the authority, say, of the President of the United States—referring to the high office; or we can, occasionally, speak of *this* or *that* President's authority, referring to features of conduct of the person holding the position. The powers of the office are often seen as existing in a defined social matrix, there to be used or ignored by any person who comes to office. Thus, if we say about a person who holds an official position (one that is to some extent "defined" by an administrative chart of functions) that "Sam's losing his authority," we may wish to call attention to the way in which different individuals function, for good or ill, when in possession of a specific office. On the other hand, someone may challenge us by insisting: "Losing his authority, you say? How's that? He still holds office and can order us about." That is, a listener can stress the *formal* aspects of officeholding, the rights and privileges that seem to go with the office. Nonetheless, we may then speak in the following way:

> Yes, you're right—Sam's still the boss here. But things are beginning to go badly. People are dragging their feet and talking behind his back. He has to buck much stiffer resistance to get his orders carried out. His ability to persuade subordinates to his point of view seems greatly diminished. Frequently, he has to give direct commands—doesn't listen to advice—acts as if he's engaged in mortal combat with his personnel. So, you're right that he still has all the official *powers* of the office. But he's losing his (personal) authority nonetheless!

Of course, in such a situation, if resistance to a leader goes far enough, a state of rebellion may occur—or a confused state in which something like a "cold war" goes on between the leader and his subordinates. If the authority is partly judged by results—including his capacity to stir colleagues to a specific course of action by persuasion rather than by direct threat and punishment—then a degree of authority may be said to be lost whenever loyal supporters become, increasingly, the objects of coercive commands. Only if all authority is judged on the model of military chains of command, in which higher offices have relatively widespread powers of "life-and-death" over their subordinates, can a person confine questions of authority to the *formal* functions of the office. There are numerous organizations, especially where democratic practices in the least prevail, in which the test of a person's authority must include *how adequately* that person is able to realize the possibilties of the office without creating widespread resistance and loss of morale.

In Plato's *Republic,* Thrasymachus argues that "justice is the will of the stronger"—showing an awareness of how rulers often determine human actions because they can exercise power or command and apply sanctions to their enemies. Plato shows that strong men may lack knowledge and wisdom—may, by virtue of their powerful positions, command courses of behavior which, in the long run, go counter to the best interests of the very rulers who command them. This is an old dispute which so-called "realists" in every age carry on with "idealists." There is much to be said in favor of the realist's view in the light of obvious facts of political life, of course—facts which idealists (those who want to judge authority by some standard other than power itself) sometimes either minimize or overlook. In political life, questions of authority are closely tied up with questions of power: how many army divisions does country X possess? how many votes can so-and-so deliver? how many "powerful friends" does Y have?, etc. Since authorities in political contexts must often command and punish in order to realize their aims, they cannot function without some reliance on force. On the other hand, since *all* authorities rely at some point on force, they must be judged also in the light of *how* force is employed, as well as when and for what ends. There are kinds of knowing, in politics or elsewhere, which help to make a man an authority: "He surely knows how to get things done!" or "Jim's a good man in a crisis—knows when to 'back off' and when to push ahead!" Quick and ready reliance on threat and force—a tendency in the mass politics of modern life—helps to create a picture of political life in which the citizens ("followers") are driven by the commanding rulers. Thus, *how* rulers achieve their results may become important in making estimates of their authority—that is, of their uses of power. And many persons in practical life act authoritatively without being able to "explain" how it is they manage to do so successfully ("Sam just has a *nose* for it, I guess!"), a feature of life remarked on by J. S. Mill in his *A System of Logic:*

> Among the higher order of practical intellects there have been many of whom it was remarked how admirably they suited their means to their ends, without being able to give any sufficient reasons for what they did, and applied, or seemed to apply, recondite principles which they were wholly unable to state. This is a natural consequence of having a mind stored with appropriate particulars and having been long accustomed to reason at once from these to fresh particulars, without practicing the habit of stating to one's self or to others the corresponding general propositions. As old warrior, on a rapid glance at the outlines of the ground, is able at once to give the necessary orders for a skillful arrangement of his troops, though, if he has received little theoretical instruction and has seldom been called upon to answer to other people for his conduct, he may never have had in his mind a single general theorem respecting the relation between ground and array. But his experience of encampments, in circumstances more or less similar, has left a number of vivid, unexpressed, ungeneralized analogies in his mind, the most appropriate of which, instantly suggesting itself, determines him to a judicious arrangement.[3]

So much of a man's life is invested in practical activity, in getting necessary things done, that idealistic talk about how they *ought* to be done (or *might* have been done) often strikes him as "empty" or "hypocritical." There simply isn't time enough to persuade men that some things must be done, especially in crises, of which even a very protected person has had some experience even by college age. Discussion cannot continue indefinitely, even if democratic policies encourage it up to a point, since the political life concerns itself with action, and talk must be shown as relevant to action if it is subject to political justification. Even if we dislike what psychologists call "an authoritarian personality" (one who relies heavily on command and

[3] New York: Longmans, Green, 1941, pp. 123, 124.

cannot tolerate other viewpoints), we can often sympathize with the irate person in certain situations who (as father, leader, boss) shouts at an argumentative subordinate or associate: "Damn it, Shultz— stop talking and *do* it!" Authorities must exercise their powers, since that is what being an authority (at least in politics) is all about—and if persuasion sometimes fails, then resort must be had to command backed up with force or threatened use of force.

Still, there is a vast difference between a political system (state, organization, family) in which coercion stands nakedly in view and one in which, though coercion is sometimes necessarily used, procedures exist for influencing actions by persuasive means, including discussion. Similarly, authorities differ in attitudes taken toward the exercise of their powers. It may even be the case that democratically minded authorities hesitate to use their coercive powers to the full because, as persons, they prefer to fail at some undertakings rather than to succeed by methods they deem undesirable. We can qualify the authoritative actions of men by different adverbs, which say something about the "human factor" in political life. Thus, about a person in authority who uses coercion to achieve some result, we may say such things as: "He exerted his full authority (reluctantly, carefully, soundly, viciously, belatedly, etc.)." Therefore, persons who maintain there is a difference between authority and power, want often to indicate how authority is an aspect of *how leaders function* and not simply a matter of the rules in a handbook. To say that an official has lost (or is losing) authority often means to make statements such as— He's lost the respect of his friends; His subordinates fear and distrust him; He's a tyrant; He rides roughshod over people. To say such things implies that the speaker wants to claim that a certain person is a "bad" authority—that he misuses his powers in some way. This value judgment implies there are other means available in which a "good" authority *would* proceed. Perhaps A. N. Whitehead's restatement of Plato's conviction about religion could equally be applied to aspects of politics: ". . . that the divine element in the world is to be conceived as a persuasive agency and not as a coercive agency. This doctrine should be looked upon as one of the greatest intellectual discoveries in the history of religion. . . ."

Democratic Authority

A cynical or realistic political theorist, like Niccolo Machiavelli (1469–1527), say, would remain unpersuaded by talk about democratic authority and attempts to separate questions of authority from questions of power. Machiavelli has given his views of political rule in *The Prince,* in which he accentuates the darker aspect of political life, arguing that a ruler is better off feared than loved if a choice has to be made. Authority is an end-in-itself for Machiavelli, and a ruler's chief problem is how to retain his power once it has been achieved. The ruler must show care in the distribution of power to subordinates, in his practice of meting out rewards and punishments. He must be resourceful, adaptable to changing circumstance (some of which result from Fortune and are, consequently, unpredictable), ever distrustful of friends and enemies. A ruler should possess a fox's cunning (a capacity to avoid pitfalls and traps) and the strength of a lion (a capacity to fight enemies when necessary). According to Machiavelli (as with the English philosopher, Thomas Hobbes [1588–1679]), men are basically unreliable—changeable, fickle, often false to their promises. Thus, a ruler must guide his decisions in the light of a pessimistic conception of human nature—something like a secularized version of the religious picture that "all men are sinners." Authority is the exercise of power toward self-perpetuation rather than towards some political goal viewed as intrinsically good. This view of man even exists in works central to democratic government (as in the *Federalist Papers* by Madison, concerned with factionalism) and operates whenever men, in discouragement, are tempted to call for quick and even ruthless use of force to achieve political ends.

"Look, the function of government is to govern!" someone may be heard to exclaim when a governing group seems to be slow to act. "There's been too much talk and not enough action!" Some democratic theorists have gone so far as to warn that, if powers are too extensively divided, a government may become ineffectual—unable to perform those necessary actions which circumstances (economic, political, etc.) call for. If democratic government is judged ineffectual, then the people will desert it—turning even to tyrannical systems in the hopes of getting what is needed. Any defense of democratic authority must rest on one or both of two kinds of argument: (1) that it is intrinsically better; (2) that in the long run it manages to produce the best results for the people. Advocates of the first view often "see" democracy as involving more than a political system—rather as being a "way of life" that is broadly social, involving customs and psychological characteristics deemed valuable. Critics of democratic views of authority can argue, similarly, either that democratic values aren't the best (as aristocrats are prone to argue, say) or that, as a political system, democracy works too slowly and is subject to domination ("behind the scenes") by special interests. Central to the democratic view is the conviction that each person counts in the determination of policy, and although this simple conviction is probably impossible of any complete realization in practice —and has been "used" by persons who pay it only lip service—it yet remains, in a rough way, indispensable to any defense of democratic practices. During the troubled period when Cromwell ruled England by reliance on an army, a significant debate occurred which involved persons from the army and two men, Cromwell and Ireton, who represented the contemporary government. A soldier named Rainboro, spokesman for the army, whose officers sometimes disagreed with Cromwell and Ireton, argued at one point: "Really, I think the poorest he that is in England hath a life to lead as the richest he." Professor A. D. Lindsay, in his *The Essentials of Democracy,* writes of this statement:

> That seems to me the authentic note of democracy. The poorest has his own life *to live,* not to be managed or divided or used by other people. His life is his and he has to live it. None can divest him of the responsibility. However different men may be in wealth or ability or learning, whether clever or stupid, good or bad, living their life is their concern and their responsibilty. That is for those Puritans as for all true democrats the real meaning of human equality. Responsibility for one's own life is something possessed by or enjoined on us all. Our equality in that responsibility is of such preponderating importance that beside it all our other differences, manifest and undeniable as they may be, are neither here nor there. That is not a

scientific nor a common-sense doctrine. It is a religious and moral principle. It is the translation into non-theological language of the spiritual priesthood of all believers. Men who could say things like that have gone deep into the heart of things.[4]

Contemporary thinkers concerned about preserving elements of democratic procedure in decision making tend to adopt realistic attitudes toward the fact of power. They realize that governments must reach decisions—that minorities, needing protection against illegitimate interference from majority opinion, must not be permitted completely to stifle action for the public's welfare. This concern is to find ways to involve persons, at varying levels of group life, in decision-making processes in first-person groups. They are suspicious of strong men, practical men who pass "down" their decisions to subordinates and then expect conformity. They worry about "rigging" of decisions under a cloak of democratic procedure. This concern touches the areas where men are most immediately affected—their jobs, their families, their education. Against the charge that treating democracy as a way of life in small groups gives too broad a view for political significance, the thinkers can argue that politics is wider than official governing and is a feature of decision making in many groups, even (or especially) professional ones. On this basis, an authoritarian system is one in which persons receive their authority from superiors (usually by appointment), are not responsible to their subordinates, and are relatively free from the need to bear criticism from their associates. Democratic systems, in contrast, limit the arbitrariness of officials' appointments by making these officials' actions subject to at least limited consultation with the members of the groups affected by the appointments.

Many factual questions about authority can meaningfully be asked, most of which are readily answerable if a questioner consults a properly informed person ("Robert knows whom to consult to find out how to get things done properly around here!") or knows which rule-book to check ("Paragraph B in the campus guidebook tells about the official hierarchy at the University."). Yet, philosophical questions are not primarily, if at all, of this factual sort. Rather, philo-

[4] London: Oxford University Press, 1935 edition, p. 12.

sophical questions tend to be concerned with how reasonable men might give justifications of specific authorities. Consider the following flow of conversation in which factual questions about authority on a fictional university campus tend to become philosophical: "How does a person register for courses at Inquiring University?" "That's simple. You consult the registrar for the rules." "Rules? Do you mean I can't simply attend the classes I want?" "Of course not! First, you have to be admitted to the university. Next, you have to enroll in some courses by requirements." "Why so? Why *must* I take certain courses? Isn't this a free country?" "Well, the faculty of the university has estab-lished a curriculum, part of which is uniform for all students. This is no limitation on your freedom, since you don't have to enroll at *this* university if you object to the general rules by which its curriculum operates." "But does a general faculty have a right to limit an indi-vidual professor's rights? Suppose I can find a professor who'll allow me in his class no matter what the university rules specify?" "An individual professor can't do that. Your grade in the course won't be official. He hasn't the authority to alter the rules." "Who has the authority?" "A faculty committee alone has the authority, so long as the general faculty gives a proper vote authorization." "Well, where does the general faculty get the right to control such matters?" "By virtue of its being a faculty! Of course, if you're asking why anyone at all should have authority to establish any rules at all, I don't know what to say to you. That's how university life runs!" "But why should it so run?" "Do you mean, 'Why should we have universities?' I think you are playing a game now!" "But . . ."

Clearly, to ask "why" about the existence of any given authority or authorized procedure need not be aimless. Perhaps the questioner thinks he has good grounds for altering some specific feature of an authoritative procedure, thus perhaps asks an ethical question of the form: "Why *should* the present procedure be continued?" He may not understand the reasons for which the authoritative procedure was instituted. If he can be given convincing reasons, he may then say: "Now I understand why!" On the other hand, if he hears the reasons stated but is convinced by none of them, he may bring forward a sug-gestion about how a more reasonable procedure can be substituted.

To do the latter, he must operate within the broader rules and channels of authority by which the community of which he is a member operates. If he is neither satisfied by the reasons given for the procedure nor willing to suggest a possible alteration, yet continues to ask "why," either he thinks good reasons can be given on behalf of the view that the procedure can be eliminated or he is asking why any authority as authority is ever needed. It is not at all clear that the last possibility is subject to any meaningful philosophical resolution.

The question "Why should there be any authority at all?" is subject to a number of replies, most of which possess a commonsense aspect. Authority is needed for reasons of efficiency, for getting things done in an orderly way. Men need authority for protection against excesses—as a means by which to achieve and maintain a semblance of social security. Part of life is rule-governed, and someone must have special authority to formulate and to enforce the rules. Human talents vary greatly; thus there are always significant differences in men's knowledge and capacities and wants, requiring that some authoritative direction be given to the organization and use of these numerous abilities. Some actions must be done even when men are reluctant to perform them, and authority is required if commands are to be given and carried out. Such general reasons for the need of some authority in social and political life are quite prosaic, perhaps even truistic. They are simply broadly stated reminders of what most men know quite well—that efficiency, order, organization of talents, and capacity to coerce some actions are, in the proper contexts, values without which social existence would be impossible.

Hearing these reasons, a person who stubbornly persisted in asking: "But why *should* there be efficiency, order, and organization of talents?" would baffle his listeners, who might feel driven to say (perhaps in exasperation): "What kind of question is that? Life is simply like that!" Of course, a person who bordered on madness, caring neither for personal security nor for any of the values which result from the orderly development of social and political processes, might reject even those arguments for authority as a necessary means by which to achieve those other values. Just as madmen need to be restrained and treated, so some persons who constantly question even reasonable kinds of authority sometimes must be coerced to act in specific ways by threats or the actual use of physical force.

"See! I told you so!" our strict rebel against the very notion of authority might exclaim. "Authority is really nothing more than force, after all!"

If human freedom is interpreted as excluding any and all authority, then authority of any kind will appear as external and even oppressive, weighing down the individual—a coercive instrument aimed solely at making a man perform those acts he does not want to do, for ends he has no desire to achieve. According to this view, freedom and authority are mutually exclusive domains and "never the twain shall meet." So individualistic a conception of freedom means that a man is free only in the absence of authority—only when he does what he wants to do, when he so wants, under the circumstances he finds compatible. If freedom and authority are absolutely distinct, then men can never meaningfully be said fully to choose authority, and the notion of cooperative human effort under recognized authority becomes a self-contradictory one. So viewed, freedom can result in social and political agreement only in contingent, nonnecessary ways—much as if, on a crowded highway lacking traffic signs and generally accepted rules of how to drive, it happens occasionally, as a matter of fact, that all the different drivers come to the same decision about when to stop or when to turn, and do so according to very similar patterns of driving behavior. An observer who then established traffic rules on the basis of how these drivers acted, and backed them with authority, could be called a threat to freedom on the grounds that these drivers, tomorrow, might desire to behave differently.

Has any serious philosophical writer ever genuinely questioned all authority as a need of stable social and political life? Probably not. Of course, some anarchists (those who reject all authority) and a few utopians (those who argue for the possibility of an absolutely ideal state of affairs) have tended toward this extreme position—although this historical fact is not evidence for the reasonableness of their views. Usually, rebels and revolutionists and utopians have argued for their own views against an existing situation which they hoped to alter. Some nineteenth-century Marxists—taking literally the notion that a purely classless communist society is possible if a complete economy based on full production for use is achieved— seem to have believed all political authority would disappear with the solution of men's economic problems. Thus, they seemed to link all authority with politics such that, given their idealistic hope for the "withering away of the state," all authority would cease to exist— presumably resulting in a social universe in which, without rules or coercion (as in the recent traffic example), all human wants would, as a matter of fact, be met automatically in the economy of abundance, and a vast technology required for such an economy would similarly operate without coercion or constraint. A sympathetic critic, hearing of so utopian a view, probably will be struck at how frustrating human social and political life actually is, even at its best, to have encouraged men even to dream of such an impossible situation.

In his famous novel, *The Age of Reason,* the first of a trilogy, Jean-Paul Sartre creates a fictional French contemporary whose attitudes and actions suggest a radically individualistic kind of freedom which seems incompatible with any type of authority. Mathieu is thirty-four, a teacher of philosophy, unmarried but suddenly confronted with the news his mistress (Marcelle) has become pregnant. Mathieu tries to arrange for an abortion, looking upon marriage as a restraint on his freedom. Similarly, when he is challenged by Brunet, a French Communist, to join the Communist party, Mathieu refuses on the ground that such a decision would limit his freedom. He tries to borrow a large sum of money to finance the abortion, finally seeking aid from his successful lawyer-brother (Jacques) who represents the stolid middle-class virtues which Mathieu so heartily detests. Yet, when he is in trouble, Mathieu willingly seeks aid from a representative of that middle class, who taunts him about this. Mathieu argues that he assumes full responsibility for his existence, for the manner in which he is condemned to be free—yet he seems unable to make any positive decision to act without risking that freedom. But what kind of freedom does Sartre's character, Mathieu, really represent? It seems to be a view of freedom which has no relation to social and political action or to making more or less reasonable choices in the light of circumstances. Sartre's Mathieu seems to view man as free to decide but, having decided, not free to seek advice or to act freely except in deciding perhaps to change his mind.

In a moving passage, Sartre has his character think to himself in the following dramatic way:

> The brake was suddenly slammed down and the bus stopped. Mathieu stiffened, and threw an agonized look at the driver's back: all his freedom had come back on him once more. "No," he thought, "no, it isn't heads or tails. Whatever happens, it is *by my agency* that everything must happen." Even if he let himself be carried off, in helplessness and in despair, even if he let himself be carried off like an old sack of coal, he would have chosen his own damnation; he was free, free in every way, free to behave like a fool or a machine, free to accept, free to refuse, free to equivocate; to marry, to give up the game, to drag this dead weight about with him for years to come. He could do what he liked, no one had the right to advise him, there would be for him no Good nor Evil unless he brought them into being. All around him things were gathered in a circle, expectant, impassive, and indicative of nothing. He was alone, enveloped in this monstrous silence, free and alone, without assistance and without excuse, condemned to decide without support from any quarter, condemned forever to be free.[5]

The radical view that a person is free in his solitariness may make religious sense (A. N. Whitehead once said that "Religion is what the individual does with his own solitariness") but seems unhelpful to thinkers concerned to make a case for social and political freedom. Social groups lead to authoritative positions and procedures—and Mathieu's anarchistic conception of freedom would lead to the absence of all authority save on the choice of a person to accept it. The point is, however, that even if a person rejects external authority, he can be affected by it even against his will (though Sartre might reply a man can even die freely on a scaffold or in a concentration camp).

---

[5] Jean-Paul Sartre, *The Age of Reason,* trans. Eric Sutton (New York: Knopf, 1947). Used by permission of Alfred Knopf, Inc. [Reprinted from the Bantam Books edition (1959), pp. 275–276.]

The point is, however, that social thinkers want to learn how to create and maintain those conditions—social, economic, political, legal—which will make concentration camps impossible and then "free" men to make genuine choices among concrete alternatives.

Conclusion

To say that "X is an authority" means that X is able to perform specific functions if called upon to do so, while to say "X has authority" means that X stands in some special relation, socially or politically, to other persons, some of whose actions he can direct or even coerce by means of political instruments. The authority may have been seized or delegated. In either event, someone who has political authority can, in certain situations, exercise powers of an office, a legal order, a military command, and so forth, against subordinates who lack that authority. Men acquire political authority in different ways, but they always gain certain powers in so doing. Political authority is usually operative only within a framework (explicit or assumed) of rules and procedures. To ask: "How did X gain his authority?" means to ask for a description of certain rules or procedures—that is to ask a question subject to empirical replies. "How did Sam get to be president of the organization?" "Sam filed papers of candidacy at the proper time and won a properly conducted election." To ask: "Why should any person hold political authority over others?" is to ask a meaningless political question in the abstract, since political life involves legitimating certain authorities. Authority rests on power but is not necessarily identical with it, since (at least for persons who use the English language) most persons want to distinguish legitimate uses of power from illegitimate ones. This means that if large numbers of persons in a political community come to question an authority's use of power, he will in time lose much of his authority —or his authority will come to rest exclusively on repressive measures enacted upon a populace filled with resentment. Such a situation may turn into a revolutionary one. In fairly stable democratic systems, authority means legitimate power to act in prescribed areas with the approval of one's subordinates.

Some Questions and Problems

1. Imagine that you read in your daily newspaper that a dictator of a foreign country made a personal appearance when, as commanded by him, a political opponent was shot to death by a firing squad. Suppose you read that the condemned man shouted, just before the bullets killed him: "You have no authority under our Constitution to put me to death!" Would you think such a shouted comment to make any sense at all?
2. In what situations might a person ask: "Where does Mr. So-and-So get his authority to act as he does?" What kinds of answers might be given to a person who asked why he should obey either (a) some specific political authority or (b) any authority at all?
3. What might be meant by saying of some other person that he just gave an *authoritative* performance (such as portraying a role on the stage or calming an angry mob)?
4. Can politicians ever act as moral authorities? Should they attempt to act as moral authorities?
5. What might be meant by a statement like: "Sam is an authority on the subject!"
6. List some ways in which conflicts between political authorities can occur. Discuss the means by which such conflicts might be handled.
7. Debate the topic: *Resolved,* That political authority is nothing more than the organized power of a dominant interest in society.
8. Where might authority be said to reside if a given state in this country successfully resists a decision of the Supreme Court or an executive order of a President?
9. Are there significant kinds of authority which are not rightly called "political"?
10. Does the effort to present a philosophical justification of authority strike you as a meaningful or as a meaningless undertaking?

Some Suggested Readings

Adams, H. *The Education of Henry Adams*. New York: Modern Library, 1931.

Adorno, T. W., and others (eds.). *The Authoritarian Personality*. New York: Harper, 1950.

Arendt, H. *The Origins of Totalitarianism*. New York: Harcourt, 1951.

Branstedt, E. K. *Dictatorship and Police Power*. London: Kegan, Paul, 1945.

Bryn-Jones, D. *The Dilemma of the Idealist.* New York: Macmillan, 1950.

Burke, E. *Reflections on the Revolution in France,* ed. T. H. D. Mahoney. Indianapolis: Liberal Arts, 1955.

Commager, H. S. *Selections from the Federalist.* New York: Appleton-Century-Crofts, 1949.

Dewey, J. *The Public and Its Problems.* New York: Holt, 1927.

Friedrich, C. (ed.) *Totalitarianism.* Cambridge: Harvard University Press, 1952.

Fromm, E. *Escape from Freedom.* New York: Rinehart, 1941.

Ginsberg, M. "The Individualist Basis of International Law and Morals," *Reason and Unreason in Society,* ed. Ginsberg. New York: Macmillan, 1960.

Huxley, A. *Brave New World.* New York: Harper, 1960.

————. *Brave New World Revisited.* New York: Harper, 1960.

Lindberg, J. *Foundations of Social Survival.* New York: Columbia University Press, 1953.

Lindsay, A. D. *The Essentials of Democracy,* 2d ed. London: Oxford University Press, 1935.

Mill, J. S. *Essay on Liberty,* ed. A. Castell. New York: Appleton-Century-Crofts, 1947.

Rieff, P. "The Theology of Politics: Reflections on Politics as the Burden of Our Time," *Journal of Religion,* Vol. XXXII, No. 2, 1952.

Riesman, D. "Some Observations on the Limits of Totalitarian Power," *Journal of Religion,* Vol. XXXII, No. 2, 1952.

Russell, B. *Power: A New Social Analysis.* London: Allen & Unwin, 1938.

————. *Authority and the Individual.* New York: Simon & Schuster, 1949.

Ryan, J. A. and Boland, F. J. *Catholic Principles of Politics: The State and the Church.* New York: Macmillan, 1952.

Santayana, G. *Dominions and Powers.* New York: Scribner, 1951.

Schaar, J. H. *Loyalty in America.* Berkeley: University of California Press, 1957.

Simon, Y. R. *A General Theory of Authority.* South Bend: Notre Dame University Press, 1962.

Weldon, T. D. "Political Foundations," *The Vocabulary of Politics,* Chap. IV. Hammondsworth, Eng.: Penguin, 1953.

Wild, J. *Human Freedom and Social Order.* Durham: Duke University Press, 1959.

CHAPTER SEVEN

The Sovereign State

Philosophical interest in political analysis has often tended to center on the notions of "sovereignty" and "state," at least since the early seventeenth century. Theorists have sought to distinguish the state's authority from other kinds of authority. Also, they have frequently argued with the aim of persuading their readers to adopt a specific attitude toward the hard facts of organized political power, advocating a particular "picture" of the individual's relation to the state, a picture which has varied significantly from one philosopher to the next. A major concern dominates the basic writings of the leading modern political thinkers—the problem of how to reconcile liberty and obligation.

According to the influential political thinker Professor T. D. Weldon, the English word "State" had a fairly recent origin in its technical status for sound historical reasons. Most ancient empires prior to the exceptional Roman period were loosely knit monarchies quite different in function and organization from modern nation states usually based on ideas of a common nationality, language, territorial limits, independence, and a fairly complex administrative apparatus. The ancient Greek city-states known to Plato and Aristotle were extremely small in territorial extent and population, units in which a face-to-face social life among the citizens was possible. Indeed, Aristotle suggested that a city's size should never exceed the capacity of a man's voice to be heard from one boundary to the next. Numerous ancient empires—like that of Alexander the Great, for example—represented makeshift affairs resulting from military conquest, hardly able to survive the temporary successes of a powerful general and his armies. Of the pre-Roman civilizations, only the Egyptian seems to have rested over long periods on a stable political and administrative foundation bringing political continuity to different generations and changing dynasties. Even the Roman political achievement, when viewed by later European thinkers, affected men's imagination as much by its disappearance as by its earlier economic, political, and military achievements. The medieval period which followed the collapse of the Roman empire in Europe may be viewed politically as a series of pragmatic efforts, under feudalism, to apply the Roman "ideal" of law and order to a chaotic and decentralized political and social situation. The medieval church brought a respect for universalism to a culture lacking political solidarity in a Europe which, relative to its earlier history, was marked by localisms and political decline. The growth of the power of European monarchs from the thirteenth century on stimulated political theorists to new efforts to understand some radically changing conditions. The eventual emergence of strong states—England, France, Spain—changed the situation in which priests and princes competed for political power even prior to the Protestant Reformation, whose successes shattered Christian religious unity and substantially aided the nationalisms appearing with the beginnings of the decline of feudal institutions and theories.

Some Models

Both ancient and modern thinkers have tended to adopt one or another model for an "understanding" of the state. Some writers have been impressed by the unity of a state's career in time as well as by its relative powerfulnesss in relation to individuals. They have recognized the state as an object of ultimate loyalty ("My country, right or wrong!"), capable of calling forth the most dedicated services of men, especially in times of crisis. Some of them have wanted to distingush the "empirical" state (the individual wills of the citizens, plus the whole factual machinery of political organization) from something known as the "real" state (the highest values plus the underlying ideal unity of political life). They have looked upon the state as a special kind of person, having a life of its own, as it were, independent of *this* or *that* citizen or any specific historical set of institutions. They have employed an *organic model* of the state, insisting it endures beyond the life-spans of individuals or particular governmental administrations and that its reality cannot be discovered simply by adding up the citizens and the political institutions of which it is taken to be the underlying reality. According to this view the state is the highest object of service as well as a unique institution which defines the legality of other existing associations. Aristotle believed that the state (or political society) is prior to the individuals and family, at least logically; while modern thinkers like Jean Jacques Rousseau (1712–1778) and G. W. F. Hegel (1770–1831) went to great lengths to subordinate individual wills to the more genuine, for them, realities of a "general will" or a "rational state" to which all else is legitimately considered secondary. Political theorists who adopt the organic model of the state often "see" it as a superperson, whose real *wholeness* is more than the reality of the several parts added together. The state is seen as an end-in-itself, intrinsically worthy, the necessary and inescapable norm in terms of which individuals can find a meaningful existence.

This organic view of the state may be viewed, even by its critics, as a dramatization of an aspect of political life. A state can sometimes call forth the most selfless devotion in some of its servants who, by serving, actually are ennobled to express a degree of individuality. Even if their model of the state is judged wrongheaded (as it is by many thinkers), the organicists do at least remind men of certain emotions they have experienced when they chose to view their political associations as the expression of their highest ideals. Professor J. D. Mabbott adds this demand to those of law, convention, and service with which society confronts its members and, in his *The State and the Citizen,* illustrates it in the following way as a power essential to any fully civilized political system:

> I may occasionally meet an Oxford College tutor to whom the College is everything. His public lectures are dull; he writes no books; he holds no university office; he has no "outside interest." But he

knows all the members of the College, is constantly consulted by them, follows their achievements in later life and wears every college success like a feather in his own cap. Every moment of his life and every ambition he has is identified with the College. Now, when a foreigner comes to Oxford and asks me about the Colleges and their powers over their members, I show him just the "College Rules," which compel early rising and prohibit matutinal gramophones. (This is parallel to the sphere of law.) Then I show him the College Hall and tell him how convention has allotted a certain table at dinner to persons of especial distinction. No rule keeps men away from it and promotion to it is conferred by tacit consent. (This is the power of custom.) Then I add that if he went about among the men he would probably discover a general opinion that everybody should "do something for the College"; still vaguer this and more easily evaded, and probably limited to games, but by no means negligible. (This is the conception of service in however narrow and misguided a form.) But I should not feel I had shown my stranger the full power of the College system unless I had let him talk for a little to the College tutor I described above. This is a power a College *can* have over its members, and I should be tempted to add that without him and his like the College system would have a short life indeed.[1]

Of course, a sympathetic reader can agree with Professor Mabbott's emphasis upon this power of a state to encourage some individuals so fully to identify themselves with its achievements and, by so doing, to enrich the lives of their admiring fellow citizens. Yet, these same readers can deny (as Professor Mabbott would himself) that the state must be viewed, literally, as a person in order for such dedicated identification with its ideals to occur.

Many theorists reject the organic view of the state, preferring to adopt some version of what has been called the *machine* model instead. The machine model pictures the state as a means to some other result—as a device which possesses only instrumental values. There are different uses of this model, as Professor Weldon has clearly shown in some of his writings analyzed in a portion of Chapter 10. A writer like Karl Marx (1818–1883) adopts the *force* conception

---

[1] J. D. Mabbott, *The State and the Citizen* (London: Hutchinson, 1948), p. 51. Used by permission of Hutchinson & Co. Ltd.

of the state, viewing it as a complicated class-dominated machinery for oppressing laborers, for him a "bad" kind of exploitation. As a revolutionary, Marx therefore sought to overthrow all political systems, believing in the possibility of a nonpolitical form of just administration in an economically sane society. Hobbes also leaned toward a force view of the state as a machine, but unlike Marx he judged the state a necessary means by which, though using coercion and force, it can bring at least a minimum amount of security to its citizens by protecting them against external and internal attacks (a matter to receive fuller attention in this chapter). In contrast to the force version of the machine model, however, has been the democratic theory in which liberally oriented thinkers like John Locke (1632–1704) and John Stuart Mill (1806–1873) argued that the state rests upon consent. On this view, the state deserves the citizens' obedience only in terms of its actions in specific areas and never, as on the organic theory, as a reality intrinsically worthy of obedience. A usual aspect of the consent theory is that some rights exist which belong inherently to individuals, meaning that the state should guard these rights as a trustee.

These models of the state are extremely simple, and it is possible no one of them fits perfectly the political views of any one great political philosopher, each of whom—on a very careful reading—may be found to adopt any one model only in a general way and not exclusively so. The important point is that, in opposition to the organic conception of the state which views the individual as totally subordinate, the advocates of the machine model grant the individual greater significance and think of the state as an association formed to accomplish some specific tasks. Some brief accounts will be now given of the thought of St. Thomas Aquinas (an Aristotelian in political thought), Thomas Hobbes (who favors the force theory of the state viewed as a machine), Jean Jacques Rousseau (who is an organicist), and John Austin (who weds both the force and consent theories of the state viewed as a machine). Some passing references will also be given to the thought of John Locke, who has been thought to have argued heavily for a consent theory of government.

Aquinas on Politics

A brief consideration of an aspect of the political thought of St. Thomas Aquinas (1225–1274) may illustrate how the quest after philosophical "justification" of legal and political practices often leads a thinker to mirror some of the settled social and cultural features of his own day and age. The greatest of the medieval scholastics, Aquinas, presents a view of law which is marked by logical clarity and an intellectual confidence in some basic philosophical principles and Christian values.[2] In the thirteenth century numerous conflicts occurred, some of which involved Aquinas as an active participant. Nonetheless, the political principles of feudalism rested securely on a public acceptance of a "natural" hierarchical structure whose clear distinctions between rulers and subordinates paralleled the subordination of theorems to certainly known axioms which characterized the deductive or geometric manner of reasoning. The earlier frictions between feudal rulers in the secular realm and bishops and popes in the spiritual had been resolved by a distinction between "secular" and "spiritual" which gave clearly defined jurisdictional functions to each. There was widespread agreement on basic principles even when, at times, conflicts occurred in practice. In a sense, Aquinas gave an unsurpassed intellectual expression to this widespread agreement by a brilliant and thorough analysis of the provinces of Faith and Reason, based on the conviction that no truth held by faith can in principle contradict a truth discernible by reason, though some truths of faith must forever remain beyond reason's reach. In a more limited way, Aquinas believed no dispute between Church and State could occur if the domain of each were properly understood. His political writings borrowed heavily from Aristotle, stressing the universality of human reasoning and the purposive human quest after seeking happiness. For Aquinas, as for earlier thinkers like Plato and Aristotle, political philosophy was an aspect of moral philosophy, presupposing a fixed

---

[2]Aquinas gives a thorough analysis of law in the first part of the Second Part of his *Summa Theologica,* found in the Dominican translation in *Basic Writings of Saint Thomas Aquinas,* ed. by A. C. Pegis (New York: Random, 1945).

human nature and a common humanity marked by "natural" reason and a "supernatural" end. The political order existed as a necessary means by which men could develop the potentialities inherent in them, and the Church, guardian of faith, represented the necessary means by which a transnatural salvation could be achieved if certain conditions of faith were realized.

In discussing law, Aquinas distinguishes four broad types of law: *eternal, divine, natural,* and *human.* The eternal law is, as it were, laid up in a Platonic heaven—existing in God who, as the universe's ruler, "has the nature of a law" but is a timeless being. The natural law is derived from the eternal but represents only that portion of the latter which is discoverable by human reason, unaided by faith. The natural law is relevant to men's natural development and happiness as members of a finite historical order, applying to them as natural entities. Divine law is that aspect of eternal law which, revealed to the Church, must be accepted only on faith, concerned as it is with a man's supernatural "end" or destiny. Human law is derived from the natural, as less general rules are deducible from more general ones, and is the application in light of reason of principles to more specific matters. However, some human laws are morally neutral, according to Aquinas, as when any one of several possible ways of expressing the precepts of the natural law is satisfactory. The model of law presented by Aquinas involves reasoning from certainly known principles, then, to more specific rules entailed by them; and then the reasonable applications of laws to varieties of cases and situations. Like Aristotle, Aquinas realizes that the practical reason (human reasoning concerned with deciding cases and judging specific actions) can achieve only general truths to which, in certain circumstances, exceptions must be made. In a succinct manner Aquinas defines law as follows: "Law is nothing else than an ordinance of reason for the common good, promulgated by him who has the care of the community."

Yet, Aquinas—like later theorists—realized that a ruler stands "above" the law in a way in which a subordinated citizen does not. Thus, a ruler coerces the actions of evil persons through the law. Coercively, the ruler (sovereign) is "beyond" the law and can even change it, ruling in accordance with law in the light of time and place.

On the other hand, for Aquinas, the ruler is subject to the directive force of the law, by his own will. The moral point here is that a ruler ought to abide by the laws he makes for others. The natural laws which are knowable to reason—common and indemonstrable principles—are the guides for rulers who promulgate human rules. These natural laws are supplemented by divine ones, taught by the Church. The divine laws are needed, first, because man seeks eternal rather than merely natural happiness; second, because human reason is fallible and only divine direction about how men are to act can be said to be free frem error; third, only a divine law can judge men's interior (hidden) acts, since human law is concerned only with externals; and fourth, only divine law can punish the entire range of forbidden evils. The natural law is public, as it were, and based on Aquinas' conviction that underlying natural uniformities can be counted on in this world. According to Aquinas (and the precepts of the natural law), all men tend to seek good and to avoid evil, especially to avoid loss of life; they have common tendencies, like sexuality and the need to educate their young; and they desire to live in social groups and to seek God.

Aquinas recognized that, however developed it may become, men's knowledge of natural laws can never exhaust the content of the eternal law—since not all aspects of God are knowable. This means, however, that knowledge of such laws can expand as, in changing situations of knowledge, men "discover" new aspects of that law. On the other hand, although the body of the natural law can change by addition, it cannot alter by subtraction. This means that, for Aquinas, the discovered natural law is not only absolute in its sphere but, like his view of human nature, unchanging. A natural law is not situational, on this view, and thus is not defensible in one time and place but not in another; nor can the accumulation of human knowledge justify men in removing an item of the natural law once it has been known by reason. There is thus a confident universalism and rationalism in the conception of law and, derivatively, of politics as formulated by Aquinas. The view contains some static elements: namely, that men everywhere share a common "nature" and that moral principles are eternal rather than situational. A scholar can say of this conception of law what Professor H. Richard Niebuhr aptly remarked about the attempt by Aquinas to produce a reconciliation of Christian faith and cultural demands.

The attractiveness of the synthesist type of answer to the Christ-and-culture problem is doubtless felt by all Christians, whether or not they are drawn to the acceptance of the Thomistic system. Man's search for unity is unconquerable, and the Christian has a special reason for seeking integrity because of his fundamental faith in the God who is One. When he has realized, in consequence of experience and reflection, that he cannot be at one with himself if he denies nature and culture in the effort to be obedient to Christ, or that such denial itself involves a kind of disobedience to the commandments of love, since the social institutions are instruments of that love, then he must seek some sort of reconciliation between Christ and culture without denial of either. The drive toward moral unity in the self is mated with the urgent quest of reason to discover the unity of its principles and the unified principle of the realities toward which it is directed. In the synthesis of reason and revelation, in which the philosopher's inquiry and the prophet's proclamation are combined without confusion, reason seems to be promised the satisfaction of its hunger. With the drives toward moral and intellectual integrity the social demand for the unity of society is inseparably connected. Society itself is an expression of the desire of the many for oneness; its ills are all forms of dissension; peace is another name for social health. The union of church and state, of state with state and class with class, and the union of all these with the supernatural Lord and Companion is the ineluctable desire of the believer. Synthesis seems required above all by the demand of God, not only as He operates in human nature, reason, and society by His unifying spirit, but as He reveals himself through His words and His Word. To the New Testament as well as to the Old Testament church the great proclamation is made, "Hear, O Israel, the Lord our God is one Lord." Because the synthetic type of answer seems to meet these needs and demands, therefore it will always be attractive to Christians. Even when they must reject the form in which it is offered they will see it as a symbol of the ultimate answer.[3]

Later political theorists, including those who retain in the language of political philosophy phrases like "divine law" or "neutral law," reflect the deeper social and political crises of a world marked by

[3] *Christ and Culture* (New York: Harper Torchlight, 1956), pp. 141–142.

powerful new monarchs and states and the altered nature of Church-State relations. The Scholastic optimism is clearly dampened in a writer like Thomas Hobbes, and even John Locke—an Englishman whose view of man's natural social nature is closer to that of Aristotle and Aquinas than to that of Hobbes—feels the need to justify political order by a contract. Also, later writers worry more about rights, suggesting a real fear that coercively stationed sovereigns may not, after all, agree to the directive force of their rulings on their own behavior. In some cases, the older classical view that politics and law are subordinate to positive moral aims is replaced (as in Hobbes) by the negative position that the state functions as a means of avoiding certain evils or (as in Machiavelli) as an expression of the amoral cunning of a prince whose primary function is to retain his power at all costs.

Thomas Hobbes and the Security State

An Englishman who lived during his country's revolutionary struggles of the seventeenth century, forced several times into exile by the changing political climate, Thomas Hobbes in his famous *Leviathan* produced a brilliant defense of a strong sovereign.[4] Some critics say that Hobbes did little more than to "justify" his private preference for a strong royal monarch, but this assertion is questionable. For one thing, Hobbes's views could justify a strong democratic as well as a royal sovereign, since he believed the sovereign might be a person or an assembly. For another, Hobbes had once translated the great *History* written by Thucydides and had been known to view the Greeks' failure to achieve political solidarity as a tragic one. How can one judge the relative influences on a man's thought? It is possible that a man who regretted the Greek failure was thereby influenced, in his own day and age, to side with the monarch in the name of sanity and order. Whatever the causes, Hobbes held a high regard for order and, in a sense, argued for a strong sovereign capable of providing security as a bulwark against disorder and anarchy. As a materialist

---

[4] A convenient selection from Hobbes's works can be found in F. J. E. Woodbridge, ed., *Hobbes Selections* (New York: Scribner, 1930).

believing that ultimate reality is really nothing more than "matter in motion," perhaps Hobbes also tended to view individuals as something like "social" atoms, needing to be kept apart so as to avoid "social" collisions (much as a harried mother, say, may try to keep peace among numerous children by keeping them in separate rooms).

Three major views are crucial to Hobbes's defense of a powerful sovereign who, coercively, protects the public peace and security. One is that of the "state of nature," the second that of a "social contract," and the last that of "natural laws." Hobbes tries to create a consistent and comprehensive political philosophy in terms of his views on these three topics. His writings are a powerful rhetorical device aimed at getting readers to agree that order is the central problem of politics, that order requires an extremely strong sovereign (state), and that a reasonable citizen of a civil order will even obey some bad laws rather than threaten the political fabric by resistance. The theme in Hobbes's *Leviathan* is that men are normally better off even in a despotic state than they would be in the absence of a political organization. Hobbes believes men are weak and cowardly, even subject to moments of sheer irrationality—thus needing for their protection a political structure which, by its coercive might, can minimize disorder by restraining the rash actions of individuals and groups as well as by laying on obligations to act when security is at stake. Hobbes is no optimist about men's nature nor about the possibility of a utopian state. Maddened by the plight of the European man of his age, Hobbes tries to shape men's vision to "see" strong sovereignty as a long-run good. As Professor J. M. Cameron has written:

> Hobbes wishes to persuade us into an ambivalent attitude towards the task of politics. The spectacle of an art practised supremely well —an intricate piece of juggling, a bridge suspended over a gorge— at once intimidates and reassures us. Given the hardness of the task, the smoothness of the performance seems miraculous, beyond human power; and yet, we reflect, this *is* a human performance, contrived by human wit and within the power of all those with the appropriate abilities.—All the same, the task is within human capacity—this is the point of the assertion that the art of constructing and governing the State is a subspecies of the art of clock-work; and

we must meet it with skill and courage or decline into the sickness of sedition and die in the agony of civil war.[5]

The attraction of Hobbes's theory is that he is convinced he can justify a strong state by convincing men that they are basically fearful and even selfish individuals. Hobbes makes clear his conception of "human nature" by asking us to imagine a "state of nature"—that is, what the human condition might be like if we imagine all political associations removed. Hobbes thinks such a state of nature would be bleak indeed—characterized by Hobbes as allowing "no place for industry, because the fruit thereof is uncertain: and consequently no culture of the earth, no navigation, nor use of the commodities that may be imparted by sea; no commodious building; no instruments of moving and removing such things as require much force." Such a state of nature would lack science, art, literature, and community. Were it to exist (an actuality Hobbes probably did not wish to assert), each man would live in constant terror of being harmed or violently killed—in short, the life of man would be "solitary, poor, nasty, brutish, and short." Moreover, in the "state of nature" individual men are lacking moral notions, living as it were in a morally indifferent and nonsocial universe, though capable of reasoning sufficiently to understand their sorry plight. The reasoning by which men in a "state of nature" could recognize their perpetual liability to harm would, for Hobbes, prove sufficient to lead men to create an artificial political system, what he terms a "Commonwealth."

The "state of nature" pictured by Hobbes is a condition of perpetual war in which men become enemies because they want identical objects which often cannot be shared or divided. Men in such a condition seek to destroy one another, quarrels arising when men invade for gain, for personal safety, or for the glory of reputation. Men need a human master who can "supervise" them, for there are no naturally moral rules since, according to Hobbes, "The desires, and other passions of man, are in themselves no sin. No more are the actions that proceed from these passions, till they know a law that forbids them: which till laws be made they cannot know; nor can any

[5]"The Justification of Political Attitudes," *Proceedings of the Aristotelian Society,* Suppl. Vol. XXIX (London, 1955), p. 96.

law be made, till they have agreed upon the person that shall make it." (Chapter XIII) [6] Thus, Hobbes pictures a "state of nature" as lacking both morality and legality, since each man has a right (a peculiar sense of "right" here: namely, a disposition or tendency) to seek by all means available to preserve and to protect his own life. This universal tendency to seek self-preservation "explains," for Hobbes, how a civil society can be understood; for the perpetual threat to life permits men, by prudential reasoning, to understand that they have more to gain by agreement to submit themselves to a strong artificially created sovereign than by living in constant terror without a ruler to maintain law and order.

The question whether Hobbes believed men at one time literally shared the natural state he describes seems philosophically unimportant. What Hobbes is attempting is to reorient men's attitude toward established political authority. Hobbes does say that the savages living in America approximate the brutish situation of a state of nature, but he also makes clear that the condition was never "generally so, over all the world." Rather, this *would* be the sorry condition if all political authority ceased to exist; and it *is* the condition which holds between one sovereign state and another, perpetually posed in a preparation for war or defense—"having their weapons pointing, and their eyes fixed on one another; that is, their forts, garrisons, and guns upon the frontiers of their kingdoms; and continual spies upon their neighbors; which is a posture of war." Yet, like the amoral character Undershaft in George Bernard Shaw's *Major Barbara,* Hobbes argues that the amorality in the relations of one independent sovereign with another does not produce the misery accompanying war between individual and individual, since the sovereigns promote industry by their warlike postures. It is clearly Hobbes' intention to get readers to adopt a realistic, even cynical attitude toward themselves and others. He insists that by locking their doors men accuse their fellows of the base motives which Hobbes portrays in his conception of human nature.

In contrast to Hobbes, John Locke held a more optimistic view of the state of nature, in which men's genuinely social instincts also

[6] F. J. E. Woodbridge, ed., *op. cit.,* p. 254.

enjoy a fair natural development. Thus, while he also thinks government must exist to restrain and to protect men, Locke believes that men possess rights even prior to their agreement to submit to a government—rights which that sovereignty must respect and protect. It is as if Locke would want to say of Hobbes's more pessimistic view of human nature, "Look, even a cat isn't always killing mice. Sometimes a cat enjoys sunning itself. There are basic animal tendencies toward herding which men in a state of nature share with one another." But, like Hobbes, Locke recognized that some men will take more than their share, thus will need to be restrained or punished by the collective power of a political sovereign. The difference between the two philosophers' views is one of degree, since even Locke recognizes that in the natural state there will be invasion of rights. Nonetheless, the difference is important. Locke's view allows for greater continuity in human motivation and action between the state of nature and that of civil society as well as grounds the subordination of subjects to sovereign on a bedrock of fixed rights. Thus, Locke is willing to encourage sovereignty based on power divided between executive, legislature, and judiciary; while Hobbes—logically able to recognize that *any* form of government can be called sovereign—shows suspicion of any system in which powers are divided.

Hobbes is clear in his contention that men act consistently with their desire of self-preservation in making a covenant with one another to enter into a contract. They have security to gain by giving up their selfish tendencies to the commanding power of a sovereign, who is not part of the contract but nonetheless is needed for its enforcement. Yet, since a contract requires a transferral of some items, the question arises what can be transferred among men in a state of nature in which no legal or moral rights exist. Hobbes is not entirely clear on this point; perhaps he is not thoroughly consistent. Apparently the men who agree to a contract give up their liberty to decide, individually, when and whom to attack (a liberty they have in the state of nature) by agreeing *among themselves* to submit to the decision of a sovereign—a sovereign which may be either one man or an assembly, and which may, strangely, come into existence either by conquest or agreement. A covenant among men must lead to a contract, since a covenant is an agreement which rests on trust and, thus, can easily be broken. On the other hand, a contract among men requires the creation of an *artificial* sovereign raised above them, able to punish those who fail to keep its terms. So long as the sovereign is powerful and can protect men from external and internal aggression, men have no right to break the contract, which is binding on all generations, so long as the sovereign's power lasts. There is, however, one basic limitation which Hobbes places on the sovereign's rightful power. The sovereign may not ask a man either to kill himself or to testify against himself, since to do so would refuse that fundamental protection for which all men agree to live in civil society. A contract presupposes creation of a sovereign who, by the sword, can keep men to its terms if later they change their minds. Where Locke granted a moral right of revolution to the subjects, Hobbes argues that no such right exists so long as the sovereign can produce security.

Hobbes elaborates on his view of the social contract and how it binds the subjects in many places in his *Leviathan*. Chapter XVII contains a passage which excellently summarizes his position, as follows:

> The only way to exact such a common power, as may be able to defend them from the invasion of foreigners and the injuring of one another, and thereby to secure them in such sort as that, by their own industry, and by the fruits of the earth, they may nourish themselves and live contentedly; is, to confer all their power and strength upon one man, or upon one assembly of men, that may reduce all their wills, by plurality of voices, unto one will which is as much as to say, to appoint one man, or assembly of men, to hear their person; and everyone to own and acknowledge himself to be author of whatsoever he that so heareth their person, shall act or cause to be acted in those things which concern the common peace and safety; and therein to submit their wills, everyone to his will, and their judgments, to his judgment. This is more than consent, or concord; it is a real unity of them all, in one and the same person, made by covenant of every man with every man, in such manner as if every man should say to every man, *"I authorize and give up my right of governing myself to this man, or to this assembly of men, on this condition, that thou give up thy right to him, and authorize all his actions in like manner."* This done, the multitude so united in one person,

is called a commonwealth, in Latin *civitas:* This is the generation of that great LEVIATHAN, or rather, to speak more reverently, of that *mortal god,* to which we owe under the *immortal God,* our peace and defence. For by this authority, given him by every particular man in the commonwealth, he hath the use of so much power and strength conferred on him, that by terror thereby he is enabled to perform the wills of them all, to peace at home and mutual aid against their enemies abroad.[7]

In the event a sovereign is created by institution, Hobbes insists that no other covenants can be made by men, since to do so means to practice disloyalty. On this basis Hobbes held that the English Puritans were in error in making a covenant with God. Moreover, the subjects must remain subservient; they cannot resign from the covenant. Those who were dissenters must accept the covenant on the grounds they were members of the original assembly. The result is, in Hobbes's view, that no sovereign can be said to act unjustly though he may commit evil; nor can any sovereign be put to death. Among the unquestionable powers of a sovereign are decisions about war and peace, the prescribing of all legal rules, the judging of all disputes, the actual waging of war, the choice of advisers, the application of rewards and punishments, the granting of titles and honors. The rhetorical sweep of the vision Hobbes held is now complete—and an artificial power (sovereign) exists to bring men the security they need so desperately.

Hobbes nonetheless lists a number of "natural laws" which a prudent sovereign, as well as prudent subjects, will attempt to honor. These are laws learned from experience—an experience which teaches men that violations of them tend to produce those conditions so deplorable in an imagined state of nature. Men's passions are so strong, their reason so fallible, that they tend to ignore such laws unless a sovereign—recognizing them by the use of prudential reasoning powers—makes them part of his commands to his subjects, supported by the threat of sanctions against those who disobey them. Hobbes fails to make clear why men should trust the rationality of the sovereign to enforce commands based on natural laws which are knowable because men possess a degree of reasoning power. After all, there is

[7] *Ibid.,* pp. 339–340.

no power above the sovereign to sanction *his* violations of natural laws. It is as if a group of men are capable of learning these laws by reason and experience, yet are too weak constantly to live by them in a natural state and must create a sovereign who is to enforce them; though the sovereign is also a man subject to passion. Some critics wonder if Hobbes can consistently justify an artificially created sovereign against a background of an amoral natural state and a defense of prudential natural laws which ought to be observed by a rational sovereign. Sympathetic readers argue that these laws are merely generalizations which, if ignored by a sovereign, will tend to produce anarchy and chaos—the very conditions a sovereign is created to avoid or ameliorate.

Nonetheless, whether consistent in doing so or not, Hobbes insists that a wise sovereign will encourage obedience to these general laws by his subjects. Among them are the following:

- to want peace and to promote it

- to defend ourselves by any available means

- to keep all contracts we make

- to show gratitude for favors and benefits from others

- to make ourselves accommodating to other persons

- to grant pardons to past offenders and to seek pardon

- to emphasize the "goodness" of future possibilities over the evil aspects of past actions

- to refrain from showing hatred or contempt of another person

- to claim no right for oneself that is denied to other persons

- to treat men equally if one is a judge

- to enjoy in common goods which are not otherwise divided

- to make first possession of non-divided goods legally primary

- to grant safe passage to all those who are on peace missions

- to submit controversial disputes to arbitration

These general laws seem like common sense formulations, so much so that a reader wonders why men in a natural state would not often live by them in the absence of a sovereign. Yet, Hobbes puts a special responsibility on the sovereign, once established, to guide his policies by them with regard to subjects who, though intelligent enough to "see" the need of a strong sovereign, are too weak in a natural state to honor them.

In contrast to Hobbes, John Locke granted to natural laws an important status even in the state of nature. His famous relevant work is *The Second Treatise of Government* (1790).[8] Locke thought that men in a natural state possess moral obligations which logically precede an established political system under a sovereign. The natural law "teaches all mankind who will consult it, being all equal and independent, no one ought to injure another in his life, health, liberty, or possessions."[9] Men in a state of nature are morally justified in punishing those who go against the law of nature, since each man has a right to act for the preservation not simply of himself but of mankind in general. Locke's conception of a state of nature differs from that of Hobbes in several important ways, then. First, it is more social— *not* a perpetual war of all against all. Second, it is marked by basic moral features which all men ought to recognize. Third, it serves as a standard by which to measure whether a contractual sovereign, once established, is violating rights the sovereign can neither grant nor deny. As a result, Locke's contractual sovereign is more limited than is Hobbes's sovereign, for his subjects possess a natural right to rebellion under certain conditions and the contract must be renewed by later generations. Locke's treatment of the basic themes in political philosophy leads to a justification of a limited government, a parliament, and invests the individual with inalienable rights—a view which greatly influenced the political thought of those Americans who signed the Declaration of Independence. This view was part of the "climate of opinion" of Protestant congregationalism, expressed well in Colonel Rainboro's statement at the Putney debates of 1647: "Really, I think the poorest he that is in England hath a life to live as the richest he."

[8] A convenient paperback edition of this work is T. P. Peardon, ed., *John Locke: The Second Treatise of Government* (Indianapolis: Liberal Arts 1952).
[9] *Ibid.,* p. 5.

Organicism in Political Thought: Rousseau and Hegel

Both Hobbes and Locke attempt to "understand" the facts of political power by viewing the state (sovereign) as a means to some end desired by men. They employed the "machine model" of the state —Hobbes arguing that the sovereign is justified as a necessary means to achieve security, Locke insisting the state functions to enforce those natural laws and protect those rights which are aspects even of a state of nature. In contrast, some political thinkers attempt to justify the state as an intrinsically valuable entity, good in itself without regard to some further values to whose existence it is instrumentally necessary. Among these thinkers, who adopt an "organic model" of the state, must be numbered Jean Jacques Rousseau (1712–1778) and G. W. F. Hegel (1770–1831), whose political thought pictures the state as possessing a reality which is more than the sum of its parts. This organic conception of the state is a very old one, of course, and deserves some special consideration here.

For what reasons have some thinkers held "an organic model" of the state? This question is difficult to answer in a precise way. A number of statements can be made, however, no one of which will necessarily prove convincing to persons who view the state as an association for getting specific tasks done. The state endures through many generations, as if having a life all its own (just as a human body, as a complex organism, endures as a unity while its individual cells die and are replaced by new cells). Moreover, the state is an activity—a *functioning* unity (again, just as a car motor *running* is an activity different from the simple form shown in a motor catalogue). A person cannot easily escape the state's functioning quite in the way he can resign from voluntary associations or sometimes successfully escape from other persons. A person is born into some functioning political order and leaves it when he dies; he does not *literally* create the state as he may sometimes form new clubs except, perhaps, in those rare historical situations—usually following on war or revolution—when he joins with others to found a new government. If a man emigrates from one state, he usually goes to another (unless he becomes a hermit and is not pursued); and if to escape the state he commits suicide, he illustrates the enduring factuality of that state by the radical means he chooses to escape. Also, the state can outlast specific governments—since even revolutionaries may find that the legal order cannot wholly be altered, nor the language and customs of the persons who compose its citizenry. Indeed, the state may come to be identical with society if the organic model is adopted—the unity of an entire culture, including its ethical, religious, philosophical, and political institutions. If this should be so, then all notions of a social compact are literally wrongheaded, since men do not contract to be born as social animals.

A profound influence on the course of the later French Revolution, Rousseau's political philosophy sought to reconcile freedom with necessity, personal liberty with inescapable obligation. Rousseau's thought has served different political traditions. His vision of an original state of nature in which men, free from political controls, lived innocently and beautifully—a vision he sometimes treated as a report of an historical fact, at other times as a helpful if fictional device—aided democratically minded persons anxious to criticize and to reform, if possible, the authoritarian class distinctions and inherited political hierarchies of the eighteenth century. This doctrine inspired some thinkers to "see" a basic human nature through the distortions of the existing social order. This contrasting of natural man with the historically developed "conventional" man occurs in Rousseau's famous *Discourse on Inequality*. On the other hand, Rousseau's attempt in *The Social Contract* to justify political authority by means of an assumed "general will" has produced both democratic and totalitarian interpretations, since the notion can be used to justify both parliamentary systems and the argument that even legislatures are subject to a more basic will than the mere factual interests their members may happen at any one moment to represent. Ultimately, Rousseau argued that genuine sovereignty resides only in the general will—a will which is very difficult to identify in the actual conflicts of human interests but is, nonetheless, said to exist "beyond" ("above"?) the empirical machinery of state politics and power. The perennial problem bequeathed by Rousseau to later thinkers is the frustrating one of trying to understand what he meant by the general will.

Admiring Hobbes as a great realist, Rousseau nonetheless wanted to reject the conclusions Hobbes had drawn from his own correct view that the state represents will to power rather than an extension of primitive social feelings. Rousseau sought to justify the *fact* of state power (coercively applied by external authority) by a notion of social contract which did not involve subordination, as in Hobbes. The *true* state is that in which, for every coercive act to direct human actions toward some common goal, each and every citizen may be said to will that coercion. Paradoxically, this means that the *source* of authority exercised in the political sphere is internal rather than external, even to the citizen whose action is being coerced. Of this peculiar argument, a doubter—Lord Bertrand Russell—has said that Rousseau's notion of freedom is a person's freedom to feel a policeman's club on his head. In defense of Rousseau, it can be argued that the general will may not necessarily be manifested in either an actual person's will or an actual act of political coercion. Sovereignty cannot be identified either with actually existing states or personal power —a view which is admittedly peculiar.

Can any sense be given to so peculiar an assertion? Actual states operate by means of legal and other coercion against the very real empirical wills of numerous individuals. Yet, recognizing this actual coercion, Rousseau sought to deny sovereignty to the actual holder of power, even when that power's exercise succeeds in crushing certain actions. Why argue in this manner? A possible answer is that, like Plato, Rousseau distinguished between an "apparent" and a "real" sovereign. Only that coercion represents a real sovereign which expresses the general will. But, since at no moment may all persons in their willing express the general will, there seems to be no empirical means by which to locate it. Thus, seeing that politics involves law and power, consequently coercion, Rousseau apparently wanted to insist that only that coercion is sovereign which would be willed by fully rational persons, if they could know what is lawful—that is, could know what is for the common interest in each situation. Fully rational beings would approve of coercion, even against their own acts, if they could know what the general will is in every instance. Professor Ernest Cassirer, in his little book *Rousseau, Kant, Goethe* (Princeton, 1947) believes this stress on law and rationality by Rousseau explains why so seemingly different a philosopher as Kant so deeply admired the French thinker, keeping a bust of Rousseau in his sparsely furnished study. Able to recognize the facts of coercive power, Rousseau wanted to distinguish rationally justifiable coercion from arbitrary force—thus, wanted sovereign coercion to represent will rather than mere force, but a will which is taken to be rational because necessary. According to the renowned political philosopher, T. H. Green (1836–1882), Rousseau realized that an individual's will may go counter to the general will such that:

> Hence the social compact necessarily involves a tacit agreement, that anyone refusing to conform to the general will shall be forced to do so by the whole body politic; in other words, 'shall be forced to be free,' since the universal conformity to the general will is the universal guarantee to each individual of freedom from dependence on any other person or persons.[10]

Green's emphasis on the word "tacit" is revealing here, suggesting an agreement which is not always directly known by the citizens!

What makes Rousseau's political view of the state an organicist one is his belief that the general will represents a unity over and against the various wills of individuals. Moreover, Rousseau saw the general will as absolutely general rather than particular, thus the actual government can never be the same as the sovereign—nor is the government established by consent or contract, for Rousseau. Governments may come and go, but sovereignty established by contract goes on forever—unified, indivisible, lawful.

Rousseau thus implies either that states can actually exist without sovereignty (since unjust "states" will never express for him the general will) or that many, or most, of the powerful political systems of his time could not on his theory really be called states. Further, even if an actual state should represent the general will, how would citizens

---

[10] T. H. Green, *Lectures on the Principles of Political Obligation* (London: Longmans, Green, 1955), p. 81.

be able to know this was the case? So metaphysical a theory, subject to no conceivable tests, suggests that Rousseau looked upon sovereignty in a Platonic sense as possibly existing independently of concrete instances of political rule much as Plato's universals existed prior to and independently of actual instances of them. It is difficult to understand why Rousseau thought this view of the general will could resolve actual political conflicts between men who are sometimes far from rational. A sympathetic writer has written as follows on this disturbing consequence of Rousseau's views:

> We may try to answer this question by distinguishing sovereign *de facto* from sovereign *de jure,* and saying that what Rousseau meant was that the general will, as defined by him and as exercised under the conditions which he prescribes, was the only sovereign *de jure,* but that he would have recognised in the ordinary states of his time a sovereign *de facto;* and that in the same way, when he describes the institution of government as arising out of a twofold act consequent on the original pact (an act in which the sovereign people first decides that there shall be a government, and then, not as a sovereign people, but as a democratic magistracy, decides in what hands the government shall be placed), he does not conceive himself to be describing what has actually taken place, but what is necessary to give a government a moral title to obedience. Whether Rousseau himself had this distinction in view is not always clear. At the outset he states his object thus: "Man is born free, and everywhere he is in fetters. How has this change come about? I do not know. What can render it legitimate? That is a question which I deem myself able to answer." (I, i.) The answer is the account of the establishment of a sovereign by social pact. It might be inferred from this that he considered himself in the sequel to be delineating transactions to the actual occurrence of which he did not commit himself, but which, if they did occur, would constitute a duty as distinct from a physical necessity of submission on the part of subjects to a sovereign, and to which some equivalent must be supposed, in the shape of a tacit present convention on the part of the members of a state, if their submission is to be a matter of duty as distinct from physical necessity, or is to be explained as a matter of right by the ostensible sovereign. This, however, would merely be an inference as to his meaning. His actual procedure is to describe transactions, by which the sovereignty of the general will was established, and by which it in turn established a government, as if they had actually taken place.

Nor is he content with supposing a tacit consent of the people as rendering subjection legitimate. The people whose submission to law is to be "legitimate" must actually take part in sovereign legislative assemblies. It is very rarely that he uses language which implies the possibility of a sovereign power otherwise constituted. He does indeed speak of the possibility of a prince (in the special meaning of the term, as representing the head of the executive) usurping sovereignty, and speaks of the sovereignty thus usurped as existing *de facto,* not *de jure;* but in no other connection (so far as I have observed) does he speak of anything short of the "volonté générale" exercised through the vote of an assembled people as sovereign at all. And the whole drift of his doctrine is to show that no sovereign, otherwise constituted, had any claim on obedience. There was no state in Europe at his time in which his doctrine would not have justified rebellion, and even under existing representative systems the conditions are not fulfilled which according to him are necessary to give laws the claim on our obedience which arises from their being an expression of the general will. The only system under which these conditions could be fulfilled would be one of federated self-governing communes, small enough to allow each member an active share in the legislation of the commune. It is probably the influence of Rousseau that has made such a system the ideal of political enthusiasts in France.[11]

Hegel's organicism appears more realistic if less hopeful to persons of democratic sympathies. For Hegel, the existing state *is* the sovereign power. Moreover, it is the very expression of rationality—its concrete manifestation. By state, of course, Hegel meant the whole unified complex of political, religious, artistic, and intellectual tendencies making up a "people" or a "culture." The state thus represents a unified way of life which pursues the inescapable path of an historical process which is logical and rational through and through. Beneath the *apparent* differences in a state exists a truly living unity which "holds them together" as it were. Each actual state in the world represents the inevitable development of an "inner" logic of an Absolute Mind. Thus, not even great men can alter the historically inevitable. Rather, they are significant pawns in the Absolute's inten-

[11] T. H. Green, *op. cit.,* pp. 90–92.

tions, operating by the "cunning of Reason"—subjectively convinced that *they* are seeking certain ends when, in fact, the Absolute is working through them to achieve its purposes.[12]

The only freedom possible is an intellectual awareness and acceptance of necessity. On Hegel's theory, a person can understand but not alter the development of the Absolute's nature in the historical order. Even philosophy can serve no practical purpose. The reason is that by the time historical understanding occurs, the Absolute is already (by its own logic) "going beyond" the cultural achievements already realized by a people. Men and cultures become like driftwood caught on a mighty wave which can be redirected neither by human thought nor will. Individuals find whatever "meaning" they may possess only as elements in a larger organic whole—and the whole, for Hegel, can change into new forms to be actualized in history.

Hegel's organicism is probably as inhospitable to practical democratic hopes as any that can be imagined. There is not a shred of practical freedom in it. Modern totalitarians have used it in defence of their own aims to enslave and control men. Yet, it is questionable that Hegel himself meant to justify any particular form of totalitarianism, though he did—as a German—look upon Bismarck's state as the highest manifestation of the Absolute ever realized.

The Command View of Law: John Austin

The special position of a political sovereign with respect to his subjects received careful attention from John Austin, a nineteenth-century English thinker especially concerned to make sense of what it is that makes a legal order distinct from other kinds of authority. Austin's theory of law combined a Hobbesian stress on the power of a sovereign to command through the existing legal system with a non-Hobbesian view of morality. It was Austin's conviction that legal and moral rules differ in a fundamental way. Legal rules are positional,

---

[12] A convenient introduction to Hegel's views can be had in his *Reason in History: A General Introduction to the Philosophy of History,* R. S. Hartman, trans. (Indianapolis: Liberal Arts, 1953).

parts of a body of public commands backed by the sovereign's power to penalize or punish offenders, while moral rules are enforceable only by the will of the community until they become actual parts of the legal order. Austin did not seek to minimize the authority of moral rules, rather he wanted as clear a notion of the legal aspect of sovereignty as he could get. The rules composing a legal order are viewed as commands of a sovereign possessing power to harm and supported by the subjects' fairly steady tendency to give the sovereign obedience. The aim here is to separate strictly legal from other kinds of law, confining legal rules to public "commands" from a superior (sovereign) to an inferior (subject). This minimized set of rules, "law properly so called," Austin termed the *positive law,* which he distinguished sharply from the *positive morality* (the rules and judgments influencing community behavior whose sanctions are nonlegal in form) and *divine law* (those maxims or rules which a wise ruler or community will follow which are what a utilitarian God, interested only in what is for the greatest happiness of the community, would exact).

The positive law is distinguishable by its special source and its sanctions. Divine laws and rules of positive morality may or may not be enforced by an existing sovereign. This means that to enforce them through political channels grants them a special status, since now the sanctions (penalties and punishments) depend on the sovereign's will and capacity. For Austin, a sovereign's commands may be unwise but never illegal. Such commands may conflict with either divine law or positive morality, or both, but remain legal even if in such conflict. Thus, legally there can exist no "bad" laws since the legal order is nothing other than what a sovereign commands.

This conception of "positive law" seeks to remind men of the peculiarly crucial relation between a legal order and political power as against those who might want to deny genuinely *legal* status to edicts or rules they judge morally unwise. Austin excludes from the legal order all instances of customary law and social practices, which for him can achieve legal status only by becoming incorporated into the positive law. Austin's positivistic conception of law "properly so called" has been said to approximate the gunman's model. To the subject the legal order stands as coercive a threat as does a gunman who demands of a victim "Your money or your life!" when pointing a gun at his ribs. Thus the legal order is something like the gunman's coercive command and the sovereign's power like the gun. Like Hobbes, Austin believed that a political system exists to promote order (thus, to punish threats to public order), but though he was suspicious of persons who emphasize only the rights-protecting function of a sovereign he did not wish to give a "black-and-white" characterization of political authority. However, if he were forced to choose between a justification of government as a rights-protecting and as a restraining influence, Austin admitted he would have to choose the latter view.

Obviously, Austin's conception of the legal order does not necessitate either a broad or a narrow view of the proper range of political sovereignty. What it does assert is that, however the range of its actual powers is defined, a sovereign is legally supreme in all those areas in which commands are given. A legal order is naturally *despotic* whether it exists, concretely, in a democracy, a monarchy, a polity (where functions are constitutionally "mixed"), or a sheer totalitarian state. Not *how often* a sovereign is to command but the peculiar status of his commands *when* he commands is Austin's major concern. There is a difference between law and morality from a legal standpoint. Until moral notions are written into the positive law, they cannot receive the important backing of a sovereign's might though, in fact, they may not always require such support to be effective in influencing human conduct.

One difficulty with Austin's analysis of the legal order stems from his exclusive insistence on *one* kind of law as being fundamental. Yet there are customary laws which, in some societies, possess a greater coercive weight than the existing legal rules. Yet they are not positive laws even if, in fact, their coercive power over human action is extreme. Another difficulty is that Austin's analysis presupposes a *unified* sovereign—and this seems difficult, even impossible to apply to the situation in the United States where different *functional* sovereigns may be said to operate and where important separation of powers exists. Further, Austin's analysis excludes from "law properly so-called" all elements of constitutional law and, as in Great Britain, is inapplicable to a system in which parliamentary acts may sometimes be subject to court review (as some acts of Congress are here subject to review by the Supreme Court).

A passage from Austin's *Lectures on Jurisprudence* persuasively expresses his awareness of the special coercive nature of a legal order. Austin wrote:

> To the ignorant and bawling fanatics who stun you with their pother about liberty, political or civil liberty seems to be the principal end for which government ought to exist. But the final cause or purpose for which government ought to exist, is the furtherance of the commonweal to the greatest possible extent. And it must mainly attain the purpose for which it ought to exist, by two sets of means: *first,* by conferring such rights on its subjects as general utility commends, and by imposing such relative duties (or duties corresponding to the rights) as are necessary to the enjoyment of the former; *secondly,* by imposing such absolute duties (or by imposing such duties without corresponding rights) as tend to promote the good of the political community at large, although they promote not specially the interests of determinate parties. Now he who is clothed with a legal right, is also clothed with a political liberty: that is to say, he has the liberty from political obligation, which is necessary to the enjoyment of the right. Consequently, in so far as it attains its appropriate purpose by conferring rights upon its subjects, government attains that purpose through the medium of political liberty. But since it must impose a duty wherever it confers a right, and should also impose duties which have no corresponding rights, it is less through the medium of political liberty, than through that of legal restraint, that government must attain the purpose for which it ought to exist. To say that political liberty ought to be its principal end, or to say that its principal end ought to be legal restraint, is to talk absurdly: for each is merely a mean to that furtherance of the common weal, which is the only ultimate object of good or beneficent sovereignty. But though both propositions are absurd, the latter of the two absurdities is the least remote from the truth.[13]

[13] John Austin, *The Province of Jurisprudence Determined* (with an Introduction by H. L. A. Hart), Sixth Lecture (New York: The Noonday Press, 1954), pp. 269–270.

Further Considerations

Professor Weldon has argued that the state is simply one of a number of associations by which men seek to regulate their social lives.[14] Yet he points out that some thinkers view the state as more important than other associations like churches, fraternities, or recreational clubs. He insists this somewhat outdated view rested on a mystical conviction that the state derived its authority from God, thus was "seen" as possessing supernatural status—a position no longer tenable now that scientific developments have shown the error in "magical" explanations of the origins of our world. Weldon also thinks the arguments for the state's uniqueness are unconvincing. These arguments are that, first, membership in a state is not voluntary (and men are unable to "resign" from a state as they can give up memberships in other associations); second, the state directly involves one's whole life-span rather than portions of it; third, the state differs qualitatively from other associations in that "it determines their legality and therefore makes it possible for them to exist at all." Against the first, Weldon argues that one can emigrate or commit suicide and that resignation from churches is also often difficult or impossible. Against the second, that even if it is true it is a trivial truth, emphasizing men's irritation at various regulations issued by the state. Against the third, Weldon insists there have been associations defined as illegal by the state which nonetheless continued effectively and influentially to function and even, in some rare instances, to gain the allegiance of majorities.

The problem of political sovereignty is one about the locus of authority and all coercive power, but it has loomed larger in some historical eras than in others, especially in those in which conflicts between groups raised questions about highest authority. Empirically, the question, Who is sovereign? is meaningless until it is placed in a context. The question can be answered, often, if we know enough details—and may turn out to be a question about who has authority to act or decide in specific cases. Thus, if asked at a baseball game when

[14] T. D. Weldon, *The Vocabulary of Politics* (Baltimore: Penguin Books, 1953), p. 46ff.

players argue, the answer may be that the chief umpire is sovereign, that is, officially authorized to decide the dispute. Or a rule book, rather than a person, which defines the nature of the game may be sovereign. In the Middle Ages, disputes about sovereignty often arose because of conflicts between Church and State, complicated by a political system—feudalism—in which the same person might function as a representative of both. Factually, to the question: "Who is sovereign in this situation?", the answer might be: "No one is!" The reason is obvious. If the situation involves a conflict between groups, neither of which can subdue the other, then in fact there is no clear sovereignty, where sovereignty is defined as authority linked with a capacity to enforce decisions.

Philosophers have sometimes tried to describe an ideal of political sovereignty—to show where, even in face of the facts, sovereignty *ought* to reside. Sometimes they described ideal states, claiming that such states would have to exist (or should be sought after) if rational political life is to occur. But, since actual political life usually reflects great factual discrepancies between ideal aims and claims and actual practices, ideal conceptions of sovereignty—where rational authority is seen as coupled with adequate capacities of enforcement—look "utopian" from the open plains of argument, conflict, and compromise. Absolutist political theorists sought to justify the divine *right* of a monarch to ultimate power, even when the tides of political fortune were adrift with parliamentarian hopes and claims. The absolutist position rests on the normative conviction there *ought* to be a universal, indivisible, ultimate sovereign in any state. In the modern world, the concept of sovereignty has fared badly in some philosophical quarters, the reasons being (according to Professor W. J. Rees) "due partly to the logical difficulties inherent in the concept, and partly to the fact that certain modern political developments, such as the growth of democracy, federalism and public law, have made the concept a difficult one to apply in present conditions." [15] The concept seems to function most fruitfully when the sovereign is pictured as a person authoritatively capable of commanding allegiance,

[15] "The Theory of Sovereignty Restated," in Peter Laslett, ed., *Philosophy, Politics and Society* (First Series; New York: Macmillan, 1956), p. 56.

thus seems best to fit a hierarchical scheme at whose summit "sits" (as it were) an ultimate, unlimited, permanent, indivisible source of command. This scheme cannot easily accommodate "mixed" political systems or parliamentary democracies, where powers of specific bodies are constitutionally defined and sovereignty is plural rather than simple and indivisible—sometimes divided among legislative, judicial, and executive bodies as well as between federal and state jurisdictional areas. In modern discussions of political theory, the word "sovereign" can mean different notions, thus can be used in more than one way whenever the question about sovereignty arises. Professor Rees has found that "sovereign" has meant: supreme legal authority; supreme legal authority which is simultaneously a fully moral one; a supreme authority of a fixed group of persons having control over specific means of coercion; a supreme coercive power used cooperatively and habitually by all, or nearly all, the members of a community; a strongest political influence; a permanently supreme authority, power, or influence. To answer any question about sovereignty, thus, would require knowledge of the meaning of the word and detailed knowledge of a context in which the question is asked.

For example, suppose a foreign visitor asks: "Who holds sovereignty in the United States?" How should such a question be answered unless the listener knows some specific issue or procedure that is supposed to be causing perplexity? The Supreme Court may (ideally) be said to be sovereign in certain legal areas but not in others. Similarly, something of this kind can be said about the Presidency or the Congress. Factually, however, even if the questioner is told that sovereignty fluctuates in the United States, the bodies having the authority to act may not always succeed in enforcement. Ideally, the Supreme Court is sovereign in defined areas, but one or more of its official decisions may meet stiff resistance. Thus, if one of its decisions cannot be enforced, is the Court *actually* sovereign because it has the authority? Furthermore, if questions of legal sovereignty arise, they may involve such widespread political effects that they are difficult to confine to the legal sphere alone. In cases where the Court, say, renders a decision which is (if only temporarily) successfully resisted by a given state, the Court has authority but not the power to enforce such that either sovereignty rests with the state (on that disputed issue) or is in a process of being located (if sovereignty means both authority and power).

Attempts to locate ultimate sovereignty in the state also produce some difficulties. What is the state? Is it one power or a function of several separate powers? Is the state more inclusive than the government? If so, is the state inclusive of the whole range of social life, incorporating family and so-called "voluntary" groups? Aren't there different kinds of state?

Philosophers tend to "see" the state in quite different lights. A few men think of the state as a superagency, almost like a person, whose reality is more than the sum of its individual parts. It has been viewed as analogous to an organism, whose parts achieve significance only as they are essential to the healthy functioning of the whole. The state, so viewed, can be treated as an end-in-itself, requiring no further justification. Thus (to give just one example) G. W. F. Hegel conceived of the state as the underlying rational unity of an entire culture, embracing not only government but art, religion and philosophy. Reality manifested its nature in and through the state, and men achieved genuine "freedom" only to the extent their activities coincided with what Hegel thought to be the inherent rationality of World Reason in the social life of a peoples' development. L. T. Hobhouse—as well as other political philosophers—is convinced that Hegel's theory of the state (and other metaphysical theories like it) is erroneous and damaging to human liberty, for he wrote:

> The best and worst things that men do they do in the name of a religion. Some have supposed that only supernatural religion could mislead. The history of our time shows that if men no longer believe in God they will make themselves gods of Power, of Evolution, of the Race, the Nation, or the State. In the name of such gods will they drench a continent with blood, and the youth will offer themselves up as willing martyrs.[16]

Like other critics of the organicist conception of the state, Hobhouse thinks it leads to passiveness before power and renders individual

[16] *The Metaphysical Theory of the State* (London: Allen & Unwin, 1918), p. 134.

political morality an impossibility. The conflict is between two views of the state, according to Hobhouse and other critics.

The alternative conception is that which "sees" a state as a means rather than an end-in-itself, a view favored by democratic theorists and by those who (like Aristotle), though seeing the state as like an organism, believe the state is a moral phenomenon whose nature involves the ethical self-realization of its members. Hobhouse advocates the democratic conception of the state (as does Weldon), writing passionately about the state:

> In the democratic view it is the servant of humanity in the double sense that it is to be judged by what it does for the lives of its members and by the part that it plays in the society of humankind. In the metaphysical view it is itself the sole guardian of moral worth. In the democratic view the sovereign state is already doomed, destined to subordination in a community of the world. In the metaphysical view it is the supreme achievement of human organization.[17]

Yet, even if the state is viewed as a means (the "machine-model," as T. D. Weldon named this view), it can be viewed so either favorably or unfavorably. Thus, democratic theorists can argue that the state is to be judged by the results in human happiness (utilitarianism), indicating that a sovereign state is never absolutely so, since it is subject to another standard of judgment. On the other hand, Marxists can "see" the state as a means which is oppressive, an agency of a dominant social-economic class which subjugates the larger class to the political and legal machinery in its control. Where the democratically minded view seeks to arrange the state's functions so as to produce the maximum of human happiness (suggesting that the "sovereignty of the people" delegates authoritative functions to the state), the rigid Marxist tends to want so to define economics that the state will ultimately "wither away" when the proper establishment of economic conditions and relations is achieved—because optimistically the Marxist believes (or pretends to appear to believe) that administration can replace politics and the coercive side of political life vanish.

[17] *Ibid.*, p. 137.

Conclusion

A number of influential philosophers have concentrated on the privileged power of those who represent the state. They have sought to persuade men to view the state in a specific way, primarily because a state possesses enormous power—a capacity to cause either great harm or widespread misery to individuals. The philosophers' concern for the special powers of a state reflect differing conceptions of the ends of political power and the relations between individuals and organized power. This concern is conveniently characterized as a concern about sovereignty.

A thinker like St. Thomas Aquinas looked on the state as a natural and inevitable aspect of human existence. Its functions were seen as justifiable only if the state encourages men's natural tendencies to seek happiness as well as reflects a knowledge of eternally existing divine and natural laws. In his turn, Thomas Hobbes emphasized the coercive power of the state and the need to justify men's subservience to so extensive a Leviathan. In one sense, Hobbes wanted to argue there are good reasons for obeying some bad laws. At the same time, he retained a list of natural laws but treated them as rough empirical maxims learned by painful experience. Both Rousseau and Hegel emphasized ways in which, according to their views, the state represents a reality greater than the sum of its parts. They insisted that the state is an integral and organic entity. Finally, John Austin identified the political order with what he called "positive law," insisting that the state is the sanctioning source of genuine legal commands given to citizens habitually prone to obey.

It is not at all clear that the notion of sovereignty can be made consistent or meaningful in modern pluralistic societies. Certainly, there may be no one central and unified sovereign. Instead, men may have to learn to speak of functional sovereigns—powers which can make only contextual sense. There are even some contemporary philosophers who believe the notion of sovereignty is no longer essential in political philosophy.

Claims about the *true* nature of the state (or sovereign power) made by philosophers do not seem subject to factual verification. Rather, the philosophers who put forth differing claims appear to seek to convince readers that they *ought,* for their own good, to accept a specific philosophical theory of sovereignty as opposed to others. Yet, each philosopher has at least illuminated some one important feature of political life which, for ordinary men and women, might have gone unnoticed. The political philosophers have brought a moral passion to the consideration of political power and the clash of political ideals.

Some Questions and Problems

1. Choose three students to represent the views of Aquinas, Hobbes, and Austin. Select some controversial political issue involving the Government and ask the students to approach that issue as they think the philosophers they speak for would have approached it.
2. Discuss the assertion: "The State is always a reality which is greater than the sum of its parts."
3. Do you agree with the critic who argued that Hobbes asks men to escape many little terrors by accepting one big Terror? Was Hobbes justified?
4. Compare and contrast Hobbes and Aquinas in their treatments of Natural Law. Which position seems to you the most sensible and defensible?
5. Discuss the assertion that the Social Contract theory makes no literal sense at all.
6. What political problem, if any, is Rousseau seeking to meet by his notion of the General Will? Is the notion helpful toward solving practical political difficulties?
7. Is Hobbes correct in claiming that independent sovereignties exist in a state of nature in relation to one another?
8. Does the notion of International Law make sense?
9. Following the Second World War, some trials were held in Nuremberg at which German officials were tried by the victorious allies. Was it wise for the allies to hold such trials? Give reasons. Can you think of moral objections to such trails? Explain your viewpoint.
10. Can a political state both preserve order and civil liberties at the same time? Discuss.

Some Suggested Readings

Aristotle. *Politics.*

Cassirer, E. *Rousseau, Kant, Goethe.* Princeton: Princeton University Press, 1947.

Collingwood, R. G. *The New Leviathan.* Oxford: Clarendon Press, 1942.

Copleston, F., S.J. "St. Thomas Aquinas: Moral Theory" and "St. Thomas Aquinas: Political Theory," *A History of Philosophy,* Vol. II. London: Burns, 1959.

de Jouvenal, B. *Sovereignty,* trans. J. Huntington. Chicago: University of Chicago Press, 1957.

Ebenstein, W. *Great Political Thinkers: Plato to the Present,* 3d ed. New York: Rinehart, 1960.

Gilby, T. *The Political Thought of Thomas Aquinas.* Chicago: University of Chicago Press, 1958.

Gough, J. W. *John Locke's Political Philosophy.* Oxford: Clarendon Press, 1950.

Green, T. H. *Lectures on the Principles of Political Obligation.* London: Longmans, Green, 1955.

Hegel, G. W. F. *Philosophy of Right,* trans. T. M. Knox. Oxford: Clarendon Press, 1942.

Hobbes, T. *De Cive or The Citizen,* ed. S. P. Lamprecht. New York: Appleton-Century-Crofts, 1947.

Hobhouse, L. T. *The Metaphysical Theory of the State.* London: Allen & Unwin, 1918.

Jones, G. "A Critical Review of R. Niebuhr's Political Theology." Unpublished essay.

Lasswell, H. D., *Politics: Who Gets What, When, How?* New York: Meridian, 1958.

Lasswell, H. D., and Kaplan, A. *Power and Society.* New Haven: Yale University Press, 1950.

Lenin, V. I. *State and Revolution* and *Imperialism and Imperialistic War,* Vols. XXI and V in *Collected Works of V. I. Lenin.* New York: International Publishers, 1932.

Machiavelli, N. *The Prince and The Discourses.* New York: Carlton House, n.d.

Mayo, H. B. *An Introduction to Democratic Theory.* New York: Oxford University Press, 1960.

Morganthau, H. J. *Politics Among Nations: The Struggle for Power and Peace.* New York: Knopf, 1948.

Niebuhr, R. *The Structure of Nations and Empires.* New York: Scribner, 1961.

Partridge, P. H. "Politics and Power," *Philosophy,* Vol. XXXVIII, No. 144, 1963.

Rees, W. J. "The Theory of Sovereignty Restated," *Philosophy, Politics and Society,* First Series, ed. P. Laslett. New York: Macmillan, 1956.

Rousseau, J. J. *The Social Contract and Discourses.* New York: Everyman's Library, 1947.

Schuman, R. L. *International Politics: The Destiny of the Modern State System.* New York: McGraw-Hill, 1950.

Strauss, L. *Thoughts on Machiavelli.* Glencoe, Ill.: Free Press, 1958.

Tussman, J. *Obligation and the Body Politic.* London: Oxford University Press, 1960.

Warrender, H. *The Political Philosophy of Hobbes.* London: Oxford University Press, 1957.

Weldon, T. D. *States and Morals.* London: Murray, 1946.

CHAPTER EIGHT

Freedom: Fact or Fancy?

Much of the literature devoted to social and political thought treats the idea of freedom as a significant one. An appeal to freedom has served as a rallying cry for movements of diverse aims and origins. Contemporary thinkers who prefer clarity to sentiment sometimes suggest that freedom is an empty notion unless carefully defined. "What do you mean by freedom?" can be a meaningful question in any context in which men use the notion in loose, generalizing ways. One man's view of freedom sometimes turns out to be another man's picture of slavery.

Psychologists also like to point out how, given a sentence like: "Harry is a free man!", we often want to ask: "Free to *do* what? Free *from* what?" Writers concerned with large-scale analysis of a human problem may worry about the issues of freedom and order, the threats to individual freedom, the paradox of freedom, and similar presumably meaningful topics. Philosophers whose job it is to analyze concepts and arguments continue to write articles about the relation of freedom and causality ("Can an act which is caused be a free act?") and about how, if a genuine moral responsibility is possible, men must in some senses be free. Political thinkers, sociologists, and practical politicians sometimes maintain that men are less free than they had supposed, or that men must choose between alternative kinds of freedom. Assuming that freedom is possible, writers can disagree about its value—some arguing to the effect that freedom can be a dangerous thing, others insisting that it is the highest end of human existence. Trying to make sense of the notion of social and political freedom is a difficult task which any intelligent citizen at some time feels the need to undertake. In this chapter, our purpose is to clarify some aspects of the philosophical and political treatments of the notion of freedom.

Philosophical Considerations

Philosophical interest in the freedom issue has tended to reflect two kinds of intellectual concern. One deeply rooted concern in the long tradition of Western thought has been the quest after a generalized description of "reality," as if in addition to the special sciences and to ordinary knowledge there might be something *like* a science—yet its own kind of enterprise—whose subject matter is "whatever is." Usually known as metaphysics, this enterprise was defined by Aristotle as an inquiry into the most pervasive traits of Being, or "whatever is." Such an inquiry has reflected a human desire for the most general kind of knowledge. Whether philosophers have concluded that the most generic feature of the universe is matter or mind, change or permanence, unity or diversity, purpose or purposelessness, they have often argued like men engaged in something like a descriptive undertaking. Of course, to describe the most general features of a universe would involve an enterprise quite different from describing, say, what a house looks like. Yet metaphysical philosophers act as if there can be descriptive answers, true or false, to a question like: "What is the fundamental nature of the universe (reality)?" just as there can be true or false replies to a question like: "What is the chemical composition of water?"

Metaphysicians like to distinguish between "appearance" and "reality." They insist that things are not always what they seem— that real structures exist, perhaps difficult to get at, which are to be "gotten at" by thought. Even philosophers sceptical about the possibility of our *knowing* what those structures are sometimes insist that they are nonetheless *there*. Thus, metaphysicians have given differing answers to the question about the ultimate nature of reality, but they have shared a common philosophic craving for a generalized description of existence. Regarding the question about freedom, they have sometimes argued that men must first know the nature of ultimate reality if they are, meaningfully, to show how and to what extent (if at all) men are genuinely free. For them, the question whether men are free cannot be answered until philosophers have determined whether they inhabit a universe in which freedom is an objective *metaphysical* possibility. The type of metaphysical "picture" one has of the universe will influence how he answers the question about human freedom.

A second broad philosophical concern with freedom has been more exclusively a moral one—an effort to analyze adequately the nature and conditions of human responsibility. Men do hold one another responsible; they do ascribe rights and responsibilities to each other.[1] For example, in a context in which an automobile driver goes through a stop sign and hits another car, a witness who says to the driver: "You did it!" is not simply describing the accident (if he can be said to describe anything at all) but *ascribing* responsibility to the driver. "You did it!" in such a situation means something like: "You're responsible for hitting that other car!" If, on hearing the witness, the driver says something like: "But my brakes failed to work—the car went out of my control!", he is not denying that he has been in an accident or that he has gone through a stop sign. He is saying that *he couldn't help what happened* because of forces beyond his immediate control. The driver is giving an excuse for what happened, as if in hopes of having the witness reconsider his judgment about responsibility. Now, an important part of the modern philosophical concern with the freedom question has been the concern with how men use language when holding others responsible or granting rights. The philosophic effort has been aimed at finding out the logic of responsibility words. Men do in fact use language in a variety of ways (descriptive, imperative, exclamatory, interrogative, ceremonial)— including its use as a tool for holding people responsible, especially in situations involving the fixing of blame. The modern philosophic

[1] H. L. A. Hart, "The Ascription of Responsibility and Rights," in Anthony Flew, ed., *Logic and Language* (First Series; Oxford: Blackwell, 1962), pp. 145–166.

concern is often to find out, given the uses of a language which make up a way of life, what assumptions they contain about human freedom.

An old and challenging "standby" in philosophy is the dispute whether there is freedom of the will. The problem has been characterized in differing ways, yet involves a common core of difficulties. It has been known as the problem of freedom of the will, freedom versus determinism, choice or necessity, causality or chance, randomness or directedness. The nature of causality has worried many philosophers, leading some to conclude that *if* all events are caused (including human acts), *then* one can argue there is no freedom. A universe pictured as lawlike, operating according to fixed regularities which universally occur, becomes for some philosophers a universe in which freedom cannot exist. "Men think they are free, or that they choose to do what they do," an imagined discussant might say in illustration of this position. "But to the extent the universe is rational, it must be explainable. To explain anything, we must show how it follows from operative general laws. Men think they are free only to the extent they are *ignorant* of the real causes of whatever happens or exists. Thus, to say that a human action is free is to admit that, as yet, we are unable fully to state the causal laws which make that action take place." In crude form, such an argument represents the "feeling" some persons have that if an event is caused, then it cannot be free. The view here is that causality is incompatible with freedom.

To counter this strict view of determinism—the view that each and every event is caused and thus not free—some philosophers argue that there are different orders of causes. For example, the German philosopher, Immanuel Kant, believed that scientific knowledge is possible only if general (universal) and necessary laws can be discovered as the bases for human explanations of events. Yet, Kant insisted in a part of his *Critique of Pure Reason* that men can never hope to discover the real causes of things. Science describes what Kant called the "phenomenal" realm, not the "noumenal" reality which, if it should exist, involves the natures of things as they are in themselves. Of course, men can never prove that such a noumenal realm exists, according to Kant. Nonetheless, Kant thought such a noumenal reality does exist and that it contains noumenal causes, including causes from

freedom. He believed that men's common moral sense indicates existence of a genuine human freedom—whose ultimate nature must forever escape the "nets" of our scientific theories and explanations.
Men can therefore act *as if* there is genuine freedom—a noumenal
freedom at the very heart of "reality." But they can never make such
freedom the object of scientific proof, nor can they fully describe its
contents. Nonetheless, Kant remained a determinist. While he insisted on the existence of two orders of causation, one phenomenal
and the other noumenal, he still spoke about a noumenal freedom
glimpsed in men's moral experience. It is as if Kant wanted to argue
that men must know the source of an act's cause if they want to determine whether it is a free act. Kant was, thus, a determinist who
thought there exists an order of causes which will forever escape the
methods of scientific inquiry and explanation—causes which, in the
human self, are not coercive of action but nonetheless make it possible.

In the nineteenth century, many thinkers despaired of making sense
out of the metaphysical dispute over freedom of the will. They went
so far as to think that determinism is, in principle, incompatible with
human freedom. Some of them argued somewhat as follows: Either
a man is free or he is not. If acts are caused, then they are not free.
Clearly, however, man is free. Therefore, some acts must be uncaused.
The position which argues that an act is free if and only if it is uncaused is known as "indeterminism." Indeterminists insist that acts
and events can occur which lack causes. This somewhat bizarre position arose, in part, from concern with evolutionary treatments of
reality which stressed the objective possibility that unique, unpredictable events can occur. Two influential American thinkers, C. S.
Peirce (1839–1914) and William James (1842–1910), concluded
that we may live in a universe whose central reality is the production
of *chance* events. They meant that in important ways the universe is
unpredictable *in principle*. To say that an act or event is free would,
on this view, mean to say that the event or act is unexplainable except
in terms of the notion of chance—that it falls outside any possible
scheme of *causal* explanation.

Now, an indeterminist defense of human freedom can be criticized as leading to no moral consequences, unless they are undesirable ones. The reason is that, if human acts are uncaused, then nothing at all intelligible can be said about them. They simply are what they are, coming as they do or not at all. They can neither be predicted nor, in scientific terms, explained. We would have no moral basis for praising or blaming persons whose acts are uncaused. Nor could individuals make sense out of their own acts, since the acts would not follow from the kinds of characters they might happen to possess. Thus, if indeterminism were true, it would present us with a defense of freedom which can have no relevance for our genuine moral concerns.

The indeterminist muddle has led most philosophers to adopt the view that acts can be caused and yet be free. Rather than argue that determinism makes moral responsibility impossible, many philosophers insist that we have an intelligible basis for making moral evaluations *only if* human acts result from causes. But this means that to say an act is caused does not entail that the act is compelled. To say: "There's a cause for Sam's action" and "Sam had to do what he did" is not *necessarily* to say the same thing in different ways. A determinist defense of freedom rests on the need to relate human character to specific ways of acting (a man's character may be said to be a "barometer" of how he will act), since the predictability of human action is a requirement of any responsible social or political system. This means that if an act results from man's freedom, then it did not have to occur ("He didn't *have* to do that, you know!") and that, in some sense, we can meaningfully say of such an act: "He could have done otherwise, if he had wanted." There are causes over which men have no control, and there are those which are subject to control. The fact that men can *learn* to act in specific ways indicates that causality and freedom need not be taken as incompatible. More than this, it can be argued that the only occasion on which the question of human freedom arises is that where parents, judges, and critics ask whether a given person should be held responsible for his acts. Our concern for human freedom shows a moral concern about how we are to justify our notions of responsibility. To say that someone is responsible for having done an act is to say that the act was neither compelled nor compulsive. We could not rightly hold persons responsible if each and every one of their acts was externally compelled or—to use psychological language—compulsive, as, for example, the stealing of a kleptomaniac.

Suppose that a mother forbids her young son to go swimming on his way home from school. Suppose, in addition, that the boy gets caught in a landslide on the way home and is hurled bodily into an adjacent pond. If, on learning about the cause of the boy's getting wet, the mother says: "I warned you not to go swimming!" and spanks the boy, she is holding him responsible for something completely beyond his control in the circumstances. The boy had no choice in the matter—getting caught up in a landslide is like that. On the other hand, a mother who issued such a command and who, then, always accepted the boy's excuse (without exception): "But, Mother, I couldn't help it!" would be held as irresponsible for failing to check up, to investigate. Not every excuse is an acceptable one, morally speaking. Nor would a legal system pass as morally adequate if it could not make reasonably defensible distinctions between acceptable and unacceptable excuses. If someone says, "I couldn't help doing what I did!", he does not rule out investigation of the claim. Such a saying usually indicates a need for investigation into the existing evidence. In a police court, many a driver of an automobile may give as an excuse for his arrest: "The car ran away from me—it got out of control!"; and yet a judge will turn to the policeman who has investigated and ask: "What does the evidence show?"

To decide whether, in a specific situation, a person is responsible for something he has done is often a difficult matter. Mistakes can be made. The philosopher concerned about the discussion of human freedom need not deny the troubling existence of such difficulties. What the philosopher can deny is that all human action must be viewed as unfree if it is the result of causes. Only if freedom is possible can a political or social system be judged as a reasonable one, permitting the exercise of powers of choice and intelligent decision by its members. There is no convincing argument to prove that because acts are caused (determinism), they are therefore unfree. The philosopher can insist that the sentences "The act was caused" and "The act was compelled" are not always synonymous.

Practical Freedom

Let us suppose an intelligent nonphilosopher to have heard the summary of some philosophical arguments about freedom up to this point and, puzzled, to burst out with some strong objections. Suppose that the objections run somewhat as follows. "But what has the philosophical analysis of freedom got to do with the genuine issue? In politics, don't men have to *make up their minds* whether freedom is possible and something to be desired? Isn't the question of freedom a practical one—a matter of holding convictions, working for those convictions by sweat and toil, trying to create institutions which can transform empty talk about freedom into an actual state of affairs? Isn't social and political freedom really a human achievement?" Such a complaint boils down to the argument that men must make up their minds that freedom is attainable and, without waiting for philosophers to show them the logic of their belief, go to work strenuously to realize it in concrete ways. Such an intelligent man wants to emphasize the importance of practice over theory, doing over talking. "Get an anchor!" he says to us, "and then put the ship of state in order!"

The practical man "sees" the question about human freedom as a matter of social and political arrangements. Men are free to the extent they are permitted to pursue certain interests without unlimited imposition of external restraints. A free political system is one which permits, and actually encourages, the creation of conditions favorable to the pursuit of human interests. Such a system permits a natural expression of those interests by limiting the authority of those who govern in such a way that rulers cannot *arbitrarily* repress peoples' legitimate desires. It will probably contain a legal system which punishes those who use raw means of force to stop public discussion of political issues. Similarly, it will tend to restrain and punish those who seek to subvert a decision of the community, once the decision has been democratically arrived at. Such a system will educate its citizens to their responsibilities in public affairs.

To the practical man, freedom means the existence of rights and opportunities available to him as steady, predictable parts of his social environment. Among these are the guaranteed right to say critical things about the government without his experiencing a club on his head; the right to meet with other citizens to organize for the protection of his and their interests; opportunities to act under courts and governmental agencies which contain a minimum of corrupt officials; the right of freedom of movement in and about a city, state, or nation without having endlessly to check with political authorities for permission so to move; opportunities to act with the assurance that law-enforcement agencies will seek to protect him in the exercise of rights which are legally his. The fair-minded common citizen will probably not expect justice never to go astray, nor deny the value and usefulness of democracy because some officials are found corrupt, nor blame the police for mistakes in judgment of a kind which can happen to the best of men and groups in difficult situations so long as, once discovered, the mistakes are admitted and amends made. Such a citizen will be something of a realist, knowing that politics involves compromises and even failures—yet be convinced that the balance sheet of a relatively free society and political system will contain positively desirable marks.

Sometimes men attempt to compare whole political systems, calling them "free" or "unfree." This is perhaps a questionable practice. Yet, as one English political thinker has shown, there are some fairly clear marks of a system which (though always imperfectly) can be characterized as freedom-oriented. Professor T. D. Weldon proposed some tests for deciding between systems, tests he thought incomplete but yet important. These tests can be put in the form of four general questions:

1. Does the political system under consideration censor the reading of those who are subject to it and impose restrictions on teaching?

2. Does it maintain that any political or other principles are immutable and therefore beyond criticism?

3. Does it impose restrictions on the intercourse of its members with those who live under different systems?

4. Do the rulers of the association which has these institutions find

most of their supporters among the illiterate, the uneducated, and the superstitious? [2]

Weldon admitted that a system could lack all of these restrictions without being fully free, but he thought any system which could pass these tests would make possible the discovery of those facts without which free citizens are unable to make proper political appraisals. To be free politically means to be in a position to act for desired ends and to have available those facts one needs to know to make sound judgments about what is desirable and also achievable. Since a knowledge of facts is always relevant to the making of intelligent choices, the extent of a system's educational facilities will provide an empirical index of its support to freedom. The *kinds* of knowledge those educational facilities make available—the educational content—and the manner in which that content is taught will also influence the extent of freedom within the society. In a system oriented to political freedom some clear distinction must be maintained between indoctrination and genuine teaching.

"Hold on, there!" our interested listener may feel impelled to break in at this point. "Not even in a democracy should citizens be permitted to fulfill all their desires. Furthermore, the desires of a majority ought not unrestrictedly to triumph, since even a majority may make mistakes. A free society will restrict certain classes of action—keeping social life from becoming a scene reminiscent of hogs rushing selfishly to the trough. In a free society a certain kind of individualism is encouraged along with an insistence on a degree of subordination of individuals to a common (public) good. Be reasonable! Be practical! A balance of some kind is needed even, or especially, in a democracy if social and political chaos is to be averted."

Probably an outburst like this would express a fairly basic kind of misgiving felt by many persons concerned about social and political freedom. The two sentences: "Harry Stalwart, American citizen, is a free man" and "The U.S.A. is a free country" look somewhat alike and yet differ in a fundamental respect. In one, an individual person is named by the subject term; in the other, a social and political sys-

[2] T. D. Weldon, *The Vocabulary of Politics* (London: Penguin, 1953), p. 176.

tem is named. A political system is made up of numerous individuals like Harry Stalwart. How can one speak meaningfully of social or political freedom if individuals are unreservedly free? If Harry Stalwart were free to drive through all the traffic lights (which, physically, he may be free to do in the sense of being able), without suffering legal penalties, then his neighbor would not be free to drive on the streets without a heightened probability of suffering serious hurt. Thus, to say "The U.S.A. is a free country" *may* often mean that in the U.S.A. Harry Stalwart is *not* free to do certain things he might otherwise be tempted to do. Harry is not free endlessly to break certain laws without going to jail, say. Any meaningful social or political freedom will thus include the notion that certain kinds of acts, as well as failures to act, must be restrained and punished. One simply cannot make social or political sense out of the claim that freedom means an unrestricted right of action.

Probably few men—including the so-called "rugged individualist" —would seriously argue that all restraints are incompatible with political freedom. Some distinction must be made between individual and social freedom. When disagreement occurs, usually it has to do with how, as well as where, to make the distinction. What interests are in principle private, and which public? How are the decisions to be made and by whom? By what procedures shall controversies about this matter reach settlement? Such questions open up a Pandora's box of political thought and controversy, allowing to fly out related problems of law and justice, punishment, rights and obligations, authority and power. John Stuart Mill—whose essay, *On Liberty,* gives the classic liberal treatment of these related problems—wrote movingly that "There is a limit to the legitimate interference of collective opinion with individual independence; and to find that limit, and maintain it against encroachment, is as indispensable to a good condition of human affairs, as protection against political despotism." Yet, the same defender of individual liberty could write just as movingly: "All that makes existence valuable to any one, depends on the enforcement of restraints upon the actions of other people." Even Adam Smith—frequently used as an example of a defender of capitalism and of limited government—insisted, in his famous *The Wealth of Nations,* that a government has not only the right but the duty "of erecting and maintaining certain public works and certain public institutions, which it can never be for the interests of any individual, or small number of individuals, to erect and maintain."

Mill's general solution to the problem of liberty and authority is based on the conviction that men tend to seek pleasure rather than pain. Therefore, that society will be the freest which permits its citizens to pursue their own pleasures within a framework of rules which minimize the production of harm to others. The *public* domain includes all those actions which affect the welfare of others. The *private* domain—to be kept inviolate from governmental or social constraint—includes all those actions which affect the individual's own personal welfare. Thus, a man should be allowed even those acts which may be destructive of his own well-being except, insofar as they have harmful affects on others. Only if fairly clear distinctions can be made between what is legitimately public and what private will the notion of freedom make sense. In parliamentary and representative political systems, this basic view expressed by Mill's political thought has functioned as a rough guide for morally concerned citizens and legislators. To be workable, the distinction presupposes the meaningfulness of several other related propositions: that some kinds of actions do not in fact harm others; that governments may rightfully persuade but not always coerce individuals to realize their own well-being; that harmful private interests must be restrained by legal and political means; that a representative political system is able to produce the needed legislation as well as to maintain a free judiciary capable of interpreting it. Mill's writings are a significant part of the literature which defends the view that liberty is essential to political democracy—a literature which argues that without political freedom, individual liberty in a whole range of human enterprises must inevitably suffer. Mill's defense of liberty therefore also requires a defense of liberty of thought and discussion as necessary conditions of the maintenance of any representative governmental system.

Two general worries have "dogged" thinkers impressed by Mill's search after a criterion for deciding between what is public and what private. The first is the worry that the criterion will not prove very helpful—that (in some sense) perhaps any human act can be harmful to others if one carefully enough defines "harmful" so as to include it. Thus, a circular argument can occur: to answer the question how men are to distinguish private from public, one argues, "Employ the criterion that what is harmful to others is a public action!"; and to answer the question about how to determine what is harmful to others, one can argue: "Any act of a private citizen which violates a public interest or rule is harmful." What has to be shown is that there are acts which do not belong to the public domain even if, on some uses of the word "harmful," other persons may experience psychological discomfort. A second worry, important to those thinkers who are suspicious of democratic political forms, rests on the fear that men in political life will in fact always seek their own interests at the expense of others, even if they are elected to office.

Mill's liberal defense of parliamentary government is eroded if men become convinced that representatives will intrude their own private interests into the legislative and judicial machinery in such a way that, in the name of the public interest, they will deceptively use political means to "feather their own nests" at the public's expense. This fear has been expressed, say, by some practicing Marxists, who are distrustful of political liberalism and see politics as an arena in which economic groups fight out a sheer power battle for the control of the government. They tend to adopt a cynical attitude toward those who insist that politics and morality can go hand in hand. "They go hand in hand, all right," a rigid Marxist might say here; "but they take the workingman right down the garden path. They confuse the real issues by imposing a class morality and persuading citizens to think such a morality expresses universal interests." Such a rigid position, if held by a critic, entails a deeper conviction (or at least a pretended conviction) that parliamentary representation of multiple interests in a society is genuinely unworkable. These two general worries about Mill's political thought deserve brief separate consideration.

Suppose that the first worrier could engage Mill in a brief discussion and that, in the light of his published views, Mill could be counted on to hold to his political faith. Such a discussion might very well sound somewhat like the following dialogue.

Worrier: Mill, you put great stress on keeping the government from interfering with those human acts which belong to the individual—which do not harm others. But what do you mean by "harm"?

Mill: I suppose the most obvious meaning is physical hurt. Society may rightfully keep individuals from doing acts which needlessly bring physical suffering to others, even if to accomplish this it must itself punish offenders even in physical ways. For example, a man has a right to pursue his recreational activities and interests; but if he happens to like hunting, he can be restrained from hunting in crowded areas. He can be required, by law, to keep his guns where children and mentally ill people can not get at them, possibly injuring themselves and others.

Worrier: What about psychological hurt? As a liberal, you defend a man's right to speak his mind on important and controversial topics. Can't what a man says sometimes hurt another person's feelings?

Mill: What a man says may influence another person to act, of course. But there must be *some* distinction between saying and doing. We restrain actions rather than what men say.

Worrier: Yet, if I have certain beliefs and I hear someone openly criticize them, may not my feelings be hurt? Isn't this a kind of harm done to me?

Mill: What you say means only that we don't like to hear our most cherished beliefs questioned. In this sense, we aren't really harmed. In fact, criticism forces us to defend the truthfulness and usefulness of our beliefs, keeping them alive and meaningful. Of course, words which incite to riot or viciously stir up others against us may at times rightfully be restrained. A community has the right to pass laws against disturbance of the peace, lying, and slander. It does not have the right to prevent quiet and forceful discussion of the most controversial issues in the appropriate situations.

Worrier: You seem to admit, then, that some cases of talking can be considered cases of harming others. That is, in some instances one finds that talking is an act, and thus subject to legal restraint. How does one decide in such cases?

Mill: I can't tell you in advance how to make such decisions. All I can say is that if *all* instances of speaking are taken to be acts, then in principle there's no freedom at all. *How* and *where* a person does his talking about controversial issues will be important. Imbeciles and children must not be allowed to exercise such rights unqualifiedly, but mature citizens should have that right. The fact that talking can lead to action, or to our psychological discomfort, is not to be interpreted as meaning that we are always harmed by someone's saying things we don't like. Falsely and excitedly to shout "Fire!" in a crowded theater, say, may be treated as threatening harm, since it may help to cause a stampede.

Worrier: Mill, I'm not sure there may not be contexts in which almost anything—overt act or spoken word—may not be treated as threatening harm. I'm not certain that the distinction between harmful and nonharmful acts can be clearly made.

Mill: But aren't you looking for an argument? Aren't you asking the political philosopher to do for you what free men must themselves do in specific circumstances?

The brief, imagined dialogue brings out the problem of how a free society is to define what makes up harmful acts. This will necessitate careful attention to procedures—legal and political—so that whatever the resulting definitions, they are not arbitrarily arrived at. The classical liberal faith has rested on the conviction that such procedures, rationally defensible, can be established if certain conditions are met and maintained. Among these conditions must be the extension of knowledge to as wide a segment of the population as is possible, since knowledge is thought to be relevant to the determination of what is for the community's good. The decision about what is harmful to others rests, in part, on the extent of the available knowledge—such that a free society may, from time to time, redefine the meaning of "harmful." One writer summarized the general position of such a liberalism by insisting that its success presupposes firm beliefs of the following kind: "the existence of a variety of social interests and values" is desirable and legitimate; rigid class and status distinctions are "gratuitous"; rational compromise can settle most conflicts of social interest; public spiritedness in politics is possible; scientific techniques are useful even in the political domain—"the best means for bringing these affairs closer to human desires"; there is a chance of continuing progress "within the durable framework of parliamentary government, civil liberty, and enlightened public opinion." [3]

In the twentieth century, exactly this liberal faith has experienced heavy and continuing criticism. "Unrealistic! Unworkable!" claim some of the New Conservatives who, defending the idea of constitutional government, yet fear that the liberal faith in politically rational compromise gives needless advantages to those interests which seek to legislate continual social reforms. The conservatives sometimes fear that such a liberalism, operating during a century marked by rigid ideological dogmatisms seeking mastery of the world, will undermine the social basis needed for political order—helping a victory for the revolutionary rather than the evolutionary procedures all genuine liberals prefer. They also fear too great a reliance on reason in matters which, as viewed by Edmund Burke—a leading historical spokesman for the conservative attitude—are more influenced by custom, prejudice, and prescription than by reason. Reason can undermine authority, which is needed as one source of the habit of obedience. Reason can also weaken the social manners without which a relaxed, natural social and political existence becomes impossible. The modern conservatives fear that modern liberalism takes "tradition" much too lightly, assuming that intelligence plays a greater role in human affairs than it does in fact. Conservatives insist that change must occur unevenly, even slowly, and that politics is an art of balancing interests more than it is a science by which to frame rational blueprints for social reform and progress. Such a spirit of conservatism appeals to men's real fears that, in seeking to improve social conditions, men may destroy the traditional moral foundations without which a sane social order can never exist.

The arguments of the New Conservatives are receiving wide hear-

[3] Charles Frankel, *The Case for Modern Man* (New York: Harper, 1955), pp. 33–37. Used by permission of Harper & Row, Publishers, Incorporated.

ing in American life. Even their critics admit they are often able men. Perhaps as well as any conservative spokesman, Russell Kirk has attempted to list what he considers to be the basic beliefs of conservatives in the contemporary world. These include:

- belief in a divine intent ruling society and human conscience, meaning that political problems are always ultimately grounded in religious and moral problems;

- fondness for the plural forms of traditional life and opposition to "levelling" uniformity;

- belief in the need of classes if social order is to prevail;

- a conviction that property and freedom are inescapably linked, thus that "economic levelling" is a threat to freedom;

- belief that prescription more than reason is needed if men's appetites are to be curbed and directed;

- insistence that change need not mean progress.[4]

Radical critics—like the Marxists, say, who demand a thorough revision of social and political institutions in the contemporary world —have a different reason for their criticisms of the liberal's faith. Marxists and others insist that liberalism underestimates the resistance to needed social and political changes which, in a parliamentary system, eventually comes from conservative groups seeking to maintain the *status quo*. Too many traditional interests and prejudices can get a hearing which radicals think deserve no hearing at all. More than this, liberals are charged with failing to take contemporary economic dilemmas seriously enough. The aim of government is to govern in the light of objective necessities, and these are matters of knowledge, not merely matters of opinion. The problem of the age is to control the vast economic as well as military forces which threaten a worldwide chaos. It is also to produce justice in the economic realm—to replace a commutative view of justice by a distributive one. The commutative view of justice sees it as a right to reward and to punish strictly in terms of individual merit and deservingness, which means

[4] Russell Kirk contrasts basic conservative and liberal beliefs in the first chapter of his *The Conservative Mind* (London: Faber, 1954), pp. 17–20.

that many individuals and even classes will receive a disproportionate share of available goods and services. The distributive view of justice "sees" each and every man, whatever his native talents or lack of them, as having a right to share in the productive benefits of a society. As asserted by Professor W. B. Gallie, a contemporary English thinker, the socialist wants to replace "the right to get" by "the right to be" by creating a political and legal system which makes the individual's self-realization its basic aim. This means that many radicals want a government which regulates and directs the economic life of a nation rather than one which merely referees in that life. According to this view, freedom is not an intrinsic value. Freedom is rather a value only to the extent that it results in the fair distribution of material goods and services to all, regardless of individual merits as judged by noneconomic standards.

Perhaps an imagined dialogue between Mill and a Marxist will help to illuminate the general nature of one influential source of the radical criticism of classical liberalism in this century.

Marxist: Mill, you underestimate the influence of economic classes on human action. You are much too individualistic. The economic class to which one belongs determines its members' interests as well as their conflicts with other classes. The historical record shows that class conflict is the basic motivating force in politics.

Mill: I disagree to an extent. Economic interests are always central, but there can be others. After all, any important economic class can tyrannize over others once it gets political power. The object of politics is to prevent any single dominant class interest from wholly dictating the nature of society.

Marxist: What a peculiar and naive view of government! You sound as if you think political leaders are not, themselves, members of distinct economic classes.

Mill: Not at all. But the aim of a liberal society should be to have a number of such interests politically represented.

Marxist: It won't work out that way. The owning classes will always control the legislative and judicial processes. The legal weight of the system will be against the interests of the most numerous class—the laboring class. What is required is a revolution which will wrest control from the rulers and place it in the hands of the laboring class.

Mill: A distinction between economics and politics will always be needed. After a successful revolution, even the laborers would have to face the problem of establishing a legal system—of defining justice. Not all questions of justice are economic, you know. A legal order must be prepared to handle a wide range of problems and interests—surely, more than the interests of the immediately dominant class if it's to be a just order.

Marxist: So long as there are multiple classes, this won't happen. Even the legal order expresses the class interests of a society. Legal justice means whatever is to the interest of the most powerful class, which means that until the laboring class dominates government the legal order will be weighted against them.

Mill: You argue more like a dogmatic theologian who claims to possess an unqualified truth to which no counter argument is possible. Justice is not a class but a human concept. Justice is a peculiar combination of sentiment and obligation —the basic human awareness that certain types of acts threaten the welfare of persons in a specially vital way. Of any class morality or legal order, including a Marxian one, we can say that it is just or unjust depending on its contents.

This imagined dialogue is presented to suggest that Marx and Mill would have understood one another's arguments, if confronted in a political discussion, without fully agreeing about the most basic problem in political life. For Mill, the possibility of freedom presupposes that, in principle, any set of legal and moral ideas is to some extent subject to discussion, analysis, and criticism. Only if Marx's economic position could be applied within a framework permitting the continued exercise of political rights and governmentally protected debates about official doctrines would Mill have considered it a worthwhile position. About some basic beliefs associated with Marxism, Mill would always raise one central question: Does Marxism permit the continuation of democratic as opposed to authoritarian modes of ruling? A negative answer to this question would lead Mill to warn men that authoritarianism of a new kind could suppress their political liberties in the name of economic necessity.

Conclusion

The problem of political freedom, as a practical one, involves the establishment of institutions, legal and administrative procedures and rules, public statements about rights and obligations, and facilities by which to permit sober citizens to develop their capacities. This is always a piecemeal matter, since men never get the chance to begin over again "from scratch." Practical freedom in the political arena means that men may seek to achieve at least some of their more valued goals without having to risk serious deprivations or punishments for trying to do so. To answer the specific question asked about any man, "How free is Liberty Smith?", we need to know much about the man as well as many details about the society in which he functions. We need to know the answers to other questions such as: "What things or goals does Liberty Smith want?", "What has he done to try to get what he wants?", and "What still remains for him to do to try to get what he wants?" To say that a man is politically free is to assert that he has desires, some of which can be met if he is willing to take the appropriate steps to realize them, individually or through group action. Political philosophers concerned to defend a practical view of freedom therefore tend to view the state as an association which functions to establish the rules by which competitive citizens may "play the political game," whose aim is the realization of some of their vital interests. Beyond this, to say that a man is free means that he is protected, legally and politically, from experiencing certain kinds of abuse—like having his house searched for no legitimate reason or losing his job because he has voted for a given political candidate or joined a union. It means that his rights are not lightly to be violated, since even governmental power will sometimes be available to help protect him in the exercise of those rights.

"Thus, we see that political freedom is a practical matter," our imagined listener might say in summary. "It is not a deep philosophical mystery. To be free politically means to have the power to seek goals within stated systems of rules as well as to be protected from certain orders of abuse. How well men maintain their freedom is therefore a matter of political intelligence—knowing what one most genuinely wants as well as what is achievable within clearly established limits and procedures. Political intelligence is also the constant re-evaluation of the existing institutions in terms of what they are supposed to make possible. Beyond this, the notion of freedom has no important political significance."

Sometimes, men who admit the possibility of a degree of political freedom ask the embarrassing question whether such freedom need always be a value. "Is a politically free society a better or more worthwhile one than a rigidly authoritarian society?" might be one way of stating this challenge. The implication seems to be that a free society may produce consequences which intelligent men will not always desire—thus, that even freedom cannot unqualifiedly be desired for itself. In the contemporary age, many persons have pondered this matter, aware that some conceptions of political freedom can produce economic chaos as well as lead to deep-seated psychological anxiety and insecurity. Many sensitive persons fear that too great a freedom may dissolve the restraining power of traditional authorities, needed as a basis for social solidarity and habitual obedience. Only if free political systems can produce the needed minimum of economic and psychological security will they prove workable and enduring. The supposition is, of course, that some other system can *in the long run* avoid the pitfalls risked by free men. The historical record indicates that political freedom does not ride the crest of the historical wave, since in only very special circumstances—and for relatively brief periods—has political freedom found a hospitable reception. This means that, to answer the value question, persons interested in defending free political systems must possess a reasoned faith that the conditions needed for social solidarity can be maintained if freely choosing citizens exercise intelligence.

"Yes, but how often do freely choosing citizens use intelligence?" can be a possible adamant demand at this point. "What is the guarantee they will do so?"

The defender of political freedom must admit there is no such guarantee. Still, the average man has grounds for hoping that freedom is the proper means to the achievement of his legitimate wants—that unfree societies always threaten him with the loss of what he has in the way of rights. In free political systems care must be taken that men understand the relative values of different ways of seeking their goals. The citizens must be aware of the inescapable anxieties which free men must always face, learning how to live adequately without authoritarian absolutes. Men must be raised up and educated who can stand ambiguity. Otherwise, in every crisis situation, men will trade in their freedoms for the solaces of authoritarian rule, thus abdicating their responsibilities to a savior. To defend the notion of political freedom men must show that it is a workable means to create the conditions needed for making human existence fruitful and meaningful. If free men are unable to do this, they will produce the nihilistic anxiety expressed by a phrase like "dreadful freedom," causing citizens to look to alternative political systems in their search for well-being. Any generally acceptable defense of political freedom can probably be stated thus: "Political freedom is a value because it permits the fullest realization of the conditions needed for human self-realization."

Whether in fact a free political system can produce such conditions in the modern world is an empirical matter, to be decided by evidence and not by rhetoric, either political or philosophical. If free men cannot meet the demands of the times by intelligent, relevant actions, then the result may well be what Jacob Burckhardt gloomily prophesied in 1871 in a letter written to a friend.

> I have a premonition, which sounds like utter folly and yet which positively will not leave me: the military state must become one great factory. Those hordes of men in the great industrial centers will not be left indefinitely to their greed and want. What must logically come is a fixed and supervised stint of misery, glorified by promotions and uniforms, daily begun and ended to the sound of drums.

Some Questions and Problems

1. Discuss the following fictitious situation, making sure to touch on questions of legal and moral responsibility:

Private O. B. Orders was a soldier in an army whose leaders sought to destroy all members of a minority religion. Private Orders did not share their prejudices, but he was a member of a military chain-of-command. Private O. B. Orders found himself in charge of a faucet which controlled the flow of gas into gas chambers in which, daily, members of the minority religion were put to death, though they had committed no crimes. Following the war, Private Orders is tried by the victorious allies who have defeated his country in war. He pleads that he was merely following out orders in turning on the gas.

Assume, next, that O. B. Orders was a military general. Would this fact alter your views? Why or why not?

2. Imagine that you are a practicing psychiatrist (or psychoanalyst) who, while treating a patient, learns from him that this patient has committed several murders. Convinced that the patient acted compulsively, thus could not help doing what he did, should you turn him over to the proper police or legal authorities? Discuss.

3. In a country giving constitutional protection to freedom of religion, should atheists be allowed openly to teach their doctrines? Should they be excluded from office on the basis of their religious attitudes?

4. List those basic personal freedoms which, on your view, should not be subject to legal or political interference.

5. Write a dialogue between Marx and Mill on the topic of human freedom.

6. Discuss the claim, advocated by some thinkers, that sexual practices should never become matters of police or legal coercion.

7. Can the demands for order in a society be made compatible with man's need for freedom? To what extent? How?

8. Either discuss or debate, in class, the assertion that a philosophical concern over the freewill-determinism issue has no practical relevance to the facts of political existence. Make sure to see that opposing views are represented.

9. Consider the following fictitious case:

Professor I. M. Vulnerable once belonged to the Communist Party. He claims to have left it. There is no evidence he had advocated Communist doctrines unfairly in his classroom performances. Nor has he violated any criminal laws in his life as a citizen. Professor Vulnerable also admits he was once a Communist. His college officials suspend him from his teaching position and threaten to fire him.

Should Professor Vulnerable be fired from his job? Give supporting reasons. Next, assume that Professor Vulnerable still admits to being a Communist. Would this fact affect your views if other facts in his case remained the same?

10. Discuss the following imagined situation:

> Fred Patriot is a private businessman who never graduated from college. As a member of an extremely conservative political group, he demands a right to speak on his local college campus to counter what he terms the "radicalism" of the faculty. He insists that he is determined to see that some members of the faculty, whose political views he dislikes, shall be subjected to public criticism by him on the campus.

Should Fred Patriot be allowed to speak? Necessarily or only contingently so, if at all? Give supporting reasons.

Some Suggested Readings

Camus, A. *The Rebel,* trans. A. Bowers. New York: Knopf, 1954.

Dewey, J. *Freedom and Culture.* New York: Putnam, 1939.

Frankel, C. *The Case for Modern Man.* New York: Harper, 1955.

Greene, W. C. *Moira: Fate, Good, and Evil in Greek Thought.* New York: Harper, 1963.

Hart, H. L. A. "The Ascription of Responsibility and Rights," *Proceedings of the Aristotelian Society,* Suppl. Vol., 1948–49.

———. *Law, Liberty, and Morality.* Stanford: Stanford University Press, 1963.

Hook, S. *Political Power and Personal Freedom.* New York: Collier, 1962.

———. (ed.) *Determinism and Freedom in the Age of Modern Science.* New York: New York University Press, 1958.

Kirk, R. *The Conservative Mind.* London: Faber, 1954.

Melden, A. I. *Free Action.* London: Routledge & Kegan Paul, 1961.

Oppenheim, F. *Dimensions of Freedom: An Analysis.* New York: St Martin's, 1961.

Pears, D. F. (ed.) *Freedom of the Will.* New York: St Martin's, 1963.

Polanyi, M. *The Logic of Liberty.* London: Routledge & Kegan Paul, 1951.

Viereck, P. *Conservatism Revisited: The Revolt Against Revolt 1815–1914.* New York: Scribner, 1950.

White, M. *Social Thought in America.* Boston: Beacon, 1957.

CHAPTER NINE

The Justification of Punishment

In the world of ordinary men and women, punishment exists both as a physical and a psychological fact. To say that someone has been punished means usually to say that someone has been made to suffer pain, inflicted by another person or usually by an institution legally representing persons, for having done some act forbidden by an existing rule or for having thwarted the desire of some other person holding a power to harm in return. Ordinary uses of the English language do not fully support the thesis that punishment occurs only between persons. Sometimes people may speak of the terrible punishments suffered by men at the hands of nonhuman forces. Suppose we overheard the following comment: "The sailor fell into the angry sea and finally got hurled, half dead, upon a rocky beach. He suffered horrible punishment!" We would understand what was being said, if we had a knowledge of stormy seas and their great, surging power. Natural forces possess the capacity to hurt fragile human beings in certain circumstances, and ordinary English expresses this fact.

Normally, however, men talk about punishment as a fact of their *social* lives—a consciously directed harming of (giving pain to) another person or group by an authority for some disapproved act of that person or group. In the social realm, punishment is a means by which to influence others to act in specified ways in the future as well as a means of retaliation for wrongful acts already committed. To the question "Why is that person being punished?", one can give two broad replies: "To make him change his past behavior" or "Because he broke the law." Often, we will want to give both replies when asked the question. Punishment is effective only when pain (including remorse) can be produced in an individual who, if he is healthy, prefers to avoid pain. Punishment means the production of pain (physical or psychological) for something which an agent has done which someone else, usually a legally approved agent of a community, judges wrongful and blameable.

To say that pain is a necessary condition of the existence of punishment does not entail the view that an individual must always know in fact that he is being punished. A person may be punished without knowing it. Thus, in some imagined circumstances, a punished person may not actually be in "pain." Suppose an employer refuses to promote an otherwise deserving man because he has learned facts—declared punishable by a legal order, say—about the man which he does not divulge. The employee feels no (psychological) "pain" *if* quite humbly he is not expecting a promotion. Yet, in this case the employer may be said to be punishing him by the employer's standards nonetheless—refusing him a promotion he would otherwise have received. In this case to say the man is being punished means that he *would* feel pain (as well, probably, as resentment) if he knew the facts in the situation. If the employee could know that his promotion was being denied because of some facts in his record, then he would feel (psychological) pain. This explanation makes sense only if there can be circumstances in which it is proper to say that someone is being punished without knowing it. In some cases, individuals who do feel pain or discomfort because of the course of events may raise the worrisome question: "Is it possible I'm being punished?" That is, given the existence of painful circumstances, a person may wonder about their causes. Thus, an unfaithful wife may mean to punish her husband by her acts even if he should be the last to know; and if he does learn what is going on, he may think to himself—trying to "understand" his wife's motivation and assuming he still cares about his wife: "Is she doing this to punish me, or does she genuinely love another man?"

The Philosophical Issue: Formalists and Utilitarians

When philosophers discuss the problem of punishment, they refer to a fairly restricted subject matter. Their concern is not with how to establish a penal system or how to run a local police department. Nor is it necessarily a concern for what should be the content of the laws whose breach results in punishment. The philosophical problem arises when, confronted by the *fact* of punishment, someone asks: "What is the proper *justification* of the fact? For what good reasons and in what circumstances ought persons to be punished?" If the questioning is taken to be meaningful, then it must be the case that the same facts are sometimes subject to differing kinds of justification—that the giving of reasons for the facts may be of different kinds. The philosophical pursuit shows more interest in the giving of reasons than it does in the facts. Moreover, many persons think that it would be a better world if punishment were not a necessity. This means that they recognize the existence of punishment rather reluctantly, much as if they were to shrug their shoulders, sigh and say: "That's just the way the world happens to be. It would be better if punishment weren't needed, but . . ."

To the question Why should men punish? philosophers have given differing answers. On one view, an act of punishing is justified if someone has broken a rule, or gone against a command of someone in authority, or failed to perform in a manner appropriate to his function. *Legal* punishment occurs when someone is guilty of a breach of law—the legal rules. Punishment is said to be justified because someone has done (or failed to do) some act clearly forbidden (or clearly required.) Consider the following fictional dialogue:

Sophomore: Why did Professor Ulcer punish Harry?

Freshman: I didn't know he had.

Sophomore: Oh, yes. He refused to accept Harry's finished term paper, the hard-nosed authoritarian. Harry gets an automatic F.

Freshman: Automatic, you say? Then it's clear why Harry was punished.

Sophomore: Oh?

Freshman: Surely. He was punished for failing to meet a deadline. Isn't that obvious?

Sophomore: I knew that much when I asked my original question. I meant, why *should* anyone want to punish a peach of a guy like Harry?

Freshman: Knock it off—that's a funny question! That's like asking why anyone ought to be punished even when, clearly, they're guilty of breaking rules.

A *formalist* in ethics usually argues that the answer to the question "Why is that man being punished?" should be some such answer as: "Because he's guilty." The punished person has done, or failed to do, something forbidden or required, thus acquiring either legal or moral guilt (or both). When generalized, this formalist argument becomes known as the *retributivist* position in punishment theory. The position entails the view that guilt is a necessary condition of justified punishment, plus a subordinate argument that we ought not (indeed, logically cannot) punish a person who is innocent.

A second great theory of punishment is the *utilitarian*. It argues that punishment is justified only if it leads to the broad improvement of the community. Given this view, there may be instances when the guilty ought in fact not to be punished, though they qualify for punishment. Thus, it would not be contradictory in some cases to make a statement such as: "Well, old Harry Wicked is guilty. He even deserves punishment. But we oughtn't to punish him, nonetheless, since nothing's to be gained by it!" We ought not to perform acts which are self-defeating in their consequences, bringing greater suffering to those who administer the punishment than to those who are punished. In other words, we ought not always to give others what they deserve—either in the form of reward or of punishments. To a retributivist who replies that such a view of punishment overlooks a feature of our moral experience, the utilitarian can reply that rigorousness in this matter can turn out to be a case of "cutting off one's nose to spite one's face." The utilitarian finds a flaw in a retributivist argument which so emphasizes doing what is right that the total happiness of a community seems to be sometimes thereby decreased. For this reason Jeremy Bentham (1748–1832) insisted that, as an unavoidable form of mischief, punishment should still never be used when it is "groundless," "inefficacious," "unprofitable," "too expensive," or "needless." [1]

If guilt is taken as a necessary condition of punishment ("Never punish someone unless he's guilty!"), then the utilitarian position seems to maintain there are occasions when one ought not to punish even the guilty. It is right for a policeman to shoot a murderer seeking to escape arrest, but there may be concrete occasions when a policeman ought not to shoot at a fleeing jailbird or murderer. Perhaps women and children in the vicinity may be injured. A perceptive critic may argue that judges, not policemen (as in this example), mete out punishment. Generally, the critic would be correct; for there are strong if not overwhelming reasons for trying to locate *legitimate* acts of punishing in public practice, legal or (administratively) quasi-legal. However, a policeman carrying out his legally defined duties may, at times, be said to punish a person who resists arrest, though in a technical sense what he does is legitimated by a legal system. It is not contradictory, in some cases, to say an individual, X, may be "punished" in different ways for the same act—by being shot at by the policeman (for seeking to resist arrest) as well as, later, by a judge's sentence. In a weaker way, someone might argue that men ought not on all occasions to give others their just deserts. Thus, to say that someone deserves punishment need not entail either that it is right to punish or that one ought to punish. "That robber deserves to be shot!" a heated citizen may shout to an officer, to himself adding: "But he oughtn't to shoot him now, since it wouldn't be right to endanger the citizens standing between the robber and me." On hearing a retributivist justification of punishment, a utilitarian would feel that it is too much a purist or rigorist one, seeming to imply the view expressed in the imperative: Punish the guilty regardless of the consequences.

[1] Bentham's views on punishment are found in his famous work *An Introduction to the Principles of Morals and Legislation,* Chapters XIII and XIV especially, published in 1789.

A more imaginative "case" to illustrate the claim that on utilitarian grounds some guilty persons should not legally be punished—at least according to the usual sentence for the case—might involve setting aside a death penalty for a murderer, in a system where this is usual for murder, who is a biological genius thought by professional colleagues to be on the verge of discovering a readily usable cure for multiple forms of cancer. The judge might set aside the penalty entirely, or substitute a weaker one, on the grounds of public welfare.

A Problem for Utilitarians

On the other hand, a retributivist can accuse the utilitarian of holding to a position which sometimes justifies the punishment of the innocent. If punishment is justified in terms of its beneficial consequences to a community, then, in principle, cases may occur when it is to the community's benefit to punish innocent persons. This possibility disturbs most utilitarians, who are willing to admit that it runs counter to our moral experience. That the innocent sometimes *do* suffer is a factual claim; that the innocent *should* suffer is a moral one, yet a strangely "immoral" one at that. Mistakes are sometimes made, for life is like that. But usually, if we find that a mistake has occurred, we feel regret and want to say something like: "Well, I know I did it. I made a mistake. But if I had known the facts, I wouldn't have done what I did." Thus, *unknowingly* we may think an innocent person to be guilty. In such a case, most persons would probably say that if our mistake is discovered in time, some restitution should be made to the injured person even if, accidentally, good to the community has resulted from the mistake. What the retributivist wants to emphasize is the fact that any community which *knowingly* imposes suffering on the innocent is one which violates a moral principle clearly understood by the average man. The American philosopher, William James, wrote movingly about this kind of moral injustice:

> Or if the hypothesis were offered to us of a world in which Messrs. Fourier's and Bellamy's and Morris's utopias should all be outdone, and millions kept permanently happy on the one simple condition that a certain lost soul on the far-off edge of things should lead a life

of lonely torture, what except a specific and independent sort of emotion can it be which would make us immediately feel, even though an impulse arose within us to clutch at the happiness so offered, how hideous a thing would be its enjoyment when deliberately accepted as the fruit of such a bargain? [2]

The utilitarian justification of punishment, thus, arouses our hostility to the extent it seems to justify even the possibility of a *knowing* and *deliberate* punishment of the innocent.

"Don't talk to me about the rightness of punishing the innocent, or the value of sometimes creating scapegoats for the long-range benefit of society!" an imagined citizen might say at this point in the discussion. "Look—I'm a realist. I know that life doesn't conform to the theories in idealistic philosophy books on ethics. Sure, I realize that innocent persons sometimes get hurt. That's how the ball sometimes bounces! To this extent perhaps we live in a tragic universe. Certainly there are many minor tragedies when men are forced to do things quickly, without adequate planning, such that the consequences may get out of hand. A policeman is at times going to shoot an innocent person, accidentally, in the line of his regular duties. But what I can't accept is that men ought knowingly and intentionally to punish the innocent. Call a spade a spade—if you think the world has some very bad features. But don't try to call such a world a *moral* one!"

Agreeing with the speaker's sense of injustice, a utilitarian can attempt to show that his position in ethics need not entail the rightness of knowing punishment of innocent persons. He can defend what has sometimes been termed "ideal utilitarianism"—a doctrine that *in fact* no community will be better off if it permits judges knowingly to punish the innocent. To do this, an ideal utilitarian must require a critic to point out a concrete instance in which the knowing punishment of an innocent person has led to the greater happiness of the community. If the instance should be the hypothetical one in which a judge, alone aware that the person he condemns is in fact innocent, declares the person guilty in order to avoid panic in a community,

---

[2] From the essay "The Moral Philosopher and the Moral Life" in *The Will to Believe and Other Essays in Moral Philosophy* (copyright 1896 by William James), pp. 184–210.

then the person who uses the instance must explain the details of the situation. What sorts of crime have brought the community to the verge of panic? How can the judge rest in his decision, knowing that the real culprits causing the panic are still at large to do their dirty work? What will eventuate if the community should ever learn that the real culprits have not been found and punished? Does not this hypothetical instance try to picture a judge who, by his very decision, makes a mockery out of the notion of justice? The ideal utilitarian can operate on the assumption that no *actual* case can be found which will prove convincing in fact.

"You say that the utilitarian position entails the rightfulness of punishing the innocent," our ideal utilitarian may want to argue. "But give me the actual case. I'm contending you can never produce a convincing one. The reason is that obvious acts of injustice cannot *in the long run* produce the genuine betterment of a community."

A defender of the utilitarian justification of punishment can, then, accept the view that one ought to seek the betterment of his community and yet deny that knowing punishment of the innocent will do so. Similarly, he can insist that men ought to do what is right while denying that doing the right can ever lead to genuine unhappiness of the community. This is what Professor Brand Blanshard has done, when he argues: "Now the keeping of engagements, the telling of truth, and the doing of justice are essential parts of the community's plan of life. To violate them officially is to do far more than to injure a particular person; it is to challenge and disrupt this plan of life as a whole." [3] On this view, then, it will always turn out that a just community is superior to an unjust one. Blanshard's conclusion is that anyone who admits this argument to be sound "would be admitting that even here the right derives from the good." Against the retributivist who insists that utilitarianism justifies the punishment of the innocent, a philosopher can argue that no actual instance of this kind can be discovered which actually produces the greater good of the community.

Professor John Rawls has employed an imaginative example in his

[3] Brand Blanshard, "Justice and the Good," in Frederick A. Olafson, ed., *Society, Law and Morality* (Englewood, N.J.: Prentice-Hall, 1961), p. 440.

Two Concepts of Rules to cast doubt on the argument that an un-restricted utilitarianism could be used to justify instances of punish-ment of persons known to be innocent. Distinguishing between utilitarian justification of individual acts and rules covering many in-stances, Rawls suggests a utilitarian reply to the charge. He asks his readers to imagine a community which permits a group, institution-alized for this specific purpose, to institute proceedings which may lead to "punishment" (what for good purposes Rawls terms "telish-ment" to distinguish it from punishment of guilty persons or those thought guilty on grounds of evidence by judges). The fear that such a "practice" can some day strike anyone will lead persons to under-stand that such a practice as "telishment" cannot be for the general welfare, since it must place too much power in the hands of a very small number of men.[4]

For his part, a utilitarian can say to a defender of the retributivist justification of punishment: "You're simply a rigorist. You're obsessed with the punishment of offenders without regard to the consequences. It's even possible that many of the rules in terms of which you make your decisions of guilt are themselves needless. Perhaps you should take a more generous attitude toward guilt. If you find yourself having to punish many people—rather continuously—perhaps you should ask yourself whether your notion of guilt doesn't rest on an overly devoted allegiance to the existing rules." Since the retributivist says that punishment is justified if someone is guilty—if someone has broken a rule or convention—then perhaps the fault may lie in the rule or convention rather than in the "guilty" person. In other words, a critic of the retributivist view may agree that guilt is a *necessary* condition of punishment and yet argue (a) that not all rule breakers are genuinely guilty, since some of the rules may be bad ones and (b) that even if the rules are sound we should not always punish offenders. A utilitarian may want to emphasize the way in which, in developed legal systems, those who judge offenders often possess discretionary powers. That is, the judges are often in a position to make an exception of a specific case—to find that an instance does

[4] Professor Rawls's essay appeared in *The Philosophical Review*, Vol. LXIV (1955), pp. 3–32.

not fall under a rule. Such a man can argue that the two sentences "Only the guilty should be punished" and "Those who are guilty should not always be punished" are not necessarily inconsistent. To such an argument the retributivist (as well as the formalist in ethics) can reply that judges should have good reasons for declaring a case to be an exception and that too many exceptions to an existing rule will inevitably weaken it, destroying its usefulness to the society that saw a need to establish it.

Swayed this way and that by the arguments for retributivism and utilitarianism in punishment theory, an interested reader may feel at this point that he has lost sight of the original issue. He may experience a peculiar disquietude of a kind which accompanies many a serious involvement in philosophical discussions. Our observer thought a problem existed to which a clear-cut solution could be found, only to discover that the apparently differing solutions need not be taken as contradicting one another. "In the beginning I thought that *either* retributivism *or* utilitarianism had to be correct," our reader may say in discouragement. "Now, I wonder if they may not even be compatible." Such a person may wonder what all the shouting was about in punishment theory. How could philosophers have come to think their differing positions involved serious disagreements which could not be reconciled? Many contemporary philosophers suspect that the disagreements are apparent rather than real—resting on misunderstanding of the genuine issues. A brief treatment of two efforts to "get to the bottom" of the apparent disagreements should here prove helpful.

Rule-Utilitarianism

One contemporary way of "solving" the retributivist-utilitarian impasse is that of Professor John Rawls, who defends a position sometimes known as "rule-utilitarianism." [5] His argument is that there are rules requiring justification and decisions about the cases which fall under the rules. Professor Rawls insists that utilitarianism should be treated as a philosophical doctrine which is adequate to answer a

[5] *Ibid.*

question like: How are rules (laws, practices, procedures) to be justified? Once rules exist which have been justified by the utilitarian standard, then (according to Rawls) formalism becomes the relevant philosophical means by which to answer a question like: When ought we to punish? We ought to punish persons who break existing rules *if* those rules (or a larger body of practices of which the rules are instances) serve the purpose of promoting the interests, welfare, and happiness of the members of the community in which they operate. On this "rule-utilitarian" position, the legislator makes rules as a utilitarian (looking to future consequences), while judges apply the rules as retributivists (looking to past legislation). Of course, this supposes that judges never perform a quasi-legislative function.

This position may at times lead to the complication that a specific rule can be justified independently (in the light of its own nature, so to speak) or, in a given situation, in the light of its importance as a member in a whole body or set of rules. Thus, if some evidence exists that rule X, taken individually, does not necessarily lead to the greater happiness of the community—yet sound evidence also exists which shows that its removal from a body of rules will adversely affect that whole body of rules—then rule X can be said to be justified on utilitarian grounds. Yet, if this is so, the argument suggests the peculiar situation in which a specific rule intrinsically does not promote the general happiness and yet is, as a member of a set of practices, nonetheless justifiable. On this basis, either a conservative (rigorist) or a liberal (permissivist) view of rules could be justified by the rule-utilitarian position. It is not clear, however, that Professor Rawls would think that a whole body of rules (rather than specific rules) is subject to such justification in any meaningful sense.

Perhaps a hypothetical example will help at this point to bring out the issue. Suppose one belongs to a social club, one of whose rules is that no member of the opposite sex may be brought to the clubhouse after midnight. Suppose, in addition, that the members of the club are mature, responsible persons who can be counted on to behave decently toward members of the opposite sex either before or after midnight and that the reason for the rule is the members' desire to please a certain kind of public opinion. The club is honored in the community because it is looked upon as one whose members live up to the standards of conduct approved by the community's members. However, in this particular community many persons would look unfavorably on a club possessing too permissive rules regarding the entertainment of the opposite sex. In this situation, one might retain the rule (*might,* it should here be emphasized) if to change it would bring the body of rules under some unfavorable comment by outsiders. In addition, some club members might prefer not to liberalize the rule, because they like the old way of managing affairs. Their attitude toward other rules might alter for the worse if this one questionable rule were either dropped or altered. An officer could thus say to those members of the club desiring a liberalization of this rule: "It's to our mutual advantage to retain this rule because of its place in a whole body of rules—the rest of which we want to be honored." In simpler terms, a utilitarian can agree to honor what he considers a "weak" rule because he wants to maintain obedience to a community's *set* of rules and believes that, as a social creature, it is wise to consider other persons' judgments in this matter. "I *am* a good member of the club," a person might reason to himself, "and that means I'm not just a freewheeling individualist. I'll go along with this bad rule for the good of the club, whose body of rules is *on the whole* a fine one."

If, on the other hand, this particular rule is only one of several under criticism, and if a number of other rules are judged unsound along with it, then the members may question the soundness of the whole set of existing rules. On utilitarian grounds they may then seek a fairly sweeping reform in a segment of the rules. In a specific legal system some rules which made sense in one situation may, at times, become useless or pointless because of changes in the social order and in the community's needs and problems. Every advanced legal system contains rules still on the statute books which, in fact, no reasonable judge attempts to apply except perhaps for purposes of a very special kind. The rules simply become inoperative even if, in a formal and public manner, they are not removed from the books. Thus, in a community containing a large number of automobiles and few horses, perhaps a rule still exists relevant to the riding of horses on the streets. Either no one rides horses in town any longer or, if one does, the riding no longer constitutes a genuine issue requiring legal control.

A second way in which to handle the apparent conflict between utilitarian and retributivist views of punishment is to treat the latter as concerned with the logic of the word "punish." This involves arguing that one simply cannot rightfully (and logically) punish an innocent person. This means that to say to a person: "I am punishing you, although I know you're guiltless" is to misuse English. The reason is that someone could reply: "You're hurting me, or abusing me, or doing me an injustice. But that's not really punishment!" This argument entails the claim that anyone who understands how to use the English language will not, in the first-person, ever say: "I punish you . . . though you're innocent." Nonetheless, an onlooker who is not himself doing the punishing (or, rather, the abusing) may say: "He (she, you) are punishing an innocent man!", without misusing the English language. This general argument seeks to point out what is sound in the retributivist conception of punishment: that guilt is a *logically* necessary condition of one's first-person use of the word "punish." This view need not entail the stricter claim that guilt is, taken alone, always a sufficient condition of punishing someone—that we must always punish a person because he is guilty. One may defend this logical point contained in the retributivist position and still remain a utilitarian in deciding when to punish those persons known to be gulty. On utilitarian grounds we may decide, sometimes, to excuse even the guilty person from punishment. Thus, Professor A. M. Quinton has recently argued that though retributivism makes a sound point about the logic of "punish," it still fails to give an adequate analysis of the grounds to be considered when we decide *whether* the guilty are to be punished.[6]

It turns out that some arguments advanced on behalf of retributivism are claimed to be consequentialist rather than formalist in nature. For example, if someone argues that we ought always to punish the guilty as a means of "balancing out" evil, then we are

[6] See his "On Punishment" in P. Laslett, ed., *Philosophy, Politics and Society* (First Series; New York: Macmillan, 1956), pp. 83–91.

claiming that punishment is right because of its consequences—the achievement of such a balancing. Again, an argument to the effect that a retributivist view of punishment produces a more just community is one which seeks justification because of its consequences, implying that if retributivism were to produce a less just community it should be abandoned. The strict retributivist doctrine seems, therefore, to insist that one must in principle punish anyone who is guilty *regardless of the consequences;* and it is this version of retributivism which receives most criticism. The idea that we should perform acts of punishment which clearly go counter to the community's genuine interests strikes discordantly on our consequentialist (perhaps utilitarian?) sense of morality.

Additional Considerations

Professor Quinton has, for one, raised other interesting points relevant to the retributivism-utilitarianism issue in punishment theory.[7] There is the claim, sometimes made, that any specific act of punishing must be proportional to the crime—a matter which cannot always be done. The reason is that in the order of nature there is no absolutely proportional compensation for "murder, wounding, alienation of affection or the destruction of property or reputation." Also, on the basis of the primitive *lex talionis* view ("an eye for an eye and a tooth for a tooth") in some codes the punishment was not applied to the actual offender. Rather, under these codes, sometimes if a man harmed another, then the law required that someone similarly related to the offender be so harmed. This meant instances in which punishment was inflicted on otherwise innocent persons because of their relation to an offender. The mountaineers who practiced blood feuds sometimes got caught up in this kind of retribution—shooting the first cousin of another family, say, if one's own first cousin had been shot by a member of the other family. To say to someone: "I'll knock out your cousin's right eye if you knock out my cousin's right eye" means to say that for a given offense an innocent person will be harmed.

[7] *Ibid.,* pp. 84–87.

Professor Quinton has also called attention to a strange attempt to defend the retributivist justification of punishment on the ground that it better protects our human dignity. The argument here is that, *as a moral agent,* a person has a *right* to punishment. This claim seems to emphasize the supposed fact that a man's moral development cannot occur unless, in some sense, he is seen as having a right to punishment. A man may be said to have a right to punishment because he has a broader right to realize his moral capacities. Such a defense of retributivism appears to rest on the conviction that men are freely able to act morally—thus, that a guilty person could have acted otherwise than he did in fact act. But such a defense leads to either a utilitarian or teleological justification of punishment, since to defend a man's right to punishment as a necessary means to the realization of his ethical stature means to justify punishment because of its moral consequences. A brief and hardly believable dialogue between two imagined persons can here clarify the issue:

Sam Utility: Why do you insist that Henry Misconduct has a right to punishment?

Ted Retribution: Because he has a right to moral betterment, and if he isn't punished there'll be no pressure put on him to change his behavior for the better.

Sam Utility: In other words, you say his right to punishment follows from his right to that kind of treatment which helps him to act morally in the future.

Ted Retribution: Now you're on the mark!

Sam Utility: But then you're defending a Utilitarian or teleological rather than a retributivist position. You're saying that Henry's right to punishment follows from the beneficial *consequences* of that punishment—not from the mere fact that he's guilty.

Ted Retribution: You're trying to "put the skids" under me. I mean that, yes; but I also mean Henry has a right to punishment just because he's a human being.

So peculiar an argument—about "an odd sort of right whose holders would strenuously resist its recognition"—may require an understanding of what is termed the "reformist" conception of punishment. Reformism is the doctrine that society has an obligation to alter offenders' behavior for the morally better by whatever means are at its disposal. Sometimes the doctrine is applied to a specifically extreme criminal case, like that of murder, where—if the death penalty is permitted—the offender is removed from any possible social influence for his improvement. Its use often occurs when evidence exists that the offender is "sick," perhaps thus not morally responsible for his criminal action. In this instance, reformism seeks to argue that society ought to attempt the reform and cure of an offender—in the case of murder, excusing him from any existing death penalty. Reformists do not deny that murderers deserve serious punishment, but often they insist the death penalty should be abolished. The reason is that by imprisoning a murderer, society can then proceed to attempt the reformation of his character. Treated in this manner, however, reformism seems to fit in best with a utilitarian theory of punishment, since it emphasizes the beneficial consequences to society which follow from the rehabilitation of criminals.

Another possible meaning of the "punishment-as-a-right" view, possibly fitting the retributivist position, is that a relevant proportion should exist between a given offense and its accompanying punishment. This would mean to argue that an offender has a right to a punishment which fits his crime—plus a right not to be excused from punishment even on reformist grounds. Here, the right would presumably reside with the individual offender and not with society or the legal system. But if the reason given is the moral regeneration of an offender, then once again the argument falls into a utilitarian (or, most broadly, a consequentialist) rather than a retributivist pattern. "Look, the offender's right to punishment cannot here fit a retributivist argument," an imagined discussant can say. "Either the punishment is the right of society and thus does not reside with the offender (whether that right is viewed as intrinsic or as based on the beneficial results to the society) *or* the right resides with the individual offender. If it is the latter, and if from such a right no benefit ensues to the man's character, what sense does it make to talk about one's moral right to punishment?" If someone now replies that an individual can possess a right which he fails to claim, and which he and others like him will never actually want to exercise, the critic can say that such a right is empty. Any answer to the question: "Why punish?" which is: "Because it's the offender's right!" seems to lead to a position which, when developed, is utilitarian rather than retributivist in nature.

There remains yet one other possible way in which, sympathetically, to try to make sense out of an otherwise confusing argument. This is to treat the "punishment-as-a-right" view as morally in *opposition to* the doctrine of reformism. One must "see" the offender as possessing a certain human dignity *even as an offender* such that, if he goes unpunished, that (inherent, potential) dignity is challenged or frustrated. The picture here operating seems to involve something like the following one. A man breaks an existing law because he chooses to do so, thus by his criminal action operating as a free man. If as a free man he chooses to break the law, then he is responsible for his action and yet may still desire to refuse, in future, to conform to the existing law. He has a right to protest the law by his action, in other words. To use reformist techniques by which to alter his character, and in turn to change his behavior, will mean to deny him the right under some circumstance to choose to remain a criminal. Peculiarly, then, the "right-to-punishment" view seems to entail the right as a free man's possession—his right to do criminal acts by choice and to suffer the accompanying punishment. The offender, as a free man, is seen as having a "right to punishment" rather than to be reformed by "treatment," if his breach of the law happens to be a morally responsible one rather than a compulsive act. It is as if one wanted to argue that to punish the offender, rather than to reform him, is in some circumstances more humane, more genuinely to treat him as a moral agent—as a free, dignified human being. Professor J. B. Mabbott, a contemporary and influential English philosopher, has attempted to bring to light what may lurk at the background of such a puzzling argument by writing:

> But the question "who is a criminal?" is itself determined by government; and the belief that men can be cured of anti-social tendencies by punishment leads irresistibly towards "Brave New World" and

"1984." What is shocking to most people about these Utopias (and about the confession, stage-trial, and brainwashing techniques which are their actual counterparts) is not the cruelty (for there need be none), nor the falsity of the creeds thus imposed, but the degradation and violation of human personality. What is often forgotten and is still more shocking is that, towering over these ordinary citizens, who are no longer men but material-for-moulding, are other men—"Big Brothers"—men who have usurped the throne of God.[8]

This kind of argument in defense of the view that men have a right to punishment appears, then, to claim that the retributivist conception of punishment may sometimes have more humane consequences than either the utilitarian or the reformist. It is a strained way of asserting that, sometimes, it may be wiser for society to take the risks attendant on society's failure (indeed, refusal) to reform the criminal than to risk a socially induced conformism which—while possibly lessening breaches of the law—decreases the ability of free men to choose to do their own acts, including even criminal ones. Put baldly, the "right-to-punishment" view reduces to a defense of a man's right to do criminal acts, if he chooses to risk suffering the consequences of such acts. Presumably, then, society has a right to imprison and to restrain such criminals but not, while persons are so imprisoned, to seek to reform them.

In criticism of Professor Mabbott, a critic can point out that any society whose laws are so questionable as to seek protection of human dignity by punishing rather than reforming offenders approximates conditions in which its judges could hardly be expected to honor even this peculiar plea on behalf of human dignity. In such a society—feared as willing to misuse "reformism" as a means to total control over men's minds and bodies—it is hard to understand how any discussion of punishment theory, including Professor Mabbott's, can make a difference in how the (vicious) authorities will behave. For this reason, Professor Mabbott's defense of a criminal's essential "right to punishment" appears unfruitful. Nonetheless, what of Socrates who, on reformist views, would not have been sentenced to

[8] J. B. Mabbott, "Freewill and Punishment," in H. D. Lewis, ed., *Contemporary British Philosophy* (New York: Macmillan, 1956), p. 308.

death in ancient Athens? This case should trouble philosophers. However, as an agnostic friend said on this point, "Well, given reformism,
we would have a different Socrates, true—but then we'd have none
of this silly 'Jesus business,' either!" One makes his choices and
suffers the consequences!

In developed legal systems the retributivist insistence that guilt is
a necessary condition of punishment seems to have gained general
acceptance. Just as the dictum "Ought implies can" is said to operate
in moral thought, so the dictum "Punishment implies guilt" does so
in most legal systems. This notion seems to make up part of the very
fabric of justice. Often, it leads to the argument that guilt involves
some actual act—something actually done—which some authority—
the legal system usually—condemns and can punish. Of course, inno-
cence should be presumed until guilt is established; and persons
should be punished for what they've done, not for what they may
be planning to do. Here, however, a crucial question arises. Can a
legal system legitimately "punish" someone for what he intends to
do? Logically, if the retributivist insistence on guilt is correct, and if
a man is not guilty until he has actually done an act, then a legal
system cannot morally punish someone for intending wrong acts. "We
must always wait until a person actually makes a move," a citizen
might say in resisting his neighbor's desire to punish someone whose
intentions he fears. Semantically, the puzzle can perhaps be solved
if we distinguish between "punishment" and "restraint." On this basis,
one can restrain another person when evidence shows that the person
intends to break a law or to harm a citizen. But this would not constitute punishment. Thus, if some person says: "You are punishing
me for something I've not (yet) done!", we can sometimes reply:
"No, we're not punishing you. We're restraining you *now* so that,
later on, we won't have to punish you."

Adequately structured legal systems will always contain procedures
by which persons who intend certain kinds of harmful acts can be
made to feel the restraining weight of rules and threats. These procedures will make up an inescapable part of the adequacy of such
systems. This fact is emphasized by the dictum: "In the law, procedure is everything." *How,* as well as the ends for which, restraining

procedures function will touch the lives of a community's citizens in countless ways. Outside any existing legal system, moral forms of restraint will also continue to operate. For example, suppose a parent directs a child to mow the grass by a certain date but, prior to that date, "punishes" the child and gives as the reason: "The child will not do what I tell him to do. I know this from past experience. So, I'm punishing him now for what I know will be his future blameworthy conduct." Any listener in possession of a sense of justice will want to say to such a parent: "You can't really punish a person for a future act or failure to act. You can only punish for past misconduct —perhaps, in this case, for the child's laziness." In addition, if we try to "punish" someone for what we think he plans wrongly to do in the future, we may in fact bring harm to an innocent person. There is always the chance the person will perform the ordered act when the proper time arrives. If we restrain a person for threatened future acts, we should always be required (morally and legally) to give reasons (thus, in a legal setting, to present evidence that the restraint is justified). Here, knowledge of the person—details of his past behavior and awareness of what he says he intends to do or not to do—must form an unavoidable, necessary part of the evidence.

In some situations, blameworthy acts can be defined in terms of what is said. Normally, a legal system distinguishes between "what a man says" and "what a man does." That is to say, a legal system usually refuses to treat instances of saying as instances of doing, unless good reasons exist for the identification. A man who says he will kill someone is not *yet* a man who has killed. What a man says may indicate that restraint is in order, but what he says is (if at all) a *verbal* action. On this basis, a community may protect its legitimate interests by listing those forms of utterance (saying) which, in stated contexts, are subject to specific punishments. Thus, while no absolute distinction between acts and speaking can be made, nonetheless there is such a distinction in any functioning legal system. At what point speaking constitutes a punishable act will constitute a difficult decision for any legal system to make. Clearly, a man who shouts falsely: "Fire!" in a crowded theater, causing a panic, is a man whose utterance may legally be subjected to punishment.

The discussion of the justification of punishment theory by contemporary thinkers has become closely linked with the freedom-responsibility issue. For example, the English ethical philosopher Professor P. H. Nowell-Smith argued that, in one sense, a person may be said to be guilty because punishable.[9] Indeed, Professor Mabbott's insistence on a criminal's "right to punishment" *instead* of his right to be reformed was partly directed at what he considered a mistake in Nowell-Smith's position. What Nowell-Smith sought was an elucidation of "voluntary" as opposed to "involuntary" acts, since moral philosophers have generally insisted that moral judgeability can apply only to acts which might not have occurred. Thus, Nowell-Smith wanted to make sense of a statement like "X could have acted otherwise, if he had wanted (chosen)." How to determine in individual cases whether a given act, Z, was voluntary? Nowell-Smith wanted an external (behavioral) criterion. He thought he had located such a criterion in a person's response to punishment. In one example, given two students who are doing poor work in school, Nowell-Smith argued the one whose performance improves *after punishment* was morally responsible, while he whose work does not improve was not. Thus, Nowell-Smith, probably too hastily, made punishability the condition of guilt (since the student who failed to respond could not rightly be said either to have been guilty or, it follows, punished). Two problems arise, if no more. What should one call what was done to the student who failed to improve? The other is that, on this view, since psychological therapy sometimes alters peoples' behavior it might be called "punishment" when successful—a view most therapists and moral philosophers would want to reject. Also, Professors John Austin and H. L. A. Hart, philosophical powers in the Oxford University renaissance in philosophical analysis (Chapter 15, "Language Analysis and Politics"), have sought to throw new light on an old and vexing issue by discussing notions like "excuses" and "defeasibility" in considering legal and moral questions.

[9] See his essay "Freewill and Moral Responsibility," *Mind,* Vol. LVII, N.S., No. 225, conveniently reprinted in M. K. Munitz, *A Modern Introduction to Ethics,* (Glencoe, Ill.: Free Press, 1958), pp. 387–399.

Conclusion

The consideration of the problem of justifying punishment has brought out how some contemporary philosophers seek to suggest some general conclusions which they hope they can "persuade" reasonable men to accept. An influential position is that punishment should occur only when someone is thought guilty on good evidence and where, in a strict sense, the guilt involves a breach of existing laws or rules. Nonetheless, the utilitarian position seems correct in insisting that (a) the guilty should not always be punished, especially in situations which would bring needless suffering and inconvenience to the punishing community, and (b) the rules governing a society should themselves be justified in quite clear ways showing they are for the betterment of the community. Utilitarianism thus is said to give a basis for deciding what laws to establish while retributivism is said to provide a criterion for deciding when one should punish but need not entail the obligation to punish. Laws justified in utilitarian terms define situations of guilt, while retributivism emphasizes the moral rightness of the fact that those who break such laws are alone the proper objects of punishment. Important discussion of punishment theory has led some thinkers to conclude that a politically organized community should give careful attention to the justification of its rules and, having done so, then insist that its judges should consistently punish only those who have violated the rules.

A general moral assumption functions as the background to discussions of punishment theory. The assumption is that men can, at least within limits, act freely and that morally (if not always legally) it would be wrong to punish those who are not responsible for their acts. Nonetheless, a community which restrains its fanatics and lunatics is not so much "punishing" them as protecting both them and itself from harmful consequences. If human action were not free at all, then no system of punishment would make moral sense; and the efforts of reformists to alter a criminal's past behavior for the better would hold no moral significance. As our discussion of freedom has already shown, only if responsible human action is an objective possibility can a morally responsible form of punishment theory exist.

Some Questions and Problems

1. Should citizens ever be "punished" for their political views by private persons like employers and neighbors? Should the right to punish belong exclusively to the representatives of a legal order?
2. Can the retributivist view of punishment ever be made compatible with humane ideals?
3. Must a contemporary utilitarian in punishment theory accept the view that the death penalty must be abolished? Give supporting reasons.
4. Can you think of a convincing situation in which it might be for the betterment of a community if its judges knowingly convicted innocent persons? Can you think of such a situation which might involve authorities other than the judges?
5. Can war against an offending country ever be viewed as a form of "punishment"? Why or why not?
6. Is Country X, which seeks to harm Country Y, ever justified in invading a neutral Country Z in order to get to Y? What might a utilitarian say to this question?
7. On utilitarian grounds, some seriously made promises should never be kept. Who should have the authority to decide the instances when promises may be broken for utilitarian reasons? Can a person who has made a promise ever excuse himself for keeping it on utilitarian grounds?
8. Discuss or debate the assertion that retributivists are right in claiming murder always deserves punishment by death.
9. Is it possible to "punish" an innocent person? Can this be done knowingly?
10. What kinds of punishment are available to political authorities? How do they differ, if at all, from legal punishments?

Some Suggested Readings

Austin, J. L. "A Plea for Excuses," *Philosophical Papers*, eds. J. O. Urmson and G. J. Warnock. Oxford: Clarendon Press, 1961.

Bentham, J. *A Fragment on Government and Introduction to the Principles of Morals and Legislation*. Oxford: Blackwell, 1948.

Brandt, R. B. "Retributive Justice and Criminal Law," *Ethical Theory*, ed. R. B. Brandt. Englewood Cliffs, N.J.: Prentice-Hall, 1959.

Cahn, E. *The Moral Decision.* Bloomington: Indiana University Press, 1955.

Fitzgerald, P. J. "Voluntary and Involuntary Acts," *Oxford Essays in Jurisprudence,* ed. A. G. Guest. London: Oxford University Press, 1961.

Fromm, E. *Man for Himself.* New York: Rinehart, 1947.

Hart, H. L. A. "Legal Responsibility and Excuses," *Determinism and Freedom,* ed. S. Hook. New York: New York University Press, 1958.

———. "Negligence, *Mens Rea* and Criminal Responsibility," *Oxford Essays in Jurisprudence,* ed A. G. Guest. London: Oxford University Press, 1961.

Honore, A. M., and Hart, H. L. A. *Causation in the Law.* Oxford: Clarendon Press, 1961.

Mabbott, J. D. "Freewill and Punishment," *Contemporary British Philosophy,* ed. H. D. Lewis. New York: Macmillan, 1956.

Madden, E. H. "Psychoanalysis and Moral Judgeability," *The Structure of Scientific Thought,* ed. E. H. Madden. Boston: Houghton, 1961.

Munitz, M. K. (ed.) "Free Will, Responsibility, and Guilt," *A Modern Introduction to Ethics,* Sec. V. Glencoe, Ill.: Free Press, 1958.

Quinton, A. M. "On Punishment," *Philosophy, Politics and Society,* First Series, ed. P. Laslett. New York: Macmillan, 1956.

Rawls, J. B. "Two Concepts of Rules," *The Philosophical Review,* Vol. LXIV, 1955.

Rieff, P. *Freud: The Mind of the Moralist.* Garden City, N.Y.: Doubleday, 1959.

Zilboorg, G. *The Psychology of the Criminal Act.* New York: Hogarth, 1955.

CHAPTER TEN

Justice

At the heart of much philosophizing about social and political topics is a concern, expressed or tacit, about the notion of human justice. Men complain about unjust treatment or make demands for different kinds of reform in the name of justice. The notion seems clearly related to many otherwise distinct topics in social and political philosophy—topics like rights, equality, punishment, and law. "Demonstrators" against racially segregated practices often *justify* their conduct by calling attention to the injustice of such practices, as well as their illegality in some cases. Legal thinkers debate the question whether a legal rule is really ("justly") a law in cases where the rule produces consequences they consider unfavorable to morality. Often, when someone says: "The police had no right to arrest that man!" he means that, in a specific situation, since the person appears to be innocent of a charge, an injustice has been done in this instance. Plato sought for a fundamental definition of justice which would, apparently, permit men to recognize any specific instance of just behavior; while Aristotle and others introduced numerous distinctions to show there are different senses of justice. The topic of justice sometimes even permits an exercise of ironic observation as illustrated by the professor who, when asked by a friend "What if any is the relation between justice and merit?", replied by saying: "I'm not sure I know what justice *is*, but whatever it is, wouldn't it be terrible if all of us got just what he deserves?"

Justice is a social concept. This much has been admitted by thinkers whose philosophical orientations are otherwise disparate. Justice seems to have to do with specific kinds of relations between men living in politically organized communities. If we should hear a stranger remark that some person has been unjustly treated, we would want in normal circumstances to know more details about what has happened to the person and what the community believes. If the stranger should attempt to satisfy our curiosity by saying: "Harry was unjustly treated because the recent earthquake has destroyed his house!", we would probably want to say that the speaker must mean to say something quite different. An earthquake is a natural event. It can cause misfortune, even tragedy, but as such it can meaningfully be the source of neither justice nor injustice. On the other hand, how men treat the victims of such natural disasters can very readily lead to charges of injustices. If following an earthquake thieves should rob the homes, and the police stood idly by while the occupants of the houses remained in a condition of shock, we could very well speak of the injustice of it. In doing so, however, we would be commenting not on the natural effects of the earthquake but upon the action, or lack of action of men living in a community affected by the earthquake. Justice as a social concept seems concerned with how men treat one another in specified circumstances.

Justice seems also related to ordinary notions of fairness in human transactions. Ordinary ways of speaking may here mislead an unwary thinker. If we should learn about a person said to have suffered exceedingly at the "hands" of nonhuman forces, we would often want to say: "It doesn't seem quite fair. No man should have to endure so many personal tragedies as that!" But unless like Job in the Old Testament we identify a person's misfortunes with the causal agency of a (perhaps vicious) personal deity—thus raising the perplexing problem of evil in a theistic context—it is difficult to make literal sense out of an assertion such as: "It's a naturally unjust world!", unless what we mean to say is something like: "It would be better for man all around if the world were naturally different—perhaps if there were a just personal God." A person who lacks religious belief may experience evil, if evil is here defined as any terrifying extreme of personal pain or any threateningly radical alteration in the course of events in an otherwise impersonal universe, but we cannot very well call that universe "unjust" except in the light of standards which apply to *human* relations essentially but which, in some important sense, are found not to be objective characteristics of the nonhuman world. To say the world is unjust means to make a disparaging judgment about nonhuman affairs with reference to standards which are themselves human and social.

Justice also seems related to notions of proportion and balance. A criminal may be unjustly treated if his sentence is too extreme, or an injustice may occur if some person is given an honor he does not deserve, where circumstances are such that the sentence and the awarding of the honor are human actions. Justice seems to have to do with weighing and measuring according to standards. Thus men sometimes speak of "the scales of justice" or of "meting out justice." Justice may be viewed as a special harmony between persons and groups—allied with the classical concern about order in human relations. Justice is that portion of morality devoted to the balancing of claims and burdens among different individuals and groups. Consistency and coherence are important, although they need not be synonymous. Coherent rules may be characterized as those which "hang together" in some sensible manner—thus lacking vagueness and arbitrariness. Of course, at this point a critic might argue that the notion of coherence here employed is a moral rather than a strictly legal one, a charge which would be acceptable by the author. A *consistent* application of a rule may be unjust because the law lacks coherence, as in a case where X, a blue-eyed child, is put to death where a rule exists to the effect that all blue-eyed children in a community are to be put to death. The rule is arbitrary even if consistently applied, and even if in a specific community there happens not to be enough food to feed all citizens. If some citizens must be put to death, why pick on the color of their eyes to decide on whom the awful sentence is to fall? We sense at once that if someone must die for the welfare of the community, surely some fairer criterion of selection is available, if any at all is available. Perhaps the citizens may be encouraged to volunteer or required to draw lots. On the other hand, a *coherent* rule may be unjustly applied if (a) it is applied only occasionally or (b) it is applied to a case which it does not at least fairly clearly cover. Consistency may refer to the manner in which rules are applied or to the logical relation between rule and rule, while coherence may have to do also with the content or meaning of a rule. Men concerned to reduce the factor of arbitrariness in human relations and judgments about them therefore usually seek both for consistency and coherence.

Merit and desert (*deserving-ness*) are important for an understanding of the notion of human justice. Many ordinary beliefs are indicative of this. An innocent man does not deserve legal punishment. An unqualified student should not graduate with his class—he deserves to fail the graduation tests. Any qualified candidate for a job, even in highly competitive situations, deserves a careful consideration by the employing authorities. Yet, a person who violates a clearly established rule may not always deserve reprimand or punishment, since there may have been excusing circumstances which need appraisal. Justice may fail to be served in a number of ways when the matter of desert is relevant. A person may receive something (goods or praise or blame) he does not deserve, or he may fail to receive what he does deserve. Moreover, a person's case may be judged without due regard to peculiar circumstances which can be offered as excusing conditions bearing upon adequate judgment. Of course, if the excusing circumstances indicate that the violation should be forgiven or overlooked, it would follow that other persons similarly circumstanced in the future should receive the same kind of treatment.

Merit and Contemporary Society

The increasingly complex nature of a technologically organized society can raise problems about merit and desert when questions about social justice are considered. One perceptive English writer, Professor W. B. Gallie, has discerned two moralities operating in contemporary Great Britain which may possess counterparts elsewhere. In an essay, "Liberal Morality and Socialist Morality," Professor Gallie redefines the older notion of distributive justice to mean that "rewards or returns should be proportional to merit." [1] He names this view of

[1] Printed in Peter Laslett, ed., *Philosophy, Politics and Society* (First Series; New York: Macmillan, 1956), pp. 116–133.

justice *commutative* and identifies it with liberal morality, a morality in which emphasis is placed on individual worth, the freedom of choice in the making of contracts, the notion of limited government, and the value of merit. In contrast, he defines as a *distributive* view of justice that which is entailed by what he terms socialist morality, in which the aim of government is seen as the creation of maximum conditions of human happiness and welfare (defined in material terms) and the nature of freedom as confined to the ability and opportunity to create and enjoy those conditions of life without which a genuinely human existence is impossible. For Professor Gallie, the distributive and the commutative conceptions of justice conflict under conditions of modern social-economic existence. Liberal morality emphasizes the "freedom to get" while socialist morality, according to Gallie's interpretation, stresses the "freedom to *be*." On this interpretation, many things considered "just" in liberal morality will appear "unjust" in socialist morality. The reason is that in the latter, the direction of economic life will often involve a disregard for an individualistic notion of merit.

Probably any welfare state in the modern world can produce examples of the kinds of dilemma which arise if justice in the social sphere is narrowly tied to an individualist view of merit. Let us consider a few which, though quite ordinary and well known, can sharpen the issue. There is a conflict between the view that a worker who produces more deserves the higher pay and the union view that full employment, rather than sheer quantity of production, should be the aim of an industrial economy. There is a difference between economic welfare for unemployed persons who have unsuccessfully sought work and unemployed persons who, lazily, have made no search at all. Given the individualistic assumption, the best-producing worker does deserve more pay, since he is more talented and perhaps works harder and longer than others. Similarly, even persons who favor unemployment benefits recognize the difference between the wastrel who doesn't want to work and the conscientious person who, through no fault of his own, can find no work. Yet, given the assumptions of socialist morality, all men deserve the minimal conditions of a human life even if, to attain this end, individual effort and merit are to be given little emphasis as such. If the unequal distribution of talent and effort are a threat to the creation of those minimal conditions, then a socialist morality must produce rules which minimize talent and effort as possible obstacles to their realization. In Professor Gallie's words, to advance a socialist morality in the economic sphere ". . . it is our duty to ensure by whatever means we can devise, that the most obvious obstacles to it shall be removed. Among these are the economic waste and insecurity involved in every form of competitive (liberal) economy."

The problems of welfare economy are complicated by the fact that welfare legislation concerns large classes of individuals and permits some abuses which even its supporters would prefer not to exist. Take for example the argument that financial support to children under a certain age means that illegitimate (as well as legitimate) children shall receive support. Yet a community may feel that its burden of welfare taxation should be limited—that women who bear children illegitimately do not deserve the same kind of support as, say, women who are married. Even married women may not have an unrestricted right to community protection if, in an age of birth control techniques, they raise large families. But to stop payments to the mothers would mean to harm the children, toward whose welfare the legislation has been directed. A person can argue that children as children *deserve* food and shelter and clothing without regard to their individual talents; and that their parents, without whom their lives will often be less happy, deserve support as parents whose happiness is crucial to that of the children. This means to talk about classes of persons—children and parents—without specifying limiting conditions. As it has in some communities in the United States, however, the question can arise whether, as a protection to the community's tax resources, women who are a burden on the welfare rolls may be required to be sterilized. If the socialist morality sees the government's role as protective and positive, rather than negative and limited (as Professor Gallie claims is the view of liberal morality), then how far may it legitimately intervene in the direction of its citizens' lives in order to realize their "freedom to *be*"? May it take children from parents and place them in state-supervised homes? May it do this coercively? Can it permit a parent who does not believe in birth control to choose to introduce illegitimate children into the world who will be a further drain on resources? Can it permit persons benefitting from welfare payments to choose to lose those payments by refusing to consider, say, sterilization or abortion? Of course, the advocate of what Gallie terms liberal morality will not have this problem, since he can deny that any person deserves support by the government.

A critic of Gallie's interpretation can argue that even socialist morality involves a commutative rather than a distributive view of justice. He can do this by saying that all persons *deserve* certain minimal conditions of life. But this means to separate desert from individual talent and effort, thus to lose the force of the emphasis which in liberal morality is placed on merit and desert as properties belonging not to classes but to particular individuals. It is also to make equality more fundamental in economic justice than liberty, without first showing that there may not be occasions when liberty, even if it produces some undesirable consequences, is more valuable than equality. And even in a welfare state whose legislators pass a law to the effect, say, that each child under fourteen shall receive financial assistance from the government, we will feel a difference between the justice of giving the payment to a child whose parents are wealthy and to the parents who are distressingly poor. That is, even if we favor a welfare state under conditions of modern life, we may sometimes want to say it produces some injustices. Perhaps this can be illustrated by the legislation, after World War II, which permitted weekly payments to veterans who had not secured work, that was known as the 52–20 Club ($20 a week for 52 weeks). Even veterans who did not wish to work, and who avoided finding work, were given the benefits—and no distinction was made between needy and wealthy veterans.

Of course, given Professor Gallie's interesting if controversial differentiation of socialist from liberal morality, the notions of justice in the criminal sphere could remain unchanged. For in the criminal sphere, the commutative view seems sound, namely, that desert is always and necessarily relevant to punishing and penalizing. But with the advent of automation in industrial life, it seems clear that the commutative view of social justice in the economic realm loses much of its earlier attractiveness when men, freely contracting with employers, could hope for improving conditions. As machines take over more and more of the work formerly done by men, and as unskilled labor produces enforced leisure through large populations, the idea that social justice involves a proportion between individual effort and talent and the distribution of income and economic reward will become questionable. An unemployed engineer may then be said to deserve as much material comfort as, say, an employed engineer in earlier times. If individual talents become economically useless, then reward will have to be based on something else instead. On the other hand, should such a highly automated society occur, the question of justice in economic relations may arise only among the small numbers of those hard-working members of an elite managerial class who work long hours while the rest of the population visits the beaches and the parks (or, on a more pessimistic view, the madhouses and the psychiatrists).

Thus, if talent and effort in a future society serve no direct economic function save for a very small minority of managers, the liberal morality's sense of commutative justice can have no significance. Every head will count as one, as well as every stomach, when the question of dividing up the economic pie arises. The motivation to secure education may also suffer. It is questionable, as one author has suggested, that school children will be motivated to work hard in school if their parents are working only a few hours each week in an organized and automated industrial society. Again, however, there is no reason to believe that criminal justice in such a society can give up the commutative view that punishment is proportional to merit (that is, in this case, to deserved punishment because of guilt). Nonetheless, many other significant issues will probably arise which will require serious consideration. Mr. Donald N. Michael has suggested what some of these may be like:

> In twenty years, other things being equal, most of the routine blue-collar and white-collar tasks that can be done by cybernation will be. Our schools will probably be turning out a larger proportion of the population better educated than they are today, but most of our citi-

zens will be unable to understand the cybernated world in which they live. Perhaps they will understand the rudiments of calculus, biology, nuclear physics, and the humanities. But the research realm of scientists, the problems of government, and the interplay between them will be beyond the ken even of our college graduates. Besides, most people will have had to recognize that, when it comes to logic, the machines by and large can think better than they, for in that time reasonably good thinking computers should be operating on a large scale.

There will be a small, almost separate, society of people in rapport with the advanced computers. These cyberneticians will have established a relationship with their machines that cannot be shared with the average man any more than the average man today can understand the problems of molecular biology, nuclear physics, or neuropsychiatry. Indeed, many scholars will not have the capacity to share their knowledge or feeling about this new man-machine relationship. Those with the talent for the work probably will have to develop it from childhood and will be trained as intensively as the classical ballerina.

Some of the remaining population will be productively engaged in human-to-human or human-to-machine activities requiring judgment and a high level of intelligence and training. But the rest, whose innate intelligence or training is not of the highest, what will they do? We can foresee a nation with a large portion of its people doing, directly or indirectly, the endless public tasks that the welfare state needs and that the government will not allow to be cybernated because of the serious unemployment that would result. These people will work short hours, with much time for the pursuit of leisure activities.

Even with a college education, what will they do all their long lives, day after day, four-day weekend after weekend, vacation after vacation, in a more and more crowded world? (There is a population explosion to face in another ten to thirty years.) What will they believe in and aspire to as they work their shorter hours and, on the outside, pursue their "self-fulfilling" activities, whatever they may be? No one has ever seriously envisioned what characteristics these activities might have in order to be able to engross most men and women most of their adult lives. What will be the relationship of these people to government, to the "upper intellectuals," to the rest of the world, to themselves?

Obviously, attitudes toward work, play, and social responsibility will have changed greatly. Somehow we shall have had to cope emotionally with the vast gap in living standards that will then typify the difference between us and the have-not nations. We shall presumably have found some way to give meaning to the consumption of mass leisure. It would seem that a life oriented to private recreation might carry with it an attitude of relative indifference to public responsibility. This indifference, plus the centralization of authority, would seem to imply a governing elite and a popular acceptance of such an elite.

If this world is to exist as a coherent society, it will have to have its own "logic," so that it will make sense to its inhabitants. Today, for most of our population, our society makes sense, even though some other eyes hardly see us as logical in the formal sense of the word and the eyes of some of our own people look on us as a more or less pointless society. We make and solve our problems chiefly by other than mathematical standards, and so must the cybernated generations. What these standards might be, we do not know. But if they are inadequate, the frustration and pointlessness that they produce may well evoke, in turn, a war of desperation—ostensibly against some external enemy, but, in fact, a war to make the world safe for human beings by destroying most of society's sophisticated technological base. One thing is clear: if the new "logic" is to resolve the problems raised here, it will have to generate beliefs, behavior, and goals far different from those which we have held until now and which are driving us more and more inexorably into a contradictory world run by (and for?) ever more intelligent, ever more versatile slaves.[2]

But the peculiarly complex circumstances of a future automated society probably should not be expected completely to alter the philosophical issues to which thinkers will give their attention. Questions about human justice will continue, no doubt, to send some philosophers to classical views on the subject as well as to reconsiderations, from their *then* existing perspectives, of the historical traditions in social and political philosophy. Among these classical views, a few will probably continue to serve as touchstones of intellectual inquiry. Plato's imaginative dramatization of philosophical themes, including that of Justice—as already discussed in an earlier chapter—will no

[2] Donald N. Michael, "Cybernation: The Silent Conquest," A Report to the Center for the Study of Democratic Institutions, The Fund for the Republic, Inc., Santa Barbara, Calif., pp. 44–46.

doubt stimulate human thinkers just as fruitfully as it has through various cultural and historical situations in the past. So, too, probably, will the long-established dialogue between those who defend a natural law position and those who "see" the law as a thoroughly human set of conventions. Unlike some scientific theories, which may sometimes replace older and even erroneous views, philosophical knowledge does not appear to be cumulative, nor are philosophical "theories" clearly falsifiable quite in the ways in which scientific views sometimes are.

The Aristotelian Analysis

Long ago Aristotle struggled with moral and political themes which are still alive, introducing fundamental distinctions which have attracted philosophers time and again. For Aristotle, justice is necessarily linked with morality yet is not coextensive with it. Justice is rather an important aspect of morality. The reason is that, for Aristotle, a distinction is needed between complete justice and particular justice. Complete justice concerns what is lawful and is the same as complete virtue, though not absolutely—for justice has as its *essential* concern men's relations to their neighbors. In Book V of *The Nichomachean Ethics* Aristotle explains this distinction:

> If it be asked what is the difference between virtue and justice in this sense, it is clear from what has already been said; they are the same, but the underlying conception of them is different; the moral state which, if regarded relatively to others, is justice, if regarded absolutely as a moral state, is virtue.[3]

But virtue is in part an individual matter requiring existence of stable political conditions without which it cannot be achieved. Particular justice is concerned with what is fair and equal, such that the unjust person is he whose motive is specifically gain, resulting in unfairness and inequality in his relations to other persons. There are other motives, of course. Two men may commit the same act (adultery, say) such that one whose motive is gain is unjust, while one whose

[3] J. E. C. Welldon, trans., *The Nichomachean Ethics of Aristotle* (London: Macmillan, 1934), p. 138.

motive is passionate love is immoral but not unjust. For Aristotle, justice is crucially relevant to the political sphere, since he views the state as prior to the individual at least in the sense that a state is essential for the perpetuation of cultural order and the existence of external goods necessary to a reasonable life. Moreover, since conflicts among a plurality of citizens will arise in any political system, justice is relevant to the state's need to balance and redress the relations which hold between citizen and citizen. Particular justice is especially concerned with this balancing function of the political system, while universal justice is concerned with custom and general criminal rules bearing upon the activities of all citizens individually in pursuit of (complete) virtue.

In its concern for what is fair and lawful, particular justice can be of two basic kinds. *Distributive justice* is concerned with the distribution of benefits (and burdens also in a modern state) among the members of the political community in the light of some rule of proportion which need not be simply arithmetical, since it may involve a proportion between intrinsic unequals. *Remedial justice* has to do with the remedy of conflicts between one individual and another. Remedial justice involves a contextual rather than an ideal proportion, since the many relevant differences between men must be considered and the element of human failure adjudged. Remedial justice concerns voluntary actions of men (as in contracts, which for Aristotle seem to have had primarily a commercial status) and their involuntary actions (instances of force or fraud or violence). In a famous passage, Aristotle summarized the kinds of particular justice in the following manner:

> There are two kinds of particular justice and of the just action which corresponds to particular justice, one consisting in the distributions of honour or wealth or any other things which are divided among the members of community, as it is here that one citizen may have a share which is equal or unequal to another's, the other kind which is corrective *of wrong* in private transactions. This latter again has two subdivisions, private transactions being (1) voluntary, (2) involuntary. Voluntary transactions are such as buying, selling, lending at interest, giving security, lending without interest, depositing money, hiring; and they are said to be voluntary because the origin of these

transactions are voluntary, i.e. *people enter upon them of their own free will.* Involuntary transactions again are either (1) secret, as e.g. theft, adultery, poisoning, pandering, enticing slaves away from their masters, assassination, and false witness, or (2) violent, as assault, imprisonment, murder, rape, mutilation, slander, and contumelious treatment.[4]

Presumably, in here calling one class of actions involuntary, Aristotle meant to refer to the victims in what are at least two-person trans-ations, although even this interpretation raises a few difficulties. Obviously, cases of "adultery" and "procuring" can occur in which both parties agree to the transaction—are not, as it were, coerced or deceived into the transaction.

Aristotle also believed in a fundamental political justice: part natural—universally and everywhere binding without regard to exist-ing human conventions; part legal—initially indifferent to human conventions which when published cease to remain indifferent. Legal conventions need not everywhere be alike, just as political constitu-tions may vary from place to place, time to time ". . . though there is but one which is everywhere by nature the best." In addition, Aristotle's basically teleological conception of the political order as a necessary means to virtuous activity permitted a further, perhaps a too neat clarification of three fundamental kinds of just actions, in an organized state, as the special concerns of three types of persons. Thus, a *statesman* functions primarily as a dispenser of distributive justice—the "sharing out" of honors and rewards. The *judge* func-tions as a rectificatory agent to assess damages and decide conflicts between persons. Finally, the *manufacturer* and the *farmer*—as repre-sentatives of economic functions—concern themselves with the ex-change of goods at fair prices. The forms of particular justice received their further justification, in Aristotle's ethical and political views, as necessary supports of needed conditions of individualized moral life.

Aristotle possessed a fine sense of individuality, nonetheless. This led him to introduce the further notion of justice as the *equitable*. This has to do with difficulties which arise because of the universality of law and the individuality of the cases to which any law may have to

[4] *Ibid.,* pp. 141–142.

be applied. As Aristotle well understood, men (acting as legislators) must render universal rules when, because of peculiar cases to arise, these lead to incorrectness. The law is based on the notion of "the usual case," even though legislators cannot always form universal rules which are correct for all instances. Equity involves a correction of legislation in terms, for Aristotle, of what the legislator is considered to have meant by the legislation. There can be errors in law because of law's universality. Thus, a special aspect of particular justice is concerned with the correction of faults in the law resulting from its universality. Aristotle did not believe that politics or ethics should be expected to achieve a greater degree of certainty in their conclusions than the subject matter of practical life permits. It is, therefore, wrongheaded to read his classificatory schemes in ethics and politics as being rigid and exceptionless in application.

What Aristotle termed justice as equity has, in contemporary literature, sometimes been treated as the problem of "the core and the penumbra." Professor Lon Fuller and H. L. A. Hart (some of whose views have already been mentioned) discuss this issue in their respective analyses of the relation, or lack thereof, between legal and moral rules. Legislation creates rules which apply clearly to cases which tend to be standard; but difficult cases arise which, for a judge obligated to decide the application of the rule, raise the issue whether in fact they fall under the rule. How is the judge to decide? If he interprets the rule in relation to the case, what kinds of reasons is he to give? Is his decision to be arbitrary? One possible answer is Aristotle's which, very much like Professor Fuller's, suggests the judge must attempt to understand the intent of the rule. Another possibility is for the judge, in such cases, to decide on the basis of social utility or social reality. In either event, the judge acts at least in part as a legislator.

Of course, it is not easy to understand what may be meant by the intent of the law. Does this mean the intent of the lawmaker, to be learned from diaries and biographies? Or the intent of the law itself, presumably to be determined by an examination of its actual language in the context in which it appears? It may occur that a penumbral case arises such that the lawmaker's intent is difficult to decipher in that case or, if it is clear historically, would lead to consequences which either the lawmaker would not have wanted (because he could not have foreseen this kind of consequence) or would be, from the judge's viewpoint, unjustifiable under the circumstances existing in his own time. An imagined example may help to clarify this issue which Aristotle grasped in its outlines, an issue which still produces discussion among philosophers of law.

Consider the possible case where a wealthy person bequeaths much land for the creation of a private university. But suppose also that, many decades after his death, the financial demands on the trustees for the maintenance of a sound university require that some land be made income-producing. Suppose the benefactor's will makes it absolutely clear that he intended the land never to be sold for any purpose. If the university goes to court in an effort to learn whether it can make some of its land income-producing, how is the judge to decide? If he is convinced the university will cease to exist unless it can receive income from its land (a result the benefactor could not have wanted, obviously), should he read the will literally? Should he permit the land to be rented rather than sold, thus technically meeting the conditions of the bequest (even if literally circumventing it) and also meeting the contemporary university's financial situation? Can he decide simply on the basis of contemporary notions of utility even if the benefactor clearly would have disagreed with some of these? In cases like this imagined one the judge must decide how, and on what criteria, existing rules or decisions are to be applied to specific cases and circumstances. The fact that such cases may arise suggests that an absolute distinction between judge-made and legislator-made law is not possible.

Mill's Utilitarian Analysis

Another influential conception of justice is elaborated by J. S. Mill who, as a defender of a utilitarian social philosophy, understandably showed a sensitivity to the charge that the notion of justice cannot fully be explained in utilitarian terms. Mill realized that strict utilitarians need to account for the peculiar sentiment which accompanies the notion of justice without invoking any arguments used by advocates of natural law. Mill aimed to show how the special force of the feeling of justice, whatever its origin, could be accounted for without appeal to the view that "the just must have an existence in nature as something absolute, generically distinct from every variety of the expedient, and, in idea, opposed to it, though (as is commonly acknowledged) never, in the long run, disjoined from it in fact." This aim Mill sought to accomplish in the fifth book of "Utilitarianism" ("On the Connection between Justice and Utility") by (1) stating some of the common views of justice held more or less universally; (2) looking to etymology to illuminate the meaning of the notion; and (3) presenting a utilitarian characterization of justice as a highly important, though special branch of general morality.

Historically, Mill found that ordinary persons have shared some general opinions about what makes actions and arrangements in social life "unjust." Men tend to regard certain kinds of action as unjust, among them at least the following. It is thought unjust, according to Mill's analysis of common notions, if:

- Someone deprives another of his legal rights (to personal liberty, possession of property, or any other entity granted him by the legal order).

- Someone is granted legal rights which, morally, *ought not* to be granted or denied legal rights which he ought to possess.

- Someone is either granted what he does not deserve, or is frustrated from obtaining what he clearly deserves.

- Persons knowingly break faith with another by failing to keep an engagement or by frustrating others' expectations about their conduct, "at least if we have raised those expectations knowingly and voluntarily."

- A person acts partially toward others, in situations in which impartiality should reign.

- Equal protection is denied to some members of the community where the community recognizes at least some general rights.

Etymologically, Mill finds that in most languages the word "just" is connected with a respect for the law. (Here, as also in some other regards, Mill's view of justice is close to that of Kant.) Justice is viewed as a conformity to law. But in some communities this association of the just with what conforms to law tended to take on a moral as opposed to a legal stance: ". . . And hence the sentiment of injustice came to be attached, not to all violations of law, but only to violations of such laws as *ought* to exist, including such as ought to exist, but do not; and to laws themselves, if supposed to be contrary to what ought to be law." The difficulty with identifying justice with general moral obligation is that, though men might like to inhabit a social world in which complete justice were minutely enforced by law, there are good reasons for fearing that too great a coercive power in the magistrate might produce too many inexpedient consequences in the whole realm of private life. Although it might be considered morally just to enforce complete lawfulness in human conduct, it would often prove politically and, perhaps, personally inexpedient.

A vexing contemporary illustration of this too complete identification of legal and moral constraint may be had in the matter of legal control over individuals' sexual practices. There are even moralists who, holding to rather conventional and even puritanical views of sexual morality, nonetheless fear the evil consequences of extending the legal arm into this area. They would prefer that persuasive methods rather than legally coercive ones direct the sexual lives of persons. Indeed, on grounds of social utility, many persons today are convinced that sexual practices between mature individuals, where coercion and violence do not occur, should not be made to feel the weight of the legal order.

Yet, since the notion of justice is closely tied to the question when, and for what purposes, men should legally be permitted to interfere with the actions of others, there is a problem of how to distinguish the notion of justice from that of morality. Mill recognizes the importance of legal constraint, for he writes: "Thus the idea of legal constraint is still the generating idea of the notion of justice, though undergoing several transformations before that notion, as it exists in an advanced state of society, becomes complete." The notion of justice here propounded by Mill is thus closely linked with the notion of general rights. Mill's conception is very much alive today when

Professor H. L. A. Hart, in his essay "Are There Any Natural Rights?" [5] distinguishes general from special rights by arguing that, in the case of the former, a special bond seems to hold between concepts of justice, fairness, rights, and (restricted) obligation. About this bond Professor Hart claims that the essential ingredient of these moral notions is "that there is no incongruity, but a special congruity in the use of force or the threat of force to secure that what is just or fair or someone's right to have done shall in fact be done; . . ."

Mill's position requires that there be some differentiation of the realm of justice from that of morality. He finds this in the opinion, held by many men, that justice is that sphere of morality in which it is proper to use coercion to secure those acts which others are considered bound to perform because someone has a right to the performance. This means, naturally, that not all duties which we would like to see performed shall be viewed as subject to legal coercion. For Mill, then, justice is the area of action where we, or other persons, may be legitimately coerced to behave in specific manners. Not all things we think good or proper to do can be classed as things we would want to see persons coerced into doing. Justice is linked with legitimate constraint of action in special situations, while morality has to do with all those obligations it would be desirable for men to meet but not right always to coerce. A famous passage from the last section of "Utilitarianism" makes this abundantly clear:

> This, therefore, being the characteristic difference which marks off, not justice, but morality in general, from the remaining provinces of expediency and worthiness; the character is still to be sought which distinguishes justice from other branches of morality. Now it is known that ethical writers divide moral duties into two classes, denoted by the ill-chosen expressions, duties of perfect and of imperfect obligation; the latter being those in which, though the act is obligatory, the particular occasions of performing it are left to our choice—as in the case of charity or beneficence, which we are indeed bound to practice, but not towards any definite person nor at

[5] This essay appeared in *The Philosophical Review*, Vol. LXIV (1955) and is reprinted in Frederick A. Olafson, ed., *Society, Law and Morality* (Englewood Cliffs, N.J.: Prentice-Hall, 1961).

any prescribed time. In the more precise language of philosophic jurists, duties of perfect obligation are those duties in virtue of which a correlative *right* resides in some person or persons; duties of imperfect obligation are those moral obligations which do not give birth to any right. I think it will be found that this distinction exactly coincides with that which exists between justice and the other obligations of morality. In our survey of the various popular acceptations of justice, the term appeared generally to involve the idea of a personal right—a claim on the part of one or more individuals, like that which the law gives when it confers a proprietary or other legal right. Whether the injustice consists in depriving a person of a possession, or in breaking faith with him, or in treating him worse than he deserves, or worse than other people who have no greater claims, in each case the supposition implies two things—a wrong done, and some assignable person who is wronged. Injustice may also be done by treating a person better than others; but the wrong in this case is to his competitors, who are also assignable persons. It seems to me that this feature in the case—right in some person, correlative to the moral obligation—constitutes the specific difference between justice, and generosity or beneficence. Justice implies something which is not only right to do, and wrong not to do, but which some individual person can claim from us as his moral right. No one has a moral right to our generosity or beneficence, because we are not morally bound to practice those virtues toward any given individual.[6]

At this point, Mill must show the distinctive relation between justice and utility. His major "move" in seeking to accomplish this is to define the notion of justice as involving both a rule of law and a human sentiment (feeling) which sanctions that rule. The sanction arises from men's natural desire to seek their self-defense against aggression as well as from their capacity to experience a feeling of sympathy for others. The desire to punish those who produce pain and suffering is a natural one. According to Mill, it has nothing moral in it considered purely as a feeling. Its morality results from its being tamed by what he calls the social sympathies of men who, as reasoning animals, can identify their interests with those of broader groupings—like families, tribes, nations, or even mankind. (Of course,

[6] Mill's *Utilitarianism* in E. A. Burtt, ed., *The English Philosophers from Bacon to Mill* (New York: Modern Library, 1939), p. 935.

at this point some critics, like the natural law thinkers, will object that reasoning plays a necessary role in the directing of the sentiment to specific ends.) It turns out, as a matter of fact, that this sentiment results in the welfare of mankind even though individual men, acting in terms of it, may not actually be thinking of others. Justice is concerned therefore with men's feelings that certain pain-producing action of others ought to be constrained since the security of large numbers of men is involved. Thus, the possession of a right is "to have something which society ought to defend me in the possession of." Justice concerns those rights without which the security of men, perhaps of all men, would be placed in jeopardy. Realizing that some critic may claim that this notion of society's obligation is not fully justified, Mill replies:

> The claim assumes that character of absoluteness, that apparent infinity, and incommensurability with all other considerations, which constitute the distinction between the feeling of right and wrong and that of ordinary expediency and inexpediency. The feelings concerned are so powerful, and we count so positively on finding a responsive feeling in others (all being alike interested), that *ought* and *should* grow into *must,* and recognized indispensability becomes a moral necessity, analogous to physical, and often not inferior to it in binding force.[7]

In brief, then, Mill's conclusion is that justice is concerned about those types of (rules and) acts which most crucially affect human welfare. The worst injustices that men can enact are wrongfully to attack others and knowingly to keep from someone what is due him. Similarly, breaches of friendship or promise are important kinds of injustice, since few acts can so affect an individual's expectations of welfare in extreme conditions. In a like manner, when it comes to judging, impartiality is a major virtue just as is the right of each person to equality of treatment according to the greatest happiness principle. This does not mean there can never be exceptions. Rather it means they must be justified in the light of special circumstances if they do occur. Nonetheless, even the maxims of justice are for Mill

[7] *Ibid.,* p. 939.

derived from the general notion of utility, as summed up in his assertion:

> It appears from what has been said that justice is a name for certain moral requirements which, regarded collectively, stand higher in the scale of social utility, and are therefore of more paramount obligation, than any others; though particular cases may occur in which some other duty is so important, as to overrule any one of the general maxims of justice. . . .
>
> Justice remains the appropriate name for certain social utilities which are vastly more important, and therefore more absolute and imperative, than any others are as a class (though not more so than others may be in particular cases); and which, therefore, ought to be, as well as naturally are, guarded by a sentiment not only different in degree, but also in kind; distinguished from the milder feeling which attaches to the mere idea of promoting human pleasure or convenience, at once by the more definite nature of its commands, and by the sterner character of its sanctions.[8]

The Matter of Fairness

Can all the maxims of justice unqualifiedly be derived from the notion of utility? In the chapter on "Punishment," this issue was seen to arise given the possibility that a judge, in the name of the community's welfare, might knowingly convict an innocent person. If a person worried by the possibility is dissatisfied with the solution offered by an ideal utilitarian: namely, that as a matter of fact no community's welfare will be improved by an act of this kind, how may he—doubting that justice and utility need always coincide—account for his dissatisfaction? One way might be to imagine the possibility that some unjust acts are morally justifiable. An example might be that of a citizen in a country marked by racial prejudice and racial inequality who, thinking laws which segregate classes purely on racial grounds are unjust laws, nonetheless favors this particular injustice at least contextually defensible on utilitarian principles. The other would be to argue that the notion of justice involves a broader concept, like that of fairness, such that while it may at times be useful to be unfair, it can never be just to be unfair. As a possible example,

[8] *Ibid.,* pp 947–948.

consider the instance of promoting a less qualified candidate in a competitive professional situation in which, if the clearly superior candidate should be promoted, the other members of the group will experience dissension and, perhaps, the destruction of what they now judge a sound functioning group.

The issue is even more complicated. It is possible that, on grounds of social utility, a specific rule or practice may be judged unjust. Yet, a person agreeing with this judgment may believe that the practice would be unjust *even if* it were to lead to social utility. So to believe, however, means to commit oneself to the position that, though utility may be a sound general guide to just action, there will be reasons of justice which possess a conceptual priority independently of utility. To accommodate this possibility, a utilitarian would need to redefine utilitarianism so that general satisfaction of human desires could not, unqualifiedly, serve as the test of the justice of rules and acts within a social framework of practices.

Mill's distinction between duties of perfect and duties of imperfect obligations may be taken as indication that he had not overlooked this problem. He could imagine situations in which it would be desirable that citizens be charitable, yet not just to coerce the citizens to perform their duties of imperfect obligations. But, suppose a society is marked by extreme economic disparities in wealth and poverty. Suppose the wealthy portion refuses to contribute to the poor minority, arguing (in this instance) that more persons are wealthy than are poor. Mill would say, morally, they have an obligation to be charitable, even if they are not. Mill would also admit the social utility of the effects of such charity. Yet, apparently, he would hesitate to claim that it is always just to coerce actions which are morally desirable. (Mill would *philosophically* hesitate, that is. Actually, Mill's politics often tended toward what today is called "welfare politics" and even socialism.)

Mill's distinction obviously presupposes a "picture" of a politically organized society as already meeting some minimally necessary conditions of economic welfare and political liberty. This is the liberal picture. The consequences to personal liberty which would result from a strict coercion of a wide range of morally desirable acts would, at some point, given this liberal view, militate against the general welfare of the community. Yet the tension between the demands of liberty and those of equality are difficult to reconcile. If a society operates minimally because persons do in fact give charitably, there is no need of coercion to secure the useful social consequences of charity. But suppose the charitable persons cease to give in the future? Or suppose that the charitable ones sense an injustice in the fact that equally wealthy persons in the community give nothing? It is often the case that the persons who object to charities like local welfare "Community Chest" campaigns, will not object to higher taxes imposed on all who qualify for the support of those agencies now privately aided by such campaigns. If private institutions are goods, is it necessarily just that private institutions are supported very unequally by contributors deriving similar benefits from them and enjoying relatively similar incomes? Is it just for nonunion workers to accept wage increases obtained by union activities supported solely by the dues of union members? Even if it is a good, is it clearly fair that of a number of members of a church, say, of those making the same annual income, 10 per cent contribute more than the remaining 90 per cent in the category? On Mill's view, if justice concerns only those areas where men may coerce the actions of others, then how does one contextually decide when coercive taxation is permitted in a community where charitable giving fails to produce stipulated goals? Apparently, Mill would have to hold to the standard of social utility in determining duties of perfect obligation, the economic members of which can be coerced—consigning charity to appropriate moral behavior beyond the call of such obligation. This would mean, however, that even in the economic realm the values of personal liberty would sometimes outweigh the claims on behalf of an unrestricted economic equality. Justice even in the economic realm would be a minimal rather than a complete affair.

Commenting on the relation between notions of justice and social welfare, Professor H. L. A. Hart has reminded men:

> Very few social changes or laws are agreeable to or advance the welfare of all individuals alike. Only laws which provide for the most elementary needs, such as police protection or roads, come near to

this. In most cases the law provides benefits for one class of the population only at the cost of depriving others of what they prefer. Provision for the poor can be made only out of the goods of others; compulsory school education for all may mean not only loss of liberty for those who wish to educate their children privately, but may be financed only at the cost of reducing or sacrificing capital investment in industry or old-age pensions or free medical services. When a choice has been made between such competing alternatives it may be defended as proper on the ground that it was for the "public good" or the "common good." It is not clear what these phrases mean, since there seems to be no scale by which contributions of the various alternatives to the common good can be measured and the greater identified. It is, however, clear that a choice, made without prior consideration of the interests of all sections of the community, would be open to criticism as merely partisan and unjust. It would, however, be rescued from *this* imputation if the claims of all had been impartially considerad before legislation, even though in the result the claims of one section were subordinated to those of others.[9]

Similarly concerned about the way in which laws create inequalities, Professor Ralph Dahrendorf in his inaugural lecture at the University of Tübingen in Germany argued that Kant was essentially correct in reminding men that inequality is a "rich source of much that is evil, but also of everything that is good." If justice is only a part of morality, and if justice as fairness is not always equal distribution of goods and burdens, then in a just society numerous inequalities may very well exist. In his lecture "On the Origin of Social Inequality" Professor Dahrendorf observed that, though many sound reasons exist for resisting extreme and arbitrary forms of inequality, nonetheless: "That social inequality exists at all is, however, an impetus towards liberty because it guarantees the historical quality of societies. The perfectly egalitarian society is not only an unrealistic, it is also a terrible idea. Utopia is the home not of freedom, the for ever imperfect scheme for an uncertain future, but of the perfection either of terror or of absolute boredom." [10]

---

[9] *The Concept of Law* (Oxford, Clarendon Press, 1961), pp. 162–63. Used by permission of the publisher.
[10] The text of Professor Dahrendorf's lecture appears in Peter Laslett and W. G. Runciman, eds., *Philosophy, Politics and Society* (Second Series; Oxford: Blackwell, 1962), p. 109.

The United States Supreme Court, in an opinion written by Justice Earl Warren, 1954, argued that racial segregation in public schools denies equal *opportunity* to children of minority races: thus, judicially called for an end to such racial segregation in the schools. The court's decision contained a rejection of the notion that equality of "physical facilities and other 'tangible' factors" in segregated schools can provide equality of opportunity and benefits. In this decision, the court appealed to the idea of inherent inequality. Apparently, even if it could have been shown (which the court's decision denied) that racially segregated schools produce desirable social consequences, the practice would have been held unjust.

A crucial paragraph in the court's decision reads: "We conclude that in the field of public education the doctrine of 'separate but equal' has no place. Separate educational facilities are inherently unequal. Therefore, we hold that the plaintiffs and others similarly situated for whom the actions have been brought are, by reason of the segregation complained of, deprived of the equal protection of the laws guaranteed by the Fourteenth Amendment. This disposition makes unnecessary any discussion whether such segregation also violates the Due Process Clause of the Fourteenth Amendment."

The court's decision implies that some forms of inequality are inherently unfair, thus unjust. This notion that justice primarily involves fairness has led some thinkers to doubt that the maxims of justice are fully derivable from considerations of social utility, as Mill had claimed. There can be some social practices which, even if they could be shown in some sense to possess utility, are inherently unjust because unfair. Justice as fairness involves some principles to which questions of utility are irrelevant. Among these principles of justice—where justice is conceived as a virtue, though not the only one, of social institutions—are two which Professor John Rawls, a contemporary philosopher teaching at Harvard University, has put forward. One principle is that given any social or institutional practice (game, ritual, trial, parliament, market, property system) whose participants are affected by it, each participant possesses an equal right to the most complete liberty which does not interfere with a similar liberty for all the others. A second principle of justice is that unequal treatment of participants in a practice is unjust if such treatment cannot be expected to produce *everyone's* advantage in cases where the positions and offices marked by the inequalities are open to all.

To these principles of justice the standard of social utility is sometimes irrelevant, according to Rawls. Thus, justice as fairness leads to a slight modification of the utilitarian conception which, nonetheless, fundamentally alters that conception of justice. Its significance is, as shown by Rawls, that *some* practices would remain unjust *even if* they could be shown to possess social utility. Professor Rawls insists that slavery is one such practice. Although utilitarians historically favored the abolition of slavery on grounds of utility, they erred in thinking that utility of slavery is relevant to the question about its justice. If some desires and wants happen in fact to be satisfied by a practice, that practice may still be unjust. This is a point at which, according to Rawls, the classical utilitarians went wrong—though their attempt to make justice coincide with utility is *generally* adequate.

Conclusion

To conclude a chapter which has sought to indicate some important ways in which philosophers have treated the theme of justice, a brief selection from Professor Rawls' "Justice as Fairness" should prove thought-provoking. The reason is that the meaning of the selection indicates that a conceptual analysis of justice in terms of fairness shows that not all principles of justice can be derived from ideas of social utility. Moreover, the selection indicates that, while justice is related to numerous concepts in a family way, it has a unique relation to the notion of fairness. Whether the philosophical issue here may be said to lead to *practical* social, economic, and political consequences must be left to readers to consider and debate. The passage from the essay by Professor Rawls reads:

> But as an interpretation of the basis of the principles of justice, classical utilitarianism is mistaken. It *permits* one to argue, for example, that slavery is unjust on the grounds that the advantages to the slave-holder as slaveholder do not counterbalance the disadvantages to the

slave and to the society at large burdened by a comparatively inefficient system of labour. Now the conception of justice as fairness, when applied to the practice of slavery with its offices of slaveholder and slave, would not allow one to consider the advantages of the slaveholder in the first place. As that office is not in accordance with principles which could be mutually acknowledged, the gains accruing to the slaveholder, assuming them to exist, cannot be counted as in *any* way mitigating the injustice of the practice. The question whether these gains outweigh the disadvantages to the slave and to society cannot arise, since in considering the justice of slavery these gains have no weight at all which requires that they be overriden. Where the conception of justice as fairness applies, slavery is *always* unjust.[11]

Some Questions and Problems

1. Is justice the highest social value? If so, on what grounds? If not, what ideal is the highest social value?
2. If you overheard a person remark: "Justice is due only to those persons who possess a sense of justice!", what might you say? Be prepared to discuss this assertion at some length, both favorably and critically.
3. Imagine that you represent St. Thomas Aquinas and are asked to criticize Mill's conception of justice. Prepare a brief speech which you can read in class.
4. Discuss the assertion: "A man who constantly demands justice is someone to be suspected."
5. How may automation raise serious problems of social justice? What should individual citizens do about these anticipated problems? What active role should government play?
6. Is property the highest value in a system concerned about social justice? Give supporting reasons for your answer. If you answer in the negative, indicate what value you consider the highest if social justice is at stake.
7. Imagine that you belong to a religious group whose beliefs conflict with some of the laws you are expected to enforce and interpret as a judge. How would you handle such a situation of conflict?
8. Should a judge ever refuse to enforce what he considers to be a "bad" law? Defend your viewpoint.

[11] From "Justice as Fairness," *The Philosophical Review,* Vol. LXVII (1958); reprinted in Peter Laslett and W. G. Runciman, eds., *op. cit.,* p. 152. Used by permission of the Editorial Board of *The Philosophical Review.*

9. Does it make sense to talk about international justice?
10. Can a system ever be legally just but morally unjust? Is justice primarily a legal notion? A moral notion?

Some Suggested Readings

Aristotle. Book V of *The Nichomachean Ethics,* trans. J. E. C. Welldon. London: Macmillan, 1934.

Brandt, R. B. (ed.) *Social Justice.* Englewood Cliffs, N.J.: Prentice-Hall, 1962.

Ginsberg, M. "The Concept of Justice," *Philosophy,* Vol. XXXVIII, No. 144 (1963).

Hart, H. L. A. *The Concept of Law.* Oxford: Clarendon Press, 1961.

Hegel, G. W. F. *Philosophy of Right,* trans. T. M. Knox. Oxford: Clarendon Press, 1942.

Hobhouse, L. T. *The Elements of Social Justice.* London: Allen & Unwin, 1922.

Lindberg, J. *Foundations of Social Survival.* New York: Columbia University Press, 1953.

Maritain, J. *Scholasticism and Politics.* New York: Macmillan, 1940.

Mill, J. S. *Utilitarianism.* Reprinted in *The English Philosophers from Bacon to Mill,* ed. E. A. Burtt. New York: Modern Library, 1939.

Olafson, F. A. (ed.) *Justice and Social Policy.* Englewood Cliffs, N.J.: Prentice-Hall, 1961.

Plato. *The Republic,* trans. F. M. Cornford. London: Oxford University Press, 1941.

―――. *Crito, Euthyphro, Laws* in *Plato: The Collected Dialogues,* eds. E. Hamilton and H. Cairns. New York: Bollingen Foundation, 1961.

Rawls, J. "Two Concepts of Rules," *The Philosophical Review,* Vol. XLIV, 1955.

―――. "The Sense of Justice," *The Philosophical Review,* Vol. LXXII, 1963.

Ross, W. D. *Aristotle: A Complete Exposition of His Works and Thought.* New York: Meridian, 1959.

CHAPTER ELEVEN

Equality

Consider the plight of a person who, at a gathering of his friends and acquaintances, argues that all men are created equal. Some wit who is present can probably be counted on to reply: "You're right—and some are more equal than others!" To say that men are equal means to raise a host of troubling issues rather than automatically to resolve an argument. Indeed, some philosophers have maintained that social equality would be an evil if pressed to an extreme. In any event, it is quite evident that in ordinary uses of the term men are very often unequal. Indeed, passionate claims of equality often, perhaps even usually, occur in social and political contexts marked by existing inequalities which bear heavily on some persons or groups. Yet, the notion of equality as well as the claims that all men are *in some senses* equal, or ought to be so, form significant elements in the history of social and political thought and action.

Even if a person falsely believed that men are *literally* created equal, he would face a serious difficulty. This is the undeniable fact that, even if an initial equality existed, it would probably disappear in the course of historical development. All newborn babies may be said to be equal in their nakedness, but as they grow up, some stronger and more talented than the others, the rich and powerful and gifted will end up with more and better clothing than will the others. On this basis, a purported original equality would not be incompatible with a present inequality among men. Oliver Wendell Holmes, father of the late famous Supreme Court Justice, gave a moving illustration of this point in his *Autocrat of the Breakfast Table* when, thinking of the experience of a spectator at a college graduation ceremony, he wrote:

So you will not think I mean to speak lightly of old friendships, because we cannot help instituting comparisons between our present and former selves by the aid of those who were what we are; nothing strikes me more, in the race of life, than to see how many give out in the first half of the course. "Commencement day" always reminds me of the start of the "Derby," when the beautiful highbred three-year olds of the season are brought up for trial. That day is the start, and life is the race. Here we are at Cambridge, and a class is just "graduating." Poor Harry! he was to have been there too, but he has paid forfeit; . . .

But this is the start, and here they are,—coats bright as silk, and manes as smooth as *eau lustrale* can make them. Some of the best of the colts are pranced round, a few minutes each, to show their paces. What is that old gentleman crying about? and the old lady by him, and the three girls, all covering their eyes for? Oh, that is *their* colt that has just been trotted up on the stage. Do they really think those little thin legs can do anything in such a slashing sweepstakes as is coming off in the next forty years? Oh, this terrible gift of second-sight that comes to some of us when we begin to look through the silvered rings of the arcus senilis.

Ten years gone. First turn in the race. A few broken down; two or three bolted. Several show advance of the ruck. *Cassock,* a black colt, seems to be ahead of the rest; those black colts commonly get the start, I have noticed, of the others, in the first quarter. *Meteor* has pulled up.

Twenty years. Second corner turned. *Cassock* has dropped from the front, and *Judex,* an iron-gray, has the lead. But look! how they have thinned out? Down flat,—five,—six,—how many? They lie still enough! they will not get up again in this race, be very sure! And the rest of them, what a "tailing off"! Anybody can see who is going to win,—perhaps.

Thirty years. Third corner turned. *Dives,* bright sorrel, ridden by the fellow in a yellow jacket, begins to make play fast; is getting to be the favorite with many. But who is that other one that has been lengthening his stride from the first, and now shows close up to the front? Don't you remember the quiet brown colt *Asteroid,* with the star in his forehead? That is he; he is one of the sort that lasts; look

out for him! The back "colt," as we used to call him, is in the background, taking it easy in a gentle trot. There is one they used to call
the *Filly,* on account of a certain feminine air he had; well up, you
see; the Filly is not to be despised, my boy!

Forty years. More dropping off,—but places much as before.

Fifty years. Race over. All that are on the course are coming in at
a walk; no more running. Who is ahead? Ahead? What! and the
winningpost a slab of white or gray stone standing out from the
turf where there is no more jockeying or straining for victory! Well,
the world marks their places in its betting-book; but be sure that
these matter very little, if they have run as well as they knew how! [1]

Clearly, an argument that men are equal goes counter to many
commonsense facts. It cannot be taken literally except in limited
respects. Probably no philosopher has ever meant the argument for
equality to be so taken. What, then, can help a person to make sense
of the notion of equality? The notion belongs to the sphere of values;
it is used in *moral* judgments to the effect that equality is a good, that
it ought in some senses to exist, and that this is so in spite of obvious
ways in which men are unequal in strength, talent, and intellect. Nor
have most philosophers wanted an equality which is total. The claim
that men are equal is a claim that *in fundamental respects,* regardless
of obvious differences between one man and another, all men deserve
to be given certain kinds of treatment. They have a *right* to certain
kinds of equal treatment in crucial aspects of their lives, though not
in all. This moral claim need not be a description of an existing fact
unless it be taken as a peculiar kind of *moral fact*—about whose
existence many philosophers would have serious doubts.

Kinds of Equality

In the realm of justice, equality of certain kinds is a good in that
fairness sometimes requires such equality. In the ardent claims of
natural rights proponents, men are said to possess equal rights to "life,
liberty and the pursuit of happiness" even if they are, in fact, unequally endowed for pursuit of such values. Equality is thus an ideal

[1] Philadelphia: Henry Altemus Co., n.d., pp. 97–98.

which often fails to find an extensive place in actual social and political situations. As an ideal, it is usually restricted to certain classes of rights viewed as belonging to all men by virtue of their very humanity. Derivatively, a social inequality may exist in a system in which special groups are said to deserve, for *their* members alone, equal treatment. Professional ethics is a subject matter confined to the study of the rights and obligations of special classes of persons, especially those whose professional roles are defined by clear standards—like professors, doctors, lawyers, clergymen. To argue for equal treatment in terms of existing standards need not mean to argue for equal treatment of all men, since very often there are special ethical considerations which apply to persons by virtue of their social roles in a broader society. Thus, academic freedom may be a right of qualified professors in a way in which it cannot be claimed as a right by other persons or groups.

1. *Equality of legal treatment*. Persons similarly circumstanced, whose actions are covered by official rules, are said to deserve equal treatment. This is part of the notion of justice. All men may be said to be equal in the sense of deserving equality before the law. On this view, no exceptions to the rules should be admitted unless other persons who meet the excepting conditions are also removed from the application of the laws. ("I know it was wrong for me to fail to cut the grass, Dad, but you didn't whip my brother when *he* forgot to cut it last month! Why treat us so differently?") However, equality before the law may itself imply the existence of basic inequalities—since laws bear more heavily on some persons than on others. To say that certain acts shall be considered criminal means potentially to divide a society into criminal and noncriminal groups. Moreover, to make a different point, to argue that all persons should pay income taxes according to fixed schedules—as well as that offenders should be treated equally by the punishing authority—need not entail the view that all persons' incomes should be identical. (This should not be interpreted as meaning that an argument for equal incomes for all members of a society cannot be made.)

An argument for equality before the law need not entail a belief that social equality is unrestrictedly an intrinsic good. Social equality would be a good only in the case of those basic rights protected by general laws. Thus citizens may be said to have an equal right to public education, in a specific country; but this need not mean that once enrolled in schools they deserve to receive equal grades without regard to their performances. Most philosophers have therefore concentrated on those basic rights in which, on their view, all men should be considered equal in any fair legal system. These are rights in which the special differences among men seem irrelevant. If the law is that murderers are to be given a specific sentence by a court, it would seem absurd to exempt persons who happen to be white, say. On the other hand, it would not seem arbitrary to consider psychological conditions as relevant to the question whether a given murderer should be treated in a special way.

2. *Equality of basic needs*. This topic has been tangentially considered in Chapter 10, "Justice," especially in regard to welfare economics. Since men possess some basic needs in common, they may be said to deserve equal treatment at least until those needs are *minimally* met. Men need food, shelter, some human companionship, sexual life, and the like, simply because men are what they are. If these needs are accepted as deserving satisfaction, and if political processes are taken as necessary to their satisfaction, then whatever inequalities that may defensibly exist in a society must occur only in so far as these basic needs are met. In the name of this type of equality, others may unequally be taxed by the government or required by legislation to live up to social obligations which fall to their lot because they are more wealthy or more gifted.

The problem has been to determine, in specifically historical situations, which needs are to be considered basic and, where they are viewed as numerous, which are to be met if not all can, at any one time, be satisfied. It is one thing to seek equality of education; it is another to define "equality" here as the same for all in content and duration. All men may equally deserve an education but not qualify for the same kind of excellence of education. Only a person who wanted to make men as alike as possible would seek to achieve a total equality, and in so doing he would no doubt require a strict totalitarian regime to maintain this levelling equality. To argue for a total equality would mean to argue that equality is the only worthwhile ideal value —since its actualization would involve the elimination of other important values. As Professor Isaiah Berlin has argued, "Equality is one value among many: the degree to which it is compatible with other ends depends on the concrete situation, and cannot be deduced from general laws of any kind; it is neither more nor less rational than any other ultimate principle; indeed it is difficult to see what is meant by considering it either rational or non-rational." [2] This means only that, if conflicts between ideals like equality and justice occur, persons must decide which value to emphasize—that there will be situations in which equality would be unjust. This need not mean that a society, faced with serious inequalities too long accepted, may not need to emphasize equality to right the disproportion. It may be unjust to use a racial yardstick as the primary basis for assigning children to public schools. Yet, given the situation which prevails in the United States, a good case can be made (as it has by many persons) that though this yardstick may cause some injustices, it is preferable to a continuation of the racial injustices which exist quite broadly in the society.

3. *Equality of opportunity.* This is a difficult notion to clarify. It may be treated as a limited instance of a basic need. On the other hand, since the public school system, for example, exists for all persons in the United States but must be maintained by coercion against those who do not wish to continue, it is not clear that education is felt by all as a need. The state coercively defines it as a requirement as well as a need. Thus, a truant officer calls at the homes of students under sixteen who absent themselves from formal schooling. Equality of opportunity can be treated as a right rather than a need, such that *if* a person wants to pursue a certain goal, he shall be free to do so insofar as the laws are drawn up. Those persons who want a college education will be free to seek admission to state institutions; they will have an equal opportunity to apply, if not necessarily to be accepted.

[2] "Equality as an Ideal," in Frederick A. Olafson, ed., *Justice and Social Policy* (Englewood Cliffs, New Jersey: Prentice-Hall, 1961), p. 144. Professor Berlin's essay appeared originally in *Proceedings of the Aristotelian Society,* Vol. LVI (1955–56).

Equality of opportunity treated as a need or a right, or as both, need not involve the view that men are entitled equally to succeed in what they undertake.

Equality of opportunity as need and as right can sometimes come into conflict if opportunity is confused with success in achievement. The contemporary racial situation in this country may be used as an illustration. Suppose the aim is the achievement of integrated housing. The legal order can make it possible for persons of different races to buy houses in all neighborhoods if they have the economic resources. The legal order can provide equality of opportunity for the purchase of housing. But this may not produce racially integrated housing, since others may move from the neighborhoods. Persons may be said to have a right to equality of opportunity in buying houses; but if they are also said to have a need of equality of opportunity in living in racially mixed tracts, then there may occur a conflict. To secure the latter opportunity, further laws may be needed to restrict the rights of others—thus, to keep them from having a right to move from a neighborhood just because they do not wish to live in racially mixed areas. This is a difficult problem, one about which many persons are understandably exercised today. The point here is that equality as a need and as a right, in the area of opportunity, may sometimes lead to conflicts.

Some Problems with Egalitarianism

Among the advocates of the doctrine of egalitarianism—the doctrine that men should be as equal as possible in all respects—even the Communist theoreticians have "hedged" the notion of equality with crucial, perhaps irreconcilable, restrictions. In illustration, the following selection from a speech by Joseph Stalin, at one time leader of the Soviet Union, can be offered as a telling instance:

> By equality Marxism means, not equality in personal requirements and personal life, but the abolition of classes, i.e., (a) the equal emancipation of all toilers from exploitation after the capitalists have been overthrown and expropriated; (b) the equal abolition for all of private property in the means of production after they have

been transformed into the property of the whole of society; (c) the equal duty of all to work according to their ability and the equal right of all toilers to receive according to the amount of work they have done (*socialist* society); (d) the equal duty of all to work according to their ability and the equal right of all toilers to receive according to their requirements (*communist* society). And Marxism starts out with the assumption that people's tastes and requirements are not, and cannot be equal in quality or in quantity, either in the period of socialism or in the period of communism.[3]

Thus, on this view, to achieve equality among classes by the abolition of classes means to introduce other kinds of "inequality" into a social order. Perhaps—as the history of the arts in the Soviet Union has illustrated in this century—artists (painters, writers, poets, musicians) must conform to an established ideological "line" in order to submit their works to a broader public. Such "producers" will not have an equal right to express their artistic genius as they see fit, in other words.

Since the doctrine of equality has usually been asserted against prevailing abuses in a political system, it has functioned historically to announce to the world the demands of submerged groups for amelioration of distinctions in the social-economic order which, to these groups, have seemed unjustified. Yet, the doctrine can sometimes produce a tyrannical political control rather than an "open society" in which many freedoms exist. One discerning analyst of American democracy in the nineteenth century, the French aristocrat Alexis de Tocqueville, recognized the fundamental role played in the society by the notion of equality. He predicted that the quest for an ever-widening equality in all phases of life could not be stopped. Yet, though he favored the equalitarian values, de Tocqueville worried whether equality in America would lead to a genuine independence rather than to a total servitude before centralized political power. He saw how the equalitarian passion, sweeping like a tidal wave through human affairs, could also blur customary distinctions which reflected important differences in talent and quality. He warned against the

[3] "Report at Seventeenth Congress of the Communist Party of the Soviet Union, 1934," in Emile Burns, *A Handbook of Marxism* (New York, 1935), p. 938.

threat of what he called "the tyranny of the majority"—a majority which might insist on conformity in tastes and thought as the necessary price to be paid for other kinds of economic and social equality. Equality as a value often conflicts with freedom. To guarantee a person's rights, for example, the political order must often interfere in the lives of others, if need be, coercing certain kinds of action. Alexis de Tocqueville wondered how well the United States could continue to introduce social equality and, at the same time, protect certain basic individual freedoms—including perhaps what might be termed the freedom to be different from others. He insisted that the abuses and misuses of freedom take time to be discovered, while the values of equality always appear immediate. But the immediate equalities achieved and enjoyed may lead to abuses of other kinds of liberty. Thus, de Tocqueville's judgment about independence in America was not a flattering one:

> I know of no country in which there is so little independence of mind and real freedom of discussion as in America. In any constitutional state in Europe, every sort of religious and political theory may be freely preached and disseminated; for there is no country in Europe so subdued by any single authority, as not to protect the man who raises his voice in the cause of truth from the consequences of his hardihood. If he is unfortunate enough to live under an absolute government, the people are often upon his side; if he inhabits a free country, he can, if necessary, find a shelter behind the throne. The aristocratic part of society supports him in some countries, and the democracy in others. But in a nation where democratic institutions exist, organized like those of the United States, there is but one authority, one element of strength and success, with nothing beyond it.[4]

However questionable de Tocqueville's historical judgment may appear, his emphasis on the problem of relating equality to freedom has represented a theme in American intellectual life carried over into the contemporary sociological analyses of the group pressures in the social life of the nation.

Egalitarianism was the central doctrine which animated the revolu-

[4] Richard D. Heffner (ed.), *Democracy in America* (New York: Mentor, 1956), p. 117.

tionaries in France in the early nineteenth century. They failed clearly to understand the numerous possible conflicts between equality and liberty, both of which values they preached. So much so, indeed, that the French Revolution called forth the passionate rhetorical outburst from Edmund Burke, for whom an unexamined doctrine of equality threatened to submerge valuable institutions and practices and to let loose chaos into the existing political situation. Equality as a value can be achieved at what critics might call a low level—a sameness among persons in which mediocrity triumphs over what, potentially, might be a higher level of achievement possible to large numbers of persons. Equality threatens to produce what some have named "mass culture," such that many refinements in taste and judgment must bow before the sheer counting of heads. Thus, an equal opportunity to experience leisure and entertainment—via the television medium, for example—may result in programs addressed to a so-called "average" viewer, denying any choice to vast millions of persons who would prefer other programs if they could be made available. Obviously, a price must be paid for human equality: but the perennially troubling question is to determine how high a price *should,* in any period, be paid.

Edmund Burke's criticism of egalitarianism rested on an aristocratic estimate of what constitutes value. In addition, he was not a believer in the view that values can be derived purely from reasoning processes. He was a political conservative. Nonetheless, his estimates of the way in which cultural values develop need not be tied to his political conservatism. Like other empirical thinkers, among them David Hume, the Scotch philosopher, Burke believed that society rests more on sentiment and custom than on reason. Even if social equality is a good, it may not be an unrestricted good in all times and places—since its existence must be evaluated in light of the consequences which will follow from the methods used to achieve it. It is not enough, then, for Burke's critics to reject his philosophically and politically conservative views; they must always labor to show, in detail, how advances in human equality can be achieved without resulting anarchy and the destruction of already existing values. Burke was not alone in rejecting the eighteenth-century view (perhaps "myth") that society is a reflection of a universal Reason, subject to rational manipulation for achievement of intrinsically worthwhile sets of immediate goals.

In his *Reflections on the Revolution in France,* first published in 1790, Burke expressed his anxiety about the French happenings of his day:

> I do not know under what description to class the present ruling authority in France. It affects to be a pure democracy, though I think it in a direct train of becoming shortly a mischievous and ignoble oligarchy. But for the present I admit it to be a contrivance of the nature and effect of what it pretends to. I reprobate no form of government merely upon abstract principles. There may be situations in which the purely democratic form will become necessary. There may be some (very few, and very particularly circumstanced) where it would be clearly desirable. This I do not take to be the case of France or of any other great country. Until now, we have seen no example of considerable democracies. The ancients were better acquainted with them. Not being wholly unread in the authors who had seen most of those constitutions, and who best understood them, I cannot help concurring with their opinion that an absolute democracy, no more than absolute monarchy, is to be reckoned among the legitimate forms of government. They think it rather the corruption and degeneracy than the sound constitution of a republic. If I recollect rightly, Aristotle observes that a democracy has many striking points of resemblance with a tyranny. Of this I am certain, that in a democracy the majority of the citizens is capable of exercising the most cruel oppressions upon the minority whenever strong diversions prevail in that kind of polity, as they often must; and that oppression of the minority will extend to far greater numbers and will be carried on with much greater fury than can almost ever be apprehended from the dominion of a single scepter. In such a popular persecution, individual sufferers are in a much more deplorable condition than any other. Under a cruel prince they have the balmy compassion of mankind to assuage the smart of their wounds; they have the plaudits of the people to animate their generous constancy under their sufferings; but those who are subjected to wrong under multitudes are deprived of all external consolation. They seem deserted by mankind, overpowered by a conspiracy of their whole species.[5]

[5] T. H. D. Mahoney (ed.) (Indianapolis: Liberal Arts Press, 1955), pp. 143–144.

The general principles on which Burke criticized the events in revolutionary France included the view that government is an experimental affair. Thus, by implication, even if equality is often a good, if its achievement requires reforms, then agreement on the worth of equality is not sufficient to the realization of those reforms. Competing interests must be taken into account. A passage which expresses Burke's sense of the experimental side to politics as well as any number of others might be the following:

> The science of constructing a commonwealth, or renovating it, or reforming it, is, like every other experimental science, not to be taught *a priori*. Nor is it a short experience that can instruct us in that practical science, because the real effects of moral causes are not always immediate; but that which in the first instance is prejudicial may be excellent in its remoter operation, and its excellence may arise even from the ill effects it produces in the beginning. The reverse also happens: and very plausible schemes, with very pleasing commencements, have often shameful and lamentable conclusions. In states there are often some obscure and almost latent causes, things which appear at first view of little moment, on which a very great part of its prosperity or adversity may most essentially depend. The science of government being therefore so practical in itself and intended for such practical purposes—a matter which requires experience, and even more experience than any person can gain in his whole life, however sagacious and observing he may be—it is with infinite caution that any man ought to venture upon pulling down an edifice which has answered in any tolerable degree for ages the common purposes of society, or on building it up again without having models and patterns of approved utility before his eyes.[6]

Literal Equality

To say that men are not literally equal in all fundamental respects does not say whether men are literally equal in any. Even as an ethical ideal, equality would be a peculiar value if men argued "All men ought to be equal in some respects" while believing that, in point of fact, they are not so equal; or that there is no literal equality which holds between man and man which can serve as the basis for an argument that it should be extended by legal and moral means. Dogs

[6] *Ibid.,* pp. 70–71.

aren't cats and cats aren't chickens, thus to say that one *ought* to be the other would mean to speak in a peculiar way. However, though they are different, cats and chickens may have some qualities in common—be alike (say, in having legs, being animals rather than rocks, possessing limited intelligences). Similarly, however different one man may be from another, all men may literally possess some common qualities or characteristics.

One contemporary American author has insisted that unless there exist some basic equality of all men, the notion of equality as a normative good would become a senseless one. Professor Joseph Margolis has argued that at least four traditions regarding the literal equality of men can be discerned.[7] The *religious* tradition, at least in what is loosely referred to as Western civilization, has affirmed that "before God men are equally sinful; and all are equally able to be saved, though God does not save all. Alternately, all men are equally subject to the limitations and evils of finite existence and all are equally able to accept their life under these conditions, though not all actually do so with the same adequacy." There is also a *tragic* tradition in which men are viewed as subject "to their destruction and death through the dedication of their own commitment and all equally exhibit admirable promise in the equality of their lives." The third tradition, that of a *comic* perspective on life, affirms the equal chance of all men "being exposed as absurd and capable, in spite of that, of being loved, respected, and tolerated." Finally, a *scientific* tradition affirms an equality of all men with respect to the possibility of knowledge. The reason is that scientific knowledge "depends on confirmation within a community of scientific workers from which, in principle, no one may be arbitrarily excluded." In a persuasive essay devoted to an unusual, even existentialist analysis of a literal human equality, Professor Margolis concluded:

> Here, then, we have four powerful traditions of thought which agree on the actual and fundamental equality of human beings. The attractiveness, for ethical theory itself, of their correspondence is precisely due to their avoidance of even covertly ethical attitudes.

[7] "That All Men Are Created Equal," *The Journal of Philosophy,* Vol. LII, No. 13 (June 23, 1955), p. 343.

Their contributions can be made ethically useful, but this is not their essential concern. Science can be turned to good or ill, but its procedures, are socially open; the religious problem persists for every human existence, no matter how worthy; tragedy can find admirable promise in every life, even those that are apparently "evil"; and comedy does not admit that any aspect of human existence is exempt from absurdity.[8]

Even Holmes' reflections on a commencement exercise, quoted early in this chapter, contained a reference to how after fifty years the original graduates limp toward a common death. However extensive the inequalities between man and man, all men are equal in their inevitable proneness to die. Is this really an important point? The answer will turn on whether, as Professor Margolis argues, the significance of certain ways in which men are alike in the human condition is taken as a highly important affair. Religious and quasi-religious writers who argue for equality want to emphasize how the *differences* between men come to appear unimportant, even trivial, from a specific perspective. Modern writers like Jean-Paul Sartre (whose views are considered in Chapter 16, "The Existentialist Protest") want to derive a universal human ethic from the way in which all men share a basic condition. Sartre seeks to argue that men, in choosing their projects, will do so with others in mind—thus, will choose for all men. There is no logical necessity in their so choosing; rather, given an existentialist picture of the human condition, it will follow from that picture that men's social sympathies will be quickened. This metaphysical defense of an ethic of equality seems to operate also in Professor Margolis' analysis.

Perhaps some practical examples may help to make a persuasive case for this approach to men's basic and literal equality. Most persons have confronted specific situations in which the usual distinctions (class, sex, economic, etc.) are made to appear unimportant by virtue of some more pervasive threat which they face. Among them the following might be included:

1. An aristocrat wounded on a battlefield finds himself next to another wounded man, an uneducated "peasant." Both need but lack

[8] Joseph Margolis, *op. cit.,* p. 345.

water. Their pains are similar, their crisis before a possible death a personal tragedy equally for each. In such a plight the equality of their crisis situation seems to make what in other circumstances would be significant social differences seem unimportant.

2. Several years ago, an advertisement for a New York City newspaper showed a drawing of a prosperous subway commuter, well-dressed, reading a paper under a poster depicting a nuclear explosion. Persons from various walks of life were seated about him in the subway car. The poster was titled "Hero." The equal vulnerability of the prosperous man to a nuclear war along with all others sustained the comic point of the drawing.

3. A story circulated during the years of the sustained economic depression in the United States whose effect depended on a person's immediate sensitivity to men's equal exposure to economic need. According to the story, an employed professor came to a party of friends and, exhilarated by a walk through a newly fallen snow, said: "What a beautiful night it is! The sky is brilliant with glittering stars, the air crisp and cold. It's a lovely night!" Then the speaker hesitated and remarked: "Oh, I shouldn't have said that. So many persons are without heat and food tonight! They must be freezing!" The sudden awareness of the terrible plight of the unemployed led him, thus, to feel guilt that as an individual he had found the night a beautiful one.

4. An insurance agent, freshly trained to show aggressive confidence in selling policies, rings a doorbell in a poor neighborhood. He has read that the inhabitants have had a new baby, thus should be promising prospects for a sale. The door opens, and to the young woman who appears the insurance agent says: "Congratulations, Mrs. Jones, on your new baby boy. I'm sure you'll want to consider taking out an insurance policy for his future education!" The woman colors, then replies softly: "Oh. The baby died yesterday!" The insurance agent can think of nothing adequate to say.

This religious or quasi-religious sense of men's basic equality is sometimes too easily overlooked or forgotten. The doctrine of equality may depend on a certain "picture" of the human scene, and a person probably must appropriate something of that picture if, in spite of evident inequalities of all kinds (many of them quite rationally defensible), he is to consider equality a fundamental value. The picture suggests that equality makes sense as a value *if we look at things in a certain important way*. It is not that differences do not exist as a basis for legitimizing inequalities but, rather, that these differences are *in some respects* hardly worth emphasizing. Thus, the English Puritans defended a doctrine of equality on the grounds that as compared with the distance between God and man, the differences between man and man are trivial and (relatively) unimportant. Generalized, the basic equalities between men are such as to make existing inequalities often seem irrelevant and foolish. Even his critics can occasionally sympathize with Jean Jacques Rousseau, who looked upon the wide inequalities in his day and age and found many of them false and useless. It is even possible that a certain mystical sense stands behind this quasi-religious awareness of basic human equality.

How sound is this "picture" which makes the ideal of equality so persuasive even to minds convinced that many specific social, economic, political, and other inequalities are justifiable? This is again difficult to answer. There have been mystical thinkers who, impressed by a basic equality among men, turned away from ethical and political considerations. The reason is that they looked upon existing inequalities as unimportant, as argued here, but then decided that they need waste no effort to remedy them. Contrariwise, others have judged the inequalities unimportant in one sense but requiring elimination just *because of that fact*. There seems no clear *logical* way in which to get from the "picture" to either political activism ("Let's roll up our sleeves and do something about it!") or to political quietism ("It doesn't really matter in the long run, you know!"). Apparently, those thinkers who have had this "picture" of man's equal condition have gone down either of these roads. The difference is that for a man like Sartre, man's basic equality in a troubled human situation is supposed to lead to a need of *action* on behalf of all men.

Sartre seems to have an important point. It is not that a person *must* (logically) treat others as intrinsically important in his decisions just because he has a deep sense of how all men share a certain situation. Rather, Sartre believes those who "see" the equality of the human situation adequately will, being men, respond to human problems in a more responsible and sympathetic way. Possessing a vision of how things are, men will in fact (Sartre seems to argue) want to de-emphasize the inequalities and choose for all men. Given this argument, however, a historian must conclude that, since most of us do not so act, we must lack the true "picture" of the human condition of which Sartre so movingly writes. Although Sartre insists his philosophy rejects "quietism," the difficult question is whether this follows from Sartre's own personality rather than from his philosophical principles.

In any event, equality as an ideal can be defended in the following way. Agreed, there are many inequalities. Agreed, also, that some inequalities may be justified as goods. However, the doctrine that equality is a value emphasizes the view that, though men differ in important ways, their differences are (and ought to be) less important than their likenesses in those fundamental human ways in which they are equally vulnerable to certain threats. Men must be reminded of their basic likenesses again and again. Why? Because they tend to lose sight of the way in which, in the long run, all social and economic differences are as nothing in significance compared to their common and inevitable exposure to death, possible disaster, and absurdity. Moreover, men ought so to be reminded. The reason is that truth is a value, and the truth of the human condition is such that inequalities come to appear conventional and unimportant in light of the basic equality of all men.

Contextual Considerations

Equality as an indeal functions to persuade men to adopt a specific vision of the social scene—to minimize the many obvious differences among men and to maximize men's significant similarities, especially their basic human needs and their tragic human vulnerabilities. How to translate the ideal into practical consequences has divided man against man, class against class, perhaps historical epoch against historical epoch. Abstractly, equality may not necessarily constitute an unquestionable value. Claims of equality normally occur in concrete contexts, and thus discussion of equality by philosophers often seems less moving and important than examples of the struggle for equality contained in literature or, perhaps, in one's daily newspaper. Judgments about the value of equality also require a context, as do actual demands for just treatment require a functioning legal system.

Only in a world in which unequals of some type exist does equality provide an ideal capable of moving men to action. It is not inequality as such which stirs moral protest but inequalities which, in a given time and place, strike us as vicious or unfair or arbitrary. Imagine a society to exist in which a citizen is not only denied admission to college because his IQ is too low but is, on the same ground, denied use of the public medical facilities. There is a *justifiable* inequality between men in a society which establishes public criteria as a necessary avenue to advanced education. On the other hand, a society in which large numbers of sick persons are denied medical attention because of intelligence, race, or economic status perpetuates *unjustifiable* inequalities. Only if medical supplies are insufficient, or there are too few trained physicians, or some unusual calamity has swamped the existing facilities, will it seem defensible to decide that this as opposed to that person shall receive care. Even in the case of a calamity which overwhelms the facilities, if the physicians treat only white persons to the neglect of all persons of other races, men will want to say that an unjustified inequality has been introduced.

To be in a position to decide whether a specific existing inequality can be justified means to know the details of the context in which it occurs. Equal treatment even of suffering persons is not always a possibility, even if in ideal circumstances it would be thought a value. If a train wreck occurs in which numerous persons are injured, a doctor would not rightly be subject to criticism for giving more (unequal) attention to some persons than to others so long as, if asked to justify this inequality of attention, he could produce convincing reasons. As justification for the treatment of women rather than men injured in the wreck, the doctor could not legitimately give as his reason that he likes women. Where there is not enough of a commodity or a service to go around, it is not always justifiable to give out equal shares. For example, it would be indefensible to give inadequate amounts of medicine to all sick persons if all may die as a result while some could be saved by giving more medicine to them and none to others.

The moral argument for equality requires that, if inequalities exist, they can be justified by the giving of reasons. Moreover, some statements can never function as reasons. This is at the heart of the contemporary quest of racial groups in the United States in so far as nonwhites insist that the reason for inequalities in educational, employment, housing, and health opportunities can never defensibly be exclusively a racial one. To describe features of the racial situation in this country as involving a moral crisis means to assert that, behind all the necessary technical legal and political "moves," social inequalities exist which immorally bar some racial groups from a full participation in the life of our society. On the other hand, it does not follow that in the case of positions for which clearly stated criteria are relevant persons should be assigned the positions because of the color of their skin. Thus, if it should be shown that too few negroes are practicing medicine, the solution would not be to allow untrained negroes to put out doctors' shingles but, rather, to make it possible for many more negroes to pass through approved medical schools. Recognizing areas in which morally unjustifiable inequalities exist is one matter. Finding the appropriate means to remedy these unjustifiable inequalities is another, and not an automatic, issue.

Contextually, what supports the claims of nonwhites to greater equality in the United States is a growing mass of statistical evidence which shows how, in area after area of national life, they are represented in indefensibly small numbers. To critics who say they agree but that more time is required for the amelioration of existing ills, the nonwhites can reply that such reasoning is often employed in order to escape the need of immediate decision and action to right oppressive inequalities. Nonwhites are accused of a moral failure to "understand" adequately the injustice of the existing racial situation. They are also accused of failing to mean what they sometimes say when, shown the existing inequalities, they call them unjust. When persons have waited a long time for the redress of obvious moral inequalities, they can reasonably accuse those who call for continued patience either of gross self-deception or of conscious moral indifference.

Even if there are some objective grounds for the exclusion of persons from equal participation in all ranges of a nation's life, the existing inequalities sustained by emphasizing those grounds may not be justifiable. Professor Bernard Williams has argued:

> Suppose that in a certain society great prestige is attached to membership of a warrior class, the duties of which require great physical strength. This class has in the past been recruited from certain wealthy families only; but egalitarian reformers achieve a change in the rules, by which warriors are recruited from all sections of the society, on the results of a suitable competition. The effect of this, however, is that the wealthy families still provide virtually all the warriors, because the rest of the populace is so undernourished by reason of poverty that their physical strength is inferior to that of the wealthy and well nourished. The reformers protest that equality of opportunity has not really been achieved; the wealthy reply that in fact it has, and that the poor now have the opportunity of becoming warriors—it is just bad luck that their characteristics are such that they do not pass the test. "We are not," they might say, "excluding anyone for being poor; we exclude people for being weak, and it is unfortunate that those who are poor are also weak."
>
> This answer would seem to most people feeble, and even cynical. This is for reasons similar to those discussed before in connexion with equality before the law; that the supposed equality of opportunity is quite empty—indeed, one may say that it does not really exist—unless it is made more effective than this. For one knows that it could be made more effective; one knows that there is a casual connexion between being poor and being undernourished, and between being undernourished and being physically weak. One supposes further that something could be done—subject to whatever economic conditions obtain in the imagined society—to alter the distribution of wealth. All this being so, the appeal by the wealthy to the "bad luck" of the poor must appear as disingenuous.[9]

In the discussion about equality as an ideal, there comes a point at which the moralist must argue that to "see" the inequalities in today's

---

[9] "The Idea of Equality," in Peter Laslett and W. G. Runciman, eds., *Philosophy, Politics and Society* (Second Series; Oxford: Blackwell, 1962), p. 126. Reprinted by permission of the author.

racial situation in the United States, a person must understand what morality is all about—otherwise he will fail to understand what is at stake. So, too, in all cases in which a moralist seeks to reform society in the name of greater equality among men. Whether and to what extent the moralist can persuade men to remedy existing inequalities is to some extent a function of his persistence and imagination, as well as of his political shrewdness. In any event, equality as an ideal takes on life in specific historical contexts when concerned persons mount a sustained political effort to remove inequalities which, in those contexts, have come to be seen by anyone with moral sense as affronts to human dignity and intelligence.

Thus, while equality is only one ideal among others, it is a crucial one in a world in which so many differences exist among men that too many persons tend to forget that they are often used to justify moral indifference and even viciousness. Social, political, educational, and other equalities are ever in need of reenforcement and reinterpretation by each new generation. Thus, the ideal of equality constantly erodes the foundations of every *status quo*.

Utopianism

Fervent believers in the possibility of a realizable human perfection have written some imaginative accounts of ideal societies. Not all utopian writers have identified perfection with complete equality. Consequently, a perceptive critic can legitimately question the inclusion of the theme "Utopianism" in a chapter devoted to the notion of equality. The perfect community developed in Plato's *Republic* made justice, rather than equality, the central human value. Indeed, Plato's *Republic* involved a class inequality, since at least three distinct classes would function harmoniously under a philosopher-king to produce a just society. Nonetheless, at least one prominent thinker has tended to identify Utopia (whose literal meaning is "nowhere") with widespread human equality. Sir Thomas More (1478–1535) lived during a period when the living conditions were for most persons just short of unbearable. Large numbers of persons remained hopelessly unemployed, religious intolerance was rampant, the existing criminal code contained oppressive and excessively cruel elements, and democratic notions of equality received little respect. In his famous *Utopia*—a major portion of which contained a detailed model of an imagined perfect society—More managed to suggest, against the existing situation in the England and Europe of his day, that a society based on reason and equality might prevail. More's social idealism, later joined with an unexamined faith in historical progress, permitted men to criticize the existing social order and, in some cases, to plant the seeds for later reforms. Indeed, in the late eighteenth and early nineteenth centuries, various groups of disillusioned persons banded together in experimental communities in a quest after a more reasonable pattern of social existence.

More's picture of a perfect society—presented by him as existing in fact in a faraway location—belongs to the socialist-communist versions of utopian societies. Men are to be made as equal as possible by virtue of training and the distribution of social duties. Wealth is to be as fairly divided as possible. The life of the mind as well as the pursuit of relatively simply pleasures are to hold a higher value than material prosperity. Leisure and educational opportunities are to be available to all. Indeed, More's humanistic faith leads him to indicate that all citizens in Utopia will be philosophically inclined, anxious to take part in intellectual discussions without academic prodding. There is to be equality of religious belief. However, there is one modification: namely, atheism is not to be permitted. Doctrines of a religious kind are to be subordinated to the application of their moral principles to the daily tasks of living morally. Certain basic kinds of labor, especially agricultural work, are to be done by all persons during fixed periods of their lives. A total specialization of labor is to be avoided as much as possible. Apparently, More feared the inequalities which might result from too rigid a specialization of work.

In Book II of *Utopia* (Book I is, in its part, a philosophical discussion of theories of governing and of criminal punishment) More sketches rather fully the geographical and administrative divisions of his perfect society. The model is a geometric one, with cities limited in size and magistrates chosen annually to govern municipal affairs. From the body of each city's magistrates three representatives are sent each year to meet as an executive body in a capital city. Hours of daily labor are limited—astoundingly for More's period—to six hours a day. The remainder of a person's time is spent in reading and lectures, all of which are voluntary. A system of scientific farming as well as a reformist theory of criminal punishment operates in Utopia.

The Utopians' disdain of material possessions is evidenced in their attitude toward gold, a symbol of wealth. Gold is used for the making of chamber-pots in Utopia, and when visiting dignitaries from other countries come wearing rich robes and ornaments, the Utopians view them with amusement. The basic values of food, health, exercise, and learning far outweigh the values of material goods. There are no extremes of wealth, and most physical labor is done on a rotational basis save for certain hard work done by criminals assigned to act as servants. Sexual codes are relatively strict, since in Utopia premarital sexual experiences bring harsh punishments. However, some divorces can be granted by the senate. The point is mentioned here to indicate that equality in More's Utopia did not include sexual permissiveness. But the Utopians' attitude toward sexuality was healthy, since More liked their practice by which a man, before marriage, was permitted to see his future bride in a naked state.

More's stress on equality in his *Utopia* is interesting in that other imaginative writers have not made equality the central value. In the present century some writers, known as anti-Utopians, have lost More's optimistic sense of progress toward a reasonable development of ever greater social rationality and equality. More represents a view in which equality is seen as one of the highest values. In contrast, the late George Orwell—critic of totalitarian tendencies of this century—looked towards a future in which human equality would probably entail an extensive totalitarian coercion in the name of obedience and absolute uniformity. For More, equality would emerge as a voluntary choice by rational men, holding before their eyes the model of Utopia. Thus the value which led More to criticize the irrational inequalities in his age can, in another age and for a different thinker, raise fears of a terrifying kind of imposed equality or uniformity which is not voluntary.

The point is that utopian writers who have emphasized equality are worth study and consideration, especially in a sometimes cynical age. Their passionate concern to stress the similarities among men, rather than their differences, needs perennially to be understood if the theme of equality is not to lose its driving power.

Conclusion

To argue on behalf of equality as a value need not require that a person argue for complete social equality. Justice viewed as equality seems to mean that individuals will be treated equally by the law. It need not mean that all individuals are alike in worth and status. On the other hand, some philosophers have meant to emphasize the value of equality as an ideal, seeking to encourage men to look upon existing social differences among men as unimportant in the light of some permanent similarities among them.

It is possible that a full understanding of the stress on equality as a value requires a distinction between a religious and a nonreligious outlook. Religiously, perhaps it could be argued that equality is so high a value that it ought consistently to be purchased at the price of what, in nonreligious eyes, might appear as injustices. Some utopian literature has attempted to picture social equality as an intrinsic good, when in fact more realistic thinkers can always look upon a utopian equality as an evil.

To say that men are created equal seems to mean that, though in fact they are very unequal, as moral beings they have more in common than the usual existing social distinctions make evident. The problem of social philosophers concerns how to relate equality as a value to other enduring values with which, at times, it may be in conflict.

Some Questions and Problems

1. Can you think of some situations in which equality is not a major value? List them.
2. Is the notion of human equality compatible with exceptions to existing rules? If so, on what grounds?

3. Discuss the assertion that anyone who claims all men are created equal is talking foolishly, since it is obvious many men possess talents which are lacked by others.

4. Is the philosophy of the Declaration of Independence fully compatible with the political philosophy which supports the U.S. Constitution? Show how the documents may conflict with one another.

5. What is meant by the phrase "equality before the law"?

6. What kinds of considerations should apply to the unequal treatment of men? On the other hand, what criteria should not justify unequal treatment of men? Should race, sex, or religion ever be grounds for treating persons unequally? Why or why not?

7. How alike and unalike are the notions of justice and equality? In what ways may the two conflict?

8. Is equality a reasonable economic ideal in a contemporary society? If not, to what extent does equality have value for determining how to distribute economic goods?

9. How might contemporary liberals and conservatives disagree on the value of equality? Try to be specific.

10. Discuss or debate the assertion that men should be made as much alike as possible.

Some Suggested Readings

Allen, C. K. *Democracy and the Individual.* London: Oxford University Press, 1943.

Becker, C. *The Declaration of Independence.* New York: Knopf, 1945.

Berlin, I. "Equality as an Ideal," *Justice and Social Policy,* ed. F. A. Olafson. Englewood Cliffs, N.J.: Prentice-Hall, 1961.

Dahrendorf, R. "On the Origins of Social Inequality," *Philosophy, Politics and Society,* Second Series, eds. P. Laslett and W. G. Runciman. Oxford: Blackwell, 1962.

Hobhouse, L. T. *The Elements of Social Justice.* London: Allen & Unwin, 1922.

Kateb, G. *Utopia and Its Enemies.* Glencoe, Ill.: Free Press, 1963.

Lindsay, A. D. *The Essentials of Democracy,* 2d ed. London: Oxford University Press, 1935.

――――. *The Modern Democratic State.* London: Oxford University Press, 1943.

Mannheim, K. *Freedom, Power and Democratic Planning.* Oxford University Press, 1950.

Margolis, J. "That All Men Are Created Equal," *Journal of Philosophy,* Vol. LII, No. 3, 1955.

More, T., *Utopia* in *Three Renaissance Classics,* ed. B. A. Milligan. New York: Scribner, 1953.

Williams, B. "The Idea of Equality," *Philosophy, Politics and Society,* Second Series, eds. P. Laslett and W. G. Runciman. Oxford: Blackwell, 1962.

Wollheim, R. "Equality and Equal Rights," *Justice and Social Policy,* ed. F. A. Olafson. Englewood Cliffs, N.J.: Prentice-Hall, 1961.

PART III

Contemporary Issues and Movements

CHAPTER TWELVE

Historicism

Contemporary thinkers have learned to adopt a specifically historical attitude toward men and events. They are conscious of the historical dimensions of events much in the way a seasoned fisherman knows the whereabouts of reefs and coral formations beneath the immediately visible waves. Over enormous stretches of historical time men possessed only a most rudimentary, fragmented, and localized "picture" of their historical origins and development. The capacity to see events in their historical contexts was, itself, an historical achievement—an experience known only to a very few gifted thinkers before the nineteenth century, when historical knowledge became more readily accessible to an ever-widening audience of literate persons.

Yet, the growth in historical knowledge—the very mass of details about many phases of the past which scholars continued to unearth—produced a cluster of questions which, for our purposes, may be re-referred to as "the problem of history." Among these questions, one assumed central importance for many thinkers. This was the supposedly meaningful concern whether any clearly discernible purpose or pattern may be detected amid the welter of particular historical happenings. However different scholars attempted to resolve this quandary—whether claiming to find some fundamental pattern or, as sceptics, denying that such a pattern exists—their actual disagreements seemed to emphasize the basic meaningfulness of the question about purpose. Apparently, the concern about historical purpose reflected a deeply rooted anxiety which the normal methods used in gathering historical knowledge were unable fully to resolve. Thus, the question whether human history manifests a basic purpose seemed, itself, to be other than an historical question, though it purported to be about history. What kind of question or concern, then, was it? About this latter question also philosophers are not agreed.

The nineteenth century witnessed a quiet revolution in historical knowledge and techniques which has probably influenced contemporary intellectual life at least as significantly as, say, Darwin's proposal of an evolutionary hypothesis and Einstein's contributions of relativity theories in physics. The present practical world of ordinary men seemed now to constitute a small "moving edge" in an enormously extended flow of historical time whose origins reached, ever beyond the reach of the latest researches, into the dim recesses of a possibly limitless past. Cultural historians, who borrowed from the specialized investigations of a growing horde of patiently laboring historians, began to trace the major outlines of the appearance and diminution of political states and peoples. Even the Greek civilization so dear to the humanists of the Renaissance has been viewed as itself a relatively late stage in the history of human thought and institutions. Increasingly, thoughtful scholars worried whether in the ebb and flow of historical circumstances there were not discernible signs that the highest achievements of civilization had ever foundered on the shoals of political and social strife. The greater the knowledge gained about the large-scale picture of historical development, the more some reflective historians and philosophers wondered whether the historical process is not, in some sense, an ultimate and undesirable fact of basic importance. As historians filled in the details of the last four thousand years in human historical experience, they also made men aware of the larger background to the rich, teeming activities of their own contemporaneous times.

Some Thinkers on History

A towering figure in the early development of philosophizing about history was G. W. F. Hegel (1770–1831), who believed he had discovered the logic in terms of which the discrete happenings in the historical order occurred as the necessary manifestations of an Absolute Mind ever in the process of a fuller realization of its inherent nature. Hegel was at least clear that knowledge of the *ultimate* pattern in historical occurrences could not be learned empirically by a study of *this* or *that* specific historical period. Philosophical knowledge of history had to be a *priori*—that is, the view that history is rational "at its core" had to function as a premise of inquiry rather than as a conclusion reached by investigation of historical facts. Thus, Hegel admitted the possibility of kinds of historical knowledge in which questions about the *ultimate* purposes of historical happenings would not arise. Indeed, Hegel implied that our ordinary empirical historical investigations failed to unearth any ultimate rationality in the historical order, for he wrote in his *Introduction to Philosophy of History* rather movingly and gloomily of the conflicts between passionate interests:

> When we contemplate this display of passions and the consequences of their violence, the unreason which is associated not only with them, but even—rather we might say *especially*—with *good* designs and righteous aims; when we see arising therefrom the evil, the vice, the ruin that has befallen the most flourishing kingdoms which the mind of man ever created, we can hardly avoid being filled with sorrow at this universal taint of corruption.[1]

Therefore, the view that this spectacle of ruined hopes is witness to some profound rational purpose must be a thought with which the philosopher approaches his speculations about history rather than an observable property of empirical events themselves. The philosopher is one who asks after some principle for which the otherwise fortuitous historical occurrences have happened—for whom, as a philosopher, "a question necessarily arises" about the "final purpose" for which individuals and states perish in conflict in the historical arena. Hegel assumed that the human mind must portray contingent events as linked by an inner necessity operating by its own logic (much as, later, Sigmund Freud assumed a "logic" of unconscious motivation beneath the more readily observable aspects of human action). For Hegel, history was the inescapable reality in terms of which rationality comes to concrete fulfillment, not of individual men's aims but of its

[1] R. S. Hartman, trans. *Reason in History* (Indianapolis: Liberal Arts, 1953), p. 26

own purposings. It is as if Hegel, much like a practicing analyst, sought to place Reason or Absolute Mind on a psychoanalytic couch in order to understand the actual workings of that mind in historical events.

Other famous nineteenth-century scholars based their programs on claims to understand the logic of historical events or to have discovered the laws of human progress in relation to historical events. August Comte (1798–1857), the French founder of positivism, argued for the view that intellectual development historically reflected a law of three stages. Modern science, the final stage, had replaced earlier theological and metaphysical explanations of phenomena by a positivistic one in which all meaningful questions had to do with the "how" rather than the "why" of things. Comte believed that a general science of sociology would supplement earlier kinds of science as the means by which to formulate the most pervasive characteristics of social existence. Comte hoped to raise the level of knowledge about society to the equivalent status with generalized knowledge in the natural sciences.

Probably the historical theories of Karl Marx (1818–1883) are most familiar to the general public of the world because so many revolutionaries, claiming to act in accordance with them, directed attention to features of modern industrial existence in need of reform and reinterpretation. This was clearly so in the nineteenth century and, in impoverished areas of the world freshly experiencing the impact of industrialization, also in the twentieth. Marx argued that a study of historical periods reveals a necessary succession of events resulting from incessant warfare between economic classes and culminating in the triumph of a scientific world view and a resolution of economic class conflicts by a socialization of the means of production—a resolution which Marx took as inevitable. Unlike Hegel, who viewed concrete social and political events as partial reflections in space and time of a fundamental "dialectic" of absolute mind, Marx "saw" the hard realities of particular economic and political stresses as the heart of the historical process itself. For Hegel's idealism, Marx substituted a thoroughly materialist conception of history such that those influenced by his views "deny the efficacy of speculative thinking and assert the all-sufficiency of scientific thinking in which theory and practice are conjoined." [2] As a passionate revolutionist calling for concerted action by politically organized men to treat problems of modern society by reliance on scientific observation and experiment, Marx viewed speculative philosophy with hostilely suspicious eyes, as a means by which to avoid concrete plans of action aimed at changing the world rather than "understanding" it. Unlike empirical traditions in politics and reform, Marxism has come to include a world view as a necessary adjunct of social action. Followers of Marx were asked not only to *act* for certain reformist ends but also to share a "scientific" ideology. As a result, some critics have viewed the world view aspect of Marxism as more like older theologies than like scientific politics. The ideological side of Marxism will receive fuller consideration in Chapter 14. Here, only the fact that Marx and his more influential followers held to a specific theory about the nature of the historical process comes into consideration. The crucial point is that, on Marx's theories, all institutions and systems of belief are seen as sharing thoroughly human origins and all beliefs are therefore subject to explanations which are scientific rather than religious, theological, or metaphysical. Social realities are reducible to arrangements of economic forces, and different historical periods are marked by important differences in the organization of the prevailing class structure. Men's ideas are casually linked (in subtle ways) to their class origin, such that a truly scientific approach to human problems can in principle introduce a genuine objectivity into our understanding of the human social world. As Professor Acton has argued, "The theory of Historical Materialism is held to unmask the deception, but it can only claim to do so on the basis of the positivist theory of science." [3]

Even established religious and philosophical views came, increasingly, to be seen as rooted in specific historical situations rather than as positions deserving consideration as expressions of more than cultural truths. The doctrine that all ideas are situated in historical epochs, that this value and truth are not eternal but relative to specific historical contexts, has been named "historicism." Ideas and values

---

[2] H. B. Acton, *The Illusion of the Epoch* (London: Cohen, 1955), p. 107.
[3] *Ibid.,* p. 109.

themselves have histories, in other words, and the historicist tends to argue that their having a history is the most significant fact about ideas, more so even than the logical consideration most philosophers want to emphasize. On this approach, to explain an idea or institution means to trace it back to its historical and social origins, and there's the end of the matter. Who introduced the idea, in terms of what interests it got believed, and the uses to which the idea was put, often become for the historicist more fundamental questions than those about its logical status. On the whole, the emphasis on historical knowledge and development tended to stress the sociological rather than the psychological, the group aspect rather than the individual elements in human existence. Thus, for Hegel the state conceived as an organic cultural entity became the basic means by which historical progress occurs. For Marx, the economic class rather than the empirically isolable individual became the crucial focus if one was to understand economic, social, and political life. For historicists, each idea and institution had to be placed in a broader historical context if its genuine significance was to appear.

In a general way, historicism is a somewhat imprecise notion which can mean one or more of the following propositions:

- that the most ultimate category of reality is the historical.
- that ideas and values are always (in some sense) rooted in a specific historical context.
- that historical events are necessarily what they are.
- that preoccupation with the nature of historical processes must replace classical metaphysics as the subject matter of philosophy.
- that reality is dynamic rather than static.
- that all human values are relative to the demands on action necessitated in concrete historical epochs.
- that no trans-historical realities exist.

The important point to remember is that, for all their differences, many nineteenth-century thinkers (like Comte, Marx and Hegel) shared a common interest in "making sense" out of the perpetual flux of historical events. They were influenced by a keen intellectual sense of the importance of history.

Social Evolutionism

Coupled with the belief in inevitable progress, the historicist position developed, in some quarters, into what is now known as the doctrine of social evolutionism. The biological theory of evolution served as the basis for an analogical argument to the effect that societies evolve according to lawlike principles as adaptations to something like a "center-line" of historical necessities. This doctrine found application in a number of sociological and historical investigations and, although its followers probably would have denied this fact, probably reflected the nonscientific views of earlier periods that contingent historical events, and epochs, follow some kind of logic of their own. Societies individually posess something like organic lives of their own, a total response to a varied set of circumstances which, if they survive, indicate that the result stands as a mark of a higher stage of social organization and perfection.

The difficulties with social evolutionism are quite readily recognizable. *First,* there is no clear way in which to judge the relative perfections of different societies, some of which are now nonexistent. Progress must always be "measured" according to some standards, and since there are no absolutes to which all intelligent scholars seem willing to agree, it does not seem possible to "verify" (in terms of evidence that is universally acceptable) a judgment to the effect that, say, American civilization necessarily represents progress over all others simply because it has occurred later in chronological time. *Second,* the sheer standard of a society's success at surviving does not logically entail this succes as a higher value, since there is the notoriously difficult problem of how to move from statements of fact to statements of value. *Third,* different scholars applied the doctrine of social Darwinism in incompatible ways. Conservatives looked upon the existing political scene and, disliking criticisms of the *status quo,* tried to argue that the existing institutions had met the test of survival—therefore were preferable to others which had failed. On the other hand, reformers and revolutionaries unhappy with established conditions looked to the future, insisting that present institutions would not be able to withstand the *future* demands of social adaptation.

One brilliant American writer, Henry Adams (1838–1919), who sought an education which would reveal whatever fundamental unities might exist, ironically illustrated the ethical problem associated with an unexamined social evolutionism. In his famous *The Education of Henry Adams,* privately printed in 1906, Adams showed the ethical perplexity of a firm believer in social evolution who abhorred the policies of President Grant by writing:

> Adams did not feel Grant as a hostile force; like Badeau he saw only an uncertain one. When in action he was superb and safe to follow; only when torpid he was dangerous. To deal with him one must stand near, like Rawlins, and practice more or less sympathetic habits. Simple-minded beyond the experience of Wall Street or State Street, he resorted, like most men of the same intellectual calibre, to commonplaces when at a loss for expression: "Let us have peace!" or, "The best way to treat a bad law is to execute it"; or a score of such reversible sentences generally to be gauged by their sententiousness; but sometimes he made one doubt his good faith; as when he seriously remarked to a particularly bright young woman that Venice would be a fine city if it were drained. In Mark Twain, this suggestion would have taken rank among his best witticisms; in Grant it was a measure of simplicity not singular. Robert E. Lee betrayed the same intellectual commonplace, in a Virginia form, not to the same degree, but quite distinctly enough for one who knew the American. What worried Adams was not the commonplace; it was, as usual, his own education. Grant fretted and irritated him, like the *Terebratula,* as a defiance of first principles. He had no right to exist. He should have been extinct for ages. The idea that, as society grew older, it grew one-sided, upset evolution, and made of education a fraud. That, two thousand years after Alexander the Great and Julius Caesar, a man like Grant should be called—and should actually and truly be—the highest product of the most advanced evolution, made evolution ludicrous. One must be as commonplace as Grant's own commonplace to maintain such an absurdity. The progress of evolution from President Washington to President Grant, was alone evidence enough to upset Darwin.[4]

[4] New York: Modern Library, pp. 256–57.

Professor Karl Popper has criticized Marx's version of historical determinism on peculiarly ethical grounds. Claiming that Marx is a "futurist" rather than an historicist, since Marx as a revolutionary predicted a necessary future state of affairs, Popper indicated that the historical determinism seemed incompatible with Marx's humane and passionate ethical concerns about the plight of modern laboring men and women. That is, Popper "sees" that Marx seems passionately convinced that the capitalist order is morally condemnable. Yet, if that capitalist order is itself the inevitable product of operative historical forces, Marx cannot consistently condemn capitalism. Nor can he consistently advocate the ethical superiority of either socialism or communism—only predict what will inevitably, on his view, occur in the future.

Professor Popper argues that Marx's writings at least imply an ethical theory. Marx does not simply condemn the existing social-economic order because it has outlived its historical necessity (which would follow from a purely nonevaluative historical determinism). He condemns the system because of what it does to human beings, thus finds it morally wanting. Moreover, a good case can be made that—regardless of the theories he advanced—Marx loved freedom and addressed men as responsible persons judgeable in light of how they react to existing conditions. Notoriously, however, if men's actions are simply reflections of inevitable social situations, they cannot be held morally responsible for their actions and beliefs. Professor Popper therefore concludes that Marx's ethical condemnation of lamentable economic conditions is not fully compatible with his later, and more thoroughly developed, theoretical writings on historical determinism.

How would Marx perhaps have responded to the kind of criticism presented by Professor Popper? The latter has attempted to suggest a possible reply. Popper has stated that Marx would have insisted that, as a scientist, a person would recognize the inevitability of the future (as described in this case by Marx) and, then, *decide* to go along with it. This would be a scientific and not a moral decision. This reply would constitute what Popper terms "historicist moral theory." But it would be inadequate. First, it would presuppose a degree of historical prophecy which cannot be substantiated in purely scientific terms. And, second, such a reply, if made, would still imply for a future-not-yet-realized the moral position that might makes right. And this position seems incompatible with that aspect of Marx's writing which, in the face of a powerfully established capitalist order, sought to change the *status quo* and called for revolution. As a consequence, Popper prefers to emphasize the lasting values of Marx's emphasis on freedom and human equality, values which continue very much alive in a contemporary world to which the rigid determinism of Marx's historical materialism is now inadequate. In a crucial paragraph, Popper argues against Marx's moral futurism in the following manner:

> In previous chapters I have mentioned *moral positivism* (especially that of Hegel), the theory that there is no moral standard but the one which exists; that what is, is reasonable and good; and therefore, that *might is right*. The practical aspect of this theory is this. A moral criticism of the existing state of affairs is impossible, since this state itself determines the moral standard of things. Now the historicist moral theory we are considering is nothing but another form of moral positivism. For it holds that coming *might is right*. The future is here substituted for the present—that is all. And the practical aspect of the theory is this. A moral criticism of the coming state of affairs is impossible, since this state determines the moral standard of things. The difference between "the present" and "the future" is here, of course, only a matter of degree. One can say that the future starts tomorrow, or in 500 years, or in 100. *In their theoretical structure there is no difference between moral conservatism, moral modernism, and moral futurism.* Nor is there much to choose between them in regard to moral sentiments. If the moral futurist criticizes the cowardice of the moral conservative who takes sides with the powers that be, then the moral conservative can return the charge; he can say that the moral futurist is a coward since he takes sides with the powers that will be, with the rulers of tomorrow.[5]

Popper's critique of Marx's brand of historicist moral theory rests on the commonsense belief that the plea to adopt the morality of the future, simply because that morality is bound to win out, would not be viewed as a genuinely moral plea. A person might on moral

[5] Karl Popper, *The Open Society and Its Enemies,* Vol. II (London: Routledge, 1945), pp. 206–207.

grounds choose to resist even that which he thinks is inevitable. On the other hand, if the plea is addressed simply to the self-interest of a group now out of power, it may make sense, though remain subject to moral condemnation. It is always the case, perhaps, that those who are *out* of power stand to gain advantages if they achieve power by "throwing the other rascals out," as it were. Nonetheless the total social result might be no improvement whatever, indeed might involve deterioration in the welfare of large numbers of persons. Moreover, groups which act only to seize power at whatever cost can, in time, be studied and their anticipated actions predicted by those who wish to retain power. Thus, there is no reason to suppose that their aims cannot be diverted by wise and prudent resistance from other political quarters.

The Threat of Nihilism

The sometimes unexamined respect for historical knowledge so prevalent in nineteenth-century intellectual circles, as well as the emphasis on the need of historical modes of explanation, encountered some serious questioning and criticism. As early as 1874, a German philosopher, not famous for a faith in classical metaphysics, scrutinized some consequences of the historicist position. In his brilliant polemical essay *The Use and Abuse of History,* Friedrich Nietzsche argued that Europeans could have too much of a good thing—that too much historical learning may, in certain circumstances, function as a sign of cultural sickness. For Nietzsche, since life entails decision and action, historical studies can produce a culture in which the necessary conditions of healthy action are ended by a constant preoccupation with the past. Nietzsche recognized a relation between historical knowledge and the nihilistic belief, or "feeling," that there is nothing new under the sun. To place all value in historical contexts means to suggest that one's own values in the present need not be eternal, thus to dampen the dedication of the young to the pursuit of these values. If all the striving of past men for meaning in existence possessed only historical significance, then the ideals and conflicts of the present age are only subject matter for the footnotes in future historians' accounts of our present quests for social and political and religious meaning in life. Psychologically, men here face a danger. The danger is that men will place too much value on the intellect, forgetting that in a healthy life there is need to view goals and ideas as if they are more than transitory historical phenomena. The living generations may experience a self-defeating tedium. Men may substitute a disinterested historical mode of knowing for immediate action and even "see" themselves as actors in a drama whose meaningfulness is in doubt. Action is oriented on future expectations, but to treat such expectations as already past, as it were, means to cast a pall over the decisions of men, in what should be a "living" present. According to Nietzsche, a necessary requirement of happiness in action is "the power of forgetting, or, in more learned phrase, the capacity of feeling 'unhistorically' throughout its duration."

Too much history can sap the energies needed by men and cultures for the healthy action required by the inescapable tasks needed to be accomplished. As a philosopher wanting to make health central to human existence, Nietzsche warned that historical knowledge may help to make men diseased. In his essay *The Use and Abuse of History,* Nietzsche wrote movingly:

> Every one has noticed that a man's historical knowledge and range of feeling may be very limited, his horizon as narrow as that of an Alpine valley, his judgments incorrect and his experience falsely supposed original, and yet in spite of all the incorrectness and falsity he may stand forth in unconquerable health and vigor, to the joy of all who see him; whereas another man with far more judgment and learning will fail in comparison, because the lines of his horizon are continually changing and shifting, and he cannot shake himself free from the delicate network of his truth and righteousness for a downright act of will or desire.[6]

If knowledge should be judged in terms of its value for furthering the life-giving human functions, then historical knowledge must serve as a means, never as an end. Therefore, witnessing the widespread triumph of the historical point of view in Europe, Nietzsche warned

[6] A. Collins, trans. (Indianapolis: Liberal Arts, 1949), p. 16.

that "Historical culture is really a kind of inherited grayness, and those who have borne its mark from childhood must believe instinctively in *the old age of mankind*." [7]

To show a continual awareness of man's historical condition means to see man as perpetually in transition—as caught between a past and a not yet realized future which, when it shall have been achieved, will also prove to have been itself a transition. Nietzsche was keenly aware that men who act require a horizon of values—that their happiness wants "deep, profound eternity." By historicizing every event, value, and institution, one tends to evade the problem of a hierarchy of valuations. One man's evaluations become as important as any other man's in the peculiar sense that no values are ultimately seen as lasting because they are all historically conditioned. Profoundly pessimistic persons sometimes become wearied of effort when they contemplate the flux of historical happenings, failing to understand that they must, by their own courage and willing, assert the values to be sought and cherished. Thus, historical modes of knowing raise rather than solve the problem of valuing—much as a well-travelled man accustomed to a diverse range of cultural values as a traveller must in some sense render his own judgment if he asks: "What should I most value?" To argue that values are relative to historical and cultural occasions means, often, to raise the philosophical question about values or, if one is not himself deeply rooted in an existing value tradition, to succumb to the attractions of nihilism—the view that no values are ultimate and that "nothingness" is the basic category of existence, hovering as a threatening reality in the background of every human achievement. Persons who find themselves living in times of radical social change and upheaval, struggling to bring sense to life and to escape from outmoded interpretations and often overcome by a deep and lonely sense of isolation and hopefulness, may find that an excess of historical knowledge accentuates rather than resolves their rather agonized efforts to find a meaningful set of values in life. The great Russian novelist, Ivan Turgenev, portrays aspects of nihilism (as a Russian phenomenon of the pre-Communist period) in his novel *Fathers and Children*. In one place in the novel Arkady explains the

[7] *Ibid.*, p. 55.

beliefs of his friend Bazarov to the former's aristocratic uncle, named Pavel.

"What is Bazarov?" Arkady smiled. "Would you like me to tell you, uncle, what he really is?"

"Please do, nephew."

"He is a nihilist!"

"What?" asked Nikolai Petrovich, while Pavel Petrovich lifted his knife in the air with a small piece of butter on the tip and remained motionless.

"He is a nihilist," repeated Arkady.

"A nihilist," said Nikolai Petrovich. "That comes from the Latin *nihil, nothing,* as far as I can judge; the word must mean a man who . . . who recognizes nothing."

"Say—who respects nothing," interposed Pavel Petrovich and lowered his knife with the butter on it.

"Who regards everything from the critical point of view," said Arkady.

"Isn't that exactly the same thing?" asked Pavel Petrovich.

"No, it's not the same thing. A nihilist is a person who does not bow down to any authority, who does not accept any principle on faith, however much that principle may be revered."

"Well, and is that good?" asked Pavel Petrovich.

"That depends, uncle dear. For some it is good, for others very bad."

"Indeed. Well, I see that's not in our line. We old-fashioned people think that without principles, taken as you say on faith, one can't take a step or even breathe. *Vous avez changé tout cela;* may God grant you health and a general's rank, and we shall be content to look on and admire your . . . what was the name?"

"Nihilists," said Arkady, pronouncing very distinctly.

"Yes, there used to be Hegelists and now there are nihilists. We shall see how you will manage to exist in the empty airless void; and now ring, please, brother Nikolai, it's time for me to drink my cocoa." [8]

Himself a troubled thinker, said by many critics to have written sometimes in a way to encourage pessimism and nihilism, Nietzsche possessed a fine psychological sense of human despair in the face of collapsing political and religious standards. He realized that a mean-

[8] Ivan Turgenev, *Fathers and Children* (New York: Rinehart, 1948), pp. 24–25.

ingful human existence requires a balancing of action by contemplation and that a culture in which the latter predominated would lose its life-furthering tendencies. Thus, he viewed his contemporary European culture as too deeply marked by the critical scientific spirit —a Socratic culture which too extensively subordinated willing and acting to demands of intellectual analysis.

To see man as an *historical* animal, born in a specific period and in some sense limited by its possibilities, means to raise the question whether any more enduring nature is part and parcel of the human situation. Nietzsche believed that men had to create a new religion of health, based on a myth of the eternal recurrence of all things— and then hereby to face the fact that all valuations must come from man himself. A whole new set of values would be needed, Nietzsche thought, if men were to cease being the sick animals. Men must draw a horizon of new values around themselves if they are to act spontaneously and happily. This predicament so crucial to modern man's efforts at self-understanding has been clearly stated by Professor Emil L. Fackenheim, who writes:

> History is a predicament for man who must live in it. In order to act in history he must seek to rise above it. He needs perspectives in terms of which to understand his situation, and timeless truths and values in terms of which to act in it. Yet the perspectives which he finds often merely reflect his age; and what he accepts as timelessly true and valid is apt to be merely the opinion which is in fashion. Thus while man must always try to rise above his historical situation he succeeds at best only precariously.[9]

To many men, living in crisis situations marked by war and revolution, the historical facts suggest that something almost like fate has produced the conditions which seem to dominate their lives, restricting their possibilities of action and confronting them with very restricted ranges of choice. In periods of widespread upheaval, affecting the lives of many millions, a deeply pessimistic mood may prevail because men can see no immediate or promising way out of their terrible circumstances. History then is viewed as something like an

[9] *Metaphysics and Historicity* (Milwaukee: Marquette University Press, 1961), p. 1. Used by permission of the publisher.

oppressive cage which confines men—and beyond the cage, as it were, is only darkness and uncertainty. Often, there seems to be no meaning to one's personal (and perhaps ghastly) involvement in events, which in their mightier outlines seem beyond the control of human intelligence. The obdurate facts of the historical situation are seen simply as *being there*—much as for a shipwrecked crew the reef is *there*—and men can choose to adopt certain attitudes toward the facts, attitudes which may barely affect the facts if they affect them at all. The order of historical happenings comes to appear as inevitable, like the steady pressures of the surf upon the slowly eroding shorelines. Men come to feel that their puny efforts to withstand historical tendencies will come to naught, that they will "go under" to inescapable and hostile (or, more weakly, indifferent) historical forces.

Suppose you had been present at a battlefield scene in 1942, say, and you heard an American soldier say, "Why was I drafted? How did I get into this foxhole, facing death?" Suppose you attempted to reply by explaining the ideals for which Americans were fighting the war, the consequences of allowing the enemy to win, the obligations men hold to protect certain freedoms—only to be told by the soldier: "That's not what I meant! I've heard all that 'guff' before. I mean why does it have to be me who's here?" The soldier would have been complaining about his personal involvement in the war—perhaps implying, say, that if he'd been born a few years later, he would have been ineligible for military services because of age. The lamentful statement "Why was I drafted?" was not a request for information or for explanation, nor was it a gesture to initiate a speech on the glories of Americans at war or about a citizen's responsibility. Rather, the statement was an expression meant to emphasize a sense of the *inescapability* of a certain involvement which functioned as a crisis in a human life. It was also an expression of a man's helplessness in the face of a threatening necessity, as war is to those who finally find themselves directly confronting an enemy capable of shooting back at them.

So, in a similar way, contemporary men often see the historical situation as a threat to personal life and personal meaningfulness.

They feel like "rats caught in a trap" not of their own making. Political affairs and theories then come to reflect the sense of the threatening nature of large-scale historical events, and some men even turn to political platforms to find personal meaning in their lives or to locate an authoritative world view and set of directions when, in the past, brave men acted without the need of such a world view or with the willingness to take free risks and the responsibility for such decisions. It is as if men want to get from political platforms what formerly they managed tolerably to live without or they obtained from religion—authoritative answers to questions like "What must I do?" and "What's the world like?" In periods of cultural chaos and collapse, many men want "quick" solutions to their philosophical and religious queries, a way out from their loneliness, bewilderment, and "lostness." They turn to political leaders who, now in possession of techniques of mass persuasion through propaganda and force, are sometimes only too willing to organize masses of men to serve their own purposes at whatever cost in truth and human suffering. In this way, the philosophical problem of meaning in life can assume political significance, especially if the attempt by individual men to make sense of the historical situation leads to frustration and, at worst, hopelessness and nihilism. Men may give up their freedom—"dreadful freedom," as one writer has called it—and find meaning by "going along with the crowd in power," donning a uniform and losing themselves in the anonymous mass. (Later chapters will analyze the rise of political ideologies in the present age as well as the totalitarian ["totalist"] tendencies in aspects of contemporary political life.) In this way, the fact that large numbers of men find old beliefs and values no longer operative in their personal lives can hold great psychological significance when the established political worthies begin to founder or fail to produce satisfactory results. There is a vast difference between doubt about particular political questions and political despair. The latter occurs only when whole areas of human life are left directionless, for as Professor Karl Mannheim has stated in *Freedom, Power and Democratic Planning,*

> People may occasionally be uncertain about what is right or wrong and this may be taken as a matter of course. But when mass anxieties

prevail, because the general ideological upheaval leaves no sound basis for common action, and when people do not know where they stand or what they ought to think about the most elementary problems of life, then again we may rightly speak of the spiritual disintegration of society.[10]

One response to the historical predicament of humanity is a nihilistic one—to give up the question after ultimate values and a general, intellectually satisfying account of the nature of social existence. Such a response opens the door to the activistic seekers of power who rush into the social vacuum and, often by force and deception, shape institutions to their own ends. The nihilist may become indifferent to the kind of political system he finds operative in his state, much like a man who shrugs his shoulders and says: "All political systems, parties, and platforms are the same." The genuine nihilist may cease asking value questions and thus become a passive, if unwilling, tool of those on the scene who are willing to give direction to affairs. As one writer has claimed, "The peak of nihilistic skepticism, and therefore of anxiety, is reached, not when a person answers the question of the meaning of life by hopelessly declaring that it has no meaning, but rather when in utter hopelessness he simply stops asking the question at all." [11]

This kind of hopelessness Nietzsche wanted to combat. Yet, he could admit the facts of the loss of faith and cultural meaning of contemporary Europeans ("God is dead!" Zarathustra hears from one of his acquaintances) and still believe, heroically, that men could hide the awareness of ultimate meaninglessness by creating a whole new set of values. Nietzsche did not spell out the detailed political aspects of this new class of breathing men, but he was sure they would reject an ethics of pity and sympathy. They would also create a new hierarchy of values, these "supermen"—subordinating the sympathetic virtues to the demands of rigor and aristocratic differentiation. They would reject democracy and socialism which, for Nietzsche, represented secularized remnants of a "sick" Judaeo-Christian concern for equality and the welfare even of troubled individuals. In

[10] London: Oxford University Press, 1950.

[11] Helmut Thielicke, *Nihilism—Its Origin and Nature,* trans. John W. Doberstein (London: Routledge, 1962), p. 138.

other words, Nietzsche did not believe that all men can stand the heroic awareness of ultimate cosmic "nothingness"—that only those so able should hold command over the others. His views seem to refine, then—if applied to practical political life—an ethical code for the rulers which differs from that for the masses, many of "those stunted men" whose poor health should not, for Nietzsche, be allowed to pollute political life.

Another response to the problem of man's (political and) historical predicament is that of positivists and Marxists who, viewing historical events as absolutely determined, think men can formulate "laws" of historical development. Thus, the Marxist view is that, given an "objective" set of circumstances, historical development must lead to a worldwide economic communism, that this outcome is necessary because the fabric of history is, so to speak, "cut that way." According to this view, man is free to comprehend true objective necessities and to adapt to them, but he is not free "in the long run" to avoid the final historical outcome. This need not mean that the economic and political decisions of men make no difference to the "short-run" historical consequences but, rather, that "in the long run" the outcome is already determined by the basic forces at work. Men can rashly fly in the face of objective historical necessities. They can even delay or postpone the final historical outcome, but they cannot defeat the ultimate triumph of those forces which represent the future. As William James said in his essay *The Dilemma of Determinism,*

> Suppose two men before a chessboard—the one a novice, the other an expert player of the game. The expert intends to beat. But he cannot foresee exactly what any one actual move of his adversary may be. He knows, however, all the *possible* moves of the latter; and he knows in advance how to meet each of them by a move of his own which leads in the direction of victory. And the victory infallibly arises, after no matter how devious a course, in the one predestined form of check-mate to the novice's kind.[12]

The irresistible movement of historical processes to a given end may, on a "weak" interpretation of the Marxist position, entail the possi-

[12] William James, *Essays in Pragmatism* (New York: Hafner, 1955), pp. 62–63.

bility of numerous changes in direction but *not* a capacity in men to alter the nature of the ultimate outcome.

The response to man's historical predicament in terms of an interpretation of history as reflecting lawlike necessities has also received a number of serious criticisms. Some scholars have argued that historical inquiry is more like art than like science and that no science of historical laws makes sense. Historical events are in some sense unique and nonrepeatable, thus not subject to rigorous explanation in terms of lawlike generalizations comparable to those, say, in physics. Historical knowledge is used much as is a man's experience gained from widespread travel, as a tentative guide to our expectations about possible happenings in specific circumstances. Others (like Karl Popper), whose second volume of *The Open Society and Its Enemies* is a criticism of the political theories of Hegel and Marx) argue that if all historical events are inevitably determined by preceding happenings, then no ethical justification of our individual decisions can be produced; for if events could not have happened otherwise, then our decisions had to assume the form they did and "freedom of choice or decision" is an illusion. If this is so, then a determinist like Marx could justify someone's joining his camp only by appealing to a desire to be on what he thinks is the winning side—surely not the usual model men take in their ethical decisions, since there is often a difference between what we take *to be* the case and what think *ought* to be the case. Thus, Popper has argued that the Marxist call to action in politics to change existing affairs is incompatible with the strictly determinist view that history is inevitably moving to a specific goal.

More significantly, if man's social ideals and theories are themselves historically determined, we are faced with a set of alternatives, no one of which may prove satisfying. (1) If different social theories are in conflict, then different historical tendencies, perhaps equally "true" or "ultimate," must be at work; and to say of any one of these theories that it will win, or lose out, is to utter a statement of our faith and hope rather than to make a scientific prediction. Men engaged in important political contrivances tend to believe what their interests influence them to *want* to believe. (2) On the other hand, if we argue that one social theory or interpretation of history is the correct one, we are again reflecting our historical conditioning and cannot show one theory to be true transhistorically. For such a theory states something about expected future events and does not simply describe a present state of affairs. (3) If we admit the provisionality of our expectations of future developments but insist that a careful study of the historical record reveals a basic trend or tendency, we must (a) disprove or counter any alternative readings of that record and (b) show that, even if no disagreement exists among scholars (a situation which has never yet occurred), the empirical evidence that a tendency is at work is not the same as showing men cannot change their minds tomorrow or that unforeseen "contingencies" (like atomic weapons or new scientific discoveries) will not affect the direction and pressure of such a tendency. (4) Finally, if political activists like Marxists encourage support of their programs of social revolution and reform by appealing to something like an inevitable tide in history, they must argue like men who cannot, on independent grounds, show how their views are reasonable and sensible. Nor can they show the logic by which their descriptions of an existing situation are truer or more comprehensive than other ones. As Popper claims, historical determinists who organize political programs usually act like men who hold certain beliefs, including: that some descriptions of a situation make more sense than others (they "fit the facts" and do not simply express the hopes of suffering people); that human action can actually influence at least the rate if not the final direction of social change; and that one interpretation of what needs to be done politically can be "better" than other competing (and inadequate) ones.

Historical "Presentism"

Many philosophers have confined their attention to the status of historical statements. While they are not "historicists," since they are concerned with epistemological rather than speculative issues, their inquiries have sometimes led to the conclusion that historical knowledge is perspectival—knowledge in relation to the "present" in which the historian operates. If this claim were accepted, then—even if history-as-reality existed "out there," so to speak—men could never know the historical past in its actuality. This would represent a "methodological" historicism, since the "objectivity" of historical statements would be a contextual affair of the present. This position requires a careful examination, since its acceptance would mean that present politics illuminates historical events; but historical knowledge cannot, in itself, ever serve as a "check" on present political aims and activities.

If asked the question "What are historical statements about?", anyone who knows anything at all about written histories can reply, somewhat cagily: "Why, they're about many kinds of things." One can even elaborate on this reply, dredging up remnants of one's notes from the old required course in History of Civilization. One can safely enumerate some of the kinds of things which serve as objects of the *aboutness* of historical statements: specific wars and revolutions, dynastic rivalries and marriages, economic institutions and policies, individual men and women (from kings, queens, and courtesans to the duller "garden-variety" ordinary persons), intellectual discoveries, and mistakes, *ad infinitum*.

If the original questioner wants yet more information, the speaker can say that existing written histories must serve as the models for deciding what historical statements are about—making sure to add that they vary in type depending on the given historian and his interests, the nature of the subject matter, and the availability or lack of documentary and other forms of evidence. If the questioner still looks perplexed, one can point out the titles of some histories one has read (or meant to read), using a kind of bibliographical ploy to impress the other: "You're genuinely interested in what historical statements are about? Try reading Thucydides or Gibbon, Macaulay or Adams, Herodotus or Pliny or Tacitus. Better still, as an educated person interested in what the 'educationists' call the deposit of the West's intellectual labors, read them all!" Should the questioner smile and say: "But I've read all of these histories, and more!", one can regroup from the surprise of such "one-upmanship" by saying something like: "Now I understand your original question. You already know quite a bit concerning what historical statements are about.

You want to know what their *aboutness* has in common in all these differing instances of written histories. Isn't the answer you are looking for this: that historical statements are about the *past* features of any subject matter involving human action and agency?" Given a questioner who *now* replies, "I was afraid you were going to say something like that!", one can surmise one is in the presence of a philosophical mind—or about to hear a lecture on some aspect of the problem of historical knowledge. One would surmise correctly.

Even prior to the contemporary age of philosophical therapy, with its accompanying emphasis on peculiar forms of "mental cramp," it was obvious to critics that some philosophers worried in a peculiar fashion about the objects of historical statements. They wrote and talked as if there was something strange about an historian's saying that historical statements are about the past. The problem seemed not that such a sentence may express a truism, nor that seldom would one find occasion for an historian to utter it. The problem seemed "deeper" than that. Consequently, several philosophers went out of their way to correct such a statement. The pragmatist Dewey wrote: "All history is necessarily written from the standpoint of the present, and is, in an inescapable sense, the history not only of the present but of what is contemporaneously judged to be important in the present." [13] Collingwood gave some partially approving attention to Michael Oakeshott's assertion that "The facts of history are present facts." [14] In one of his essays Isaiah Berlin is said, by C. K. Grant, to have insisted that "Propositions about the past were required by the more uncompromising among the early positivists to become ('in some sense') propositions about the future or else to be eliminated." [15]

Such statements seem to suggest that historical statements are about the present or the future. Taken literally, they do ring strangely in unphilosophical ears. It is as if the statement: "From Cheshire the King turned southward, and, in the full belief that the Fellows of

[13] John Dewey, *Logic: The Theory of Inquiry* (New York: Holt, 1938), p. 235.
[14] R. G. Collingwood, *The Idea of History* (London: Oxford University Press, 1946), p. 154.
[15] C. K. Grant, "Polar Concepts and Metaphysical Arguments," *Proceedings of the Aristotelian Society,* Vol. LVI (London, 1955–56), pp. 103–104.

Magdalene College, however mutinous they might be, would not dare to disobey a command uttered by his own lips, directed his course toward Oxford" [16] might mean either that, if one were at Oxford right now, one would see James II approaching; or that if he got there in the future (perhaps tomorrow) he would be on hand to see a king meet a mutinous faculty. Indeed, even philosophical ears seem occasionally to respond when such assertions about the present-centeredness of historical statements are heard, but for different reasons. The philosophers seem to want to start talking just when the practicing historians think it time to go home.

The philosophers who make such arresting assertions often act like men who realize they are making peculiar claims which, in fact, are not intended to be as revolutionary as they at first sound. For example, Dewey says "Every history is a history of the present" in a context which fairly shouts: "But allow me to explain what I mean by saying that!" A good part of his explanation is nonphilosophical. It involves making a number of statements which practicing historians would find quite sensible and even trivially obvious. For one thing, he seeks to remind readers of the indubitable fact that historians reflect particular intellectual interests and write always in a given time and place. Historical statements reflect the interests of their authors, in other words. An idealist like Collingwood (who says a number of different and often incompatible things in his *The Idea of History*) suggests that historical statements are a function of certain historians' abilities at "entering into" the experiences of previous historical epochs by virtue of knowing how, in their own epoch, to ask the right questions. His point is that no one historical epoch can permit the asking of a sufficient range of questions about past actions to produce equally adequate accounts of all past periods. In each case, however, the philosophers concerned defend the scientific integrity of historiography. Neither denies that historians must submit their evidence to the rigorous tests by which reliable evidence is separated from unreliable. The decision about what shall pass for evidence is independent of the historian's interests, never an arbitrary matter to be

[16] Douglas Jerrold (ed.), Macaulay's *History of England from the Accession of James II* (London: Dent, 1953), Vol. II, p. 161.

decided by someone's saying: "As a contemporary historian, living in my own epoch, I happen to want X, Y, and Z to count as evidence and not W, T, and Q." Yet historians must *do* something with the evidence in making their historical statements, and what they do is said to reflect the present range of knowledge. This means that when historians make interpretations of past events they do so in light of explanatory norms and moral evaluations which must supplement the existing evidence. Dewey refers to this interpretative function as involving the historian in a *conceptual* (or a *methodological*) present.

Emphasis on the way historical statements depend on evidence can here prove quite misleading if one wishes to stress also the present-sidedness of the reference of such evidence. Many statements not themselves historical (including many statements of ordinary life) also depend on evidence. ("Aunt Lysistrata called here yesterday while we were out." "Oh? Can you be sure?" "Well, she left a note in the mailbox, bearing yesterday's date and it's in her handwriting." "Might someone have been playing a dirty trick on you?" "Oh, go to the devil!") What is at stake here is the extent to which men can rightfully claim to know something to be the case when direct observation is not now taking place (assuming that the sceptical philosophical worry about the certainty of first-person sensory perception is not here raised at all). Think how much practical knowledge rests on the reports of others who have observed events or received reports from others who did. Often to say that one knows something to have happened (or to be happening) means to assert, in answer to the question "But how do you know, really?", some such statement as: "Well, I know that Adam Smith is feeling poorly because Sam Schopenhauer—who has always been reliable in such matters—told me Smith gets feeling poorly when the stock market goes down drastically, as it has."

Of course, there is an important difference between many common-sense reliances on authorities for one's knowledge-claims and the historian's. In many of the former instances (though not in all) one can, in principle, "check up" on what has been reported by finding someone who did observe the event or activity. The historian cannot interview dead witnesses. Still, many of the statements made by historians are found *in* the evidence—letters, diaries, dated newspapers and magazines, almanacs, and the like. Historians can only "check up" on such statements in terms of what they call "internal criticism" (consistency of the reporting) and by finding other documents, say, which report the same events in similar ways. It is obvious that this is no easy matter—that historians must learn to discriminate among existing authorities (quite reliable; reliable with known exceptions a, b, c (say); generally unreliable). But similarly, if a court calls in witnesses who claim to have observed past events their memories *now* must be assumed relevant to what they observed *then*. So the difference between the historian's and the average man's reliance on evidence for many statements turns out to be one of significant degree rather than kind.

Surely John Austin argued rightly when he insisted that one uses "know" correctly in many cases involving claims that something has happened (or is happening) when direct observation has not occurred (or is not occurring) for the claimant. Austin's words are helpful here: "Among the cases where we give our reasons for knowing things, a special and important class is formed by those where we cite authorities. If asked 'How do you know the election is today?', I am apt to reply 'I read it in *The Times,*' and if asked 'How do you know the Persians were defeated at Marathon?', I am apt to reply 'Herodotus expressly stated that they were.' In these cases 'know' is correctly used: we know 'at second hand' when we can cite an authority who was in a position to know (possibly himself also only at second hand)." [17] Like Mr. Average Man, the historian can claim to know many things, even though he may in some instances have to say later, "I see I thought I knew, when I didn't." The fact that new evidence may lead an historian to admit former mistaken knowledge-claims does not require him to stop using "know" and to preface all historical statements with "I believe that . . ." or "Probably it was the case that . . ." If I discover I have made a mistaken claim about some aspect of my grandfather's life (say, the sentence: "My grandfather burned down the old covered bridge connecting Phoenixville

[17] John Austin, "Other Minds," in Anthony Flew, ed., *Essays in Logic and Language* (Second Series; Oxford: Blackwell, 1955), p. 128.

with Mont Clair, Pennsylvania"), I do not go sceptical in a philosophical way about other knowledge-claims about him and say things like "I *believe* my grandfather lived in Pennsylvania," "I *believe* my grandfather was married to my grandmother," and the like. Is the lesson taught by any one memory lapse on my part that I must never trust my memory in making later knowledge-claims?

If an historian explains how he knows by a statement like "We have it from Herodotus," he makes use of present evidence which includes the observations of a man long dead. Imagine the consequences of failing to recognize that Herodotus died long ago. In his *History* Herodotus tells, for one thing, about the interesting Babylonian religious custom by which, once in a lifetime, each married woman went to the temple, waited to be taken away by a strange male, and after fulfilling the sexual role of her religion went back home to remain forever faithful. One can picture a healthy fraternity male, mistaking the account for a present one, preparing to go to Babylon when he reads that "Such of the women as are tall and beautiful are soon released, but others who are ugly have to stay a long time before they can fulfill the law. Some have waited three or four years in the precinct." One would say to the fraternity male: "Don't make the trip. Keep your present religion. Herodotus is recounting a custom of the *ancient* Babylonians." [18] It is an interesting aspect of historical evidence *in the present* that it carries often the marks of age—*worn* and *marred* pages, *weathered* houses and *eroded* monuments, *moss-grown* grave markers on battlefields, *dated* letters. One has occasionally heard quite ordinary people make a statement such as: "Look at that old battleaxe! She carries her past in her face and bearing!" *Historical* evidence often brings its own credentials from a past. Of course, the philosopher will note that historical statements can never achieve certainty save in relation to authorities and that authorities are sometimes found to have erred. In this the philosopher will be right. But the conclusion should not then be that historians speak strangely when they claim to possess historical knowledge. As Austin observes: "It is fundamental in talking (as in other matters)

[18] The quotation from Herodotus is found in George Rawlinson, trans., *The History of Herodotus* (New York: Tudor, 1928), p. 75.

that we are entitled to trust others, except in so far as there is some concrete reason to distrust them." [19]

Nonetheless there are understandable reasons why the historian's picture of events before one's own time, in principle now removed from possible observation, causes men to worry. The reasons are primarily moral and political. There is no album of originals against which we can check our pictures, only the evidence used in the creation of accounts of vanished events. This makes us subject to possibly grievous errors in our characterizations of past actions if the evidence is itself faulty or distorted. The imperative for historians should run somewhat like: "Make sure to exercise rigorous standards of evidence in making statements about the past." The historian's imperative should *not* be: "Stop talking about the past." Philosophers concerned about the present-centeredness of historical evidence make good moralists to the extent that they wish to remind men of their vulnerability to lost or distorted evidence. Lose the evidence and men cannot even hope to construct an historical account. On the other hand, men can imagine the possibility that they could, though slowly and painfully, relearn the whole extent of physical knowledge if all physics books were somehow destroyed. The physicist's evidence would in principle remain, awaiting the right questions from a race of men newly emerging on evolutionary legs from a Post-Nuclear New Stone Age. But a good part of historical evidence is not like that. One would suppose that philosophers who emphasize the need for evidence for historical statements would, as moralists, "see" clearly that its importance *in the present* is related to the making of historical statements about the past.

Imagine the following fantastic situation. A war occurs involving use of powerful chemical agents which have two effects, one temporary and the other permanent. The temporary effect is the total collective amnesia of the war's human survivors. The lasting effect is the disappearance of all print and writing from existing books, monuments, and documents of all kinds. This would involve the total abolition of all written evidence relevant to the historical reconstruction of happenings up to the occurrence of this particular war. This fan-

[19] John Austin, *op. cit.,* p. 129.

tastic story illustrates the point some philosophers want to stress in arguing that historical statements are in some sense always about present evidence and presently accepted methods of interpreting the evidence. But it also points out the moral they should draw from their own concern with historical evidence: namely, that historical evidence is required if men are to make statements about the past as historians.

The claim that historical statements are, *in some sense,* about the future loses its paradoxical sound when one understands that logical positivists made it to emphasize the difference between factual statements and propositions in logic and mathematics. The point here is that historical evidence includes statements which are presumed to be factual, thus subject to certain empirical tests. It is a characteristic of our knowledge that new empirical discoveries may show earlier factual claims to have been wrong. Mr. C. K. Grant writes of this point. When referring to Isaiah Berlin he says:

> He asserts that early positivists held that *all* propositions are in an abnormal sense 'about the future,' with the result that 'the future' can be contrasted with nothing and is therefore meaningless. No positivist, to my knowledge, has ever believed this; what has been maintained is that all *empirical* propositions are 'about the future.' The point behind this paradox is that all factual propositions, even historical ones, are liable to falsification by empirical information that may become available in the future, unlike logical and mathematical propositions that are not empirically falsifiable—or verifiable either. There is thus a contrast between propositions that are 'about the future' in this sense, and propositions that are not about facts at all.[20]

In principle, then, one might argue that all factual claims are subject to possible future empirical correction.

This is a bad argument with reference to historical facts, of course, since it would make it impossible for men to give any use to the word "evidence." It seems to give us an interpretation of factual statements such that, given any instance of a historical statement, men would have to make a statement comparable to: "The First World War began in 1914, though future evidence may show that it did not." To argue that all factual statements are in principle subject to future

[20] C. K. Grant, *op. cit.,* p. 104.

falsification means to commit a fallacy analogous to the kind Ryle discusses in his handling of the sceptic's worry about the dubitability of all sensory knowledge—trying to make sense out of the notion of counterfeit coin in a country with no coinage at all. It is hard to form a picture of present evidence, each and every item of which in principle is subject to possible future falsification. Likewise is it hard to ignore the fact that every possible future falsification of a present factual statement must occur in a present-yet-to-be which, itself, becomes subject in principle to future falsification. Thus, to say strainedly that historical statements are about the future means that they concern future judgments about the evidence by which *now* they are said to be justified. It is difficult to take this view seriously to the extent it casts a sceptical doubt over all our knowledge-claims about matters of fact. To take the view seriously, one would have to believe that all historical evidence, now on hand, has been manufactured by an Orwellian superideologist hidden away in a special rewrite section of the "Big Brother" Historiographical Falsification Room. Still, the positivist seeks to emphasize the point that factual statements are meaningful only if subject to specific tests as well as to remind men that present factual assertions are subject to *continuing* future tests. His paradoxical way of saying this proves less disturbing once one realizes he worries about tests and not about the reference of historical statements.

Too much has been made by some logical positivists of the argument that only those knowledge-claims are factually sound which can, in principle, be corroborated by sense experience. "Go and look!" this group says (though often in a more sophisticated way) to the sceptic who doubts some report of present fact. But the advice is for any one person impossible of practical application. One can only "look and see" in a given place, at a given time. The advice can be stated in a weakened form: "Have someone whose observations you trust go and look." This restates the argument to assert that those factual statements are sound which can be checked by *someone's* observations. If I reject this weakened form of the argument, as a sceptic I must refuse to believe anything in my newspapers and magazines; and I find I know almost nothing of the "present" in which some philosophers (though not the positivists) find the locus of the interest of historical statements. So many events get reported, in any one day, that I can check on only a few (preferably close at hand). On this view, much of historical evidence can be taken to be sound to the extent it reflects what were observations of then-living persons. Clearly, our sense of evidence will eliminate those reported items which make us incredulous—as exemplified by the current joke of the man who says: "I don't care who you are. Stop walking on the water while I'm fishing!" As a matter of fact, the kinds of reports in historical evidence can be stated: (1) Describes what happened and includes first-person statements that something of the sort was intended; (2) Presents statements of intention but lacks reports on what exactly happened; (3) Presents forms of evidence which—in the absence of reports of what happened as well as of first-person statements of intention—constitutes historians' generalizations about probable happenings, derived from agents' actions in other contexts.

Insofar as the philosophers mentioned say peculiar things about historical statements, they do so to dramatize the crucial way in which historical statements presuppose existing evidence. The philosophers also want to remind men how standards of evidence sometimes alter. This seems sane and tame enough. They are in error, however, if they think that their views show it is the wrong thing to say about historical statements that they are about the past. The extent to which the surprising statements with which we began are subject to nonphilosophical explanation or elaboration is an important aspect of the effort to understand which one-sided feature of historical knowledge the philosophers were attempting to illuminate. This task is rather a "meat-and-potatoes" one, showing that what seems to express a peculiarly philosophical problem is often a condensed and sometimes garbled version of a number of quite understandable judgments about evidence.

Common Sense and History

There is another approach to these philosophers' statements about the present-sidedness of history which must be considered. This has reference to their possible argument that historians make many different kinds of statements. Some are singular ones; others comparative; some are actually dated or involve contexts clearly implying datedness (like Macaulay's chapter on the state of England in 1685). Others are causal statements, some of which trace relations between past events and present happenings. A pragmatist like Dewey, for instance, also likes to emphasize how historians must make selective judgments about beginnings and endings, inevitable choices of initial and terminal foci for any given written history. This is particularly true of what is sometimes called "history in the grand manner" in which an effort is made, say, to trace the development of parties or institutions from one temporal period to a later one.

The pragmatist says that such histories are always of the historian's present in the sense that *his* selection of consequences becomes normative for the materials treated in the written work. The historian decides what are the *important* consequences, and he does this by virtue of an advantageous stance denied to many of the human characters involved in the events he wishes to characterize or explain. The historian can sometimes explain features of eventful institutional history in a way which would have been impossible for the individuals whose temporal life-spans were not equal to the temporal period under historical analysis. The historian *now* knows something the historical figures could not in fact then have known—much as a pilot can actually see the traffic jam shaping up while Harry Humperdink, say, drives blissfully up Bayshore Highway unaware that the jam lies ahead. The pilot, like the pragmatic historian interested in tracing the history of his worrisome "big problems," actually sees a consequence of the activities of agents *at that moment* not directly known to them. But this pragmatic position simply argues for the significance of a special kind of written history. It does not invalidate the claim that, given the historian's judgments about those problems he thinks important, what makes his finished account historical turns on the statements he makes about the past of that problem's development. The historian's account of that problem's emergence may involve historical statements which are relatively general and embracing, but they will nonetheless be concerned with the pastness of features relevant to that problem. One of the leading "fire-eaters" in this pragmatic camp has written:

> If this selection is not to be merely of what is important *for him*, it must have an objective focus—something to be done, some problem he sees forced on men. The history of what is important for that problem, of its materials and conditions and resources, will then be perfectly objective—in a sense in which no mere recording of arbitrarily selected facts ever could be.[21]

A more impressive methodological point some philosophers make, along these lines, is that *how* historians explain (or "understand") events is a function of present knowledge. Suppose today I say about American policy in relation to Cuba during the past decades that the (temporary) loss of Cuba to elements aggressively hostile to the United States results from serious kinds of indifference to the social aspirations and problems of great numbers of the Cuban people. What makes this function as an explanation of a present state of affairs (if it can be taken to be adequate) surely is the increased awareness men now have of the way in which bad economic conditions have spurred revolutionary regimes even in small countries. Probably this explanation would not have proved convincing to my grandfather, say. Nonetheless, if asked to support the explanation by historical statements, I must make statements about past situations which (on my view) have helped to produce the situation which now, pragmatically, worries me. If I wish to do more than make a generalization, I must gather the evidence and attempt to learn if it does support the generalization. Unless I am simply a propagandist, I must make historical statements about a wide range of issues relevant to the present situation. What will be provided is a whole series of statements about acts, or lack of acts, in the United States and in Cuba during a specified temporal period.

Pragmatic historians make much of the way in which the consequences of acts get worked out, influencing men to pay attention to features of events which, earlier, our prevalent norms of explanation and judgment permitted men to overlook. The "logjam" treatment

[21] J. H. Randall, Jr., "On Understanding the History of Philosophy," *The Journal of Philosophy*, XXXVI (1939), p. 472.

of history simply emphasizes how, given certain consequences, we want to pay attention to previously overlooked features of eventful happenings. This does not so much mean that old histories get re-written as that new ones are written. A course in pragmatic philosophy will never solve the historian's problem, which is (in his present; concerned with specific consequences of past acts) to place those consequences in a historical setting. To do this he must make historical statements about the past. If different historians emphasize different problems, they may write differing accounts of the same general span of events, but this need not mean that one account contradicts the other. "Every shift in the course of events changes the bearing of the past upon the present," one writer, S. P. Lamprecht, has argued, "and so makes imperative the writing of history. Just because historians deal with particulars that are, so to speak, dripping with alternatives or even plural potentialities, they may legitimately view the past as prelude to two or more different futures and hence as possessing two or more different significances." [22]

But even this does not fully consider what some men mean when they argue that historical writing reflects the present range of knowledge. They sometimes mean that not all statements in any given written history are *historical*. Rather, the statements in any history make up a bedraggled collection—including generalizations about human motivation, sketchy characterizations of situations, ascriptions of responsibility to human agents whose decisions (or lack of decision) influenced the affairs of the day. One may even claim that many written histories are peculiar kinds of sustained arguments in which, independently of obvious historical references to individuals and times and places, the historian seeks to make men "see" events in another light from the customary ways. The historian has reasons for his persuasive effort, of course. They may be moral, religious, economic, or political. He wants to convince readers that his approach "makes sense" of the events about which he writes; and if he is writing a History of Civilization, say, he often provides his reasons for some of the interpretations he gives. The historian often attempts to supply

[22] S. P. Lamprecht, *Nature and History* (New York: Columbia University Press, 1949), p. 71.

the "rules of the court" for handling the evidence on hand. He wants —as Collingwood so ably points out—a history more full-blown than mere chronicle, more comprehensive than a lengthy presentation of conjunctions of singular statements. It is obvious that competent historians concerned with relatively the same periods and materials do not "make sense" of them in the same way. A Marxist "sees" the Protestant Reformation in a light different from a devout Lutheran or a convinced Catholic. Yet, the three historians can "understand" one another's perspective on events while not agreeing (though they may refuse to admit this fact). How they "understand" events is a function of their beliefs about human nature, motivation, institutions, and the like. They differ in their judgments of importance.

But it is only to the extent that different historians agree on some historical statements about the past that their differing arguments about these statements can make a dialogue possible. Their histories must contain some *normative* historical statements to which their nonhistorical statements are relevant. This is what historical argumentation is about. One judges his argument in relation to the historical statements which are taken to be sound. Suppose several historians "understand" the divorce of Restless and Clytemnestra Shultz in differing ways. Only to the extent that they agree on some historical statements about the couple's relationship can their different interpretations seem relevant to historical considerations. It is also possible that different explanations of the divorce are equally true: "Restless was an extremely possessive and jealous man—one to whom Clytemnestra gave cause for provocation by her behavior"; "They could never settle their arguments by kissing and making up"; "Restless' restlessness disturbed Clytemnestra, who had another personality entirely"; and so on. If these explanations did not satisfy a listener, one would have to "fill out" the picture in more detail. If the listener still did not understand, one would wonder how much he knew about divorce proceedings and causes. It is doubtful that if, after the picture had been filled out, the listener still seemed perplexed one could help him by saying: "Under such circumstances, couples often tend to divorce." What one who is interested in the history of the couple's divorce would want is fuller details, not more generalizations. Scriven may be right when he argues that most historical explanations are nontrivial truisms; [23] but this does not mean a truism must be stated in a form prefaced by words like "all" or "most." Once the historian has filled in the details, he cannot make a baffled reader understand more adequately by producing a truistic explanation in the form of a universal generalization. A person who does not understand the sentence: "The couple divorced because Restless was jealous" cannot be helped by a further sentence: "Most jealous husbands divorce their wives given proper provocation."

The point of all of this is that, though seldom need he do so, the historian can rightly say that "historical statements are about the past." This is preferable to saying they are either about the present or the future. A commonsense conception of historical knowledge operates here, of course. This conception assumes that, in previous times and places, human beings lived out their fretful existences around their interests in family, friends, and personal aspirations. How their lives passed reflected the institutions and customs of their day. Some were more fortunate than others in experiencing prosperity rather than depression, relative peace instead of war, domestic administrative continuity and tranquility in place of revolutionary turmoil. Men are able to know something about how they passed their lives by virtue of a wide variety of documents and other evidential remains, including (perhaps especially so) the literature some of their compatriots wrote. The historian's task is to reconstruct features of their lives, at many levels of historical generality. His function is to provide a selective characterization of their aims and achievements in conformity with what the evidence indicates the case to have been. The historian should do this in such a way that, if we read Thucydides, say, on putting down the account of the destruction of the Athenians at Syracuse, we can say something like: "Poor lost, dead rascals!" MacIver has it right when he argues: "Oakeshott or Collingwood calls the history (let us say) of the Peloponnesian War a 'mode of experience,' meaning by this his own experience in his

---

[23] Michael Scriven, "Truisms as the Grounds for Historical Explanations," in Patrick Gardiner, ed., *Theories of History* (Glencoe, Ill.: Free Press, 1959), pp. 443–475.

twentieth-century Oxford or Cambridge college room, forgetting that what made the history was experience all right, but the experience of thousands of poor devils two dozen centuries ago." [24]

If someone should, at this juncture, wonder how on this view men can legitimately speak of "contemporary" history, the explanation would have to go something like this: Contemporary history is written by historians as if posterity peers over their shoulders. Such history stresses what, as important in the present, a later generation will judge in a similar light. It is an attempt to view events, even *now,* as if they are in a sense already past—to achieve a disinterested pose in relation to them. Thus, Thucydides wanted to preserve a record of the greatest war of all time. Thus, also, one keeps his snapshot collection with future grandchildren in mind, who will ask: "What did daddy look like as a boy?" This is not too good, perhaps; but it will have to do.

The point is simply that if a characterizing statement about historical statements is needed at all, it is much better to say that historical statements are about the past than to say they are about present or future. Such a truistic thesis needs summary restatement. Of course, for the satisfaction of any sceptic in the reading audience, one can end by saying something like: "Let us, you and I, take down Gibbon to read about what happened today!"

Historical Interpretation

Political uses of historical world views and claims about the future are, after all, interpretations. Their appearance in aspects of twentieth-century political life and struggle suggest something more like theological views in politics than scientific hypotheses. Hypotheses are subject to verification and are, by practicing scientists, held tentatively—such that in principle scientists can suppose that evidence may arise requiring a change in the hypothesis. Historical interpretations when used to "back" specific political programs can become dogmas, held on faith, even blindly—and thus in principle not subject

[24] A. M. MacIver, "Historical Explanation," in Anthony Flew, ed., *op. cit.,* p. 187.

to alteration. This need not mean that such dogmas are unimportant or unenlightening, only that they are not (as is often claimed for them) scientific hypotheses. They can complicate the open discussion of political differences too. Suppose that one voted for political candidates *not* on the basis of their stands on specific issues (like farm legislation, public medicine, tax programs, etc.) but in the light of their views of history? Empirical treatments of political issues would become most difficult if not impossible, and political disputes would look like theological conflicts in the past, marked by bigotry and intolerant sectarianism.

In our century, many men have become discouraged with attempts to find the underlying purpose in the historical arena. They have argued that, in any event, science is unable to answer what may be a religious or philosophical question about the meaningfulness of human history. Some philosophers of history have, like Professor W. H. Walsh, a contemporary English thinker, distinguished between *speculative* and *critical* philosophizing about history. Speculative thought seeks to find an underlying *pattern* to empirically observable events and is marked by the view that there is one historical reality, however plural the particular occurrences. Critical philosophy of history rather asks more limited questions about the nature and extent of historical knowledge, whether historians can achieve "objectivity" in their treatments of past events, how the explanations employed by historians are like or unlike those of people working in the physical sciences, and what historians mean when they speak or write about truth or fact in history. Such critical inquiries aim more at a clarification of the possibilities in historical inquiry rather than at sweeping statements about History (with a capital H) and where it is inevitably tending. They believe that philosophers can unearth no new knowledge about history and its processes but can, given the actual works of practicing historians, help to make clearer the logical side of historical knowledge.

Careful scholars who study the details of controversial past conflicts of wide historical scope also caution contemporaries that large-scale events call forth passionate partisanship. So, too, political uses of philosophies of history seek more to achieve conversions than to "explain" events for their own sakes. A contemporary English historian, Professor Herbert Butterfield, has shown how later generations are sometimes able to achieve greater clarity in appraising the diverse conflicting strands which make up important wars and revolutions— a clarity which, in the thick of the battles, even historians often lack. There may not even be *one* true interpretation of a great historical event—like the Renaissance, say, or the Protestant Reformation.[25] Even the actors in the original drama may not clearly have understood what the real issues were, for as defined by Santayana, the fanatic is one who redoubles his effort after he has lost his aim.

Nonetheless, a preoccupation with the problem of history has marked modern life and politics. Even a liberal in politics like Charles Frankel, trying to restate the hopes of liberals for a sane evolutionary rather than revolutionary, democratic rather than totalitarian solution of the world's difficult problems, has argued:

> Philosophy is reviving in America, and it is reviving mainly in the shape of philosophies of history. Our phrases are the phrases of philosophers of history, old and new—"Crossroads of History," "The End of an Era," "A Time of Troubles," "The Illusion of Progress." They resound from the pulpit, echo in editorials, and whisper between the lines of sober estimates of the business cycle. The novels of contemporary experience, with their parade of bare, uninterpreted events, of actions that are meaningful, at best, only as elements in a struggle for personal integrity, suggest how bitterly men are reacting to a world from which a sense of direction seems to have vanished.[26]

Conclusion

Men's theories of history many times influence their actions. Current discussion within the Communist ideological "camps," between the Russian and the Chinese theorists, may be taken as one example of this possibility. Contemporary scholars are more conscious of history than were most thinkers of the past, chiefly as a consequence of

[25] Professor Butterfield has written extensively, but his *History and Human Relations* (London: Collins, 1951) gives careful attention to the problem of making fair judgments about past happenings.
[26] Charles Frankel, *The Case for Modern Man* (New York: Harper, 1955), p. 11. Used by permission of Harper & Row, Publishers, Incorporated.

the historiographical developments of the last century. However, "historicism"—the doctrine that all truths are historically rooted, that a thing's history is the fundamental element of that thing—became a fairly widespread viewpoint in which philosophical and historical issues are often lumped together and often confused. This chapter has attempted to indicate how historicism—both as a doctrine about processes and as a specific treatment of the problem of historical knowledge—contains some conceptual difficulties and confusions. The aim has also been to indicate how, under the name "historicism," quite different views have existed which may, logically, have little in common with one another.

Primarily, however, this chapter has sought to show how a widened sense of history has, at the very least, influenced the intellectual "climate of opinion" in which talk about politically important notions and events has increasingly taken place. The attitudes men take toward historical events may profoundly affect their expectations about the future, thus sometimes influencing their actions.

Some Questions and Problems

1. If all historical knowledge is taken as reflecting the historian's "present," can written histories provide an important map for politicians trying to render judgments about men and events?
2. Suppose that you are attending an international student conference to which delegates have come from colleges and universities all over the world. How would you reply to a delegate who spoke as follows?

    > Contemporary men often make wrong political judgments because they misunderstand the conflicts of their day and the onward sweep of the historical current. They possess no theoretical grasp of the movement of historical forces. Until contemporary men understand the direction of historical tendencies, they will continue to make political blunders, mistaking symptoms for causes. Without a true and comprehensive theory of history, politics remains the unconnected practices of fools and idiots.

3. Write out your reply to the following charge:

    > Americans are today too politically innocent for words. They see international issues in too black-and-white a fashion. They

are terrible moralists, unaware of the obdurateness of evil and too convinced that moral judgments are important in politics. Americans are sometimes really insufferable moralists when they take up problems of international politics. Until they become realistic, they cannot lead themselves let alone Europe or the world.

4. List some ways in which citizens of this country could have altered the historical record by acting differently from how in fact they did act in the past. Make sure to consider some actual historical situations important in American history.

5. What would you say to the person who asserts that, no matter what they had done, Americans would have had to experience the Civil War?

6. Choose any one of the following counter-factual statements and be prepared to discuss it in class. What might have been the historical outcomes *if*—
   a. President Roosevelt had lived longer and been elected to a fifth term?
   b. Mr. Richard Nixon had defeated President John F. Kennedy in the 1960 election?
   c. The United States had actively joined in the League of Nations after the First World War?
   d. The United States had refused to use the atom bomb and, even during the Second World War, announced to the world it was destroying its nuclear bomb-making capacity?
   e. The United States had supported Fidel Castro both before and after his successful revolution in Cuba?
   f. The South had won the Civil War?
   g. The U.S. Constitution had abolished slavery?
   h. Germany and Japan had defeated the United States in the Second World War?
   i. Advanced education had not been made available to large numbers of American citizens?
   j. The Marshall Plan for Europe had not been created after the last war?
   k. The United States had not sent troops to fight in Korea?

7. In your opinion, what will happen in the future of American politics *if*—
   a. Latin and South America either "go" Communist or radically socialist?
   b. An extreme political Conservative becomes President of the United States?

   c. There is a serious depression?

   d. Any major European power votes a Communist party into political office?

   e. Disarmament occurs on a wide scale?

   f. A revolution occurs either in China or in Russia?

   g. Automation continues to put people into the unemployment category?

   h. The labor unions become weak and small in numbers?

   i. Private colleges and universities all but disappear from the American scene?

   j. Nonwhites fail to make large advances as a result of their fight to achieve civil rights?

8. Discuss the role played by ideas in political life. How important are ideas in contrast with other important political influences?

9. Discuss the following assertion: "Nothing like the Nazi movement can conceivably succeed in the United States because its political tradition is different from that which existed in Germany."

10. In what concrete situations do hopelessness and nihilism come to influence men's political actions?

Some Suggested Readings

Beard, C. A. "That Noble Dream," *American Historical Review,* Vol. XLI, 1935.

Becker, C. *Everyman His Own Historian.* New York: Crofts, 1935.

Berlin, I. *Historical Inevitability.* London: Oxford University Press, 1954.

Butterfield, H. *Christianity and History.* London: Bell, 1954.

Collingwood, R. G. *The Idea of History.* London: Oxford University Press, 1946.

Dray, W. *Laws and Explanation in History.* London: Oxford University Press, 1957.

————. *Philosophy of History.* Englewood Cliffs, N.J.: Prentice-Hall, 1964.

Fackenheim, E. L. *Metaphysics and Historicity.* Milwaukee: Marquette University Press, 1961.

Gardiner, P. (ed.) *Theories of History.* Glencoe, Ill.: Free Press, 1959.

————. *The Nature of Historical Explanation.* London: Oxford University Press, 1952.

————. "Metaphysics and History," *The Nature of Metaphysics,* ed. D. F. Pears. London: Macmillan, 1957.

Lovejoy, A. O. "Present Standpoints and Past History," *Journal of Philosophy,* Vol. XXXVI, 1939.

Lynd, R. *Knowledge for What?* Princeton: Princeton University Press, 1946.

MacIver, A. M. "Historical Explanation," *Logic and Language,* Second Series, ed. A. Flew. Oxford: Blackwell, 1953.

McKeon, R. *Freedom and History.* New York: Noonday Press, 1952.

Popper, K. R. *The Open Society and Its Enemies,* rev. ed. 2 vols. London: Routledge, 1952.

―――. *The Poverty of Historicism.* London: Routledge, 1957.

Randall, J. H., Jr. *Nature and Historical Experience.* New York: Columbia University Press, 1958.

Renier, G. J. *History: Its Purpose and Method.* Boston: Beacon, 1950.

Social Science Research Council. *The Social Sciences in Historical Study.* Bulletin 64, 1954.

―――. *Theory and Practice in Historical Study: A Report of the Committee on Historiography.* Bulletin 54, 1946.

Stern, F. (ed.) *The Varieties of History.* New York: Meridian, 1956.

Walsh, W. H. *An Introduction to the Philosophy of History.* London: Hutchinson, 1951.

CHAPTER THIRTEEN

Politics and Contemporary Value Problems

Historians undertake a difficult task whenever they attempt to describe the moods or emotional attitudes which have characterized specific periods or provided a psychological accompaniment to the rush of social and political events. Sometimes historians want to reconstruct the kinds of outlook on events held by persons who were contemporaneous with those events. How men have interpreted their problems —the emotions they felt or did not feel, the presence or absence of concern, despair, even panic perhaps—are often as much important aspects of social and political reality as are those more easily recognized facts contained in public records.

In one situation, men may become upset by a prevailing mood or attitude which, in other times and circumstances, some men have tolerated without misgivings or accepted with positive satisfaction. The view that all human values are relative rather than absolute has been judged quite differently from period to period. The relativistic "doctrine" has often disturbed men in a community; in other situations it sometimes refreshed the community's members. Persons struggling against some oppressive absolutism (economic, political, religious, moral) sometimes become relativists in order to loosen the authoritative ties of the *status quo* or tradition, although they may do so in order eventually to establish absolutes of their own. Some rebellious persons may experience a new sense of freedom, the discovery that they have been "taken in" by rules and authorities which, they now judge, never were really needed. They may conclude that individual tastes and preferences should be granted a freer rein in society—that types of behavior previously subjected to restraint should be removed from authoritative interference. On the other hand, if men sense they are witnessing a loss of that value consensus without which a society can be threatened with chaos, they may come to look upon the relativistic doctrine with fear and trembling, convinced that such a doctrine may contribute to the absence of strenuous efforts to "shore up" a sagging morality or to unite individuals in needed cooperative undertakings based on deeply shared convictions. The very attitudes valued as freedom-producing in one set of circumstances may, in a later generation, seem a serious threat to social survival.

Men cannot live effectively without some basic convictions about values, nor can they perpetuate social, economic, and political institutions if they refuse a minimal degree of obedience to the authorities identified with their functioning. The troubling question is whether men must convince themselves of the absolute as opposed to a provisional acceptance of the value of desired ends if they are to act effectively on behalf of those ends. Absolutists tend to argue that men require some fixed stars by which to guide their lives—that there are, in fact, values which are absolute, eternal, unchanging, part of the very order of things, ignored only at men's peril. Relativists, on the other hand, tend to deny there are eternal values, though they may sometimes want to claim that values are objective in the sense that knowledge of a specific situation leads reasonable men to understand how some values, for *that* situation, are clearly discernible. Relativists also confront absolutists with the claims that no convincing *proof* of the eternality of values can be presented—that even if there *should* be such values, men can never for certain know what they are and, simultaneously, know that they know. The philosophical problem of values is not whether men may feel better or more secure by *believing* their values are absolute. It is rather the problem of how to show that such a belief (which is a psychological matter) can be said to constitute genuine knowledge. Absolutism in values requires not only argument for the position that values are unchanging but a demonstrable means of showing what some of these values are. Thus, unless the absolutist can give convincing answers to the question, "How do you know that your values are absolute?" his position seems empty, since he will be reduced to saying something like: "I know there are absolute values, but I can't name them for certain!"

In some historical situations men cease to worry about whether their values are absolute, yet manage to live satisfactorily with a sense that their goals are worthwhile, their efforts are at least partly proportioned to the achievement of those goals, and the prospects of the future are fairly inviting. A perceptive analyst, Professor Robert L. Calhoun, has characterized this attitude as "modernism," writing as follows:

> Modernism as used here means neither a formal school of thought, nor a vague whole that takes in all civilized life of recent date. It means a particular recurrent mood of temper which in essence is very old, which during the past two hundred years has become more widespread than ever before, but which has never been in any sense universal. Its keynote is active, conscious preoccupation with the present, that is, with affairs in the forefront of one's own time, and comparative disregard for their larger backgrounds. Its disregard extends both to supra-temporal being, the very existence of which it commonly denies, and to the more fateful and tragic aspects of temporality itself. The past, especially the obstinate, urgent past embodied in living tradition, is disparaged; and the incessant surveys of temporal process toward the future is treated as though it were, in all essential respects, compliant to human understanding and control. A tendency to glorify man and his works, though not indeed universal, is typical of the modernistic temper. A strong sense of emancipation pervades it; a sense of having outgrown traditional ideas and obligations by new critical insight. Such insight may issue at the moment in dogmatic rationalism, in positivism or in skepticism. But in each case, the modernist takes pride in having cut away spiritual bonds which else would hold the present and future to the past. This cutting of bonds affects also group solidarity in the present, and modernism usually tends away from the more exacting kinds of group loyalty toward self-reliant individualism and cosmopolitan tolerance. All this converges, for awhile, into an expansive kind of optimism, which may be thought of as modernism in its more naive, "healthy-minded" phase. Among the most thoughtful modernists,

however, skepticism and disillusion grow, and a phase of world weariness or pessimism sets in, to be succeeded by a new period of more radical dogmatic self-commitments.[1]

Professor Calhoun's analysis also contains some statements about the conditions in which the modernist attitude gains form—urban living centers, periods of exploration, the rise of a new class to a position of power, improved material standards of life, ever-widening contacts between previously isolated cultures. His general thesis is that modernism is a consequence of an earlier, less tolerant faith—that the beneficiaries of this earlier faith rather than its creators enjoy the world. Modernism, in Professor Calhoun's view, is sometimes the creator of later revolutions but is not itself revolutionary, since modernism values toleration and moderation. In contrast, religious or semireligious faiths like Christianity or Marxism are more genuinely radical in temper.

A number of thinkers have expressed concern over what they consider the loss of consensus about moral values in the twentieth century. They suspect that moral relativism, as a doctrine influential in the age, is causally related to some economic and political consequences which, in their eyes, reasonably sensitive persons will view with alarm. Professor W. T. Stace suggests that future historians will lament the absence in this century of fixed moral codes by which men might have conducted their lives in times of change and widespread crisis. He also criticizes the philosophers who, speaking with many tongues on basic moral issues, have added intellectual confusion to the extensive moral bewilderment which has sapped the sense of social obligation and of moral order. Professor Stace's rhetoric is powerful when he charges: "But those who preach the various relativisms have taken upon themselves a heavy load of responsibility. By formulating abstractly the defeatism of the age they have made themselves the aiders and abettors of death. They are injecting the poison into the veins of civilization. Their influence upon practical affairs may indeed be small. But it counts for something. And they cannot

[1] "The Dilemma of Humanitarian Modernism," *The Christian Understanding of Man*, T. E. Jessop and others, eds. (New York: Willett, 1938), pp. 45–46.

avoid their share of the general responsibility. They have failed to do what little they could to stem the tide." [2]

On the other hand, a sociologist like Morris Ginsberg points out in his essay "Moral Bewilderment" that general diagnoses of the whole mentality of a period, though rather easily made, are extremely difficult to prove, especially if they argue for the view that moral degeneration is a widespread phenomenon. Such diagnoses often emphasize only a few factors in a society while completely over-looking others. Ginsberg argues that there is really no readily convincing evidence that contemporary morals are, *on the whole,* worse than those of a previous generation—though in a functional way a community's notions about morality may change, people becoming less exercised morally about specific sexual practices, say, but more morally concerned about economic morality. Moreover, in contrast to Professor Stace, Professor Ginsberg insists: "There is no evidence that doctrines of this kind necessarily affect the working code of the people who teach them. For philosophical analysis is one thing, actual morality another. There is still less evidence that such doctrines are at all widely accepted by nonphilosophers or that they make articulate a widely diffused belief that the distinctions between right and wrong are ephemeral and arbitrary." [3] Yet, Ginsberg admits that our century is marked by what he terms a "moral malaise" some of whose aspects can be recognized—a malaise which establishes the environment in which men must wrestle with their moral perplexities and dilemmas. However, this concern can be treated as a sign of "moral ferment" rather than as an indicator of moral decay, showing that men are bothered by the lack of clear moral guidelines rather than indifferent to them. Among the causes of modern moral bewilderment, according to Professor Ginsberg, are the failure of religious leaders success-

[2] W. T. Stace, *The Concept of Morals* (New York: Macmillan, 1937), pp. 60–61.

[3] Professor Ginsberg's "Moral Bewilderment" appears in his *On the Diversity of Morals,* volume one of his *Essays in Sociology and Social Philosophy* (New York: Macmillan, 1957), pp. 1–9. Other relevant essays in this volume are "The Moral Basis of Political Conflicts" (pp. 10–25), "Ethical Relativity and Political Theory" (pp. 26–40), and "On the Diversity of Morals" (pp. 97–129). Volume two of Professor Ginsberg's collected essays is titled *Reason and Unreason in Society* (New York: Macmillan, 1960), and volume three, *Evolution and Progress* (New York: Macmillan, 1961).

fully to point out how their congregations can use the moral principles they are taught in facing extremely complex problems; the involved way in which questions of fact are "interweaved" with ethical questions; the peculiarly disturbing way in which modern propaganda seeks to influence behavior by emotional uses of moral appeal, suggesting a basic insincerity; and the extent to which some moralists stand forth as fanatics, tending to condone or even to encourage the open resort to force and violence for the realization of their aims.

Relativism

Different types of arguments in support of relativism can be given, some of them based on factual material, others on logical and philosophical considerations. The factual arguments rest on the surface obviousness of the diversity of moral and other values in different cultures or societies. As any student of anthropology knows, if he has read no more than Ruth Benedict's *Patterns of Culture,* different cultural groups reflect varying "ways of life." What the Kwakiutl tribe value is not necessarily what is valued by the Zuni or the Dobu. Cultural groups also arrange their values in widely differing hierarchies of importance. A person raised in a society which is, at least verbally, monogamous in its view of sexuality and marriage will be surprised to learn that a Dobu male, living in a tribal culture which values hostility, must marry that girl with whom he has slept but failed to rise early enough to leave still a single man. Many a college freshman or sophomore, guilt-ridden by thoughts about the allurements of premarital sexual attachments (perhaps only in a pre-Kinsey era?) must have considered a trip to Dobuland, for in the words of Professor Benedict, in the Dobu culture:

> Marriage is set in motion by a hostile act of the mother-in-law. She blocks with her own person the door of her house within which the youth is sleeping with her daughter, and he is trapped for the public ceremony of betrothal. Before this, since the time of puberty, the boy has slept each night in the houses of unmarried girls. By custom his own house is closed to him. He avoids entanglements for several years by spreading his favours widely and leaving the house well before daylight. When he is trapped at last, it is usually because

he has tired of his roaming and has settled upon a more constant companion. He ceases to be so careful about early rising.[4]

Even if the different cultures of the world have shown, as many an anthropologist has claimed, a "basic culture pattern"—a pattern by which needs are met—they have often given a variety of contents to the pattern. A specific culture marked even by a fairly high degree of continuity may also experience an important shift in some of its values from one historical period to another. The Victorian Age in England valued sexual conformity in women more, probably, than did the postwar age in England; and David Riesman in *The Lonely Crowd,* a sociological interpretation of changing American values, has argued that thrift and independent enterprise were more highly valued in an earlier period than they are valued in a contemporary affluent society which prizes adaptation and "other-directedness" over "inner-directedness" and individualism.

A person who is sceptical of the claim that there are absolute moral values can embarrass the absolutist by a number of factual "moves." The sceptic can call attention to the historical record as evidence for *historical relativism.* To give just one example, the pre-Restoration period in England witnessed a rigidity in moral evaluations because of the great influence of Puritan ideas on the active politics of the day, while after 1660 a revulsion from Puritan standards led to a great laxity in manners and public morals even in the same country. The sceptic can argue for what is known as *sociological relativism,* since he can show how as a matter of fact different cultures—and different subcultures within a single society which is pluralistic—actually reflect differing codes of conduct. Or the sceptic may argue for the doctrine of *psychological relativism*—the position that moral evaluations stem from the individual's preferences and choices. A sociological relativist may explain an individual's values by saying they reflect the standards of some group to which he gives primary loyalty, while a psychological relativist may argue that group standards happen to be empirical and not necessary reflections of persons whose evaluations happen, his-

---

[4] Ruth Benedict, *Patterns of Culture* (Boston: Houghton, 1959). Used by permission of Houghton Mifflin Company. [Reprinted from the Mentor edition (1959), p. 124.]

torically and sociologically, to be in agreement on some fundamental issues. Even when groups and individuals behave fairly consistently according to either group or individual codes or standards, these standards may change in the future. This means, of course, that the standards of the group (or of the individual) are what at any given time they happen to be, and those of one period have no necessary normative claim on those of a later period. Those actions and intentions are better (or worse) which a group, or an individual, at a given point believes to be better (or worse).

A number of philosophical (as opposed to "factual") arguments favorable to the doctrine of relativism can also be given. Three of these deserve consideration. One is the famous point made by David Hume (1711–1776), the influential Scotch philosophical sceptic, that descriptions of fact are significantly different from statements of a morally normative kind. A second is the argument that value assertions, including moral evaluations about "good," "ought" and "right," are neither true nor false and thus lack cognitive significance. A third is the argument that moral assertions are really not assertions at all but, rather, imperatives or commands having prescriptive force. These three arguments actually overlap and reflect the general view that no one can give a universally convincing "proof" that moral assertions are objective or absolute, including the absolutist who insists there are such moral norms or rules and the agnostic, who isn't sure, yet who keeps trying to show that there are.

David Hume's moral philosophy denies the possibility of a rational morality whose principles (like "Lying is always wrong" and "Fairness is always morally right") can be universal. Rather, he thought that morality represents a certain expression of human sentiment and a peculiar kind of disinterestedness with respect to interests. Morality is founded neither on reason nor on the relations between objects which can be objectively described and measured. In a famous passage in his *A Treatise of Human Nature,* Hume argues that it is logically impossible to derive "ought"-statements from "is"-statements. The passage reads:

> In every system of morality, which I have hitherto met with, I have always remark'd, that the author proceeds for some time in the ordi-

nary way of reasoning, and establishes the being of a God, or makes observations concerning human affairs; when of a sudden I am sur- priz'd to find, that instead of the usual copulations of propositions, *is,* and *is not,* I meet with no proposition that is not connected with an *ought,* or an *ought not.* This change is imperceptible; but is, how- ever, of the last consequence. For as this *ought,* or *ought not,* ex- presses some new relation or affirmation, 'tis necessary that it shou'd be observ'd and explain'd; and at the same time that a reason should be given, for what seems altogether inconceivable, how this new rela- tion can be a deduction from others, which are entirely different from it. But as authors do not commonly use this precaution, I shall presume to recommend it to the readers; and am persuaded, that this small attention wou'd subvert all the vulgar systems of morality, and let us see, that the distinction of vice and virtue is not founded merely on the relations of objects, nor is perceiv'd by reason.[5]

The implication is that moral judgments do not describe objective properties of things or relations between things, but express the desires of individuals or the values possessed by members of a specific group or community. Hume's position has had a continuing influence on thinkers concerned with value theory, since the position entails that moral assertions are different from propositions which are true or false. The consequence is that, since Hume, it has been difficult for absolutists or objectivists in morals to show how, if at all, value judg- ments can have universal cognitive significance.

Hume's emphatic disclosure of the difference in the logical force of descriptions and evaluations ("The book is about the French Revo- lution" as distinguished from "This book about the French Revolu- tion is a good one"), need not lead to ethical relativism unless this doctrine is to mean absence of a clearly rational demonstration that some moral principles are binding universally on men, in all times and places. Nonetheless, Hume's position has often influenced thinkers— whether rightly or wrongly—to draw relativistic conclusions from it. Hume himself thought that political life rested on a "way of life" in which customs and traditions functioned to direct and influence be- havior. These customs were conventions, as it were, made up by men as means to a relatively pleasurable existence; but they were not

[5] *A Treatise of Human Nature,* ed. L. A. Selby-Bigge (Oxford: Clarendon Press, 1955), pp. 469–470.

thereby necessarily arbitrary. Like Edmund Burke, Hume was a political conservative who cautioned men against the attempt to "deduce"
social and political institutions from "pure reason" rather than to
judge them in the light of their usefulness in the production of minimal happiness and order and the restraint of basically hostile and
destructive human tendencies. Yet, Hume's position places him in the
camp of the moral noncognitivists—those thinkers who deny that
ethical evaluations (or assertions) are strictly true or false, a peculiarly "factual" description of a moral state of affairs "out there," so
to speak, to be apprehended by reason (as natural law thinkers have
sometimes argued).

In this century the noncognitivist position has flourished quite con-
spicuously in some philosophical quarters. Existentialist writers (like
Sartre, for example) have stressed decision as the core of morality,
doubting that any essential morality exists independently of human
willing, insisting that men must accept the risks and responsibility of
decisions in a universe which is otherwise morally purposeless and
marked, for men, by many moral ambiguities to which there are no
objectively certifiable "keys." More powerfully and analytically, a
number of thinkers subscribed, to one degree or another, to the basic
tenets of a position known as "logical positivism" or "logical empiri-
cism." In England, A. J. Ayer, and in America, C. J. Stevenson, to
name only two influential popularizers of this viewpoint, helped to
make logical positivism a philosophical force which reached readers
beyond the fairly narrow confines of academic halls. Ayer's *Language, Truth and Logic* (1936) and Stevenson's *Ethics and Language,*
(1944) are historically significant works for the way in which the
former traced the implications of logical positivist thought in a number of areas and the latter wrestled with its implications for ethics.
Science, rather than religion or common sense, served as the model for
many logical positivists, whose aim was to make philosophy as scientific as possible—thus the title of one of Hans Reichenbach's books,
The Rise of Scientific Philosophy (1951). Wearied by the "nonsense"
and obfuscation contained in many philosophical writings, as well as
enamored of the laudable aims of clarity and rigor, these philosophers
wanted to find out—once and for all, if possible—which kinds of

statements can be said to make rational sense and which, if any, make no such sense. If genuine philosophical questions could be resolved in the fairly satisfying ways in which many scientific questions had given way to logic and experimentation, then philosophy might make a limited and public kind of progress; if not, then "so much the worse for philosophy" was the verdict which should be rendered.

The logical positivist position involved the view that meaningful statements (assertions, propositions) must be either true or false if they are to have cognitive significance. They found two major types or classes of cognitively meaningful statements to exist—logical statements which are true by virtue of their form alone, which they called *analytic* truths since their truth reported nothing about the world of ordinary fact; and factual (or empirical) statements which are true or false according as they do, or fail to, report or describe actual features of the world. These empirically meaningful statements must, in principle, be subject to experimental and/or observational verification, either directly or indirectly. Examples of logical truths would be statements like "If Tom is a bachelor, then he is unmarried," "If Tom is shorter than Bill, and Bill is shorter than Frank, then Tom is shorter than Frank," and "A red object is a colored object." Examples of empirical statements would be assertions like the following: "Water freezes at 32° Fahrenheit," "Bachelor Tom is thirty years old, a Democrat, and more than six feet tall," and "Men live on the moon." Empirical statements need not be testable immediately, but for them to qualify as empirical, men must be in a position to know the conditions under which they could be verified or "checked."

The implications for ethics and politics are almost self-evident. We can have empirical knowledge of moral codes and political institutions if enough social scientists undertake regulated investigations and ask questions subject to verifiable answers. *That* the Kwakiutls practice certain rituals can be observed and described by anthropologists, and *that* the Hopi Indians favor certain ethical views can also (though in a weaker way) be learned if sufficiently sensitive social scientists patiently study both cultures. But to say that the Hopi's ethical views are right or wrong is to render a *normative* judgment about what can, in its own terms, be described. A troublesome question is *how* to validate such a normative judgment, since it may express or evince an attitude of approval or disapproval of a person who belongs to another culture or ethical "way" of seeing things, a "way" which itself is not necessarily universal, but partial and culture-bound. Noncognitivists in ethical theory maintain that *normative* ethical judgments are neither true or false, thus are not really statements at all but expressions of interest or approval, subject to challenge by others and not resolvable, in the case of conflict, by ordinary scientific or common-sense means as are factual disputes to which evidence is relevant. Indeed, some noncognitivists in ethics have advanced a restricted view known as "ethical emotivism"—a position which argues that the use of ethical terms (like "good," "wrong," "right," "bad," "evil," "valuable") is purely emotive in force, expressing a speaker's feelings.

Some thinkers influenced by the central doctrines of the logical positivists became radical noncognitivists. Professor A. J. Ayer presented a brief version of such a radical noncognitivism in ethics. According to Ayer, there are no genuinely ethical propositions or judgments, thus ethical expressions cannot be statements about an independent reality nor can they be a peculiar kind of description. Ethical expressions are literally meaningless—though they are not, on that account, unimportant. They are expressions of emotion, thus extremely important—but they cannot be shown to be either true or false. Indeed, so anxious to appear consistent in his brand of ethical emotivism was Ayer, that he willingly classified himself, at the time, as a "subjectivist" in ethics, writing as follows:

> Thus, although our theory of ethics might fairly be said to be radically subjectivist, it differs in a very important respect from the orthodox subjectivist theory. For the orthodox subjectivist does not deny, as we do, that the sentences of a moralizer express genuine propositions. All he denies is that they express propositions of a unique non-empirical character. His own view is that they express propositions about the speaker's feelings. If this were so, ethical judgments clearly would be capable of being true or false. They would be true if the speaker had the relevant feelings, and false if he had not. And this is a matter which is, in principle, empirically verifiable. Furthermore, they could be significantly contradicted, for if I say, "Tolerance is a virtue," and someone answers, "You don't approve of it," he would,

on the ordinary subjectivist theory, be contradicting me. On our theory, he would not be contradicting me, because, in saying that tolerance was a virtue, I should not be making any statement about my own feelings or about anything else. I should simply be evincing my feelings, which is not at all the same thing as saying that I have them.[6]

Ayer's position is, clearly, that ethical expressions are neither expressions of feelings nor necessarily propositions about feelings—a position which, as Ayer recognized, is subject to the criticism that men cannot genuinely argue about value questions. This is a conclusion which Ayer was ready to accept.

Ayer argues that men do seem to engage in arguments about value questions, but he denies the arguments are *ultimately* about values. Rather they are about facts. Disagreements which are subject to argumentation cannot be about moral values but, in the language of C. L. Stevenson, must be about "beliefs"—where beliefs are assumptions men make about what the facts in a situation are. To change someone's value orientation (including his moral notions) means to argue about the facts—to point out how he has overlooked some feature in a specific situation, some motive or some consequence of action—rather than to lead the person to "see" his ethical feelings as mistaken. The aim of argument is, thus, to alter a person's knowledge of the facts such that he *may* change his ethical position. Unless persons and groups (or "interests") engaged in ethical and political disputes can transform such disputes into considerations of facts, there can be no "solutions" to such disagreements. Psychologists and sociologists and economists thus will be needed, rather than moral philosophers, if apparent ethical disagreements are to be analyzed as expressive of peoples' desires and aims. As Ayer expressed this view, "The further task of describing the different feelings that the different ethical terms are used to express, and the different reactions that they customarily provoke, is a task for the psychologist." If two persons cannot agree on the facts of a case, thus perhaps coming to agreement, they will continue to share different moral "viewpoints" or attitudes,

[6] A. J. Ayer, *Language, Truth and Logic* (London: Gollancz, 1951), p. 109. Used by permission of Victor Gollancz Ltd.

and no amount of moral argument will alter the disagreement. Ayer insists that an "opponent" whose "moral conditioning" has differed from ours may even agree to the facts of a *case* and *still* disagree about their moral significance. Two persons who so "disagree" in moral attitude rely on different sets of values, and there is no way for one to "prove" to the other that his set of values is superior.

Not every logical positivist ethical writer is as extreme in his emotivist position as is Ayer. Professor C. L. Stevenson thought that ethical "assertions" not only express or evince feelings and attitudes but, in disputes, themselves function as persuasive devices to win another to one's moral viewpoint.[7] Similarly, philosophical definitions of ethical terms like "good," "right," "ought" contain a persuasive aspect, since philosophers seek to persuade their hearers to adopt these specific definitions rather than other (possible) ones. Stevenson's *Ethics and Language* also develops more fully the degree to which ethical disputes may be about matters of belief, revealing a profound awareness of the complexity in the relations between "beliefs" and "attitudes." Stevenson appears to argue for two major, perhaps incompatible points. One is that men's "beliefs" (factual in principle, thus either true or false) do *as a matter of fact* usually influence their moral attitudes. A second is the logical point that, still, it is possible in principle for two persons to agree on matters of fact—thus share the same "beliefs"—and yet remain in fundamental moral, or attitudinal, disagreement. The general position of Stevenson is that even disagreements of moral attitude can sometimes be resolved by patient analysis of the disputants' beliefs but that, even if factual agreement is reached, a moral disagreement *may* still remain. Disagreements of moral attitude are not resolvable, however, by a scientific "proof" which can show that one attitude is intrinsically right and the other wrong. Reasons for each can be given, but these cannot be like logical or scientific proofs. The implication is, then, that the more knowledge men gain the better are the chances they can in fact resolve many of their moral disagreements, even though there is no logical guarantee that this *must* be so.

[7] *Ethics and Language* (New Haven: Yale University Press, 1944).

A perceptive writer has neatly stated the ethical positions of persons like Ayer and Stevenson in the following way:

> At this point you might like to ask: Is there no objective standard for the truth or falsity of moral evaluations or judgments—a standard that would in some absolute sense prove that some actions are right and others wrong? The answer of the positivist is no. To the extent that ethical judgments express attitudes, they are, like imperative statements, neither true nor false. This, however, is no reason to regard our moral choices and evaluations as irrational and to give up any attempt to guide conduct by reason. In many cases moral conflicts arise not from conflicting attitudes but from disagreements in belief, and even where attitudes are in conflict, they may to a large extent be altered by rational persuasion. Of course, in so far as people are in agreement on all relevant facts and still disagree in attitude and refuse to be moved by any form of persuasion, there is nothing that can be done about the matter. Moral conflict in such cases is inevitable.[8]

Are logical positivists like Ayer and Stevenson, say, necessarily ethical relativists? This is not a question to which a simpler answer can easily be given. It all depends on what one means by "relativism." If a relativist is defined as one who denies there are eternal values, then these men are relativists. Or if relativism is defined as involving any view which denies that ultimate moral standards are subject to universal "proof" by varying men, then these men are relativists. On the other hand, if a relativist is a person who must deny there is even an empirical (as opposed to a logical) relation between our knowledge and our moral views, than Ayer and especially Stevenson are not relativists, since they think we can often resolve ethical disputes by appeal to facts. They are, however, relativists if relativism is a doctrine to the effect that our moral judgments do not report independent or, in G. E. Moore's phrase, "objective" properties of things.[9] Certainly, both Ayer and Stevenson clearly deny that there are "unique"

---

[8] John L. Mothershead, Jr., *Ethics: Modern Conceptions of the Principles of Right* (New York: Holt, 1960), p. 123. Used by permission of Holt, Rinehart and Winston, Inc.

[9] G. E. Moore defended ethical "objectivism" in his now famous *Principia Ethica* (London: Cambridge University Press, 1903).

or privileged value-facts, as it were, which discerning moralists discover and report.

Thus, in this century the "cognitivist" position in ethics and value theory—that moral *knowledge* is a possibility—has received a searching critical analysis. Many thinkers have come to doubt that values are objective properties of things and events, even unique ones, and as such subject to true or false, correct or mistaken description. It it far from clear how a convincing proof can be produced to show that values are objective, even for those who remain convinced, on some grounds, that moral judgments are not simply relative to persons, or to times and places. But, does the embarrassment of the cognitivist in value theory harbor practical consequences? Does it matter "in the market place" that noncognitivism has won a wide following among contemporary philosophers? Professor Sidney Zink has argued, forcefully, that it does. In his *The Concepts of Ethics* (1962) Zink has faced, candidly and worriedly, the disturbing fact that in considering ethical judgments men uniquely experience the conviction that "some of them must be mistaken" but also that they "cannot establish or get agreement that they are such." In contrast with science, disagreements in ethical (and other value) judgments are not subject to a convincing test by which they can be resolved. Facing the question whether men must decide between the cognitivist and the noncognitivist positions, Zink argues that the answer must be in the affirmative, reasoning as follows:

> Perhaps we need not decide? We might treat values as a borderline case, and say that in one respect value judgments are like claims to knowledge, while in another respect they are not. But there is a decision to make, namely whether we shall try to get more agreement in our value judgments. All value theorists seem to agree in this value judgment, that it would be generally good to have more agreement in value judgments. Well, if we think values are knowable, we will have more hope of getting agreement, and make more effort to get agreement, than if we think they are not. And we will be more likely to get agreement if we try to get it. There is then a pragmatic advantage in adopting the objectivist hypothesis. By trying in the concrete to obtain the agreement which would prove the hypothesis true, we are most likely to succeed in proving this. And if we do not succeed, still we will have obtained more of an end universally recognized as

desirable than if we assumed that the cognitivist hypothesis were either false or unverifiable.[10]

To act on the decision that value judgments represent a possible kind of knowledge need not commit one to an absolute position, if "absolutist" means that values as knowable are eternal or inviolable. One can adopt a position known as *situational objectivism,* sometimes —perhaps confusingly—also referred to as *objective relativism.* This position permits one to admit that values are objective in specific situations *and* that situations can change. Values would then be objective *relative* to a situation. To know those values would require knowledge of a situation, such that any well-informed person in that situation would (tend to) adopt the values of any other well-informed person in *that* situation. Thus, values would be viewed as contextually knowable. Applied to politics, this position would mean that where men are found in serious disagreement on issues, they must be viewed as in disagreement about what the situation genuinely is—or, in the "language" of C. L. Stevenson, that their differing evaluations reflect some basic disagreements in belief (as to what the facts are). Of course, they may also disagree about what the facts will be *if* certain policies or procedures are followed—just as they may (logically) continue to disagree in attitude, according to Stevenson. However, the *situational objectivist* must reject Stevenson on this last point, arguing that *as a matter of fact* men who agree about the facts of a situation will reach common agreement in their evaluations. Thus, it cannot be convincing to a situational objectivist to give as a reason for a disagreement in attitude between two men: "Oh, they simply share fundamentally opposed attitudes" unless, by this assertion, the speaker means some (as yet) undisclosed (and perhaps undiscoverable) disagreement about the situation causes the disagreement in attitude.

Social and Political Appraisals

In his *The Vocabulary of Politics,* Professor T. D. Weldon argued strongly against the view that political "scepticism" and "subject-

[10] Sidney Zink, *The Concepts of Ethics* (New York: Macmillan, 1962), p. 41. Used by permission of The Macmillan Co.

ivism" follow from a denial that political judgments about men, events, and institutions can be deduced certainly from axiomatic principles. To say that political judgments can never be shown to be cognitively absolute does not entail that they are necessarily arbitrary or without reasons. The word "subjectivist" when applied to the views of ethical or political theorists functions emotively, suggesting that unless men know *absolutely* they know nothing at all in ethics and politics. A demand for standards in politics which are objective in the sense of being absolute is an "impossible" demand. It calls for the same degree of certainty in the criteria used in politics and morals as is sometimes possible (perhaps) in the measurement of physical objects. Rather, moral and political judgments are appraisals of men, policies, and institutions—as such, neither absolute nor subjective but usually based on much empirical evidence and accumulated experience in making a fairly wide range of human judgments. What Weldon maintains, then, is that political appraisals can be based on "evidence," thus be "better" or "worse," though they cannot be shown to be true or false in the literal way that a report, say, that "the book is on the table" can be substantiated as so or not in a specific context. Judgment enters into the making of political appraisals, but it is a judgment more like that possessed by knowledgeable persons who render aesthetic judgments such as: "That's a splendid painting!" than a judgment made by geometricians who deduce sure conclusions from axiomatic premises.

To say that a given person qualifies for a job, or that a specific policy is desirable, or that a political institution functions well is to render an appraisal for which supporting reasons can be given. It does not mean to say simply: "I happen to like the person for the job, approve of the policy, prefer the institution." Nor does it mean that the appraiser is describing objective "properties" of persons, policies, or institutions in the way a philosopher like G. E. Moore argued on behalf of the objectivity of value judgments. Appraisals are neither literal descriptions of "properties" nor subjective expressions of personal preferences. They are a peculiar kind of judgment which is made contextually for which "evidence" or "reasons" can be adduced but not in an absolutely convincing way if disagreement occurs. A similar position is advanced by Professor Stephen Toulmin [in *The Place of Reason in Ethics* (1953)] who defends the "good reasons" view of ethical inquiry.

Suppose a specific community is faced with the question whether a new public hospital, maintained from public funds, is desirable. The first task to be undertaken is a "factual" one, a careful assessment of whether the hospital can be built if the citizens want it, plus a survey of citizens' preferences. A host of factual questions can be raised relevant to whether, if the decision to build is made, the project can be realized. Will the present tax structure support the project? If not, can the taxes be raised? Are there sufficient nurses available? Can equipment be purchased? Will the building of the hospital interfere with other planned projects (say, a new junior college or a new public park)? Experts can be employed to make these inquiries, which they can put in the hypothetical form: "If the citizens desire this hospital, the following conditions must be fulfilled." But, suppose the citizens are in fundamental disagreement, some saying yes, a hospital is needed, others saying no, it is undesirable. Can reasoning influence either group to give way to the other? Both Weldon and Toulmin would say that reasons for either policy decision could be given, such that one set of reasons might prove decisive with individuals though this cannot be guaranteed. Thus, if public attitudes remain sharply divided even after reasons *pro* and *con* have been given, an impasse would be reached. There would still be a difference between those citizens who reached a decision on the basis of reasons given (thus rendered their appraisals after deliberation) and those citizens who simply "held fast" to their original convictions.

Another twentieth-century philosopher who believed that "facts" and "values" are always related was John Dewey, whose social and political philosophy presupposed that intelligent men can, in some trying circumstances, handle value problems in a scientific manner. Dewey suggested that exclamations may, contextually, imply propositions.[11] For example, "Help!" is an exclamation which is neither true

[11] One important work in which Dewey succinctly developed his value position is his *Theory of Valuation,* International Encyclopedia of Unified Science, Vol. II, No. 4 (Chicago: University of Chicago Press, 1939), especially p. 12.

nor false since it asserts nothing in its starkness. However, if we hear a drowning man shout "Help!", we may assume the exclamation "implies" some (tacit?) assertions, perhaps like: "A drowning man needs help"; "Any healthy bystander is obligated to assist a person who is drowning"; "Human life is a very high value"; and so forth. On the other hand if, in another situation, we come upon a college student at a dance who, while being kissed by an extremely pretty girl, says "Help!" we may assume propositions to be implied of the following kind: "This student is pretending to need assistance"; "The English language has uses other than literal ones"; "Some students—like this one!—possess delightfully playful streaks"; and so forth. Thus, on Dewey's view, not even ejaculatory or exclamatory utterances are merely expressions of present feelings, since in specific contexts they may be said to imply other kinds of assertions—thus to have *implicitly* cognitive functions. Dewey's view was that, though factual and evaluative assertions seem logically distinct, nonetheless they are *as a matter of fact* usually, perhaps always, related. Thus, value assertions are subject to scientific and commonsense tests. Human intelligence is, on this view, an essential means for the realization of social and political values and for the amelioration of value conflicts in a very real world. Nonetheless, Dewey's value "experimentalism" involved the possibility of some failures, leading Dewey to admit that should intelligence sometimes prove inadequate to resolve great social and political perplexities all need not be lost. According to Dewey,

> When theories of values do not afford intellectual assistance in framing ideas and beliefs about values that are adequate to direct action, the gap must be filled by other means. If intelligent method is lacking, prejudice, the pressure of immediate circumstances, self-interest and class-interest, traditional customs, institutions of *accidental* historic origin are *not* lacking, and they tend to take the place of intelligence.[12]

In a century marked by many appeals to irrationalism as a way out of human problems, Dewey's pragmatism rejected the sharp separation between facts and values advocated by many and argued that

[12] *Experience and Nature* (Chicago: Open Court, 1926), p. 265.

intelligence has a directive function. Dewey refused to identify judgments that a thing is "satisfying" and that it is "satisfactory," since the former are reports while the latter are genuine judgments of value, subject to inquiry. Clearly, Dewey recognized that the fact that men desire something is insufficient to determine that the thing is genuinely desirable. Aware that philosophical critics argued that Dewey could not show that value judgments have the same logic as factual ones, Dewey continued to insist there can be genuine judgments of value, arguing in his famous *The Quest for Certainty* (1929) that ordinary speech reflects this view:

> The endings "able," "worthy," and "ful" are cases in point. Noted and notable, noteworthy; remarked and remarkable; advised and advisable; wondered at and wonderful; pleasing and beautiful; loved and lovable; blamed and blameable; blameworthy; objected to and objectionable; esteemed and estimable; admired and admirable; shamed and shameful; honored and honorable; approved and approvable, worthy of approbation, etc. The multiplication of words adds nothing to the force of the distinction. But it aids in conveying a sense of the fundamental character of the distinctions; of the difference between mere report of an already existent fact and judgment as to the importance and need of bringing a fact into existence; or, if it is already there, of sustaining it in existence. The latter is a genuine practical judgment, and marks the only type of judgment that has to do with the direction of action. Whether or no we reserve the term "value" for the latter (as seems to me proper) is a minor matter; that the distinction be acknowledged as the key to understanding the relation of values to the direction of conduct is the important thing.[13]

Moral Experiment?

Dewey's philosophy called for an "experimentalism" in social and political affairs, a reflection of a liberal view of the state as a means to enriched human existence. Probably Dewey stressed too greatly the usefulness of scientific methods to persons concerned with value issues perplexing a commnnity. Dewey resisted absolute separation of "means" and "ends," but there does nonetheless appear to be a dif-

[13] John Dewey, *The Quest for Certainty* (New York: Minton Balch, 1929), p. 261. Reprinted by permission of G. P. Putnam's Sons.

ference between learning *how* to reach a certain goal and "justifying" that goal as a worthwhile one. Experiment usually takes place within a restricted context, part of which contains "settled" theory, since not everything can be "questioned" at once. Given agreement *that* X is worthwhile, perhaps men can "experiment" with various policies aimed at X's achievement or advancement. But given a community lacking in ethical agreement (or, in Dewey's language, some "shared values"), no amount of experimentalism will teach its members *what* is worthwhile. A goodly share of Dewey's practical philosophy is concerned with questions of *how* to achieve values already agreed upon —always a crucially important philosophical matter. It is questionable that science can teach man what those values are, though it can be helpful in the realization of those values once a community decides to seek their extensions. A moral experiment which could teach a person ignorant about values which values to pursue makes no sense at all, if taken literally.

A Problematic Conclusion

Suppose a "listener" has "heard" the foregoing remarks in a public lecture and reacted to them in the following way:

> So, there are a number of thinkers—especially philosophers apparently—who are worried about relativism in values in one way or another. So what? What are the practical implications of such philosophical disputes? Why should I become agitated since I'm concerned about the *concrete* and *practical* sides of social and political matters?

Can any argument, if not conclusive proof, be produced to indicate how the concern over value relativism may have a direct bearing on actual affairs of men?

Unfortunately, the matter is not a simple one. The reader has already heard one argument for belief in value objectivism—the pragmatic one given by Professor Zink. Still, a sceptic may reply, even to Zink's argument, that fanaticism also follows from a concern with objectivism—since it is an easy step to the position that "my side" holds to an objectively sure position while "your side" is wrongheaded —that is, objectivist *claims* may be themselves the causes of certain great crises in social and political life. The broad question is, however, whether philosophical discussion of the value problem may be said to have genuine significance in practical life.

This chapter has attempted to indicate some ways in which there can be serious concern over the question *whether* a relativistic attitude is *in fact* widespread in ethics and politics in the contemporary world. This concern appears more or less factual in emphasis. Nonetheless, historians and sociologists as well as social critics can disagree about whether a thoroughly reliable answer to such a factual concern is readily available, since the "evidence" is often difficult to establish beyond a shadow of a reasonable doubt. Moreover, even if an expert decides on the basis of "evidence" that a relativistic attitude is widespread, the "question" whether this should be viewed as "a good thing" or as "a bad thing" receives differing "answers" from interested thinkers. Many social and political thinkers argue that a relativistic attitude tends to produce undesirable, even sometimes disastrous consequences. Other thinkers deny that this need be so. Assuming that ethical and political relativism is prevalent in this century, what value interpretation can a social and political philosopher render about the significance of what is assumed? To conclude this chapter, the historical judgment of a contemporary philosopher about the factual issue will be taken as true (for purposes of argument). A persuasive argument, in the form of a story, will then be given in an effort to convince the reader that the concern over the status of values is an important one in this century. Since the argument cannot be "proved," its persuasiveness is readily admitted; but it will be offered as an instance of a kind of argument which, though admittedly subject to counterarguments, has a rightful place in a book devoted to social and political philosophy.

The historical judgment which will not be questioned here is that rendered by Professor Charles Frankel in his challenging book *The Case for Modern Man*. The judgment is as follows:

> Since the early part of the nineteenth century, it is unquestionable that most philosophies of a liberal bent have been, to use the current expression, "relativistic" in their approach to all moral codes and social systems. They have denied, that is to say, that there are any

eternal moral principles which are unquestionable, or any immutable standards by which all men and all societies can be judged. In any system of values, for a philosophical "relativist," there is an element of simple preference or interest which cannot be eliminated by argument; and so in any moral system there is always something accidental or personal or limited, something wholly a-rational, which is "relative" to a man's tastes or to his special historical circumstances of a specific place or time. So there cannot be any single system of morals or politics which holds good for everyone; and there cannot be any special group of experts who can lay down the infallible last word on questions of value.[14]

If the factual estimate made by Professor Frankel should be a correct one, would any significant consequences follow for contemporary men? More precisely, could an argument be found to show how an unexamined relativism may present contemporary men with a significant problem? Could the purported fact of widespread belief in ethical relativism be taken as a starting point of something like an argument for a reexamination of the problem of values in the modern era? The ensuing story about Professor Anxious Q. Values, a fictional character, should be read as one possible attempt to form such an argument. The story presupposes the reader knows a bit about current historical and political problems and is not so optimistic as to believe "all will work out for the best" without any intellectual and practical efforts by living men. As a persuasive conclusion to this chapter, the story aims to convince the reader that, whether he chooses to side for or against the ethical relativist, he cannot do so *lightly* in the contemporary world and that, in fact, he must give careful attention to the views of those who are critical of ethical relativism.

The story goes that at a leading American university, Professor Anxious Q. Values felt pleasure at being asked by a student group to lecture on the crisis in contemporary men's values. However, he was told "not to give an entirely disinterested lecture but to take a position." He thought this would be a challenging change from his usual attitude in the classroom, in which he prided himself on his "objectivity" and philosophical aloofness from practical questions of society

[14] Charles Frankel, *The Case for Modern Man* (New York: Harper, 1955), pp. 54–55. Used by permission of Harper & Row, publishers, Incorporated.

and politics. The Professor appreciated the invitation as an opportunity for him to present, perhaps even in a forcefully dogmatic manner, his own convictions about the most enduring values for his age. Perhaps he could even try a bit of preaching! Yet, as the day of the lecture approached, he began to experience misgivings. He found that he had taught "objectively" for so long, wishing not to force his own convictions upon his students (or so he told himself!) that he was no longer sure about the values he most honored. Indeed, at one point he thought: "I shall strike a blow for absolute values, since most of my students say they are relativists. I shall attempt to shock them into awareness of another possible viewpoint!" Still, he experienced some doubts that he could succeed if he were to argue for absolute values. What to do? What to say?

A few days before the lecture, still unresolved what position to take, Professor Anxious Q. Values retired, his poor head reeling from an evening of thought about the coming affair. Falling into a deep sleep, he dreamed. And in his dream various "persons," impossible to identify clearly, made consecutive appearances, during which each spoke as if only to the Professor and about the value problem.

The first "person" to appear had (like the others to follow) an indistinct appearance, yet his voice sounded clearly and calmly. The voice announced the speaker as Value Absolutist and spoke as follows:

> Values are absolute and eternal. Moreover, they are transcendent to history, anchored in the nature of Being, which being timeless is not subject to the flux of historical occurrences. Any lasting social, economic, political order must come to terms with these absolute values. These values are discovered rather than invented by men. Either one comes to know them or one does not. Those who lack knowledge of these values live in ignorance. Each and every adequate social system must reflect these fundamental values and, to the extent it does not, must inevitably contain serious defects. In this respect, politics is a philosophical affair. Only those persons who possess the knowledge of absolute values deserve to rule, thus to hold authority over others. If democracy is to be justified as a political system, it must be shown to be a superior means by which to bring men into the knowledge of these values. Otherwise, democracy can have no basic claim to men's allegiance. Thus, knowledge of values requires knowledge of Being or God, and insofar as this is so politics and social affairs are

never finally to be divorced from knowledge of Being or God. The function of men is to learn what these absolute values are and, then, to build social and political institutions which will reflect them.

The second "person" to address Professor Anxious Q. Values in his state of dreaming spoke with assurance also. It was as if he had, like the Professor, "heard" the first speaker. The second voice announced itself as Ethical Relativist and said forthrightly:

All values are relative to time and place and viewpoint. There is no "perspective" from which all existing value viewpoints can be judged. What is "right" and "wrong" varies from culture to culture as well as from historical epoch to historical epoch. Value Absolutist cannot prove his claim to the objectivity of values, nor can he know the nature of those transcendent values about which he speaks. To change one's ethical or other value viewpoint means to adopt another existing value standard. Not only are value statements not literally true or false, they are cognitively meaningful only as reflections of some way of life of a people or culture. Social and political conflicts are likewise relative reflections of different ways by which to evaluate conditions. They can be settled by force or by emotional persuasion, not by reason as such. Personal preferences and historical circumstances play important roles in the creation of a set of values in a specific time and place. There is absolutely no known way by which to prove one way of life *objectively* better than another. Thus, it isn't possible to show that American democratic methods are *objectively* better than communist or fascist ones, or the reverse. These are very different political, economic, and social ways of life for which no independent standard exists by which to measure them comparatively and disinterestedly.

The third "person" to invade Professor Anxious Q. Values' dream announced himself as Pragmatist and spoke with a decided New England accent. Pragmatist had obviously "overheard" the preceding speakers and had their remarks in mind as he said:

Both Absolutist and Relativist are mistaken. True, values are not absolute in the sense of being eternal, nor are they necessarily transcendent to historical conditions. Nonetheless, they aren't thereby relative in the way Ethical Relativist has argued. Values are oriented on situations into which intelligent men can make properly guided inquiries. Value questions are sensible only in terms of expected consequences, and wise men and women determine their values by examining the outcomes of proposed plans of action, thus control their preferences in light of threatening facts. Values are relative to situations and, by virtue of *that* fact, may be said to be objective. In this sense, intelligence can guide action and show men which of their values are now outworn, which are crucial in changed conditions. Scientific knowledge which has helped to revolutionize human institutions and techniques has introduced the need of a sweeping re-examination of human values. Because some perennial values are not exceptionless does not mean they lack universality. For example, normally peace is better than war but there may be some situations which are exceptions. Only human intelligence directed to the solution of concrete practical problems can determine which values deserve to prevail. It may also turn out that continuing inquiry shows us some perennial values as having a very wide status in numerous situations. Thus, values are the results of inquiry into concrete situations in which men worry about how they ought to act in light of facts and consequences desired.

A fourth dream figure spoke more pessimistically than had the earlier "person." This man announced himself as Atheistic Existentialist, and while he neither looked nor sounded like Jean-Paul Sartre, the French existentialist philosopher, he sounded like someone who had read Sartre's writings. His comments introduced some of the qualities of a "quiet" nightmare into the Professor's dreaming, for he said solemnly:

> Relativist is right—there are no objective values for all men. Men must decide *as if* they choose for all men, but men make themselves in their choosing and have no eternal or objective standards by which to relieve themselves of their responsibilities in choosing. But Pragmatist is also right, although he is too optimistic and relies too heavily on human intelligence. Men's decisions should take account of facts, but the facts do not in themselves determine their choices. Man is a freedom. He can hide neither behind facts nor institutions. Absolutist is simply wrongheaded! There are no eternal values. Man is wholly alone in his decisions, fully responsible for his own character in an alien world. There are no preexisting essences or divine "plans." Man creates situations by his choices and must take the consequences, without blaming them on some God. Man continually confronts an abyss of Nothingness. He must face his own inescapable anxieties and live in spite of them. He is abandoned in the universe, meaning there is no divine guidance, no God to whom he

can turn for direction or consolation. Man is also an anguished creature, knowing that he must choose for all men in a universe lacking fixed absolutes by which he can guide his decisions. Ethics is therefore forever ambiguous. The one certainty is that in social, political, and economic matters only a "stinker"—a person who acts or chooses in "bad faith"—tries to justify his decisions by looking to external conditions as "excuses." There are no excuses. In this sense, any ideology oriented on group conformity is evidence of such "bad faith," whether communist, nazi or democratic. The awareness of his terrible aloneness is what is central to all situations requiring anguished decision. Only this human condition is universal, since there is no permanent or fixed human "nature." Thus, men must decide responsibly without a blueprint from God or a political Big Brother!

The final speaker in Professor Anxious Q. Values' dream, now a somewhat troubled one, announced himself as Religious Existentialist. Indeed, he sounded like some contemporary Christian existentialist thinkers, though in appearance he seemed not to resemble the Protestant thinker Paul Tillich, the Catholic philosopher Gabriel Marcel, or the German thinker Karl Jaspers. Nor did he look at all like the great Christian existentialist, Sören Kierkegaard. However, he spoke as one who wanted knowingly to borrow some of the emphases from men such as these, for he argued:

> There is a peculiar development in the order of the speeches you have heard in this, your dream. From confident Absolutist and somewhat contented Pragmatist we have arrived, Professor Values, at Atheistic Existentialist's terrible pessimism and anguish. Perhaps this ordering of the talks in your dream reflects a "movement" in the consciousness of contemporary men, who, having given up the quest after absolute values, may want once again—as has happened before in the history of human thought and experience—to re-examine absolutism in a changed context, in a world threatened as some say by chaos and possible social and political dissolution. Isn't there something strange in a godless existentialism which yet makes you tremble at the idea that you, like all men, are on the edge of a value abyss into which given one false move you will fall, perhaps dragging all of mankind with you? Isn't there something *dreadfully* objective about this picture? Would a man standing by the Grand Canyon, feeling the crowd's pressure pushing him toward its yawning mouth, remain an atheistic existentialist? Wouldn't he rather shout

out the stupidity of the crowd's actions in the name of some permanent values, including that of living? Isn't it possible that some classical religious themes are being rediscovered in our century, partly through the unintended influence of atheists, existentialist and otherwise? It seems to me that if we are aware of the abyss in human existence, we may be aware once again of that feature of life that led earlier men to the discovery of sane stable values, including those contained in religious symbols. I think that the present situation in political life, especially on the international scene, confronts men with the apparent need to rediscover those lasting values without which we shall all disappear into the abyss. But I claim this is not a necessary decision we must make! Before it is too late, we can —perhaps as Pragmatic Existentialists—rediscover the objective worth about which religious men have always spoken. It is even possible that we shall rediscover God, although I am not one to be too hopeful in such matters.

When Professor Anxious Q. Values awakened from his prolonged and exciting dream, he was bathed in perspiration. But the sun streamed through his bedroom window. Outside the songs and twitterings of the birds sounded reassuring. As he staggered from his bed, remembering his dream, the Professor thought that perhaps Religious Existentialist had a major point. Perhaps, after all, it was time to reconsider the usual doctrines about values in the modern world—to do this in the light of the obviously threatening circumstances the atheistic speaker had mentioned. As he dressed, thinking of the speech he was to give to his student group, the Professor said: "Well, I know what I shall do now! I shall tell the students about my dream. And I shall tell them I am partly persuaded that Religious Existentialist deserves a serious hearing again, even in political matters. But . . . I wonder if they will think me mad?"

This chapter ends with Professor Anxious Q. Values' final thought. Will contemporary students think a person mad who suggests it is time again to reexamine objectivist and religious value claims as relevant to our social and political problems?

Some Questions and Problems

1. What consequences may be said to follow for political discussion and decision making if all value judgments are simply statments of per-

sonal preference? Would the consequences necessarily be undesirable ones?

2. Can you think of ways in which some values may be said to be "objective" ones? Which values, if any?

3. Try to indicate how factual considerations should, in your opinion, influence men's judgments of value regarding some important controversial political issues.

4. Is the doctrine of ethical relativism really a serious obstacle to the human quest after agreement on values?

5. Discuss or debate the claim that a civilization will perish unless its members "ground" their values on the absolute transcendence of God (or Being).

6. Assuming you were in a position of power, what steps would you take to compromise a serious political dispute between persons sharing widely divergent value orientations? At what point would you consider using force? Are there any political disputes in which you would prefer never to use force?

7. Can the notion of absolute values be made consistent with the realities of political life in a democracy?

8. Is it possible for international law to develop in a world possessing plural value systems and widely differing cultures?

9. Does political agreement necessarily require agreement on ultimate values? If not, why not? If so, can you suggest some concrete examples?

10. Is loyalty a basic political value? How, if at all, does loyalty relate to patriotism? What values do you consider the highest social and political values?

Some Suggested Readings

Ayer, A. J. *Language, Truth and Logic*. London: Gollancz, 1936.

Bentham, J. *An Introduction to the Principles of Morals and Legislation*. Reprinted in *The English Philosophers from Bacon to Mill*, ed. E. A. Burtt. New York: Modern Library, 1939.

Brightman, E. S. *Personality and Religion*. New York: Abingdon, 1934.

Cassirer, E. *An Essay on Man*. Garden City, N.Y.: Doubleday, 1953.

————. *The Platonic Renaissance in England*. Austin: University of Texas Press, 1953.

Dewey, J. *Problems of Men*. New York: Philosophical Library, 1946.

————. *Theory of Valuation*. International Encyclopedia of United Science, Vol. II, No. 4. Chicago: University of Chicago Press, 1939.

Emmet, D. *The Nature of Metaphysical Thinking*. London: Macmillan, 1949.

Flew, A., and MacIntyre, A. *New Essays in Philosophical Theology*. London: SCM Press, 1955.

Graham, A. C. *The Problem of Value*. London: Hutchinson, 1961.

Hall, E. W. *What Is Value?—An Essay in Philosophical Analysis*. New York: Humanities Press, 1952.

Hare, R. M. *The Language of Morals*. Oxford: Clarendon Press, 1952.

Hook, S., (ed.) *Psychoanalysis, Scientific Method and Philosophy*. New York: Grove, 1960.

Lewis, C. I. *Analysis of Knowledge and Valuation*. La Salle, Ill.: Open Court, 1946.

Moore, G. E. *Principia Ethica*. London: Cambridge University Press, 1959.

Morgan, G. A., Jr. *What Nietzsche Means*. Cambridge: Harvard University Press, 1941.

Perry, R. B. *Realms of Value*. Cambridge: Harvard University Press, 1954.

Reichenbach, H. *The Rise of Scientific Philosophy*. Berkeley and Los Angeles: University of California Press, 1951.

Sesonske, A. *Value and Obligation*. Berkeley: University of California Press, 1957.

Stevenson, C. L. *Ethics and Language*. New Haven: Yale University Press, 1944.

CHAPTER FOURTEEN

Ideology

Scholars from different disciplines have during the last century and a half produced a voluminous literature concerned with the description, interpretation, and comparison of political ideologies. They have sought to compare whole cultural styles or "ways of life" (like democracy, communism, fascism) in order to mark off the boundaries of major areas of conflict in an, admittedly, troubled world. Their awareness of the contemporary anxieties which beset men, some of them fairly basic the world over in a revolutionary age of technological and social changes, helped to sustain systematic attempts to understand human action in determinate environmental situations.

Modern thinkers have shown, consequently, a deep realization of the nonrational, sometimes even the irrational factors which influence human behavior—factors which no serious student of contemporary social life and politics can safely overlook. Their attention has been directed, even in psychology, away from the isolated individual to analysis of group action and mass phenomena. In brief, scholars today have become interested to comprehend human action against a larger social, economic, and political background taken as causally related to that action. Concern over ideologies has reflected a more general judgment that any adequate understanding of man requires a thorough knowledge of the social and historical situations which exist in specific places and times. Indeed, the great popularity of the social sciences, particularly evident in academic settings, reflects this growing desire to make some sense of men's cultural and historical orientations. Classical individualism seems to be giving way to a demand for a view of human behavior which emphasizes how men's roots require a surrounding social soil.

As a matter of historical fact, the quest after knowledge of society has sometimes affected even philosophical activity. The emphasis has been concentrated on *practical* knowledge rather than on imaginative speculation unsupported, and often unsupportable, by clearly marked evidence. Action has become more central than reflection. Moreover, the successes of the natural (or "hard") sciences stimulated scholars to raise their investigations of social phenomena to a scientific status —to replace social and political philosophy by the social sciences. This hope may not have been realized in an indisputable way, since persons exist who are still willing to debate a question such as: Are the social sciences really "sciences"? Nonetheless, enormous quantities of factual and statistical information have been accumulated from empirical studies done by historians and social scientists.

Scientific and historical studies of political affairs tend to show how extensively the members of a group often share the same, or at least similar, opinions about a host of issues. These opinions form a cluster, pattern, or style of ideas which depend on one another, "hang together" in an associational if not necessarily in a logical manner. These clusters of ideas influence the action of members of a group. To any instance of such clusters of ideas scholars apply the term "ideology" —a concrete way of thinking which marks off one social group from another. Professor Louis Wirth has thus defined ideologies as those "complexes of ideas which direct activity toward the maintenance of the existing order." [1] Participants in social practices which make up a way of life often act without a fully self-conscious awareness of why they so act. They tend to reflect the values and aims which, almost like the surrounding air, make up a social environment. Thus, Professor Karl Mannheim has emphasized the ideological character of much political activity in the following way:

> The concept "ideology" reflects the one discovery which emerged from political conflict, namely, that ruling groups can in their think-

[1] Karl Mannheim, *Ideology and Utopia* (New York: Harcourt, 1951), Preface, p. xxiii. Used by permission of Harcourt, Brace & World, Inc.

ing become so intensively interest-bound to a situation that they are simply no longer able to see certain facts which would undermine their sense of domination. There is implicit in the word "ideology" the insight that in certain situations the collective unconscious of certain groups obscures the real condition of society both to itself and to others and thereby stabilizes it.[2]

Ideology and Knowledge

Whether true or not, ideas can have important consequences. So truistic an assertion has been accepted as meaningful by a number of scholars. Thus, even a scientific study of politics and society need not raise any questions about the truth or falsity of the beliefs shared by members of a group, since the study can concentrate on those ideas which seem to influence a group's actions. Yet, given a decrease of faith in philosophy as a means to disinterested knowledge, many scholars have argued that men's ideas about values (the ends thought worthy of pursuit even by political action) do not, and cannot, constitute an arena of objective knowledge in the normative sense—that no science of normative human values is possible, rather only a science which describes and compares what different sets of men happen to think worthwhile.

Moreover, since knowledge of any kind is gained in some concrete social context, human knowing may be said to have inevitable social roots. If science cannot tell men what they *ought* to value most dearly, and if social and political evaluations always reflect an ideology— some influence of class, race, sex, economic, or religious bias—then human evaluations are decisions about how to act which can be justified only in terms of the existing ideology. Men can sometimes decide *which* ideology to follow, perhaps. Yet, they cannot do this objectively; nor, having decided, can they "prove" their choice objectively and universally superior to the choices of others. If evaluations are ultimately only reflections of existing ideologies, then they represent *perspectives* which reflect prevailing *interests*. The interests cannot be said, then, to be subject to rational justification save in a hypothetical way. Thus, democracy cannot be shown rationally supe-

[2] *Ibid.*, p. 36.

rior to communism, or either of these to fascism. Inquiry can point out how democracy, communism, or fascism tend to produce certain consequences in social or political life, among which a person can choose without being able—outside of the actual choosing—to show that one set of consequences is inherently better than another. Science can help to produce factual knowledge *about* values but not, itself, either create or justify values.

There is something disturbing about this view. Persons living in what has been termed a "culture-studying culture" can amass enormous amounts of knowledge about how others live. Like an empirical anthropologist who travels to primitive tribes to learn about their diverse cultures, contemporary students can learn about competing ways of life. But if there arises the question, Which of these ways of life is the best?, they must answer, in the light of science, that they are all of equal status. Instead of aiding men to decide wisely between competing ways of life, on this view science may actually increase men's anxieties by showing that, in comparison with their own preferred way of life, many others exist whose values actually sometimes conflict. Rather than tolerance, confusion and animosity may actually result.

But, some analysts of the contemporary philosophical scene have suggested that knowledge itself is socially determined. It is not always clear exactly what such a claim means to assert. The claim may mean either (a) that the conditions under which any kind of knowledge is gained are themselves social and political; or (b) that *all* human knowledge has an ideological foundation—that ethics, philosophy, politics, even perhaps science are based on perspectives which are not in some assumed nonsocial sense free of inevitable distortions. Most sociologists concerned with what is called "sociology of knowledge" —the study of the relations of knowledge to specific cultural conditions—have held to a belief in the possibility of a disinterested, culture-free science but have thought social elements important in judgments of value. They have suspected that conflicts over the good, the beautiful, the worthwhile are ultimately ideological, while disputes in the sciences are not, in the long run, necessarily so. Sociologists of knowledge have tended to stress the inescapable relation between

social and historical "situations" and the specific *interests* which influence the kinds of knowledge that get discovered. They have shown
how the production of certain kinds of knowledge would be impossible
in the absence of certain needed sustaining social conditions. However, some sociologists sometimes suggested that any attempt logically
to distinguish knowledge from the social setting in which it has been
achieved means to make some type of fundamental mistake. It is this
latter aspect of the sociology of knowledge which seems subject to
challenge.

For example, to tell a person that in Culture X a scientist seeks
after a "cure" for cancer because the culture he inhabits supports that
type of inquiry does not explain what would, if anything, make a discovery about cancer truly an item of knowledge rather than of super-
stition or wishful thinking. There is a difference between saying
knowledge is *difficult* to obtain because of our limited human perspectives and saying knowledge is *impossible* to achieve because our
perspectives, always and everywhere, reflect nonrational ideological
factors. If this latter claim were accepted without qualification, even
practicing social scientists could not consistently claim to be able to
describe competing ideologies, since their descriptions could be said
always to contain perspectival "distortions" or "biases." Thus, a non-
Communist could never give an objective description of communism,
or the reverse, since every description would ultimately involve a
"hidden" evaluation. This position would indeed undermine the possibility of even a descriptive science of human behavior.

Nineteenth-century thinkers like August Comte (1798–1857) and
Karl Marx (1818–1883) wanted a scientific study of society, thus
implying the possibility—however difficult to realize—of overcoming
the distorting ideological aspects of social and political action and
thought. In their disappointment with earlier versions of social explanation they did not, in recognizing the importance of ideological factors, appear to write as sceptics about men's capacities to achieve an
objective knowledge of social and political events. Two contemporary
scholars have emphasized this fact by writing:

> To be sure Marx believes that objective knowledge for the human
> studies is possible, but only when the distorting influence of existing

social structure ceases—that is, when the class struggle is ended. Thus with Marx, as with Bacon, the *ideologues,* and Comte, the dominating thought is that objectivity can come about only as ideas are purified, or as they break out of the falsifying ambiance of the social. Marx like his predecessors views the social perspective in pejorative fashion, as derogation from the autonomy of reason.[3]

. . . Marx and Engels regarded ideologies as systems of misleading or illusory ideas. But no one can justifiably describe something as misleading or illusory except by comparison with something he thinks is not misleading and not illusory. What, then, according to Marx and Engels, is it that is not misleading and not illusory? In *The German Ideology* they state quite clearly what they think it is. "We set out," they say, "from real active men, and on the basis of their real life-process we demonstrate the development of the ideological reflexes and echoes of this life-process. The phantoms formed in the human brain are also, necessarily, sublimates of their material life-process, which is empirically verifiable and bound to material premises." On the next page they say: "Where speculation ends—in real life—there real, positive science begins: the representation of the practical process of development of men." That is to say, there is according to Marx and Engels, a system of ideas ("the representation of the practical process of development") about man, his religions and his societies, which is not illusory, which is not ideology.[4]

If Marx's thought raises questions about the objectivity of social knowledge, then it does so not in his treatment of ideologies but (as suggested in Chapter 12, "Historicism") as a result of his materialistic and determinist conception of the historical process. If an objective social knowledge is possible, as Marx's treatment of ideologies implied, then either men can to an extent "transcend" their particularized position in the historical order *or* there must exist some basic and unchanging factors which pervade each and every historical period.

[3] Stanley Taylor, *Conceptions of Institutions and the Theory of Knowledge* (New York: Bookman Associates, 1956), p. 21. Used by permission of the publisher.

[4] H. B. Acton, *The Illusion of the Epoch* (London: Cohen, 1955), pp. 127–28.

Contributing Conditions

The nineteenth century fairly teemed with intellectual attempts to explain social phenomena. Indeed, Professor H. D. Aiken of Harvard University has dared to title an important anthology of nineteenth-century philosophical writings *The Age of Ideology*. Men reacted against the older philosophical claims to metaphyhical objectivity and absolute knowledge. They turned rather to the sciences. In addition, a profound revolution occurred in men's historical knowledge, vastly extending their conception of historical time and challenging them to discern patterns in the grand sweep of cultural development. Darwin's theory of biological evolution led some social thinkers, by analogy, to seek for an evolutionary understanding of human societies and institutions—resulting in contradictory or inconsistent versions of an intellectual movement known as "social Darwinism," containing a conservative wing which justified existing institutions as being most fit to survive by the fact of their survival and a radical wing which condemned existing institutions as going counter to the present tendencies of an evolutionary line. There is little doubt that these evolutionary views of society and history were, to an extent, influenced by the organic philosophies of Hegel and Rousseau. The notion that societies develop and progress according to their own unalterable laws became, itself, almost an ideology hardly questioned or criticized by an impressive array of hardy thinkers.

Two notable instances of expressions of this evolutionary "ideology" can be found in positivism, fathered by the Frenchman, August Comte; and in pragmatism, an American philosophical movement which emphasized how "truth" is a function of what "works" and how philosophy is, ultimately, a critique of culture and civilization rather than a discovery of eternal and absolute truth. Comte's position involved the famous "Law of the Three Stages." [5] Minutely worked out, its basic thesis claimed that men's efforts to understand reality had passed through several fundamental historical phases. The

[5] The relevant work is Comte's *Positive Philosophy,* trans. H. Martineau (London: Bell, 1913).

early phase involved a theological attempt to "explain" phenomena in religious terms, later replaced by a "metaphyhical" stage based on reason. These attempts failed because they sought to answer the question Why? rather than the question How? Comte believed a third and final stage, that of positive science, would now replace the earlier ones—ultimately resulting in a scientific society based on the full discovery of the laws of social existence and development. Comte's impact on his century was immense. Somewhat disregarded now, his ideas still stand as expressions of an optimistic and rational attempt to stem the forces of irrationality in the light of genuine social knowledge. What is now clearly seen, however, is that his claims about a positive science rested on a thoroughly *philosophical* assumption about the nature of history and society.

American pragmatism, on the other hand, challenged the idea that any kind of absolute knowledge—including knowledge of fundamental social laws—could be attained. Nonetheless, the pragmatists disdained what they considered "airy" metaphysical speculations. Especially did John Dewey attempt to produce a philosophy of culture in which the evolutionary notion played a central role. Human intelligence was viewed as functional, operating always in selected contexts, primarily a problem-solving capacity rather than, as in traditional philosophy, a disinterested instrument by which to recognize objectively eternal truths. As a result, Dewey emphasized the way in which human inquiry always operates in a *situation*. Its aims are always practical and selective rather than purely theoretical and disinterested. Whether consistently or not, pragmatists nonetheless held to the possibility of a scientific (as opposed to a philosophical) knowledge of men and events in situational contexts and, like Marx and his followers, tended to blame past intellectual mistakes on the distorting influences of institutions, especially religious ones which preached supernaturalism.

These evolutionary quests after a scientific treatment of social phenomena resulted in a sharp-edged cutting away at the prestige of traditional institutions and customs. Thus, John Dewey urged men to use intelligence in order to escape from the "dead hand" of the past —to judge values in the light of future expectations rather than in view of past precedents. Consequently, Dewey's philosophy unsettled traditions—requiring them to submit to the critical judgments of present-day needs and insistent demands. He treated past philosophies much in the same manner, leading even a staunch and loyal admirer to comment:

> Now Dewey himself has dwelt so long and so vigorously on the need of just such liberation from persistent tradition, that it is not irrelevant to ask these questions about the true nature of an experimental philosophy. Many who have found that basic drive congenial have indeed raised them. They have been sadly puzzled to find his works overloaded with references to outworn ideas of thinkers they would themselves prefer to forget. Why all this beating of dead asses? For years it was possible to reach his most penetrating analysis of the logic of inquiry, in *Essays in Experimental Logic,* only through a thick tangle of Lotze, a logician whom it is safe to say no one has seriously read for a generation. And of even his fundamental *Experience and Nature,* it has been not unfairly pointed out, each page is made up of a fresh grappling with pressing problems worthy of the best laboratory approach, and half of a wrestling with the vagaries of an ancient tradition. Why does Dewey insist on conducting his original inquiries in the musty atmosphere of a historical museum? Why does he not throw open the windows to let the fresh breezes of the present blow these dusty cobwebs away? Why, to go forward a step, must he look backward on the whole course already traversed? [6]

The author of these remarks concluded that Dewey did not seek to praise the past but, rather, to make appraisals of it to prepare against future difficulties. "Toward the history of philosophy," claimed Professor J. H. Randall, Jr., "his attitude differs little from that of the chemist or the biologist: all alike view the chronicle of man's intellectual achievement as an arsenal, or as a warning, but not as an ancestral mansion to be lovingly explored." [7]

Some critics point out how Dewey, much like Marx, failed to be consistent in holding *both* to an evolutionary, therefore deterministic view of social development *and* to a critical pragmatic version of intelligence as able to alter and direct an evolutionary development.

[6] J. H. Randall, Jr., "Dewey's Interpretation of the History of Philosophy," in P. A. Schilpp, ed., *The Philosophy of John Dewey* (New York: Tudor, 1931), pp. 79–80.
[7] *Ibid.*

The problem is that, for Dewey, intelligence is itself one item *within* an evolutionary reality. As a result, it is possible Dewey failed to achieve a balanced view of the ways in which established institutions may themselves represent a special *kind* of time-tested rationality. They were themselves the products of needs and problems which they "solved" by their very existence. Yet, Dewey blamed such historically evolved institutions as the source of much error and human blindness, when he wrote in his famous *Experience and Nature* (1926):

> When theories of values do not afford intellectual assistance in framing ideas and beliefs about values that are adequate to direct action, the gap must be filled by other means. If intelligent method is lacking, prejudice, the pressure of immediate circumstances, self-interest and class-interest, traditional customs, institutions of accidental historic origin are not lacking, and they tend to take the place of intelligence.[8]

But why, on an evolutionary view of process, consider institutional adjustments "accidental"?

Many thinkers, then, pointed out how pervasively distorting influences operate to make adequate social and valuational knowledge difficult, if not impossible. In this regard, they stood in a long critical line of thinkers concerned with theory of knowledge, extending from Bacon to Kant—thinkers worried about the bases on which *claims* to human knowledge can be substantiated and defended. However, most of these thinkers did not worry about the social element in knowledge. Rather, they assumed that knowing is an affair involving an individual subject (a man) and an object (separated from him) about which either perceptual or conceptual knowledge, or both, is possible. According to this view, well illustrated by Bacon's famous "Idols," objective knowledge is difficult because individual and social perspectives often introduce irrelevant biases into the observation and "description" of what is observed. Thus, knowledge may be marred by inadequate senses in a man; or by prejudices of his tribe which influence his conclusions; or by the complexities and nuances of human language; or by the weight of philosophical and theological systems, or "convictions," which lead a man to project his wishes into what should remain a

[8] John Dewey, *Experience in Nature* (Chicago: Open Court, 1926), p. 265.

value-free object. As a result of this concern to remove distortions from human knowledge, a modern "picture" grew up in which knowledge can occur *only if* human wishes, values, desires are excluded from the subject matter under study. What the sociologists of knowledge have sought to do, as a result, is to reintroduce human desires and emotions as parts of knowledge itself—claiming that every society produces a science which, at its horizons, is marked by such valuational elements. This notion of an ultimate, though changing, social aspect to knowing may, if at all, be explained as a peculiar misuse of Immanuel Kant's theory of knowledge. Kant thought human knowledge presupposed a finite set of conceptual "categories" which function as selective limits to human knowledge. These categories are universal, operating like a selective net tossed into a possibly vaster *noumenal* sea from which phenomenal objects (those which can be captured in the "net") were, as it were, lifted out. But Kant excluded values from the categories entirely. Analogously to this Kantian treatment of the inescapable limits of human knowledge, the sociological view of social limits to knowledge makes the social ideology similar to Kant's philosophical "categories"—with the significant differences that (1) the social ideology need not be common to all men and may change from historical epoch to epoch, and (2) the social ideology constitutes a "net" of value judgments which serve as the "eyes" for the evaluating done by members of the society. These values are "given" by an existing society.

Bentham and Marx

Jeremy Bentham influenced English social thought which, while Marx lived and studied in England, influenced the latter's views in important ways. For all their differences, these two men held some common convictions. Both looked upon philosophical claims about "natural rights" with jaundiced eyes, thinking the claims nonsense at best and vicious distortion of the real situation at worst. Both wanted to achieve something like a genuine science of society—Bentham seeking a calculus of pleasures (which he termed the "felicific calculus"), Marx trying to turn Hegelian philosophy of history "upside down" and to detach—from its idealistic pockets-turned-inside-out, as it were—a purely materialistic theory of historical development which would prove "scientific" (on Marx's now questionable view of science as synonymous with unquestionable certainty). Finally, both men detested philosophy pursued for its own sake and concentrated on inquiries which would lead to social reform and human betterment. They differed radically, however, in that Bentham wanted a yardstick which legislators might use in framing general laws affecting human welfare, while Marx—embittered by the economic and social injustices he observed even in nineteenth-century England, which gave him refuge from the police of other European countries—looked upon legislatures as "fronts" for amoral capitalist aims, dominated by class interests. Nonetheless, both men held a passionate dislike of hypocrisy and pretense.

While Bentham produced no systematic theory of ideologies, he did recognize the fact that men often hide their genuine motives from themselves.[9] Bentham listed eight kinds of human motives for which, in the English language, eulogistic words—that is, words conveying approbation—were not in general use. According to Bentham, men often pursue goals to which these motives are important but, because of their refusal to admit they seek pleasure and avoidance of pain, wish to hide this fact from others as well as, sometimes, to deceive themselves. This crude form of a treatment of self-deception, as developed by Bentham, indicates that Sigmund Freud was not the only nineteenth-century thinker to be impressed by men's capacities to hide their genuine motives even from themselves. The motives for which favorable English terms were not in use were, according to Bentham, those having to do with desire for food and drink, sexual desire, physical desires as a general class of desires, desire of power, human curiosity, love of ease and rest, desire of self-preservation, personal intent as a general category. All men often act from motives like these but, in public or to themselves, "justify" their actions by stating some other (purported) motive which, given their presumed moral code, they think more acceptable.

[9] See David Baumgardt, *Bentham and the Ethics of Today* (Princeton, Princeton University Press, 1952), especially pp. 373–488.

On this score, Bentham suggested some examples of how men, either consciously or unconsciously, hide their true motives. He pointed out, for example, that men use "masks." Seeking the pleasures of sex, they may say they have a "love of children"; enjoying food, they may claim a "love of good cheer"; anxious to get and hold power, they may camouflage these desires under banners of "love of country" or "love of reputation." Thus, Bentham's keen if perhaps cynical eye for men's foibles led him to suggest there are illuminating eulogistic (favorable) terms for a number of presumed motives—motives like regard for reputation, fear of God, goodwill towards men, love of matter or wealth. Bentham did not claim that men *always* hide their genuine motives, either from others or themselves, or both—rather that they frequently do so. Indeed, he thought men acting on the principle of utility could, within limits, realize a degree of probity, defined as forebearing to diminish a neighbor's happiness; and a degree of beneficence, defined as positively seeking to increase a neighbor's happiness.

In contrast to Bentham's psychological and individualistic analysis of the "springs" (motives) of human action, Marx came to see in the actions of individuals the powerful, if shadowy, influence of social and economic classes. Thus, angered by the capitalist set of values and its economic practices which he thought living out its final "days" in a determined historical order, Marx argued that capitalist society introduced "distorting" evaluations into practically all phases of human existence, affecting religion, ethics, morality, art, law, and the whole range of intellectual life. An inevitable revolution, based, as the prophecy is now well known, on class conflict would, Marx believed, achieve *not only* a fairer economic distribution of material goods than that which he found prevalent in the unregulated capitalism of his times *but*—a remarkable hope—make possible a "classless" society in which, for the first time in human history, genuinely disinterested and unbiased art, science, and social evaluation would occur. This apparently anarchistic notion of a "classless" society seemed, in Marx's writings, to serve as a counter to the possible criticism that, even if capitalism should be supplanted by communism, one ideology would simply replace another. But, now to be developed somewhat, Marx's analysis of the notion of ideology revealed that he "saw" an ideology as a distortion of human knowledge resulting from a set of social prejudices which, in a rational society, would be removed.

In Marx's mind, English utilitarianism was linked with the established economic order—thus constituted an ideology. But, more importantly and paradoxically, for a thinker so concerned with economic classes, Marx believed that utilitarianism was not *sufficiently* individualistic, since its emphasis on pleasure as the yardstick of utility represented an attempt to "see" all men as alike in their pleasures. A revealing comment on Benthamism and utilitarianism ran as follows:

> The connection between the pleasure-experiences of individuals at any time and the class relations of their time as well as the conditions of production and communication which produce the class relations within which individuals live, the limitation of all traditional pleasures which do not flow from real life activity of the individual, the connection between every philosophy of pleasure and the actual pleasures at hand, and the hypocrisy of every philosophy of pleasure which presumes to generalize for all individuals regardless of their differences—all of this naturally could not be discovered until the conditions of production and communication of the traditional world had been criticised, and the opposition between the bourgeois view of life and the proletarian socialist and communist point of view created. Therewith all morality—whether it be the morality of asceticism or that of the philosophy of pleasure—was proved to be bankrupt.[10]

Marx's economic approach to an understanding of politics, coupled with his refusal to divorce theory from practice, helped to produce practical results because it rested primarily on a brilliantly realistic critique of a complex set of conditions threateningly new to European civilization. Consequently, Marxism operates eventually as a significant intellectual influence wherever men refuse to come to alternative terms with the kinds of situations to which Marx's analyses are relevant. Professor T. D. Weldon has reminded contemporary thinkers how, just as Sigmund Freud's unquestionable genius altered the perspectives of nineteenth-century psychology, Marx's work produced an

[10] Sidney Hook (ed.), *From Hegel to Marx* (New York: Humanities Press, 1950), Appendices, p. 317.

impressive sociology which has influenced all social democratic as well as communist movements in the world. Even critics who want to reject Marx's revolutionary "solutions" to the "contradictions" he found in the existing capitalist order usually admit that, as a *diagnostician* of the economic-political impasse faced by modern men, Marx stands among the few outstanding thinkers.

The appeal of Marxism has often rested on its corrosive critique of existing economic orders. Like two other nineteenth-century prophets alarmed by the sights before their eyes: namely, Sören Kierkegaard, the Danish critic of Hegel; and Friedrich Nietzsche, the German preacher of a transvaluation of all values—Marx forced men to recognize evils in their social order which they would have preferred to overlook. The Marxian "reduction" of political activity to one feature of an economically determined "superstructure"—practices and ideas automatically thrown up by existing economic realities—is by now a fairly familiar one. "Political power, properly so called, is merely the organized power of one class for suppressing another," as a sentence from the *Communist Manifesto,* presents the thesis adequately if baldly. On so sparse a foundation did Lenin, in *State and Revolution* (1917), seek to construct a basic Marxian teaching for a proletariat working to make a successful revolution.

Several dogmatic convictions are central to Marx's treatment of the state and political power. *First,* Marx believed that disinterested scientific inquiry might eventually discover the causal connections between economic factors of production (the "base") and a society's beliefs about value (the "superstructure") if scientists could escape the distorting lens of a capitalistic vision. *Second,* Marx found everywhere prevalent in European society a class orientation which, touched by capitalist evaluations, undermined the immediate possibility of objective treatments of philosophy, science, and religion. *Third,* the existing political system served as the organized means by which a favored economic class protected its special privileges. *Fourth,* Marx concluded that the distortion of human values was so extensive that only by a violent revolution against the capitalist order could genuine values once again appear. *Finally,* Marx thought that communism would inevitably triumph over capitalism as a consequence of class warfare but that, for this triumph, a rigidly organized proletarian political party would be needed to hasten the process.

Consequently, Marx set his sails against the winds of a prevailing ideology. He saw the ideology as something to be resisted, since it represented the oppressive weight of an established opinion based on capitalist economics. In his analysis of the notion of ideology, Marx joined with earlier thinkers who linked it with those influences which, unless eradicated, made a genuinely objective human knowledge impossible—much as a cinder in one's eye makes clear vision an impossibility. Ideology is a process in which a person may be conscious *that* he holds certain beliefs but, nonetheless, unconscious of his real reasons for holding them. Thus his consciousness is really "false consciousness." The consciousness is really a reflection of the values implicit in a specific institutional structure, in a given epoch, rather than of the truly individual capacities and strivings of the person holding the beliefs. Borrowed from Hegel, this notion of "false consciousness" has also received an original and penetrating contemporary development by Jean-Paul Sartre, the living French existentialist thinker, in a portion of his classic *Being and Nothingness* devoted to "bad faith."

According to Marx, the ideological thinker goes wrong both in theory and in practice. His actions are in some sense lacking in genuine sense, and the theories from which they follow are ultimately incoherent. Moreover, "false consciousness" is a malady affecting the whole social body rather than, say, one organ or function of that society. It represents a kind of institutional sickness. The entire social order is marked by its distortions—law, morality, religion, art, philosophy, even science. To "save" individuals, one must alter the structure of the entire society if he wants to get at the causes rather than at mere symptoms.

This analysis of ideology as produced by Marx implies the possibility of a nonideological understanding of society. For Marx, this can come about only by the removal of those economic relations of production which prevail in a capitalist society. Thus, Marx used his analysis to further his own persuasive attempt to undermine the existing order. The remaining perplexity, apparently not subject to rational removal, is that of trying to understand why Marx thought any set of social, economic, and political institutions would not, in time, develop its own ideology, its own "superstructure" whose function is to protect the existing order.

Fascism

Not many persons impressed by Marx's analysis of ideologies shared his classical faith in the possibility of a classless society. Some, indeed, became complete cynics and even nihilists—convinced that no objective truths exist, that all human beliefs ultimately reflect a set of evaluations which, unprovable and rationally unjustifiable, simply express the facts of power. Yet they turned the analysis of ideologies to their own uses. Among these in this century were those theorists of fascism —the political doctrine that force alone determines what is true and right—whose notions led to nazism in Germany and variants of this doctrine in many parts of the world. Using the power of the state to control human action, fascists sought to organize a society in a total way, often doing so by propounding myths and racist doctrines for which, in the terms of European science and philosophy, no convincing evidence existed. They sought obedience, total control by means of police and the legal order, and the submission of generous believers in the humanist notion of "universal man" to the authoritarian goals of a specific state.

Perhaps as frightening a "picture" as any of the kind of total control sought by many fascists has been created by George Orwell, whose novel *Nineteen Eighty-Four* meant to criticize the fascistic aspects of communistic regimes in the third decade of this century as well as of non-communist ones. There is little doubt that actual communist regimes—especially the Stalinist regime in the Soviet Union— in practice sought total control over their subjects. The difference between communism and fascism in theory, if it is a meaningful one, is a difference in ends sought rather than in techniques. Where the communist theorists held to a vision of a possible future state of affairs in which (at least in their claims) no such coercion would longer be needed, purely fascistic theorists believed only that force and irrationality would always prevail over reason and science. However, fascistic forms of behavior can occur in practice in any political system.

Orwell's novel confronted men with the imaginatively portrayed possibility of a type of amoral control new to the world. The regime in power, using all the sophisticated technological techniques produced by modern science solely in the service of conformity, sought not only conformity in action but absolute agreement in belief. The regime invented and directed the ideological perspective. The entire range of social life became political through and through, even to attitudes toward relations between the sexes. Moreover, opponents of the established ideology were not only punished but, by careful psychological manipulation, led to believe the very things they thought false. Names of persons out of favor with the regime because of changes in the ideological "line" disappeared from the files of newspapers as well as from the history books. A historiographical "rewrite" room functioned constantly to alter the historical records. Truth and fact became whatever happened to be put into existing men's minds by the vast propaganda organizations controlled by "Big Brother," the source of unity and proper beliefs.

On the other hand, a writer like Professor Peter Viereck associated the model of fascism particularly with German nazism and contemporary tendencies of the German mind. In his *Meta-Politics,* a controversial book first published in 1941 early in the Second World War, Viereck blamed fascism of a pronounced kind on the peculiar history of the German people. Thus, on this view, nazism represented a "natural" consequence of centuries of cultural and intellectual tendencies in central Europe. It was viewed as the result of several great revolutions, among which nineteenth-century German romanticism with its stress on striving as a value in itself and its depreciation of reason and limits, was the most conspicuous, though Viereck thought the Lutheran religious Reformation had also earlier contributed. Rather than specific economic conditions as cause, ideas and beliefs—especially distorted ones peculiar to German cultural history—were seen as the chief causes of the Nazi form of fascism.

According to Viereck, German romanticism represented a peculiar "sickness" of a whole people, different from other brands of romanticism which appeared in other nations and civilizations. Viereck is at least eloquent in defense of his view, arguing in 1941:

> In setting up meta-politics against politics, Germany deliberately turns her back on western civilization. Both Germany and the west are agreed on that—and both pugnaciously so. Is the common phrase "western civilization" mere rhetoric? Or can we not find for it a brief definition both Germany and the west will accept? A rough attempt in a single sentence: loyalty to western civilization means loyalty not to one particular portion of geography—that would be nationalism—but to a universal civilization compounded of three separate heritages: rationalism, classicism, Christianity.

Given these heritages, nazism turns out to be a peculiarly German phenomenon:

> Nazism stands for the opposite of each of these three heritages: for force against reason, for romanticism, for tribal paganism. This states the contrast a bit too naively, because, of course, the matter is hardly as simple as this. This contrast is only the framework, requiring qualification and elucidation and, above all, explanation.[11]

One problem with Viereck's analysis is that, in contrast with the Marxist view, it makes the radical economic disasters in twentieth-century Germany and the world only a minor cause of fascism. Moreover, Viereck's treatment seems to suggest that nazism naturally can be fitted into the mainstream of German history when, as many scholars would hold, it is as much a "departure" from as a "culmination" of that historical development. Finally, Viereck perhaps assumes too readily that ideas play a much greater role in political action than they actually do play. While ideas and beliefs help to shape the attitudes of a people, they do not always in themselves produce the conditions under which those attitudes can lead to fascism. Thus even if nazism was a peculiarly German expression of fascism, it was an instance— admittedly a uniquely threatening one—of a more universal phenomenon which may occur in other nations and under differing circumstances. If Viereck's thesis has a drawback, it is its (unintended) tendency to suggest that because of their peculiar history, primarily

[11] Peter Viereck, *Meta-Politics: The Roots of the Nazi Mind* (New York: Capricorn, 1961), pp. 4, 5.

Germans constitute a people and a culture in which rigorous fascism can occur. This may lead uncritical persons to fail to recognize in their own political attitudes and actions distinctive expressions of a fascistic mentality.

The Nazi phenomenon may indeed be repeatable. This is the warning which German nazism presents to other peoples in the present century. Its philosophical and value outlook may prove adaptable to different nations. As Professor Zevedei Barbu has written, in a comment about Nazism which can be generalized to cover other possible variants of the fascistic viewpoint:

> The *Weltanschauung* of Nazism rests on the assumption of the irrationality of human nature. Human action, and human will in general, is guided by instincts, intuition and feelings. Will has its end in itself, and it reaches its purposes more adequately if not embarrassed by reasoning. Though doubting the ability and power of reason, Nazis are neither sceptics nor nihilists. According to their convictions, will and feeling provide human knowledge and action with a greater degree of certainty than reason. Human action, though basically irrational, leads by itself to order, to a new type of order. For, while the fundamental category of rational order is that of equality, and agreement between equals, the order springing from the irrational factors of the human mind rests on the feeling of "distance" (Nietzsche); it expresses itself as power hierarchy. Man's most important virtue consists in the fact that he can impose his will by force, and fears force at the same time. This human quality becomes the main feature of the Nazi way of life. Man's wisdom is shown in his ability to discover the leader and to let himself be ruled by him. Needless to say, this wisdom is by no means the work of reason. For will and affection guide the people towards the choice of their leader, rather than reason. The leader himself would very seldom, if at all, use reason to get the consent of the people. His strongest weapons consist in his power and its capacity to fascinate and to dominate.[12]

Democratic Metaphysics

The Marxian solution to the intellectual problem of contemporary politics rests on the acceptance of a view of history as unquestion-

[12] *Democracy and Dictatorship* (New York: Grove, 1956), p. 131.

ably deterministic: namely, the materialist conception. On this view, the prevailing "sick" capitalist ideology will "in the nature of historical necessity" succumb to communist revolution, producing a purely scientific and nonpolitical society in which pure "administration" will replace "politics." Contrariwise, the Nazi version of fascism denied any ultimate rationality to historical development but, relying on myth and irrationality, sought to subdue politics to the dominating power of a leader and his tightly organized followers. If neither of these alternatives seems either reasonably true nor persuasive, where can a person turn for an alternative view of political life?

Apparently, the only alternative is to defend a democratic view of politics as, in principle, capable of escaping at least the extreme forms of ideological rigidity as well as of taming power by rational procedures directed to cooperative social ends. Discussion and persuasion, implying the right and necessity of opposition, must form important aspects of such an alternative way. A question arises whether democracy viewed as a specific technique for achieving common action in a society involves any necessary philosophical attitudes or beliefs. Thinkers take radically opposed stands on this issue. Professor T. D. Weldon insists that democracy does not entail any "metaphysical foundations," since it sees governing as a process of refereeing clashes between interest groups through a state interpreted as one association among others. On the other hand, the American pragmatist G. H. Mead (1863–1931) thought that democracy involved at least some minimal philosophical commitments. The difficulty arises from the way in which "democracy" is a "weasel" word, possessing numerous meanings. Democracy sometimes means something like a religion—a spiritual attitude toward the notion of equality. It can also mean a distinctive social "way of life," involving not only political organization and action but a certain relaxed tolerance toward diversity in manners and morals. Finally and most narrowly, it has often meant government which is, in some sense, subject to recurring expressions of a peoples' will.

Probably Professor Weldon is right in arguing that democracy, viewed narrowly as empirical politics, need not entail any necessary *philosophical* beliefs, though it will require agreement about some psychological attitudes toward individuals and the state. On the other hand, if democracy is treated as a "way of life" broader than the solely political structure of governing bodies, then G. H. Mead's position—like that of other American pragmatists—probably deserves at least a hearing. The pragmatists want to insist that a democratic way of life extends certain forms of association into the family, church, and professional life of a people. Thus, how persons in a large variety of social groups carry out their common functions, especially in reaching policy decisions, is a fundamental feature of a democratic society. Participation in important committees which permit some "say" about the ends, rules, and procedures to influence the group becomes a fundamental aspect of democratic experience. The officially organized political government of city, state, or nation becomes merely an important and powerful expression of the activities of millions of persons in countless organizations within the society.

To argue that a democratic *political* system requires no complete agreement about philosophical issues means usually to deny that democracy must be grounded in "metaphysical" (as opposed to everyday, "garden-variety") truths. It is not always an easy matter to clarify the intent of such an argument. Since representative political systems in the West historically emerged after long struggles against deeply rooted royalist and ecclesiastical powers, the argument tends to emphasize that men possessing a variety of *religious* convictions can, under some conditions, manage to live in a modicum of political harmony. Thus, the argument is a defense of cultural pluralism—existence of different practical interests and views of reality—against those who believe political success requires intellectual uniformity. No officially approved ideology—whether that of an established church or an omnipotent political party—is needed for democratic societies, by the compromise of competing interest-claims, to function normally. Nor should an educational system in a democratic society teach (or "preach") an official "line." In this sense, the argument that democracy entails no one set of philosophical truths seeks to separate specifically political disputes from religious and philosophical convictions held by the citizens of the state. In the United States, it has been instrumental, for instance, in attempts to control ecclesiastical groups in their efforts to dominate the curriculum in the public schools. In a like manner, this argument for democracy rejects as fallacious the view that political solutions to men's problems require agreement about something known, as indicated in the chapter on historicism, as "the meaning of history."

The view that democracy essentially involves pursuit of "a public interest" fails to satisfy some political thinkers. They are not convinced that a unique public interest can, on the basis of public evidence, be shown to exist at a specific historical juncture. The phrase "public interest" carries overtones of the earlier metaphysical doctrine of "the general will," which seems always to withstand any possible empirical validation. Instead, some political thinkers associate democracy with a political process in which leaders and political parties "take stands" on pressing issues, using their rhetorical and organizational abilities to persuade voters to permit them to interpret what needs to be done. On this view, the democratic process permits leaders to emerge whose views become politically dominant through the existing power structures in a society. Thus leaders and parties as much shape and direct opinion as merely reflect it. Finally, sometimes it develops that a public interest is nothing more than the contingent overlapping of aspects of existing, otherwise distinct separate interests. In this way, combinations of special interests can occur which reach agreement on isolated issues or in face of serious crises. In accordance with this view, a public interest need not include some minimal interest of all citizens but only of a substantial number, probably a majority. In addition, civil rights advocates "see" the democratic process as hedging minorities about with protections from existing dominant interests.

It must be admitted that the notion of "public interest" need not exhaust the meaning of democracy. To this extent the critics are not in error. However, any democratic process requires agreement that some public interests go beyond narrow confines of party, class, race, or outlook. Part of the justification of democratic procedures resides in the view that they are able to isolate those issues which affect a very wide segment of a citizenry's interests and to act to implement policies regarding them. This need not mean that special interests are wrong in lobbying for their aims, so long as the claim of a public interest to the right to permit many such special-interest groups to "pressure" legislative officials is given a realistic hearing. Given some democratic procedures, it often turns out in fact that special interests —counterbalanced by the politically powerful claims of counterinterests—learn the value of compromise in which they, as well as others, get less than what they had hoped for. Thus to argue for the notion of a public interest means to reflect how democratic practices in fact often operate, though not always.

There may well be instances when a public interest cannot be served by political compromise. There is no *a priori* rule by which to determine these in advance. One scholar who also served in the United States Congress has argued that compromise is usually to the public interest except under special conditions.[13] Compromise should not be attempted when it is needless, when peace is sacrificed by a compromise which leads to unending demands for yet further sacrifice, and when progress is blocked by a compromise which means a balanced stagnation.

In practical terms, at least in theory, supporters of democratic political institutions and procedures vote for men's stands on pressing issues rather than for candidates' religious or philosophical views. Voters do not inquire into a candidate's philosophical position—that is, they do not ask if Candidate X is a philosophical idealist, materialist, neo-Thomist, pragmatist, or Platonist. Rather, they want to know how Candidate X "stands" on questions of race, governmental support to medicine, public education, welfare benefits to workers, and any number of a host of concrete issues which pressingly confront a democratic electorate. Thus, it is more important to know what the relevant issues are and how various political figures view them than to know whether a political candidate is Protestant, Jew, or Catholic or a follower of Plato, Aristotle, Aquinas, or Kant. This, at any rate, is the theory behind the argument that democratic government requires no one ideological support.

Professor G. H. Mead, who taught for many years at the University

[13] T. V. Smith, *The Ethics of Compromise and the Art of Containment* (Boston: Beacon, 1956).

of Chicago, tended in his lectures and writings to suggest that a genuine democracy would best be intellectually supported by a belief in what Mead termed "social behaviorism." By "social behaviorism" Mead sought to deny both an *individualistic* and a *partially social* conception of the human mind. The adherents of the individualistic explanation claim that mind is, logically and biologically, a presupposition of any actually functioning social process. Thus they seek to understand the social side of human existence by questionable contract theories of political obligation. Admitting that mind realizes its powers only in a social environment, defenders of a partial social explanation of mind nonetheless claim that mind is partly prior to that social setting. Mead wanted to argue that mind and social process are dependent on each other, unable to exist alone in any sense. He believed that a democratic society most widely provided choices among numerous (possible) roles for citizens to try, thus enriches what Mead meant by the range of the mind. At times, followers of John Dewey also looked upon pragmatism as the philosophical outlook most congenial to a democratic system. Both men "saw" the life of the mind as a constant unfolding of the consequences of cooperative inquiries undertaken for shared ends in a community framework. Thus, they looked upon absolutist philosophies as obstacles to a scientific and commonsense pursuit of human truths—truths which require flexibility of mind as well as of purpose, since they are "truths in the making." Inherited philosophical traditions and opinions can blind men's eyes to the realities of the day which demand analysis and treatment by political means. In this regard, one writer has suggested that American pragmatism represented the philosophy of having no philosophy at all.

Probably few persons have wanted seriously to deny some relation between democratic politics and philosophy, if by "philosophy" is meant a set of value judgments about men and their relations to one another. This is to use "philosophy" in a nontechnical sense, of course. As Professor Zevedei Barbu has pointed out, supporters of democratic political systems have often presented a view of social life in opposition to authoritarianism. They have valued such concepts as (1) individuality, (2) critical-mindedness, (3) objectivity on the basis of facts, (4) leisure as an intrinsic value, (5) flexibility of personal character, (6) tolerance, and (7) compromise as a goal in situations of conflict. These are values which seem necessary to any adequately functioning democratic system.

Thus, John Dewey's philosophical views represented a reasoned defense of a democratic conception of social life. What Dewey recognized earlier than many is that democracy as a social phenomenon, as a way of life, required constant creation of new associations to handle mutual problems in an industrial age. The individual needed an organic context in which to function—face-to-face groups possessing genuine powers of decision. He had to be free to act. Because this kind of problem is notoriously studied today, even in corporate enterprises, and because our psychological awareness of anxiety produced by "mean" features of a contemporary society has greatly increased, we easily underestimate Dewey's contribution. Yet, democratic procedures in wide areas of modern life remain useless, and in many areas we hardly know how to create and perpetuate them. The individual today cannot protect his rights nor develop his capacities outside of group situations—and, yet, these situations become causes of anxieties such that, unless one conforms to what others want, he will suffer deprivation; or if he conforms too readily, he will lose his independence. This is not a narrow political problem but an extensive one, in labor, business, education, and in religious life. In addition, some structure is needed to protect persons in groups from the deprivatory machinations of the "operator" (as the American sociologist David Riesman has called them, the "inside-dopesters"). How to train individuals who can responsibly cooperate in groups without simply conforming or using them to their own various interests is still the dominant issue of our times. There are many who fear the consequences or the possible abuses of group function—yet their own destinies are tied up with whether democratic decision making and control can be spread through widening circles of the average citizen's life. For this reason, Dewey detested authoritarianism of any kind—but *not* authority.

Dewey is also the great leveler. In the name of Intelligence he went forth to slay dragons—of tradition. There is here a danger which Dewey perhaps did not fully understand. He wanted an orthodoxy to counter old orthodoxies—a constant treatment of history for purposes of the future. The "cash value" of an institution was its capacity to aid with present difficulties—measured in some objective way. A rigorism runs side by side in Dewey's writings with talk about pluralism. The *situation* is what counted (Dewey's realism), and any intelligence functioned relatively to it.

Whether even John Dewey's pragmatic defense of democratic values makes convincing sense in today's ideologically troubled world remains an open question. Scholars are disagreed on this point. Dewey's main contention was that political democracy can work only if sustained by a democratic social setting. Democracy can function as a valuable means only if a community's members can (1) agree on what they want according to some fairly worked out priority list and (2) agree on which of these wants most conform to their actual situation in a very real world. Some agreement about a present state-of-affairs (What's the situation?) is needed if citizens are sanely to order their wants according to the realities. Unlike many other philosophers, on this point Dewey insisted that science and value judgments are *empirically* related—that knowledge of a situation *as a matter of fact* always tells men how they should best proceed. Dewey held a strong faith in human intelligence as the means by which facts and values can be related if needless obstacles to inquiry and open political discussion are not created to confuse citizens.

This democratic faith so influentially defended by John Dewey in the first half of this century still has followers as well as critics. A friend to this philosophy has written:

> Any new individualism, hence, must realize individual liberty in terms of its relation to social change, and the lasting task of the liberal is to be alert to the process of change and to mediate the indicated adjustments. In all situations liberalism seeks to replace stasis with movement, to abolish boundaries and monopolies, to free communication, to share experience. In the schools, the implementation of such seeking is education; in the sciences it is the winning of truth, in the arts it is consummating experience, in political economy

it is democracy, in international relations it is peace, in the personal history it is growth in freedom through reason. Everywhere it is religion.[14]

But a former friend and later disheartened critic wrote:

The philosophy fell apart under the pressure of forces which its central ideas were incompetent to understand or to direct to "liberal" ends. Its "cooperative intelligence," an unstable combination of social gospel and scientific method, lost its moral bearings as "advancing social science" grew increasingly specialized, technical and noncommital as to values. Its progressive faith in "on-going forces" turned in the direction of disillusionment as the course of events was found to be on the whole unfriendly to its antecedent hopes. And its liberal preconceptions, unsupported by engineering techniques and evolutionary trends, either survived, as in Dewey, as a noble nineteenth-century attitude, or dissolved into expediency, accommodation, and a tolerance based less on principle than on the lack of it.[15]

Nonetheless, the American thinkers Mead and Dewey kept alive the faith—now come upon hard days—that democratic politics could operate successfully without ideological conformity. The anxious question asked today is: Were they right in so thinking?

This is not a new problem. In the late nineteenth century, the somewhat dour thinker, Henry Adams, worried about the prospects of democracy. In his impressive novel *Democracy*, first published anonymously in 1880, the central theme concerns the question whether democratic government can exist without the usual forms of corruption associated with other kinds of government in the world. In one place in the novel a Baron Jacobi, representing a Balkan country in Washington, D.C., speaks for the fears of Henry Adams as author when he is made to say:

"Ah!" exclaimed the baron, with his wicked leer, "what for is my conclusion good? You Americans believe yourself to be excepted

[14] Horace M. Kallen, "John Dewey and the Spirit of Pragmatism," in Sidney Hook, ed., *John Dewey: Philosopher of Science and Freedom* (New York: Dial, 1950), p. 35.
[15] A. E. Murphy, "Philosophical Scholarship," in Merle Curti, ed., *American Scholarship in the Twentieth Century* (Cambridge: Harvard University Press, 1953), pp. 185–86.

from the operation of general laws. You care not for experience. I have lived seventy-five years, and all that time in the midst of corruption. I am corrupt myself, only I do have courage to proclaim it, and you others have it not. Rome, Paris, Vienna, Petersburg, London, all are corrupt; only Washington is pure! Well, I declare to you that in all my experience I have found no society which has had elements of corruption like the United States. The children in the street are corrupt, and know how to cheat me. The cities are all corrupt, and also the towns and the counties and the States' legislatures and the judges. Everywhere men betray trusts both public and private, steal money, run away with public funds. Only in the Senate men take no money. And you gentlemen in the Senate very well declare that your great United States, which is the head of the civilized world, can never learn anything from the example of corrupt Europe. You are right—quite right! The great United States needs not an example. I do much regret that I have not yet one hundred years to live. If I could then come back to this city, I should find myself very content —much more than now. I am always content where there is much corruption, and *ma parole d'honneur!*" broke out the old man with fire and gesture, "the United States will then be more corrupt than Rome under Caligula; more corrupt than the Church under Leo X; more corrupt than France under the Regent!" [16]

Mrs. Lightfoot Lee, the central character in Adams' novel, possesses a firm democratic faith, yet wants to look all the facts "full in the face." From a personal association with a powerful practical politician, a Senator Ratcliffe who seeks vainly to marry her, she hopes to learn the secrets of practical democratic politics. Yet, she too becomes discouraged by the realities and—momentarily despairing of the democratic dream—is made to have the following feelings:

The ease with which Ratcliffe alone had twisted her about his finger, now that she saw it, made her writhe, and the thought of what he might have done, had she married him, and of the endless succession of moral somersaults she would have had to turn, chilled her with moral terror. She had barely escaped being dragged under the wheels of the machine, and so coming to an untimely end. When she thought of this, she felt a mad passion to revenge herself on the whole race of politicians, with Ratcliffe at their head; she passed hours in framing bitter speeches to be made to his face. Then as she grew calmer, Ratcliffe's sins took on a milder hue; life, after all, had

[16] Henry Adams, *Democracy* (New York: Signet, 1961), p. 48.

not been entirely blackened by his arts; there was even some good in her experience, sharp though it were. Had she not come to Washington in search of men who cast a shadow, and was not Ratcliffe's shadow strong enough to satisfy her? Had she not penetrated the deepest recesses of politics, and learned how easily the mere possession of power could convert the shadow of a hobby-horse existing only in the brain of a foolish country farmer, into a lurid nightmare that convlused the sleep of nations? The antics of Presidents and Senators had been amusing—so amusing that she had nearly been persuaded to take part in them. She had saved herself in time. She had got to the bottom of this business of democratic government, and found out that it was nothing more than government of any other kind. She might have known it by her own common sense, but now that experience had proved it, she was glad to quit the masquerade; to return to the true democracy of life, her paupers and her prisons, her schools and her hospitals.[17]

The democratic faith requires a sustaining belief that, even with the corrupting influence of power, political action can in important ways be made subject to the control of an electorate. In spite of the cynicism and the disillusionment of fictional characters like Baron Jacobi and Mrs. Lee, democratically oriented citizens even as realists must be willing to participate in the political processes which often involve compromise and the bending of fixed principles. Otherwise, the notion of a rationally justifiable democratic political system becomes meaningless and empty.

Conclusion

For numerous reasons, historical and philosophical, many modern thinkers lost faith in a ready objectivity in political and social knowledge and action. They became impressed by the extent to which social origins influence men's values and their range of knowledge. Yet writers concerned to analyze the ideological problem in its logical aspects have disagreed about the extent to which social conditions determine human knowledge. Even Karl Marx looked upon an ideology as a distorting perspective which might be overcome. Thus the central problem in ideological analysis seems to be how extensively

[17] *Ibid.*, p. 176.

human knowledge is colored by group interests. Fascists often accepted the perspectival view with delight. The democratic faith has presupposed, on the other hand, that some degree of disinterested knowledge in politics is possible, though difficult to obtain—that within limits citizens can make up their minds in the light of issues and evidence. If this faith is totally in error, then it would appear that politics can never reach beyond the adjustment of rival claims in terms of sheer power, a view which would undermine the rational traditions of Western thought.

This chapter has sought, simply, to show how ideological analysis introduced a change into the manner in which men discuss politics and power, as well as to characterize some of these changes by referring to specific men and movements. Emphasis has been directed to the value disagreements rather than to the factual question of their historical significance. The crucial point is this. It seems obvious that men cannot hope to create minimal conditions essential for a beginning solution to international problems if the past ideological age does not, rather rapidly, give way to an age of empirical analysis of common problems in world politics. Continued dogmatic argument about different "ideologies" may turn out to have been, in the eyes of some imagined future cosmic historian, the prolegomena to mankind's political obituary.

Some Questions and Problems

1. Can there be a democratic ideology? If not, why not? If so, how could an ideology be considered democratic?
2. Should schools and colleges actively attempt to teach "the American way of life"? If so, how should it be done? If not, how should democratic values be handled in classrooms?
3. From the class, choose a person to present a Marxian criticism of contemporary American life as well as a person to reply to the criticism.
4. Should any important contemporary ideology be denied a hearing on a college or university campus? Be prepared to support your decision with arguments.
5. Choose a speaker to defend the Communist view of human existence as well as a speaker to criticize that view.

6. Assume that you are a college dean or president and that a student group has invited a controversial political figure to speak on campus. Assume that an influential body of local citizens protests the appearance of the speaker. How would you handle this situation?

7. What might be some of the differences between *teaching* and *advocating* a specific ideology? Is the question a misleading one? If so, how should it be stated?

8. Are there some religious views which are really only ideologies? If so, should members of those religions be allowed to teach?

9. Is the notion of truth compatible with the notion of ideology?

10. To what extent may the social sciences be ideologies rather than "genuine" sciences? Is there any difference between science and ideology?

Some Suggested Readings

Acton, H. B. *The Illusion of the Epoch*. London: Cohen 1955.

Aiken, H. D. (ed.) *The Age of Ideology*. New York: Mentor, 1956.

Barbu, Z. *Democracy and Dictatorship*. New York: Grove, 1956.

Becker, C. *Freedom and Responsibility in the American Way of Life*. New York: Knopf, 1945.

Berlin, I. *Karl Marx: His Life and Environment*. London: Oxford University Press, 1939.

Cohen, C. (ed.) *Communism, Fascism, Democracy*. New York: Random, 1962.

Dunham, B. *Heroes and Heretics: A Social History of Dissent*. New York: Knopf, 1964.

Fromm, E. *Marx's Concept of Man*. New York: Ungar, 1961.

Ginsberg, M. "On the Diversity of Morals," *Essays in Sociology and Social Philosophy,* Vol. I. New York: Macmillan, 1957.

Hofstadter, R. *Social Darwinism in American Thought,* rev. ed. Boston: Beacon, 1955.

Hook, S. *From Hegel to Marx*. New York: Humanities, 1950.

Jordan, Z. A. *Philosophy and Ideology*. Dordrecht, Holland: Reidel, 1963.

Kornhauser, W. *The Politics of Mass Society*. Glencoe, Ill.: Free Press, 1959.

Leavis, F. R. (ed.) *Mill on Bentham and Coleridge*. London: Chatto, 1950.

Mannheim, K. *Ideology and Utopia,* trans. L. Wirth and E. Shils. New York: Harcourt, 1955.

Sabine, G. H. "The Ethics of Bolshevism," *The Philosophical Review,* Vol. LXX, No. 3, 1961.

Snow, C. P. *Science and Government*. Cambridge: Harvard University Press, 1961.

Stern, F. *The Politics of Cultural Despair*. Berkeley: University of California Press, 1961.

Taylor, S. *Conceptions of Institutions and the Theory of Knowledge*. New York: Bookman Associates, 1956.

Thielicke, H. *Nihilism,* trans. J. W. Doberstein. London: Routledge, 1962.

Viereck, P. *Meta-Politics: The Roots of the Nazi Mind*. New York: Knopf, 1941.

CHAPTER FIFTEEN

Language Analysis and Politics

Two philosophical "movements" in this century have washed like strong tides against the bedrock of older ways of philosophizing. One such movement is known as existentialism—a sustained protest against philosophical abstractions in the name of personal existence and human values. Most influential among European thinkers, existentialism is nonetheless making inroads in the United States, if not yet in England. This new humanistic protest constitutes the subject matter of the next chapter. The second contemporary movement, difficult to characterize fairly in general terms, has proved remarkably fertile and influential first in England (stemming from the great universities at Oxford and Cambridge), as well as in this country, especially during the past three decades. For purposes of convenience, this contemporary movement will here be designated as language analysis, though it has been referred to in differing ways: as "linguistic analysis," "ordinary language philosophy," or simply "analysis." Nonetheless, the language-oriented philosophers form no "school" in any usual sense. Rather they share a conviction, expressed in imaginatively differing ways, that traditional philosophical "problems" ("perplexities," "puzzles," "mental cramps") can be clarified, if not resolved, by careful attention to the ways in which natural languages are actually used.

Many gifted thinkers have become identified with language analysis in this century. Suspicious of philosophizing "in the grand manner," they have preferred to pursue topics in a more piecemeal fashion.

Consequently, many of their most valuable contributions have appeared in learned journals or in collections of original essays, to which most nonphilosophers lack a ready access. No brief listing of important persons involved in language analysis can possibly do justice to the wide range of the contributors or their many interests. Nonetheless, such a list would have to include (among those now deceased) at least the following: in England—G. E. Moore, Ludwig Wittgenstein, T. D. Weldon, and John Austin; and among the living—John Wisdom, A. J. Ayer, H. L. A. Hart, and Gilbert Ryle—all associated with English academic institutions; as well as in the United States— Morris Lazerowitz, O. K. Bouwsma, Norman Malcolm, and Frank Ebersole.[1] The investigations of men like these have touched upon nearly all the traditional subjects in which historically oriented philosophers have shown interest. About the language analysts one critical yet sympathetic scholar has written: "English philosophy, over the last fifty years, has been in a state of revolution. And this revolution has not been simply a domestic affair—a reaction against the preceding fifty years of English Hegelianism, for instance; it represents, so at least its partisans pretend, a revolution in the very nature of philosophy itself. It consists not so much in a new philosophical *doctrine*— a return to some kind of 'neo-realism'—as in a completely new conception of the kind of activity which philosophy is." [2]

Among the practitioners of language analysis a "hardheaded" and a "softhearted" division has appeared, though the division is not a rigid one. The hardheaded group tends towards the view that most, if not all, philosophical puzzles can wholly be solved by a careful attention to how language is ordinarily employed. Metaphysical "questions" are not genuine; rather, they are confusions inevitably resulting

[1] The first teaches at Smith College, the others at the Universities of Nebraska, Cornell, and Oregon respectively. Representative contributions from these thinkers' philosophical writings include: Morris Lazerowitz, *The Structure of Metaphysics* (London: Routledge, 1955); O. K. Bouwsma, "The Blue Book" (*Journal of Philosophy,* Vol. LVIII, No. 6, 1961), pp. 141–162; Norman Malcolm, *Dreaming* (London: Routledge, 1959) and *Knowledge and Certainty: Essays and Lectures* (Englewood Cliffs, N.J.: Prentice-Hall, 1963); and Frank B. Ebersole, "Whether Existence Is a Predicate" (*The Journal of Philosophy,* Vol. LX, No. 8, 1963), pp. 509–524.

[2] Maxwell J. Charlesworth, *Philosophy and Linguistic Analysis* (Pittsburgh, Duquesne University Press, 1959), p. 1. Used by permission of the publisher.

when men attempt to "use" language in peculiar and illegitimate ways. The philosopher's task, for this group, involves clearing away the misuses of language without which philosophical issues cannot arise. In contrast, the "softhearted" practitioners agree that metaphysical language is peculiar yet in some sense inevitable and requiring to be "understood" in its own terms.

Yet linguistically oriented philosophers share a number of very general attitudes. They doubt that philosophers can achieve a systematic knowledge of something classically called Reality or Being. They believe the philosopher should aim more at clarifying concepts and removing fundamental linguistic errors than at creating finished philosophical systems. The language analysts also tend to distrust philosophers who present individual interpretations of the "meaning" of human existence or who recommend, on purported philosophical grounds, moral or aesthetic "solutions" to contemporary practical issues. The philosopher is viewed as possessing no privileged station from which, in comparison with ordinary mortals, to resolve such difficulties. Thus G. E. Moore defended the claims of commonsense; Ludwig Wittgenstein argued that philosophers make no new factual discoveries, but rather can free men from their philosophical perplexities; John Wisdom believes that philosophical analysis can indicate how philosophical puzzles are unique expressions of profound anxieties; and John Austin produced careful analyses of some of the many ways language can legitimately be employed. These men "see" the philosopher's task as an analytic and clarificatory one, emphasizing critical and procedural issues and casting doubt on philosophical "constructions" and large-scale "explanations." Their aim is more to help men "get clear" about their philosophical "questions" than to assume the questions are clear ones, in demand of straightforward "answers." Often, their methods involve asking something such as: How can men seek to understand the philosophers' questions?

This need not mean that language analysts are actually uninterested in social, economic, and political issues. As men, they are involved quite often in such matters. Their belief is, however, that no special philosophical "wisdom" or "knowledge" exists which, if it could be discovered, would provide men with a sure blueprint for social and political utopia. Thus, their philosophical positions tend towards humility. They resist being cast in a role which, on their understanding of philosophical activity, philosophers are essentially ill-equipped to handle.

Types of Linguistic Philosophy

The earliest hardheaded version of language analysis, usually known as logical positivism, dominated philosophical activity in England and, to a lesser extent, in the United States during the nineteen-thirties and forties. Its central thesis (too rigidly expressed here to prove adequate to what logical positivists maintained in subtle ways) asserted that perhaps all traditional philosophical "problems" are literally "meaningless" or, cognitively, "nonsense." As has already been shown elsewhere, logical positivists shared the doctrine that only two general classes of meaningful assertions (propositions) genuinely exist. One set contains mathematical and logical propositions whose "truth" is conventional and definitional—as in "All bachelors are unmarried males" and "If Sam is taller than Harry and Harry is taller than Pete, then Sam is taller than Pete." Such truths are important in the organization of human knowledge, though they report no new facts about the existing world. They are *analytic,* thus descriptively "empty." The second class of propositions is made up of enormously varied *empirical* propositions—like "The dog is on the rug," "Albany is the capital of New York," and "Sam weighs two hundred pounds"—which report facts. Empirical propositions are subject to verification, meaning that a person can imagine the kinds of situation in which it would be possible to check up on them by sense observation. Consequently, for the logical positivists, most philosophical assertions are either analytic truths telling men nothing about the factual world; or peculiar "assertions" possessing no literal meaning. As a result, the realms of moral philosophy, value theory, and aesthetics ceased to represent avenues for literal reports about an objective world. Rather, they became the provinces in which different individuals expressed varying emotive judgments about events and issues. Professor A. J. Ayer conveys the central emphasis of logical positivism in its historically "strong" form by writing, in a chapter "The Vienna Circle" (named for the place where several prominent thinkers first worked out their characteristic doctrines) in a little book entitled *The Revolution in Philosophy:*

> The positivist flavour of their thought comes out most strongly in their hostility to metaphysics. Metaphysics, which they construed as covering such allegedly philosophical enterprizes as the attempt to describe Reality as a whole, or to find the purpose of the Universe, or to reach beyond the everyday world to some suprasensible spiritual order, was condemned by them not as being unduly speculative, or even as being false, but as being literally nonsensical. They reached this conclusion by the application of a criterion of meaning which is known as the verification principle. The precise formulation of this principle is a complicated matter: I am not sure it has even yet been satisfactorily done. But, roughly stated, it lays it down that the meaning of a statement is determined by the way in which it can be verified, where its being verified consists in its being tested by empirical observation. Consequently, statements like those of metaphysics to the truth or falsehood of which no empirical observation could possibly be relevant, are ruled out as factually meaningless. The emphasis here is on the word "factually." It is not denied that language has other uses besides that of imparting factual information. Nor is it maintained that these uses are unimportant, or that metaphysical statements may not serve them. They may, for example, express an interesting and challenging attitude to life. All that is claimed is that they are not capable of stating facts.[3]

Perhaps the most radical version of the hardheaded analysts has come from Professor Morris Lazerowitz, an American thinker who has attempted to "explain" the peculiar power of philosophical assertions in something like psychoanalytic terms. The logic of Lazerowitz's position is clear. If philosophical "assertions" are striking in contrast to assertions in ordinary language, and if on the "softhearted" analytic view they are taken nonetheless to serve some important human purpose, then the problem is to discover that purpose. The uniquely deceptive nature of philosophical "statements" may be sub-

---

[3] A. J. Ayer, "The Vienna Circle," *The Revolution in Philosophy,* Introduction by Gilbert Ryle (New York: St Martin's Press, 1957), p. 74. Used by permission of Macmillan & Company, Ltd., London, and St Martin's Press, Inc.

ject to a nonphilosophical explanation. Professor Lazerowitz suggests that every genuinely philosophical "theory" (of reality) contains three levels of meaning. Only one of these levels is obvious, while the two others are "buried" or "invisible," needing to be "dug out" and brought into the clear light of day. Grammatically, philosophical assertions (like "Reality is one" or "Every event of necessity has a cause") look like simple descriptions of a factual condition (as in "The book is on the table" or "Water freezes at 32° Fahrenheit"). This apparent simplicity hides what Professor Lazerowitz considers the significant, if buried, nature of philosophical assertions.

In a controversial but penetrating essay entitled "The Relevance of Psychoanalysis to Philosophy," Professor Lazerowitz has presented in a brief form a thesis he has extensively, and minutely, argued in numerous articles. Given the sentence "Every event of necessity has a cause," Lazerowitz analyzes its meaning into three "levels":

> The first, the uppermost layer of the structure, is the delusional appearance of words being used to express a speculation about a familiar type of phenomenon. The other two parts consist of (1) a hidden revision of terminology which expresses (2) a hidden proposition that is important for our unconscious mental life. There can hardly be any doubt that it is mainly for the purpose of expressing this unconsciously grasped proposition that language was remodeled, and it is the unquenchable interest in it that prevents us from drawing close to the deception effected by the changed piece of language.[4]

Generalized, this thesis would entail the theory that all philosophical propositions contain delusional contents.

The members of the "softhearted" camp of the language analysts are less rigid in their distinctions between meaningful and nonmeaningful uses of language than were the logical positivists. Nor are they quite as convinced as Professor Lazerowitz that the newer way of philosophizing can neatly and finally produce a single "explanatory" theory to account for the various kinds of philosophical bewilderment experienced by men. Probably the two most prominent thinkers in

[4] Morris Lazerowitz, "The Relevance of Psychoanalysis to Philosophy," in Sidney Hook, ed., *Psychoanalysis, Scientific Method and Philosophy: A Symposium* (New York: New York University Press, 1959), p. 153. Used by permission of the publisher.

this softhearted tradition of language analysis are Ludwig Wittgenstein, the troubled genius whose reactions against the hard-and-fast doctrines of logical positivism opened up new avenues of imaginative philosophizing; and John Wisdom, who finds that metaphysical puzzles are at least "important" nonsense if, indeed, they are only nonsense.

Considered by many the most creative language analyst of the century, Ludwig Wittgenstein (1889–1951) expressed a deep dissatisfaction with all previous philosophizing, including his and the logical positivists' own earlier hardheaded attempts to make sense of philosophical "questions." His important posthumously published *Philosophical Investigations* (1953) and *The Blue and Brown Books* (1958) serve as guides to original treatments of a host of philosophical perplexities. He did not think a philosophical system, if possible, is worthwhile; nor did he argue for one method in philosophizing. Rather, there are many methods and therapies. Moreover, detesting generalizations about philosophical activity, Wittgenstein preferred to work at specific topics in an effort to learn how they might be illuminated or, perhaps, dissolved. Consequently, he would have thought poorly about textbooks in philosophy—like the present one—as he would also have given a low rating to attempts at characterizing in general terms what is here termed language analysis.

Unavoidably misleading, a set of generalizations about Wittgenstein's way of philosophizing may prove at least helpful to beginning inquirers. This can be only a tentative set. *First,* philosophical doubts are deep and profound in ways in which scientific and common sense doubts are not. They reflect a peculiarly disturbing kind of mental cramp which requires its own technique for dissolution, a dissolution which if it is to occur at all will "appear" to the doubter in the actual process of his philosophizing. *Second,* a philosopher needs to pay close attention to how ordinary persons tend to use [the English] language. Probably (perhaps) by doing so, the philosopher can show how philosophical puzzles (always handled discretely, emphasizing a *specific* puzzle) arise because language which causes no difficulties when used in ordinary ways is employed out of context by philosophers. *Third,* an effort is required to avoid generalizing rather than carefully and minutely treating individual examples and cases of philosophical language or "argument." Close attention must be paid to the contexts in which ordinary assertions are made in order to provide a contrast with what philosophers attempt to do with such assertions. *Fourth,* philosophers need to avoid thinking there is only one way, or model, which can properly serve for numerous philosophical inquiries. On the contrary, philosophizing is more like an art than a science; and imagination and even genius contribute to the success or failure of specific inquiries. *Fifth,* there is no reason to believe a fixed body of philosophical problems exists to which a finitely adequate, final set of conclusions (or "solutions") can be worked out once and for all. The reason is that, for Wittgenstein, the English language is so complex that, if persons are careless in its use, a wide number of philosophical perplexities will arise. Indeed, a perplexity may be cleared up in one inquiry only to give rise later, to others.

Not too many of the original leading figures in language analysis worried about the special topics associated with social and political philosophy. They concentrated more on the central concerns such as theory of knowledge: What can one know?; ethics: What should one do?; and metaphysics: What is there? Nonetheless, later thinkers have applied some of their methods to treatments of most of the usual topics. Indeed, in places this textbook has in an introductory way made use of some of these methods. The language analysts have made their contemporaries aware of the richness of language as well as self-critically concerned to distinguish philosophizing from other kinds of activity, like what is done in the social sciences or in practical politics. In the remainder of this chapter, an effort will now be made—by means of a somewhat arbitrary selection—to indicate how one influential hardheaded analyst treated social and political philosophy as well as how a specific topic in social and political philosophy might be handled by its followers.

T. D. Weldon as Political Philosopher

The manner in which political philosophy has felt the influence of the contemporary attention to language analysis can be illustrated by

400 Contemporary Issues and Movements

a consideration of the writings of the recent English thinker, Professor T. D. Weldon (1896–1958).[5] More unreservedly than some others, Weldon joined the camp of the hardheaded analysts, writing in one place that the philosopher's *sole* task was that of clearing away linguistic muddles, that "it has done its job when it has resolved the confusions which have occurred and are likely to recur in inquiries into matters of fact because the structure and use of language are what they are."[6] Weldon wrote for persons broadly interested in talk about politics in more than immediately practical ways, neither especially for nor yet excluding technical philosophers. A legitimate question is possible about how firmly Weldon looked upon political philosophy as a valuable subject matter in the twentieth century.

Weldon insisted that politics as an activity is practical and prudential rather than theoretical and, as an academic subject matter, primarily a topic for empirical study. Statesmen and politicians "do" politics, although the statesman's appraisals are somehow worth more than those of the politician, if only to a degree. The academic side of doing politics is not doing political philosophy but is, rather, the undertaking of empirical studies of ideologies as well as of comparative institutions and cultures. The purpose of such studies is limited, aimed at showing how governing involves judgment and decision rather than the formulation of theories and explanatory models. Weldon did not much care what men call such studies. He wished rather to emphasize the perennial nature of their contextual relevance. Many of the classical texts in political philosophy were not strictly speaking philosophy but various compounds of history, persuasion, and appraisals of men and events. Thus they remain important even if their philosophical portions were confused.

[5] The analysis of Weldon's views is based upon a lengthier essay, "T. D. Weldon on Politics and Philosophy," by Whitaker T. Deininger, which appeared in *Western Political Quarterly,* Volume XIII, Number 1 (March 1960). Used by courtesy of the Editor of *Western Political Quarterly.*

[6] "Political Principles," in Peter Laslett, ed., *Philosophy, Politics and Society* (First Series; New York: Macmillan, 1956), p. 23. Other important works by Weldon include: *States and Morals* (London: Murray, 1946); *The Vocabulary of Politics* (Hammondsworth, Eng.: Penguin, 1954), and "The Justification of Political Attitudes" in *Proceedings of the Aristotelian Society,* Vol. XXIX (London, 1955), pp. 115–130.

Political Appraisals

Statesmen and those who govern do not so much make up theories as make appraisals of men and events. If they make these in light of professed political principles, they do so more for empirical than for logical reasons. The drift of much of Weldon's political writing was to the effect that principles are interesting for historical and psychological reasons but do not, so far as he could see, imply any one set of rules or any one "way of life." On this matter Weldon was not always absolutely clear. In some contexts, he indicated that specific political principles express moral sentiments which may delimit the bounds of a social situation; in others, he suggested they even exclude some acts entirely. Political principles are not so much "empty," then, as they are often truistic or trivial. Nonetheless, Weldon admitted that one could try to create a schema of fundamental general rules covering what many kinds of football games share in common, however different in practice each specific game might be from the rest. These rules would help one to realize that not all games are football, though the rules would be so broad that no one set of laws covering a specific football game could exhaustively be derived from them. The ability to recognize that X is an actual instance of a football game would still remain an empirical matter. Similarly with institutions and principles of government, there may come a point "at which one can say with considerable confidence 'I don't think *that* regime could be described as democratic in the ordinary meaning of the term.' " [7] Yet Weldon "sees" the connection between such sentiments and given political principles as having no logical status, even though most philosophies —and especially ideologies—usually contain confused empirical appraisals at their base. What Weldon wants to emphasize is that individual philosophies of the state usually make use of principles to justify a specific view of the relation of the state to the individual.

Weldon sought to follow David Hume (1711–1776)—the empirically minded sceptical Scotch philosopher—by denying the possibility of a bridge between "is"-statements and "ought"-statements, although

[7] *The Vocabulary of Politics*, pp. 98–99.

he found Hume's use of the bridge metaphor quite misleading. Yet he wants to treat morals and politics as overlapping concerns in that both involve the making and following of rules as well as the making of appraisals which need not be simply subjective.[8] Political principles are significant expressions of ways of life, and any way of life involves rules about how men should act in specific circumstances, even though knowledge of such rules cannot help one in solving *all* questions about proper action. On the other hand, Weldon sometimes makes the mistake of viewing principles as "empty." In one place he gave as examples: "All men are always to be treated as ends and never as means" and "All men are created equal." Weldon asserted that such statements are vague, since from them we cannot clearly derive exhaustive and narrow prescriptions. Here Weldon overstated his case when he argued that such high abstractions can provide us with no basis for deriving actual laws or appraising existing ones. Writing earlier in *States and Morals* (1946) he had claimed that party politics can get nowhere in the long run unless agreement on some principles emerges. What Weldon wanted especially to argue for is that the empirical connections existing between principles and ways of life can have no special logical significance. Indeed, logically, according to Weldon's view, political associations need have no rules at all, though *in fact* no such associations have ever existed.

Weldon's tendency to divorce, sharply, logical from empirical considerations stemmed from the residue of an older logical empiricist orientation existing side by side with a growing interest in ordinary usage. The two orientations just cannot be made fully compatible. The reason is that ordinary uses of language fail often to fit the neat "schematization" of types of assertions so fondly constructed by positivists in this century. The tendency followed also from the manner in which he made use of the phrase "way of life." Weldon insisted that we must not seek to render the phrase too precisely but must use it rather loosely. The kinds of behavior going to make up a way of life are, usually, less neatly connected than some *philosophical* critics

---

[8] *Ibid.*, p. 191. Of course, even Hume makes clear that though rules are artificial, they are not therefore arbitrary; cf. *A Treatise of Human Nature* (London: Oxford University Press, 1955), Bk. III, Pt. II, p. 484.

want to believe. "They overlap one another and have each some sort of internal coherence"; but the phrase "way of life" misleads if taken to refer to any one absolute pattern or ideal. Advocacy of this loose meaning of "way of life" led Weldon to argue that men can justify a principle by appealing to a way of life and yet never give a complete justification. Thus, Weldon believed that modern political philosophers in the European tradition, though disagreeing on many fundamental value issues, managed to share a common idiom. He thought this true, for example, of men like Karl Marx and John Stuart Mill. Such men could have come to understand where, and for what reasons, they disagreed; while they would have had equal difficulties in comprehending the thought of someone like St. Thomas Aquinas.

The appeal to a way of life played a fundamental role in Weldon's treatment of political principles and their justification. Holding to a loose Lockean view of social life, he preferred an "open" society in which a citizen is not expected, all the time, to rationalize all the principles influencing his life into one ideal set. This left Weldon faced with the internal problem of potential conflict as well as by the moral fact that some men, in a specific way of life, do judge one association's principles as more important than those of others to which they also belong. Weldon refused to show deep philosophical concern here— indicating that distinctions between moral and political rules are primarily religious in origin, yet too facilely proceeding to dismiss such religious origins as of negligible significance. The result is that Weldon has little to say to someone worried about the problem of determining which of the associations to which he happens to belong ought to hold a normative prestige in times of conflict and disorder. That men do make such decisions Weldon showed by arguing that appraisals need not be arbitrary or subjective. He should have argued, then, in favor of that way of life in which the making of relevant appraisals is encouraged by the principles of one's primary associations.

The possible complaint that Weldon's appeal to a way of life means simply to accept the "force makes right" theme would miss the point that a specific way of life need not lack for conceptions of better and worse. A man may even hold to customary ways of acting because he has, in a rough way, "thought it out"—that is, judged the way as significant and valuable for respectable reasons. In the case of a conflict situation, Weldon would insist that one needs to render empirical recommendations in order to counter, say, another X's way of life appeal. Mention of principles without such empirical recommendations would often prove inadequate. Seldom would X give up a complete way of life. Yet he might be persuaded to incorporate some of Y's recommendations into his manner of living, without completely uprooting his behavioral patterns.

Weldon's Chaucerian view of a way of life sees it as inevitably diversified and complex rather than simple; and his view that men often defend their value judgments by ultimate appeals to a way of life, including sometimes "principles," does not imply arbitrariness. Weldon was simply aware of the fact that a specific principle may fittingly apply to more than one empirical set of conditions, or at least to features of more than one. What Weldon did wish to emphasize is the fact that, when both X and Y justify differing ways of doing things by appeal to the same principles, not much will be gained by philosophical talk or verbal syntheses; for the ways of life will remain different for all the talk. Men's institutional attachments change very slowly as well as quite moderately. A critic of Weldon is right in seeing that an appeal to a way of life *may* represent a refusal to appraise its features; but he should also admit that use of appeals to "principle" may also indicate an unwillingness to look at the facts afresh. To judge the reasons why one man makes either type appeal, one would need much information about the man as well as about principles and a specific way of life.

To accentuate the decisional character of political appraisals, Weldon recommended that "puzzle," "difficulty," and "problem" do not belong together. He thought "problem" misleads, since it can suggest either a puzzle or a difficulty. Use of the word may indicate that calculation is the sole instrument to get men out of their difficulties. Only puzzles have solutions such that, once known, one can establish clear criteria by which others sufficiently intelligent can recognize the solutions as legitimate. This is not the case with difficulties which, according to Weldon, can have no incorrigible solutions. One lives with or through, suffers from or flees, difficulties. It is true, of course, that men struggle to turn difficulties into a series of lesser problems, often on the analogy of the inductive sciences. But such turning is itself a means of surmounting difficulties and not so much a matter of finding correct solutions as with puzzles. Weldon is stipulating a use of the word "puzzle," obviously, in that ordinary usage does not limit its functions so narrowly as, for example, in the statement "Harry is puzzled by the situation"—in which the situation may have no incorrigible solution.

This aspect of Weldon's linguistic recommendations is important in that Weldon saw active political life as "a living with difficulties." The statesman is never simply critic or consultant. Statesmen deal in difficulties; political and natural scientists in problems; mathematicians and logicians in puzzles; and philosophers in puzzles and nonsense. Thus, "insoluble puzzle" and "riddle with no answer" are self-contradictory, while "insoluble difficulty" need not be so. Weldon wanted here to resist those thinkers who identify politics too closely with a mathematical model or a narrowly experimental view of the behavioral sciences. Experts have their places as critics and consultants. On the other hand, statesmen make decisions. But Weldon did not attempt to argue that a statesman is more like an artist than like a scientist. The reason is that the artist does not deal with living beings and his final achievements, unlike those of the statesman, are sometimes much less dependent on what his own contemporaries think of them.

Politically, Weldon believed there are better and worse appraisers and appraisals, though there exists no "Grand Appraiser." Political appraisals fall unclearly between verifiably factual reports and descriptions of an agent's attitudes. Involving both, they are often reducible to neither. The argument is that appraisal words are never used simply to reflect one's psychological preferences, but rather are situation-oriented. Appeals to correspondence, histories, and biographies of politically successful performers as well as to one's own uses of appraisal words indicate clearly that some men "brought it off" better than others in their judgments about men and events. The classical political philosophers managed, in a like manner, to render significant appraisals of men, institutions and events—thus often exerting an important influence on practical life. Because he agreed with Professor Margaret Macdonald (who taught at the University of London until her death) that "as rational and responsible citizens we can never hope to know once for all what our political duties are. And so we can never go to sleep," [9] Weldon thought the continued study of the classical texts justified on prudential, historical, and empirical grounds. Yet he believed that no one of the differing models of the state advanced by political thinkers can ever receive verification as true and correct. He thought the models dangerously misleading, since they appear as grounded on self-evident axioms when there are no such axioms.

Oriented on situational difficulties, then, appraisals are much like aesthetic judgments ("That painting is beautiful!"). Adequate or not, fair or unfair, they cannot be strictly true or false, though they do involve empirical materials insofar as they are concerned with concrete contexts and the establishing of human dispositions. Favorable or unfavorable appraisals will be on the order of dispositional descriptions coupled with expressions of sentiment or feeling. If pressed hard to justify a specific appraisal, like "X is a 'good' department chairman, because he's flexible," one can point out the consequences of such flexibility in an approbatory way (a flexible man is adaptable, can respond to criticism, is able to maintain a human image) or state a principle which acts ultimately as a conversation-stopper ("Flexibility is always an intrinsic good!"). Men can appraise institutions and other men much as they do works of art, but this does not mean that universal agreement will result. There would be the "seeing" or the "not seeing" what the appraiser sees. On this point, Weldon made a somewhat peculiar suggestion that the poverty of the English aesthetic vocabulary—which he could not explain!—is interesting: a poverty which falsely suggests that all appraisals are subjective. But one need not imply he has no sound reasons for approving a specific institution or person because he answers a request for these reasons by saying: "I think X is a 'good' institution (person)!" The questioner may simply "see" the institution or person differently.

[9] "The Language of Political Theory," in Anthony Flew, ed., *Logic and Language* (First Series; Oxford: Blackwell, 1962), p. 186.

The effort to demonstrate that there are empirically relevant appraisals to a philosophical sceptic who, without regard to context, continued to ask for conclusive evidence, would be like attempting to give reasons for holding to political principles when, in the end, no one can ever arrive at absolute primitives from which those principles logically derive in a strict manner. Conversation with the sceptic must stop at some point. Relations between attitudes and empirical appraisals are not of that kind of logically deductive order. Yet no one need conclude, because of this, that appraisals are subjective or simply emotive. Quite ordinary persons use appraisal words, referring to specifiable features of situations. Thus one may say, according to Weldon, that "X is a 'good' member of the team," and agree empirically that *in part* the statement can be resolved into a series of statements about aspects of X's behavior. We must remember, however, that by such a statement we mean often to mention something about X's character. We do this not in spite of X's behavior but (sometimes) in addition to it. As a matter of contextual stress, we try to bridge the behavioral and the motivational issues and, usually, succeed only in calling attention to a problem—that is, in mentioning it. The character tends to express itself in those acts, yes; or is to an extent just those acts. Yet we often want also to stress the way in which, as well as the reasons for which, the acts get done by X.

Weldon tried valiantly to avoid an absolute dichotomizing of empirical facts and emotive attitudes when he argued that men seek to appraise an agent's reasons for acting as well as the acts done. Like the word "moral," "good" suffers from an unavoidable vagueness. Although Weldon insisted there can be no simple reply to the question, "To what do moral appraisals refer if not to qualities?" he did at least claim the intuitionists were right in pointing out how one must distinguish between *judgment* and *observation*. Political philosophies of the past remain important, then, even if their attempts to state unchanging axioms proved unsound. Their importance lies in the wide range of significant appraisals they contain and *the ways in which* they contain them for concrete situations. That is, the texts of the political philosophers make up a specially valuable literature of appraisals of men, events, and institutions.

Weldon on Language

Originally, Weldon judged that to do political philosophy meant to appraise the arguments concerning the grounds on which the state may claim to exercise authority over its members as well as to clarify issues in the discussion about what, ideally, the state ought to be like. He was then willing to admit the peculiar way in which philosophical talk about politics is an aspect of university life—a kind of talk which goes on, almost exclusively, in academic settings. Even though specific political philosophies arise in delimited historical situations, Weldon insisted nonetheless that their classical expressions—as in Hobbes or Locke, say—remain broadly relevant to later situations because they concerned themselves with the great moral issues about which men are often willing to make extreme sacrifices. Thus the great political texts constitute an important type of literature. In his *States and Morals* (1946) Weldon criticized many academic moral theorists for their refusal to discuss the problem of relevance and importance when giving concrete examples of moral perplexities in their writings. He thought the political philosophers managed, on the other hand, to stir human emotions in ways obviously foreign to tracts on moral theory. Weldon's conclusion was that political theories get accepted or rejected because they conform to, or disagree with, moral beliefs about the importance or the unimportance of the individual, rather than for their strict internal consistency or its lack.

The later Weldon—as author of *The Vocabulary of Politics* (1954) —appeared far less hopeful about the indirect influences of political philosophizing upon practical matters. This followed from his stricter conception of what is involved in the philosopher's primary function. His earlier complaint that philosophers had given insufficient attention to the question, "What is the status of the definitions from which political philosophy is derived?" becomes unimportant, since there are no verifiably acceptable definitions from which one can meaningfully derive a final political philosophy. It is not the job of the philosophers to concern themselves with factual discoveries or to claim privileged status in making recommendations as to how one should view the state.

Weldon came to believe that the classical political philosophers "went wrong" in several important ways. They thought they could discover and formulate the axiomatic grounds of politics and morals in order to escape something called "subjectivism." Moreover, they failed to realize that the quest after *the* meanings of key words in the political vocabulary (including "state," "right," "authority," "law," and "freedom") must end in failure, since words do not have meanings "in the same sort of sense as that in which children have parents." Words simply have uses, according to the Weldon who had read Wittgenstein and Ryle—important language analysts mentioned earlier in this chapter. Because there are uses of words which are simply correct in certain contexts rather than absolute meanings, political philosophers ought to have concerned themselves with matters of "more or less . . . and not a straightforward 'either-or' disjunction." [10] The traditional search after "real essences," "absolute standards," and deductively complete justifications of political systems patterned on a geometric method turned out to have been metaphysical in the bad sense, thus illusory.

A significant aspect of Weldon's concern for the key words in the political vocabulary is that he also made an important recommendation in line with democratic and empiricist political convictions. Words like "authority," "rights," and "law" are connected with one another, as well as with "state," on the condition that men use "state" to designate only one kind of an association existing alongside many others. This move indicates that Weldon thought the philosopher should consider not only singular uses of words as isolated units in a language, but also the manner in which some of these words hold family resemblances to other words in a political vocabulary. The reasons for such a recommendation are only partly linguistic. They include, *first,* the assertion that adoption of a specific use of a word allows other words to function without needless confusion in the political vocabulary; and, *second,* the *normative* statement that if "state" is

[10] *The Vocabulary of Politics,* p. 29.

used to designate one type of human association, then puzzles originally created by idealistic and organicist metaphysical "misuses" of
the word will disappear. In his later writings, Weldon held the philosopher to a strict conception of doing philosophy while, himself,
recommending a specific use of a "political" word. Such recommendations are justified only by appraisals of language which are not
strictly confined to how language is actually used. In this manner, he
continued fruitfully to do what he claimed the classical political
philosophers erred in doing, save insofar as they realized they were
not doing philosophy but rather rendering a special kind of appraisal.[11]

An exegetical consideration of Weldon's treatment of the five key
words in the political vocabulary is not here possible. His treatments
of these words led Weldon to conclude that they can cause no philosophical confusions if philosophers simply study the actual uses to
which they are put. His recommendation that men view the state
as one kind of association only, prompted him to suggest that, as
members of any association, men possess some rights, are amenable
to some authority, must submit to some laws, and will gain some
liberty. How the citizen justifies his membership in other kinds of
association in cases of conflicts among rules Weldon does not consider. His point is that, in such conflict situations, there can be no
a priori rule of deciding on action. Nor did Weldon take seriously
Professor Macdonald's comment that references to the state as an
association involve "objects which are obscure . . . and not listed
in any of the recognized dictionaries." Most associations can be legally
defined. The difficulty is that the state is often that association which
permits such legal definition in specific contexts. The fact is Weldon
stipulated a use for the word "state" which, he judged, will fit democratic, liberal, and parliamentary convictions. He failed to show how
this stipulation can be justified solely in terms of linguistic use.

Weldon reached other suggestive conclusions, two of which deserve

[11] A similar recommendation that the state be viewed as an association is
made by Professor J. Mabbott in *The State and the Citizen* (London: Hutchinson, 1948), pp. 123ff.; but Mabbott supports his recommendation in moral and
teleological terms by arguing that (a) free association permits free activity,
which is a good; and (b) the consequences of such activity tend to be good.
Mabbott realizes that he views the state as a means to moral activity.

mention. One is that questions about origins, as in "Where did X's authority come from?" make sense only if subject to vague answers like "by the consent of the governed" or "from the will of the people." Otherwise, origin-questions are peculiarly unanswerable because what they seek to know is *what* got conferred by certain rituals or performances. The second conclusion is that teleological descriptions of the functions of states and institutions are often pointless and confusing. Weldon's example here is a telling one. "Now 'Aspirins relieve headaches' and 'Parliamentary institutions promote the general good' look very much alike," Weldon admitted. "But if we ask for the evidence, we can only get back statements about how X tends to produce Y; yet, when assembled, these can never be made non-controversially and exhaustively identical with "general good." If we say that "Parliamentary government is a good thing" needs to be compared with "Basketball is a good thing," we find that persons obey the rules of basketball because they like to play that kind of game. To a question like: "What is rule X good for?" where X is some specific rule, we can perhaps reply: "In order to promote happiness." But if we don't happen to like the rule, we shall sometimes be puzzled by the assertion it can promote happiness. Also, if we ask about the reasons for which any person follows the rule, we can make only a finite range of relevant general replies "He has none"; "He likes the rule"; "He feels obligated"; "He uses it as a means to something else"; or "He has a calling" (used to emphasize someone's judgment that the rule is extremely important). Any further call for reasons would be pointless, according to Weldon. A person asked for reasons for following a rule will mention a principle as a last resort, thereby hoping to appeal to a way of life as well as to some contents of an appraisal about that way. As Weldon has maintained, "To justify a political principle is to describe the way of life accepted by all or nearly all the members of a particular state at a particular time. Political principles differ within a state because people see the state in different ways—it looks different to different people." [12]

Weldon did not claim persons should never ask "Why?" of a specific command. There will naturally be times when so to ask will

[12] "The Justification of Political Attitudes," p. 130.

prove unwise. Yet to the "Why?" of commands as well as rules, two kinds of lawlike replies are possible. If the rule should be the imperative "Don't swim in this lake," someone who questions it might be told either that if one swims here, he tends to be swept to his death by the current (Law One); or that if one goes swimming, he will be fined a certain amount of money by the guards (Law Two). Political philosophers are interested primarily in laws of a prescriptive nature, thus laws of the second type. Nonetheless, there are commands which cannot ultimately be justified save by some such statement as: "Father says so, that's why."

The result is that, for Weldon, philosophers are in no particularly favorable position for making adequate appraisals as philosophers of the men and events of their times. Nor are they equipped in any special way to pursue the empirical studies of social and political matters—studies pursued usually by historians, sociologists, economists, and psychologists. They must therefore show care in answering only philosophical linguistic questions, as in the example: "How alike and unalike are the sentences 'Is the American Constitution better than the English?' and 'Is Jones a better tennis player than Smith?'" Performing in such a limited manner, philosophers can serve to eliminate confusions, showing "that when verbal confusions are tidied up most of the questions of traditional philosophy are not unanswerable. All of them are confused formulations of purely empirical difficulties." [13]

In conclusion, a few difficulties with Weldon's particular expression of the linguistic approach to philosophy need mentioning. The first is that Weldon sometimes made a convenient use of the appeal to ordinary uses of language while continuing also to make important recommendations about how a key word in the political vocabulary *should* be employed. Weldon thought such a recommendation can sometimes be backed up by showing how its adoption will permit other important words to "fall into place." A second point is that Weldon failed clearly to show how appraisal words like "good" and "wicked," if made members of the political vocabulary, can complicate the problem of determining the uses of other words in that

[13] *The Vocabulary of Politics,* p. 192.

vocabularly. A third difficulty is related to Weldon's failure to suggest what the extent of the political vocabulary is. Where does it end, if at all? A fourth difficulty arises from Weldon's conception of the non-subjective, nonarbitrary characteristics of appraisals, for whose rendering words like "good" and "bad" will often function normatively. Sometimes men do use such appraisal words to judge a specific way of life or a full *set* of rules, as is the case when one says: "But that way of life is a 'bad' one!" It appears that—like some other contemporary thinkers—Weldon was impressed both by the logical empiricist model of language as well as by the later "ordinary use" model (if it can be said to be a model at all). Weldon appealed to that model which best met his interests at a given time.

An important upshot of Weldon's approach to political philosophy is that the breach between empirical politics and philosophizing both widens and narrows. The philosopher is to pretend no other than therapeutic linguistic aims. Nor should he as a philosopher claim any special powers to describe or judge men, events, and institutions. On the other hand, the political philosopher needs an increasing empirical knowledge of situations and the actual uses of words if he is adequately to perform his function. Thus, to the question: "How important is political philosophy?", Weldon's general answer seems to go something like: "Not very, unless those who do linguistic analysis hold an extensive first-order knowledge of problems in politics and the confusions associated with certain uses of words." If pressed hard, probably Weldon would have wanted to say that the great texts of political philosophy are important for historical and political reasons only. They contain appraisals whose significance is lasting.

Some Supplementary Considerations

Professor Weldon emphasized some of the general linguistic themes which have exercised a number of contemporary philosophers. However, even in social and political philosophy a number of stimulating examples of what has been called "language analysis" have appeared in the past decade. Philosophers have sought to appeal to our ordinary uses of the English language to elucidate "confusions" about a social contract, the problem of rights and obligation, issues of sovereignty and authority, as well as the relation of the legal and the moral order. No general introductory treatment can possibly indicate the originality in these many analyses. What the authors share is a conviction that philosophizing involves nothing other than linguistic clarification of philosophical assertions, using ordinary language as the model.

In his introductory remarks to a first edited volume of readings about politics and society [*Philosophy, Politics and Society* (First Series; 1956)], Professor Peter Laslett referred to the apparent death of political philosophy. Yet, the contents of that first volume suggested that, if philosophy was experiencing a funeral, the funeral had brought out an unusually gifted assortment of mourners. A second edited volume [*Philosophy, Politics and Society* (Second Series; 1962)], contained a somewhat more optimistic note about the philosophical prospects. Apparently, though language analysis can help to clear up some old "muddles," men still need, on a softhearted interpretation of these, to understand what led philosophers in the first place to make use of their peculiar notions. These peculiar notions seem deeply disturbing to adherents of the softhearted view—not simply easy mistakes to be cleared up "at one fell swoop," never again to trouble active thinkers.

How to account for the slight shift in emphasis, from Weldon's hardheaded to the later more softhearted emphasis in language analysis, would require a book on its own. However, it is possible that Professor John Austin's genius in numerous essays at showing the rich range of uses of English has led philosophers to a more cautious estimate of this contemporary philosophical approach. For example, Austin's discovery that some uses of language are *performatory,* actual instances of doing something by speaking or writing (as when someone in authority says at commencement exercises: "By the powers of the State of _____ I award you this Doctor's degree.") has probably helped to renew interest in nonliteral and nondescriptive aspects of language.[14] It is possible that the old philosophical prob-

[14] John Austin, "Performative Utterances," in G. J. Warnock and J. O. Urmson, eds., *Philosophical Papers* (Oxford: Clarendon Press, 1961), pp. 220–239. More fully developed in J. O. Urmson, ed., *How to Do Things with Words* (Oxford: Clarendon Press, 1962), entire work.

lems will now be illuminated, in ways difficult to predict, by this more generous conception of the uses of language. Philosophical "problems" may in one sense be nonsense, yet not only that. If so, philosophers will have the detailed task of attempting in their own terms to understand social and political philosophers' attempts to "say something" by their otherwise apparently nonsensical assertions.

Moreover, some writers have turned to the legal order in an effort to throw helpful light on philosophical issues. As a result, interest in philosophy of law—long dormant among philosophers and practised chiefly by students of jurisprudence in law schools—has revived, influencing the way in which philosophers treat topics in ethics and political thought. Professors Austin [15] and H. L. A. Hart [16] have indicated how some considerations of legal distinctions may help men to employ the notion of "excuses" in making better sense of aspects of the freedom-responsibility theme. Strangely, the language analysis which seemed to be bringing about the death of social and political philosophy as traditionally practised may actually turn men's minds, once more, to a serious reconsideration of old arguments in an effort—from an altered perspective—to try to make new sense out of them. Thus what began as a funeral may, in important ways, turn out to have been the beginning of a minor philosophical renaissance. There is no doubt that language analysis has captured the interest of a number of persons who, on independent grounds, had earlier come to believe that philosophical issues had all been resolved either by the physical or the social sciences. Whatever social and political philosophy is, it is not identical with history and the social sciences. It has its own distinctive subject matter and techniques, even if these should turn out to be limited.

Perhaps the power of language analysis in philosophy can now briefly be illustrated by showing how the notion of a social contract— so fundamental to philosophical worries about sovereignty, as an earlier chapter has indicated—can be "saved" by a softhearted ap-

[15] John Austin, "A Plea for Excuses," in G. J. Warnock and J. O. Urmson, eds., *Philosophical Papers* (Oxford: Clarendon Press, 1961), pp. 123–152.

[16] H. L. A. Hart, "Legal Responsibility and Excuses," in Sidney Hook, ed., *Determinism and Freedom in the Age of Modern Science* (New York: Collier, 1961), pp. 95–116.

proach even on the assumption that it lacks literal cognitive meaning. Professor Margaret Macdonald [17] has done work on the notion of natural rights; and Professor John Rawls [18] has indicated that, though wrongheaded if read literally, the contract view of government at least recognized that some social practices are inherently wrong.

Social Contract Theory

The pages of some philosophical works contain references to (as well as arguments for) something known as the social contract. This is a notion of a contract analogous to the understandable kinds of contract made in everyday life, yet it is *ultimately* very much unlike them. A contract is any written or spoken agreement between individuals, binding each to the other by virtue of a "promise" (legally enforceable) that each will perform specified acts under certain stated conditions or be made to pay compensation if the agreement is avoided. Not every promise need imply a contract. The reason is that contracts presuppose existence of some coercive authority recognized by each of those making the contract—or, if not so recognized by each, available to some party to the contract to enforce the terms of the contractual agreement. In developed modern societies, disputes often arise about whether a specific agreement constitutes a contract —a matter to be determined by the courts.

Suppose one sunny morning you say to a neighbor (in a fit of euphoric well-being): "Charlie, you've been working too hard. I'll mow your lawn for you during the coming month." You are making a promise. Now, is such a promise a contract? Probably not. If you fail to keep your promise, you can be made to feel the moral weight of the neighborhood's disapproval ("Sam's a promise-breaker!"), but no (reasonable) legal system can make you keep that promise or punish you for failing to keep it. For one thing, this was a one-way affair in which only the neighbor stood to gain. (Of course, the one

[17] Margaret Macdonald, "Natural Rights," in Peter Laslett, ed., *Philosophy, Politics and Society* (First Series; New York: Macmillan, 1956), pp. 35–55.

[18] John Rawls, "Justice as Fairness," in Peter Laslett and W. G. Runciman, eds., *Philosophy, Politics and Society* (Second Series; Oxford: Blackwell, 1962), pp. 132–157.

who made the promise could be said to gain or lose a certain kind of character, which is a moral consideration.) Suppose, on the other hand, you agree to mow your neighbor's lawn while he is on vacation, as well as to water it properly, in return for a fixed payment in money or services. If you forget to do so, and the lawn dies from lack of watering, your neighbor may attempt to gain a legal judgment against you. This does not mean he will succeed, since in any reasonable legal system there must be witnesses—and, if you did not sign a contract (agreement), your neighbor must produce convincing witnesses to your mutual agreement. For this reason, as legal systems develop, the tendency is to place the terms of agreement in writing.

What transforms a promise into a contract is a difficult question, but usually the transformation occurs at the point at which the promise is subject to legal enforcement. A contract is a promise subject to legal enforcement, or to legal interpretation if a dispute arises. This means there must exist some recognized system of rules and procedures capable of producing decisions which are backed by the authoritative force of the proper institutions. A contract is like a restricted type of promise-making. It involves at least two legally recognized persons in a mutual relationship. Usually, it should be voluntary—such that one party is not coerced into making the contract under duress. Each of the parties involved agrees to do something for the other's promise to do something in return. The parties must be aware of what the agreement involves or, if in fact one or the other is not (having failed, say, to "read the small print"), it must be possible to show that they *could have known* what the terms of agreement were had they paid attention.

If one accepts the moral rule that one ought to keep his promises, one is often committed also to the moral point that "ought" implies "can." Morally, it would be peculiar to argue that one ought to keep promises which are impossible to fulfill. Sometimes quite reasonable persons make promises which turn out to be impossible—often, because later events make it *now* impossible to do what *then* (when the promise was made) seemed possible. If I promise to meet you for an important engagement and suffer an automobile accident on the way, it is doubtful that anyone would say I am morally blameable for having failed to realize the promise. It sometimes happens that we blame a person for not having tried what turns out to have been impossible. "No one could have saved that drowning man, but Sam didn't even make an effort!" To say that someone ought to do a certain act is to say that the act is possible (or, that there is no convincing evidence that the act is impossible if one genuinely tries). On the other hand, persons are sometimes held liable for breaking contracts, though this is done unintentionally and it could not have been avoided. For example, an owner of a private airplane may be liable for damages if, through no fault of his own, a part of his cargo being delivered to a customer is destroyed in flight. Thus, we do find people sometimes held legally blameable (liable) when they would not, in similar circumstances, be held morally so.

In classical thought, an important distinction was made between nature and society ("what is naturally the case" and "what is socially the case"). The distinction attempts to account for differences between processes which produce specific kinds of results independently of human contrivance and processes which, while requiring some natural conditions, produce results influenced by human agency (intelligence, will, intention). Aristotle distinguished nature from art. By the latter he meant the class of all those things which, without human agency, could not exist in the forms in which they do exist. Anything in whose production men are necessary efficient causes belongs to art—from the making of a house to the writing of a speech. On the other hand, nature comprised that realm of facts which would be what they are independently of human agency. Thus, Aristotle thought an acorn naturally tended to realize its potentiality as an oak tree; and that this tendency existed independently of human agency. Aristotle viewed men as *naturally* social (political) animals, tending to live together in groups. *What* social and political arrangements they lived under were, for him, products of human agency. *How* a thing gets done by men involves, for Aristotle, a degree of art, since human agency is necessary to the doing of many kinds of things—from making furniture to living morally.

Now the existing social order appears obdurately *there* to the common man. Metaphorically, men sometimes speak of the "weight" of tradition. Tradition is seen as "heavy," especially if it happens to be oppressive to the viewer. The social habits indicate regularities of behavior in one's fellows which seem almost as steady and predictable as the course of the sun. To be told that such habits *might* be other than they are if the agents chose to act differently may, to the common man, seem a bit of nonsense. "Well, they don't choose to act other than they do," he might reply; "and they won't!" David Hume expressed this sense of the apparent unalterability (for practical purposes) of much human action when he wrote: "The same prisoner, when conducted to the scaffold, foresees his death as certainly from the constancy and fidelity of his guards, as from the operation of the axe or wheel." [19] Many of the details of social life get carried out routinely, by individuals doing their jobs without deep thought about the significance of what they do. Yet, looking for a justification of the regularities observed in social and political life, some philosophers write as if many of these activities are based upon something like a contract. It is as if they want thinking men to "see" that the social necessities of their time and place have, in some sense, been agreed to—and that they are, in some sense, voluntary participants in that agreement. This is a puzzling doctrine which goes counter to much of commonsense. Sceptics can argue that there never was such a contract in any literal sense; or, if there were, that it cannot bind them, since it was made by someone else. Yet the force of the social contract theory is that men are bound by it (within limits) and that they are not, somehow, simply passive participants in a natural process.

Sometimes the social contract theory seems to function as an answer to the peculiar philosophical question: "Why should I obey any authority at all?" The theory seeks to show that an appropriate answer might be: "Because there's a contract which binds you." That is, there is supposed to be an agreement made by persons, or made for them—such that they are *morally* obliged to abide by its terms. The peculiarities connected with this view include the fact that individuals seldom ever sign such an agreement and that if they violate the contract there is no one but the existing sovereign—with whom

[19] L. A. Selby-Bigge, ed., Hume's *A Treatise of Human Nature* (Oxford: Clarendon Press, 1955), p. 406.

they are joined by contract—to punish them. It is as if by being recipients of the benefits of social life (into an instance of which one is born without choosing the conditions or the birth) individuals in some sense assent *voluntarily* to the specific social obligations which are entailed. It is as if an individual agrees to participate in the existing social arrangements which, though he did not choose them in fact, are to be treated as if he had so chosen them. The aim of the theory is to encourage men to "see" their activities as voluntary and rational; it seeks to encourage men to assent to the necessities of their social lives *as if* they had chosen those necessities. The purpose is to dramatize for men the sense of voluntary participation in what is socially required. Though not literally true, the social contract doctrine tells us something about the obdurateness of social life and its inescapable obligations.

The social contract theory tends to counter the argument that one's actions are the conditioned results of environment—to soften the otherwise impersonalized nature of social institutions and arrangements. Man is seen as in some sense responsible for his social arrangements, even inherited ones. Thus, he has agreed to them. The social contract notion suggests that men give approval or acquiescence to the social order. They are not simply automata who react to existing conditions. Since the political order may be viewed as representing an achievement of art—a realization of aims of human intelligence—it might be other than it in fact is. Yet need of stability requires that the political order possess a high degree of enduring features and that its members think of those features as contributing to their own ultimate purposes. Moreover, any political order requires obedience from its members—a subordination to rules and procedures whose aim is the perpetuation of that order, presumably for the higher purposes of the citizens. The social contract theory attempts to account for the fact of obedience as a rational acceptance of the obligation to obey the authoritative rules which exist. The social contract dramatizes obedience to rules as an active, rational acceptance of those rules even by individuals who never made them or were consulted about them.

"What a strange contract!" the critics can rightfully object. "Here the philosophers talk about a contract which isn't like anything which goes by the word in reasonable legal systems. There is no independent neutral authority to enforce it, if broken. It is seldom written down; and even if it is, it cannot be said to bind later generations if it is like ordinary contracts. Yet this peculiar arrangement is called a social contract!"

The critic is certainly correct in pointing out these matters. By doing so, he confronts philosophers using such a theory with the need to justify the theory. They must show that the notion of the social contract is not to be taken literally and yet is not meaningless, that it says something important about social life but not what, at first blush, it may seem to assert. Also, a philosopher may conclude that the propounders of social contract views made mistakes and, yet, somehow managed to say something important without themselves clearly understanding what that was. Some contemporary philosophers think the social contract theory is basically unintelligible, even nonsensical, beyond salvation. What they and others who want to "save" the theory say must receive attention after several historically influential versions of the theory are stated. The versions important to the modern world are found in writings by Thomas Hobbes, John Locke, and Jean Jacques Rousseau. These versions also introduce the view that men do possess some fundamental *rights* as well as obligations—rights not derived from the rules of *this* or *that* existing social order. These versions of the social contract seek to show that a necessary relation exists between rights and obligations, that the two cannot be sundered. These men "see" the social contract as illuminative of the deep moral aspects of social and political existence. They seek to persuade men that certain necessities in social life which would have no moral significance if seen as purely natural processes can be both necessary and yet morally significant, since we can adopt an attitude toward them which can make a great difference to our conception of political life.

Conclusion

The concentration on language analysis, in England and to some extent in the United States, has reflected a conviction that traditional ways of philosophizing are fruitless and misleading. The quest has been after clarity. Instead of "seeing" philosophical questions as intrinsically meaningful, thus attempting to locate their "answers," philosophers have worried about how to make sense of the questions. A number of differently oriented thinkers have devoted careful attention to many traditional problems, looking to the uses of language to illuminate these in a new way.

The earlier hardheaded version of analysis insisted that most, if not all, philosophical issues are literally meaningless. The softhearted version has, on the other hand, indicated that since language can be employed in many ways, a special philosophical training and ability is needed to "make sense" out of what, if read literally, would remain philosophical nonsense. Even with the more generous minds in this philosophical camp, however, there is a suspicion of philosophical system-building and of claims to philosophical kinds of "knowledge" or "wisdom." The language analysts excel at criticism rather than at the creation of systems.

Language analysis has been a valuable movement in this century. Whether it will be able to sustain its present position in the philosophical limelight would be for a prophet to maintain. This chapter has sought, in any event, to present a brief survey of some of its emphases and of some of the persons who have brought it into prominence.

Some Questions and Problems

1. Write out a number of ordinary English sentences in which each of the following words is used: *law, freedom, power, right, state, authority*. Try to make different uses of each word. Compare your sentences with those written by others in the class.
2. Show how a person can criticize Hobbes' notion of a social contract by calling attention to actual uses to which the word "contract" is often put.
3. Imagine the kind of comment a language-oriented philosopher might make about the following assertion: "Until men discover *the* meaning of History, they will continue to wallow in the chaos of daily events, directionless and abandoned."
4. Look up the meanings of the English word *compromise*. Is com-

promise a notion important in politics? Defend whatever position you take on this question.

5. Discuss T. D. Weldon's claim that politics is a thoroughly empirical matter. Show how and why you agree (or disagree) with Weldon's position.

6. Discuss the following speech, showing your reaction to its contents:

> It is difficult to *prove* that men's philosophical beliefs necessarily influence their practical political decisions and actions. Yet, I am convinced they do so. Whether a man thinks God's existence can be proved or that a legal order rests on natural law can be more important than whether he favors social reform or protection of labor unions' rights, say. Show me a man's basic philosophy, and I say you show me how he will vote and act!

7. Would most politicians benefit from a course in social and political philosophy? If so, on what grounds and in what ways? If not, why not?

8. Is a philosophical "understanding" of the world (reality) incompatible with efforts to change the world?

9. Give some reasons how a command over one's spoken and written language can have political consequences.

10. Can you think of some ways in which social scientists may sometimes pass off philosophical generalizations as scientific truths? List some of these, if you can; and try to explain why they are not "scientific".

Some Suggested Readings

Austin, J. L. *How to Do Things with Words,* ed. J. O. Urmson. Oxford: Clarendon Press, 1962.

————. *Philosophical Papers,* eds. G. J. Warnock and J. O. Urmson. Oxford: Clarendon Press, 1961.

Ayer, A. J. *Language, Truth and Logic,* rev. ed. London: Gollancz, 1951.

————. (ed.) *The Revolution in Philosophy*. London: Macmillan, 1957.

Charlesworth, M. J. *Philosophy and Linguistic Analysis*. Pittsburgh: Duquesne University Press, 1959.

Copleston, F., S.J. "Contemporary British Philosophy" in *Contemporary Philosophy*. London: Burns, 1956.

Flew, A. (ed.) *Logic and Language,* First and Second Series. Oxford: Blackwell, 1951 and 1953.

Gellner, E. *Words and Things*. Boston: Beacon, 1950.

Hampshire, S. *Thought and Action*. New York: Viking, 1960.

Laslett, P. (ed.) *Philosophy, Politics and Society,* First Series. New York: Macmillan, 1956.

Lazerowitz, M. *The Structure of Metaphysics.* London: Routledge, 1955.

Lewis, H. D. (ed.) *Contemporary British Philosophy,* Third Series. New York: Macmillan, 1956.

Malcolm, N. *Ludwig Wittgenstein: A Memoir.* London: Oxford University Press, 1958.

————. *Knowledge and Certainty: Essays and Lectures.* Englewood Cliffs, N.J.: Prentice-Hall, 1963.

Pears, D. F. (ed.) *The Nature of Metaphysics.* London: Macmillan, 1957.

Runciman, W. G., and Laslett, P. (eds.) *Philosophy, Politics and Society,* Second Series. Oxford: Blackwell, 1962.

Ryle, G., *Dilemmas.* London: Cambridge University Press, 1954.

Urmson, J. O. *Philosophical Analysis: Its Development Between Two World Wars.* Oxford: Clarendon Press, 1956.

Weldon, T. D. *The Vocabulary of Politics.* Hammonsworth, Eng.: Penguin, 1953.

Wisdom, J. *Philosophy and Psycho-analysis.* Oxford: Blackwell, 1957.

Wittgenstein, L. *Philosophical Investigations,* trans. G. E. M. Anscombe. New York: Macmillan, 1953.

CHAPTER SIXTEEN

The Existentialist Protest

Following the Second World War, in the difficult period when many Europeans confronted a discouraging task of rebuilding ruined cities and discredited political systems, an international religious conference took place in the United States. Some participants in this conference read papers on the theological implications of contemporary man's crisis situation and possible Christian means of meeting the crisis. The story is told that one European's paper gloomily emphasized the "darker side" of man's nature—his sinfulness and perverted self-deception—while an American theologian stressed the perennial hopefulness of faith. When the European was asked to explain his pessimistic estimate in face of the American's more optimistic appraisal of the situation, he is said to have replied that—unlike the American—he had lived in a house which suffered a bombing toward the war's end. His reply implied that an individual's personal experiences tend to influence even his theological views and that persons who had experienced the terrors of war at first hand, plus a total defeat of their countries, could not respond to optimistic estimates of human possibilities in the modern world.

On a much wider scale, numerous twentieth-century thinkers experienced a growing sense of hopelessness, accentuated by revolutions, wars, and economic depressions. A continuing threat of nuclear war has helped to encourage men everywhere to reappraise traditional beliefs and attitudes. Out of this reappraisal, especially on the European continent, a deeply personal mode of philosophizing known as existentialism has emerged. Rooted in a way of thinking made famous by a few nineteenth-century figures like Sören Kierkegaard (1813–1855) and Friedrich Nietzsche (1844–1900), contemporary existentialism functions as a protest against the dehumanization of the individual by the coolly impersonal forces of industrial technology, nationalism, militarism, and a scientific "objectivism" which often seems unable to clarify the values for which men ought to strive. It is also a protest against intellectual tendencies toward systematization—"pretensions" to a total explanation of human existence in the name of a comprehensive theory or ideology. Existentialist philosophers believe that meaningful truths are "subjective"—authentic first-person experiences rather than objectively testable generalizations available to all men, in the same way, in the marketplace. Such philosophers are concerned about human values in an increasingly depersonalized natural and social universe. Their emphasis is on the personal, the authentic, the decisional side of human existence. Existentialism is made up of numerous tendencies which reflect contemporary uncertainty about the destiny of humanity in a scientific and tightly organized social situation fast becoming worldwide. Individual existentialist thinkers disagree on many fundamental problems—whether God exists, whether religion is a sign of weakness or hope, whether *this* or *that* particular political program should receive our support. What they do agree on is the desperate situation of human values, the crisis of freedom, the significance of certain pervasive kinds of human anxiety. Thus, existentialism is first of all a diagnosis of the human predicament of men living amidst rapid cultural changes and threatened by the possible loss of freedom and personal meaning. Even thinkers who doubt that existentialism has offered an effective "cure" for man's plight often respond favorably to the existentialist diagnosis which seeks to make men aware of their situation.

Existentialist writers are concerned to make clear the nature of something called "the human situation." They want to provide an authentic description of what it means to be a human being. Their writings emphasize the category of individuality—the kind of individuality which exposes man to risks as well as happiness, to the inescapable need to make choices even when "the times are out of joint." They say many things about freedom and responsibility, arguing that to be human means to be a free being. Their aim is to transform men from passive agents into responsible actors in the drama of human existence—to replace a "spectator" view of reality by a "participant" view. Negatively, they resist tendencies which provide men with "excuses" for gross mistakes and failures to act on important issues because of environment, or conditions of early toilet training, heredity, or the personal threat to security and happiness involved in acting. There is a sense in which each man must decide for himself on important issues, but do so as a responsible agent. Their emphasis on the theme of responsibility comes as a protest against those who seek to avoid *personal* involvement by appealing, for justification, to existing authorities (religious or secular) or bodies of rules. The center of the existentialist view is this insistence on individual responsibility which, as the basis of human dignity, is also a source of fear and trembling. To be responsible means to accept the consequences of one's choices without illusion or excuse or complaint that the responsibility lies elsewhere when "things go wrong."

Personal existence makes up the subject matter which most existentialist thinkers explore. And personal existence is always a "problem," for there are no authoritatively objective answers to questions like "What is the meaning of my existence?" or "Why does anything (the cosmos, the world, the individual questioner) exist?" These are questions which must be "lived with," if they are to be handled at all. They are answered only in the first-person decision called forth from the questioner. According to one scholar,

> The main business of this philosophy therefore is not to answer the questions which are raised but to drive home the questions themselves until they engage the whole man and are made personal, urgent, and anguished.[1]

The assumption here is that traditional "schools" of philosophy, as well as scientific theories of man's functions—physical, biological, psychological, and sociological—provide no adequate *philosophical* picture of the problem of human existence, since they seek to "solve" the problem in a way which is, for existentialist thinkers, impossible

[1] Harold J. Blackham, *Six Existentialist Thinkers* (London: Routledge, 1952), p. 152.

of absolute solution. Nor can the human predicament fully and finally be "dissolved." There is no permanent "cure" for the human plight, so to speak—only better or worse, wise or less wise, responses to the concrete perplexities inevitably faced in living. Existentialism thus gives a diagnosis of the human situation, not a cure.

Recognizing the existentialist emphasis on diagnosis, H. J. Blackham raises a serious point:

> But if man is a suspense of being, always in question, and if the objective world is also permanently in question because of the irremovable ambiguity of nature and of history and the enigmatic silence of the cosmos, what is the use of a philosophy which instigates and insists on questions that have no possibility of an answer? [2]

The answer is that, no matter how widely human knowledge may extend in future, man will always remain a problem to himself—partly bound to specific historical situations yet a free and responsible agent. No philosophic or scientific "system" will ever exhaust the possibilities of human choice and decision. Yet, endlessly, men will practice a self-deception, acting as if they have discovered the nature of reality or a secure basis for actions in a given political system. Existentialism functions as a perennial challenge to this kind of self-deception, confronting men with the evidences of their finiteness, contingency, and radical freedom. Especially in the present age, which contains many claimants to the throne of universal certainty, does existentialism keep alive a serious concern about ethical and other values.

> An age which has discovered and recognized absolute evil, not in the heart of man but in the contemporary deeds of men, has to come to terms with itself, and that is what we find going on in the later development of existentialism, confirming its foundations. That is why it is a call to heroism and has so little to do with average hopes and fears and with the themes of an earlier humanism. If it proposes liberation by enlightenment, as did those earlier humanists, it does not mean, as they did, emancipation by scientific knowledge of the laws of the universe and of man and of society, but awakening to total individual responsibility—"I am my own witness." If as a movement it stops short at this harsh conversion, it can hardly go

[2] *Ibid.,* p. 152.

further without going back on itself; and its individual exponents do go further in furnishing their own witness and representative example. Thus each of them makes his own contribution to the problem of civilization which confronts the modern world, and each of them must be left to his own singular fate and fortune in meeting criticism and carrying conviction in the professional controversies of the schools.[3]

The Boundary Situation

Existentialist writers are keenly aware of the crisis aspect of existence as well as of the peculiarly threatening situation of modern man. To discover what is involved in being a man is, experientially, to face a crisis. This is the perennial side of the human predicament. The "shock" of existence involves the self-conscious discovery that all previous certainties are from some perspective questionable—that is, to experience a lack, a gap, the threat of "nothingness" about which, in earlier times, religious persons had much to say. Existentialists are aware also that the contemporary economic, social, and political situation poses special threats. There is, thus, a perennial aspect to the diagnosis, plus a more restricted historical one. Men are *always* puzzles to themselves. But, because they now live amid anxiety-producing conditions which are more extensive than in the past, they are tempted to forget their ambiguous situation by "hiding," as it were, behind new authoritarian standards. Such transitional periods have occurred before, though they have never been the ordinary historical case; but never before have so many men recognized their situation for what it is. Existentialists do much to clarify the dimensions of the peculiar crisis of modern men as well as to warn them against "easy" solutions. The crisis must be faced, endured, borne, lived with by men who are responsible and free. In a practical sense concrete decisions must be made even when the evidence is never totally sufficient to justify them on objective grounds.

"But this seems to be a lot of stewing over life's problems just for the sake of the stewing," a practical-minded person might say at this juncture. "Look! Either a problem can be solved or not. If it can't be

[3] *Ibid.*, p. 164.

solved, what is gained by constantly dwelling on it? Men must still, one way or another, get on with the difficult business of living!"

"Yes, you are right," an imagined response might be. "Usually, we think of problems in practical contexts—as difficulties about which we can do something concrete if only we are knowledgable and persistent. There are better and worse solutions, we think, to such problems as how to establish an income tax policy, how to deal with facts of juvenile delinquency, how to meet the military threats of a hostile political power. Nonetheless, there are broader problems which must be dealt with and, yet, never finally or completely resolved. Take the so-called 'problem of adolescence' or 'problem of marriage,' for example."

Suppose our sceptically inclined practical man now says: "But I don't understand your position. Adolescence or marriage need not constitute *a* problem. Rather, *during* adolescence or *in* a marriage many specific problems arise which call for attention." Is there any reply which an existentially oriented thinker might make? If so, perhaps it might be developed somewhat as follows. In life there are "problems" and, then again, there are problems. They are not all alike. There is the "problem" of living with those difficulties which are not subject to ready, neat solutions. Yet they are often very real. They may even possess tragic characteristics in some circumstances. A person does not "solve" the "problem" of old age in the manner in which he solves, say, the problem of paying his income tax for a given year. The "problem" of old age is hard to define, yet it is nonetheless real. Similarly with the "problem" of adolescence. Nor are all such problems necessarily pathological, dependent on individual biographies. They may be quite objective. Thus, men often must live through trying social and political turmoil, including wars and revolutions, to which no quick solutions are apparent. They must endure. There are problems which, because they cannot readily be solved, must be borne and lived with, involving care and concern.

Sören Kierkegaard stressed one such "problem" in his classic *Fear and Trembling* (1843), whose central aim is to make sense of Abraham as the father of faith who, on God's command, is pictured as willing to sacrifice his son Isaac. Kierkegaard recognized that different types of heroism are possible—that the heroism of the man of faith and the tragic man are not identical. The tragic hero faces a "problem" to which there is no neat solution, including that of faith. He is, in Kierkegaard's view, confronted by a tragic situation in which two competing moral requirements cannot equally be met and between which he must yet make a choice. No matter which choice he makes, some unhappy consequence is sure to follow. Thus, Agamemnon as a human father wants to love and cherish his daughter Iphigenia, yet as a political leader is required to sacrifice her for the community. How does he neatly solve such a "problem"? Perhaps the political aspect of tragedy is at some time known to all political figures, who must often make choices and decisions they would prefer—as ordinary citizens often are able—to avoid making. In any event, contemporary existentialist thinkers are aware that many "problems" are not of that neatly definable kind so dear to the practical man. Kierkegaard grasped this existential aspect to human existence, in its tragic dimension, when he wrote:

> Ethics, however, has at hand no chance and no old servant. The ethical life contradicts itself as soon as it must be carried out in reality. Hence ethics requires revelation. The tragic hero displays his ethical courage precisely by the fact that it is he who, without being ensnared in any aesthetic illusion, himself announces to Iphigenia her fate. If the tragic hero does this, then he is the beloved son of ethics in whom it is well pleased. If he keeps silent, it may be because he thinks thereby to make it easier for others, but it may also be because thereby he makes it easier for himself. However, he knows that he is not influenced by this latter motive. If he keeps silent, he assumes as the individual a serious responsibility inasmuch as he ignores an argument which may come from without. As a tragic hero he cannot do this, for ethics loves him precisely because he expresses the universal. His heroic action demands courage, but it belongs to this courage that he shall shun no argumentation.[4]

Political affairs touch the average man's life at numerous points from birth to death. The citizen's expectations help to shape the "climate of opinion" in which active statesmen and politicians carry

[4] Sören Kierkegaard, *Fear and Trembling,* trans. Walter Lowrie (Princeton: Princeton University Press, 1945), p. 133.

on their never-ending strategies, manipulations, and compromises. A citizenry can often "slow" the political pace of a specific regime by indifference or quiet resistance, just as it can lend support to a regime if its expectations are closely tied to the regime's policies. Even when a citizen feels himself unable either to shape or to retard the political course of events, he needs a viewpoint from which to "understand" them—even if, like the saintly seventeenth-century Frenchman Blaise Pascal, he believes about men like Plato and Aristotle that—"if they wrote of politics, it was as if to regulate a hospital for madmen." Sometimes helpless in the onrushing stream of events, yet always affected by their political consequences, an ordinary man wants the cold shower of "truth" so that, freed from illusion and wishful thinking, he can at least "call a spade a spade." It is possible that, if a sufficiently large number of men come to "see" the hopelessness in the drift of events, they may even prevent actualization of some of the more daring possibilities of disaster looming on the horizon.

Stated briefly, men want sometimes to ask of political affairs, "How can I endure them?" as well as the practical question, "What can I do to alter events?" There comes a time when, as in personal matters, a man wants to know the facts in all their threatening obdurateness. If he cannot change the facts, he wants sometimes also to know this. Often, men sense that things are going awry, that habitual types of political action fail to produce satisfactory results, that from all sides they are given "official" propaganda which "hides" the real nature of the human situation. Contemporary existentialists write often like men who, lacking clear-cut programs of political reform and action, direct our attention to the implications of our human involvement in even the most gruesome of political happenings. At the same time, their philosophical analyses can perhaps lead men to assume responsibility for the affairs of their own day—refusing to blame the culture, state, economic class, or historical circumstances for the terrible consequences of free human decisions. The existenlialists protest against features of modern culture, but they do so in the name of a more basic and enduring human condition, which though accentuated by specific contemporary happenings nonetheless remains what it is in any time and place. In some ways, the existentialist analysis of man's condition may influence men to decrease their expectations from the political arena. Politics may be able to improve the environmental conditions amidst which men must live out their days without being able to change some permanent aspects of man's condition.

One concern central to existentialist writers is the analysis of basic human anxieties. Many men have reflected on the ways in which various types of human anxiety influence social and political affairs. Political leaders can manipulate their anxieties to their own ends, using their existence as a ready-made avenue to power by "promising" to create conditions which will relieve men of their "aches" and "pains." For this reason, men need to become clearheaded about those anxieties which can, and those which cannot, be satisfied or assuaged by purely political means. They must learn to judge political "promises"—especially across-the-board political panaceas which come as ready-made ideologies—in the light of objective criteria rather than of their personal wishes. Because contemporary men are baffled and often frustrated by the complexities of industrial life and the perplexities of international relations in a revolutionary world, they can become easy targets of crass power-hungry individuals who, speaking for powerful groups, will "say anything" in order to achieve office.

A person who asks how existentialist emphasis on human anxiety contributes meaningfully to a constructive understanding of social and political philosophy may have several matters in mind. He may question the apparent psychological preoccupations of many existentialist writers. Perhaps psychological analyses are important, yet relatively unhelpful in social and political philosophy. On the other hand, he may think that the problems central to political action and decisions are treated as unimportant, since whether men decide in "anguish" or with confidence, the emphasis in political life must fall on the need to act, for whatever reasons. In Sartre's novel, *The Age of Reason,* a Communist (Brunet) confronts the leading character (Mathieu, an existentialist) with an invitation to join the Communist party, an invitation which is declined on the grounds that such a decision would limit Mathieu's freedom. Brunet is unimpressed by Mathieu's notion of freedom, saying: "You live in a void, you have cut your bourgeois connections, you have no ties with the proletariat, you're adrift, you're an abstraction, a man who is not there. It can't be an amusing sort of life." In a final gesture

> Brunet smiled an absent smile; he was still pursuing his idea. "You renounced everything in order to be free," he said. "Take one step further, renounce your own freedom: and everything shall be rendered unto you.[5]

Many critics of existentialism insist that men must decide on entire programs—that a romantic preoccupation with the individual's "lostness" cannot alter the objective need to come to terms with pressing realties.

A possible response to such a critic might be put in terms like the following. Human action takes place against a background of hopes and expectations. Many persons expect too much (or too little) from political action. A knowledge of the "situation" in which certain pervasive anxieties operate may teach men how to evaluate the programs and the aims of existing political parties and leaders. It may also help men to accept what cannot be avoided, teaching them how to cope with *inevitable* frustrations common to their industrialized world by equipping them with the kind of self-knowledge which permits them to function even in areas where certainty and security are impossible. Citizens need some kind of *personal* orientation to the conditions in which they must live out their lives. They look to politics, but in our century also fear the possible effects of political actions on their own cherished values. Existentialist analyses of the human condition help contemporary men to understand the extent to which they must settle some problems for themselves, taking full responsibility for their decisions and their condition.

Industrialization and Alienation

Contemporary men and women are living in an age when the fact-side of the Industrial Revolution is little questioned. Rather, their

---

[5] Jean-Paul Sartre, *The Age of Reason,* trans. Eric Sutton (New York: Knopf, 1947). Used by permission of Alfred Knopf, Inc. [Reprinted from the Bantam Books edition (1959), p. 131.]

main problems are centered on how to decide *what attitude* to adopt toward the facts—*which aspects* of so enormously complicated an event to emphasize—*how to* determine the extent of their own power or freedom to control and direct some of the continuing consequences of an Industrial Revolution which has, in several centuries, almost completely altered the environments in which they live.

The Industrial Revolution has transformed more than economic and political arrangements. It has among other results shaped modern armies and means of fighting wars; introduced inescapable systematization (Max Weber, the famous European sociologist, used the term "rationalization") into all phases of contemporary human life; affected the whole style of life from the businessman's workday to his vacationing, from how parents space their children to how they raise them, and in what kinds of environment. Newspapers spew forth problems which reflect always the effects of the Industrial Revolution: problems of world overpopulation, depression and inflation, full employment, mass communication, nuclear competition. Ideologies exist which seek to deal with the effects of the Industrial Revolution in some totalistic fashion, threatening men with a kind of totalitarianism never dreamed possible in previous epochs. Even as men attempt to understand the relevant facts, the revolution in communications makes available yet more facts so that they wonder how any intelligent person can possibly catch up with the facts. The Industrial Revolution has affected scholarship, including the number of books published and the number of learned journals to which struggling young scholars can send their latest little essays in their search for promotion. Men go on vacation and, while floating in some cool lake, hear its signs overhead and all about. Even their neuroses and anxieties reflect the age of industrialization, as men have their disturbing dreams: Will the moon be turned into a gigantic used-car lot? Where will all the fissionable materials be dumped?

If men are sometimes both poetic and a bit pessimistic, they can feel—along with T. S. Eliot in *The Hollow Men* (1925)—that the epitaph for our industrial civilization may become:

> We are the hollow men
> We are the stuffed men

Leaning together
Headpieces filled with straw. Alas! [6]

Recent scholarship has emphasized the extent to which even Karl Marx, whose revolutionary ideals have usually been presented by his followers as scientific in character, protested against the unhappy consequences of uncontrolled industrialization and capitalism on humanistic and moral grounds. Scholars have returned to a careful examination of Marx's writings in which the plight of modern laborers is treated almost in existentialist terms. Professor Robert Tucker in his *Philosophy and Myth in Karl Marx* seeks to understand "Marx's own Marxism" against its historical background in German philosophy and its development in Marx's own career. He writes:

> The recent rise of interest in this circle of problems springs in part from the discovery of an early philosophical Marx about whom next to nothing was known until the second quarter of the twentieth century. Only then did we obtain access to certain previously unpublished materials of Marx's formative period that enable us to learn how he created Marxism. The most important of them is a set of manuscripts written by Marx in Paris in 1844. These *Economic and Philosophic Manuscripts of 1844,* as they have been named, contain a first version of Marxism seemingly quite different from the mature Marxian system, to which Marx and his collaborator Friedrich Engels gave the title "Materialist Conception of History" or alternatively "scientific socialism." They resurrect for us a young philosophical Marx whose central theme of human self-alienation shows affinity with the thought of our own later age and thus confers upon the first system (which I have called "original Marxism") a curious modernity across the gap of years. [7]

In the early writings, Marx appears as much a moralist and a "religious" critic of existing circumstances as a scientific socialist. He makes a philosophical diagnosis of the situation of contemporary men. A central category in his diagnosis is that of alienation. Marx "sees" the existing capitalistic order as isolating individuals from one another as well as from their potential humanity. Profit and wage relations between employee and employer become more fundamental

---

[6] *Poems 1909–1925* (London: Faber and Faber Ltd., 1932 edition), p. 123.
[7] London: Cambridge University Press, 1961, p. 11.

than human dignity, disrupting the organic aspects of social existence. The proletariat is unable to participate in the cultural and educational "values" of the social order. Thus, the capitalistic system is morally corrupt—deserving *on moral grounds* the harsh condemnation of men and, for the capitalist class which perpetuates it and its attendant social horrors, a retaliatory justice of the strictest kind. This humanistic Marxism justifies class revolution on moral grounds. It does not follow from a materialistic and deterministic conception of history (an issue discussed in Chapter 12, "Historicism"). Rather, Marxian humanism serves as the basis for the construction *of* such a conception of history.

Marx was not alone in his awareness of how human alienation occurs in a social framework. The nineteenth-century sociologist, Emile Durkheim (1858–1917), in a classic study of types of suicide, showed how one kind of suicide reflects a sense of the ultimate senselessness of things in a social order whose stable values are threatened. Other nineteenth-century thinkers and writers, including among others Soren Kierkegaard, Friedrich Nietzsche, and Fyodor Dostoyevski, examined in great detail the manifold ways in which a person's self-identity can be threatened and even destroyed. What was unique in Marx's analysis was the linking of alienation to the economic order. Marx argued that in a capitalist order the worker has no basic human status. He becomes a *thing*—a piece of property. In accepting this situation, the worker also adopts the ideology which has put him into his miserable position in the first place. He is thus emasculated, unable to revolt against the sustaining conditions which create his unhappy plight. Throughout Marx's earlier writings runs a deep moral sense of the injustice of this state of affairs. Real individual men and women are suffering—not mere abstractions. Revolution is advocated as a means to make possible conditions of full genuine individuality. About this moral protest in Marx, Professor Tucker claims that "If by moralist we mean simply a person whose thought moves in the orbit of prime concern with values of good and evil, a person whose thought-process is decisively governed by a basic value judgment, then Marx is unquestionably a moralist." [8]

[8] Robert Tucker, *op. cit.*, p. 15.

Marx's concern for the individual self as a reflection of pervasive economic and social practices suggests a viewpoint not incompatible with aspects of contemporary existentialist analyses. To understand the *living* individual, the vibrantly individual man or woman, a person must "see" that individual in a concrete situation. It is to Marx's credit that, in his early writings, he illuminated some of the existential effects on men's daily lives of economic and social conditions operating as causes. The difficulty faced by Marxian scholars concerns how, consistently, if at all, to make the early manuscripts conform to the deterministic view of the historical process which he developed later —an attempt which, as Professor Popper has been shown to claim (Chapter 12, "Historicism") is doomed to failure since historicism, in his view, leads to a complete "futuristic" ethic of success in Marx's later position. In any event, it is well to keep in mind that Marx, the man, hated subservience of any kind and felt with passion the injustice of workers crushed beneath the weight of unjustifiable economic practices.

Even the *Manifesto of the Communist Party,* first written in 1848 and aimed at stirring men to action, contains numerous sections in which man's existential alienation under a capitalist order is emphasized. Among them, two examples should at least indicate why contemporary scholars, influenced by existentialist views, have returned to the early manuscripts. Marx and Engels wrote in the *Manifesto:*

> Owing to the extensive use of machinery and to division of labor, the work of the proletarian has lost all individual character and, consequently, all charm for the workman. He becomes an appendage of the machine, and it is only the simplest, most monotonous, and most easily acquired knack that is required of him. Hence the cost of production of a workman is restricted, almost entirely, to the means of subsistence that he requires for his maintenance and for the propagation of his race. But the price of a commodity, and therefore also of labor, is equal to its cost of production. In proportion, therefore, as the repulsiveness of the work increases, the wage decreases. Nay, more, in proportion as the use of machinery and division of labor increases, in the same proportion the burden of toil also increases, whether by prolongation of the working hours,

by increase of the work exacted in a given time, or by increased speed of the machinery, etc.[9]

And, again:

> The bourgeoisie, wherever it has got the upper hand, has put an end to all feudal, patriarchal, idyllic relations. It has pitilessly torn asunder the motley feudal ties that bound man to his "natural superiors," and has left remaining no other nexus between man and man than naked self-interest, than callous "cash payment." It has drowned the most heavenly ecstasies of religious fervor, of chivalrous enthusiasm, of Philistine sentimentalism in the icy water of egotistical calculation. It has resolved personal worth into exchange value and, in place of the numberless indefeasible chartered freedoms, has set up that single, unconscionable freedom—free trade. In one word, for exploitation, veiled by religious and political illusions, it has substituted naked, shameless, direct, brutal exploitation.[10]

Tillich on Human Anxiety

Among the thinkers who have laid bare the structures of human anxiety the contemporary Protestant theologian Paul Tillich holds an influential position. His thought will be considered as one sample of how an existentialist analysis of man's plight may take form. Of course, many other thinkers loosely termed existentialists—living persons like Jean-Paul Sartre, Martin Heidegger, Gabriel Marcel, John Wild, to name a few—write on aspects of anxiety, sometimes disagreeing in their conclusions. An existentialist like Sartre is an outright atheist, claiming that Nietzsche's assertion: "God is dead!" must function as the leading assumption in any practicable analysis of the human value problem in our times. Yet, other existentialists—like the Catholic Marcel and the Protestant Tillich—are convinced believers in God. Thus, it would appear doubtful that either religious faith or its absence is a necessary aspect of one's right to claim he is an existentialist. These thinkers rather share (a) a concern to understand man's concrete situation—his human condition; (b) concern to map the

---

[9] Samuel H. Beer, ed., *The Communist Manifesto* (New York: Appleton-Century-Crofts, 1955), pp. 16–17.

[10] *Ibid.*, p. 12.

range of human anxiety and, perhaps, to address remarks to it; and (c) a tendency to concentrate on value problems as central to the modern man's predicament. All existentialist philosophers tend to reject science (at least the physicist's model of science) as the basis for adequate philosophizing. The reason for the latter, according to Professor John Wild, is that theoretical science has become increasingly remote from the "lived" problems of men. Wild argues that Plato's famous myth of the cave (in which ignorant man, confined to experience of shadows in the cave, must escape to "see" the light—wisdom—of the sun outside the cave) actually falsifies man's position. Wild writes as follows in *Human Freedom and Social Order:*

> The world that is everywhere there in the first place is not the underground cavern but the vast upper region where men work and struggle out of doors in the light of the sun. It is here that human life and history begins. Rational thinkers and scientists are a special group of men. In this respect Plato was right. But they do not climb up. They descend into a gloomy, cavernous region of their own, more adapted to the weakness of their eyes. Here they build a fire which they can look at directly, and simulate the conditions of the upper world. Taking various things down into their Cave, they examine them one by one, paying no attention to their color and subsistence and making no use of them at all. As scientists they simply regard the shadows cast on the wall, and how different successions of shadows correspond to different manipulations of things. Strangely enough, this objective information, which started as a mere game, turns out to be very useful in the upper world where luminous things, put together in various ways, continue to produce the luminous results that can be predicted from watching the order of shadows.[11]

Thus, in Professor Wild's view, the *Lebenswelt* ("lived world") of concrete experience rather than the subterranean world of the scientist's investigation—often far removed from a common sense "picture" of reality—makes up the subject which philosophers need to illumine by their reflections and analyses.

Karl Jaspers, a major German thinker who survived the Nazi regime and the war, emphasizes contemporary men's awareness that the

[11] John Wild, *Human Freedom and Social Order.* (Durham: Duke University Press, 1959), pp. 63–64. Used by permission of the publisher.

situation they share is an unfinished one—a world in which many dangers exist. A systematic, intellectually compelling "finished" philosophy can achieve no permanent success in this world, for as Jaspers wrote as early as 1930:

> The situation of philosophy is to-day characterized by three indefinite realities. First of all, the epoch has produced a vast number of persons devoid of all faith and receiving their stamp exclusively from the apparatus. Secondly, religion, though represented admirably enough by ecclesiastical organizations, would seem to have lost the power of creative expression in conformity with an actual present. In the third place philosophy has, during a whole century, become, it would appear, more and more a mere enterprize of doctrine and history, thus increasingly renouncing its true function.[12]

Because Jaspers thinks the philosopher's perennial task is to confront man with the diversity and concreteness of human experiences, rather than to offer finished systems, he joins others in support of what is called "existence-philosophy."

Thus, whether religious or irreligious in orientation, many existentialist thinkers seek to lay bare the structure of men's anxieties in a seriously disoriented world. Their view is that a portion of men's social and political dilemmas result from their lack of self-knowledge —from a need to discern a set of permanent values without which our contemporary world may experience a disaster which will be final and total.

Paul Tillich, who came to the United States from Germany because of opposition to Hitler, has contributed to this existentialist analysis of the human condition in a significant manner. Of course, Tillich's theological interests are rooted in his conviction that a renewed "understanding" of Christianity can "solve" man's estrangement from the world and from himself—a conviction which many other thinkers do not share. Nonetheless, Tillich's way of expressing some fundamental features of the human plight has attracted widespread attention even from thinkers who reject his religious "solution."

Tillich insists on a distinction between pathological (neurotic) and

---

[12] Karl Jaspers, *Man in the Modern Age,* trans. Eden and Cedar Paul (London: Routledge, 1951), p. 139.

ontological (universal) anxiety. Neurotic anxiety can vary from culture to culture and is subject to healing, since it is a manifestation of a sensitive but "sick" individual's restricted response to objective (existential) kinds of anxiety. Ontological anxiety is, in contrast, inescapable and objective—although the healthy man in his relations with the threatening aspects of existence "usually is not aware of nonbeing and anxiety in the depth of his personality"—though these are *there,* yet not usually consciously so. Even a healthy man's adjustment ("self-affirmation" in Tillich's terminology) can collapse in crisis situations of widespread consequences, when new objects of fear and a deteriorating pattern of values confront man, radically and shockingly, with the threat of nonbeing to which he makes a wrong response. In periods of vast cultural change, marked by pervasive insecurity in many walks of life, mass movements develop causing previously healthy individuals to become practically concerned to protect the *status quo.* Thus, even the healthy individuals of a society are potential subjects of neurotic behavior when a whole social order—or "way of life"—undergoes rapid and extensive changes. So aware is Tillich of the ways in which men's responses to anxiety may become neurotic that he can ask at one point, though he is himself an existentialist in the treatment of the human condition, "To what degree are present-day Existentialist descriptions of man's predicament caused by neurotic anxiety?"

Ontological anxiety is basic to man's condition, according to Tillich. As such, it is natural and not neurotic, a permanent feature of human existence in any time and place—a feature which can be recognized and lived with but never finally overcome. It requires a special kind of courage—a courage which cannot ease the threat of nonbeing but which can, nonetheless, allow a man to function "in spite of" nonbeing. This kind of anxiety Tillich calls "existential." He finds that such existential anxiety can be analyzed by philosophers, claiming that this analysis presupposes that no purely curative or scientific psychotherapy can produce the analysis. As a "state in which a being is aware of nonbeing," existential anxiety is as much an inescapable aspect of the psychologist's life as it is of that of his clients. Men everywhere are marked by anxieties of death, condemnation, and meaninglessness. Specific historical periods have accentuated one or another of these three types of anxiety, yet the three are intermingled and never mutually exclusive. Tillich believes the ending of the civilization of the ancient world tended to make anxiety of death predominant, while the collapse of medieval culture produced an emphasis on the anxiety of condemnation—as evidenced in the struggles of the Protestant era. Our contemporary world, secularized and industrialized, contains conditions which accentuate the anxiety of meaninglessness —a spiritual loss of direction and meaning which touches the arts as well as politics. Meaninglessness is the primary mode in which contemporary men become aware of the perennially available threat of nonbeing—a threat which is fundamental in each of the three types of existential as opposed to neurotic anxiety.

Professor Tillich gives a succinct summarization of his analysis of human anxiety in *The Courage to Be,* an influential book in which his existentialist approach to an understanding of the human condition is presented in somewhat popular terms:

The analyses of pathological in relation to existential anxiety have brought out the following principles: 1. Existential anxiety has an ontological character and cannot be removed but must be taken into the courage to be. 2. Pathological anxiety is the consequence of the failure of the self to take the anxiety upon itself. 3. Pathological anxiety leads to self-affirmation on a limited, fixed, and unrealistic basis and to a compulsory defense of the basis. 4. Pathological anxiety, in relation to the anxiety of fate and death, produces an unrealistic security; in relation to the anxiety of guilt and condemnation, an unrealistic perfection; in relation to the anxiety of doubt and meaninglessness, an unrealistic certitude. 5. Pathological anxiety, once established, is an object of medical healing. Existential anxiety is an object of priestly help. Neither the medical nor the priestly function is bound to its vocational representatives: the minister may be a healer and the psychotherapist a priest, and each human being may be both in relation to the "neighbor." But the functions should not be confused and the representatives should not try to replace each other. The goal of both of them is helping men to reach full self-affirmation, to attain the courage to be.[13]

[13] Paul Tillich, *The Courage to Be* (New Haven: Yale University Press, 1952). Used by permission of the publisher. [Reprinted from the paperbound edition (1961), pp. 77–78.]

Existentialism's Political Uses

The implication for politics stemming from Tillich's analysis is that some types of anxiety are beyond the reach of strictly social and political treatment. If men seek to overcome these anxieties by reform in the social order, reforms which may be quite justifiable for other reasons, they will inevitably fail since existential anxiety must appear in any historical or cultural setting as the barometer of the "human weather." Yet, Tillich's analysis possesses a clear significance for contemporary thought about politics. The reason is that men, in ignorance of an enduring feature of the human condition, can contribute to political disaster by putting their trust in organization and ideology for the wrong reasons. They can attempt to "cure" a situation by inadequate means, becoming fanatical whenever, as eventually it must, such misdirected effort fails to produce the hoped for results. As George Santayana once remarked, the fanatic is a person who redoubles his effort when he has lost his aim. Probably a connection exists between the harsher forms of totalitarianism, so prevalent in this century, and the kind of misdirected effort referred to by Tillich. Social and political reforms are desirable if they are sought for the right reasons and with proper prudential regard to the circumstances in which men find themselves living. The attempt to create and perpetuate stable forms of social life is always an important quest central to the practical aspirations of each generation. Nonetheless, men often tend too radically to divide the "ends" sought from the "means" employed, trying to convince themselves that the intrinsic value of their goals justifies almost any action undertaken to achieve them. Often they turn to the "ideas" of nationality, economic class, party, race, seeking to drown out the deeper "voices" of frustration and despair. They even forget their original gods, respectively responding to their existential anxieties by yet greater emphasis on conformity and coercive treatment of their contemporaries. No matter how loud the cries of distress or how extensive the cemeteries in which they bury their enemies, they act as if directed by a "good conscience," when insistence on certainty is, itself, a manifestation of a "sick" situation in which man's existential freedom is denied.

Since the actions of political leaders require at least the acquiescence of large numbers of citizens, the responsibility for political crimes rests partly even with those "good" persons who, living obediently by the rules, refuse to speak out against abuses of authority. These "good" citizens often fail to take risks against existing abuses, though it is true they seldom instigate the more vicious actions which mark what Toynbee calls a "Time of Troubles." They sit on the sidelines, as it were—spectators but not participants, ready when social or political chaos threatens to say, amorally, "We didn't do it! We didn't want it to end this way!" Yet their very indifference to the "signs of the times" always constituted an item in the more calculated planning of those who harbor authoritarian aims. Tillich's analysis of human anxiety points to a possible kind of self-knowledge which, if it cannot guarantee a clear-cut guideline to economic, social, and political decisions, can at least bring men to an awareness of the pitfalls to be resisted and avoided.

Karl Jaspers has also helped to accentuate the tendencies toward dehumanization prevalent in an age of advanced technology and mass movements, standing as a giant among numerous thoughtful men concerned to mark certain contemporary pathways with danger signs. Many human values appear threatened and dying in a universe which appears devoid of purpose. Technical civilization and scientific "objectivism" produce demands for unity and conformity, and men feel themselves swallowed by the structures surrounding them. "The new world which has arisen as an apparatus for the supply of the necessaries of life compels everything and everyone to serve it," Jaspers has written in *Man in the Modern Age*. "It annihilates whatever it has no place for. Man seems to be undergoing absorption into that which is nothing more than a means to an end, into that which is devoid of purpose or significance. But therein he can find no satisfaction." [14] The very devices sought by modern men to extend control over nature, once hopefully viewed as a means to a new paradise on

[14] Karl Jaspers, *op. cit.,* pp. 79–80.

earth, can threaten man's very selfhood so that, waking of a sudden in fear and trembling, he wonders if instead of paradise he may not end as an inmate in a worldwide prison house. Existentialist writers diagnose a cultural situation in which men's responses to crises may add to the crises rather than resolve them.

The French atheistic existentialist Jean-Paul Sartre has emphasized man's inescapable individuality by presenting a radical view of human freedom. Sartre insists that man is a freedom—that to be a man *is* to be free. This is an unusual conception of freedom, since most men believe freedom is a function of circumstances and capacities. Sartre's view is reminiscent of some earlier theological views which "see" God as possessing unlimited possibilities and powers. According to Sartre, man is free to make of himself whatever he wills. Man creates his own values by deciding on his own "projects" and commitments. Yet, ultimately, man is forlorn and abandoned, a freedom in a universe lacking God or universally objective standards. Sartre "feels" the anguish of this situation but fails to relate his notion of freedom to the practical demands of ethics and politics, except to argue that men are responsible for *all* their decisions and the consequences resulting from them. No matter what these consequences may be, men cannot give up their freedom—since freedom for Sartre is not a property of some acts as opposed to others but the very definition of what it is to be a man. Thus, if Sartre is to be consistent, man is a freedom whether he lives in a relaxed and tolerant society or finds himself in prison or standing on a scaffold about to be hanged.

Comparing two extremes of modern philosophical thinkers, one of which seeks to understand human action in purely behavioral (bodily and environmental) terms, Professor A. C. MacIntyre writes:

> At the other extreme, there are those who admire the Cartesian autonomy of mind* so much that they reject any suggestion of

* *Author's note:* Rene Descartes, a seventeenth-century French philosopher sometimes called the father of modern philosophy, asserted the existence of a radical dualism between mind (mental phenomena) and matter (physical phenomena). Thus, he bequeathed to modern thinkers impressed by his views the problem of how one or another of these kinds of phenomena can affect the other. One result is the attempt by later thinkers to explain mental phenomena either exclusively in physical terms alone (behaviorism, materialism) or in mental terms alone (mentalism, idealism) or some form of interactionism.

dependence upon or interrelation with the physical at all. Such are the French existentialists of the present day, Sartre and his disciples. For Sartre all important human behaviour is the fruit of human decision. You are what you are because of what you have decided. This is asserted not just of actions but also of attitudes and emotions. Your sadness is the result of your choosing to be sad. There are no antecedent conditions which determine human behaviour.[15]

Another analyst of Sartre's philosophical position has brought out his radical view of freedom in the following succinct way:

> The real tragedy of Sartrean man is a theistic one. His alliance with both being and the nihilating power of consciousness drives him toward transcendence, so that the most radical passion of his life is to be a God who does not and cannot exist. This is the very essence of the human structure: "Man fundamentally *is* the desire to be God." The touchstone of sincerity is our readiness to face up to this truth and to abide by its moral consequence, which is that man must create his own values without any sanction from an already existing divine standard.[16]

Can so radical and nonpolitical a view of freedom help in the least to clarify the social and political plight of contemporary men? The answer depends on how one "sees" that political plight in the specific historical period in which men are seeking to avert nuclear war and to direct the growing urbanization and industrialization of the world's different cultures. If a person "sees" a problem in the numerous threats to human individuality rather than in the question how to further the organization of resources and human actions, then he may value Sartre's conception of freedom for its emphasis on an aspect of man's existence which can never fully be subjected to organization and control. Sartre's philosophy can, in this way, function as a dramatic reminder of men's need to express their essential freedom by action. Yet, insofar as Sartre defines man as a freedom, it appears that man-as-a-freedom can exist in any social or political situation—thus, that man is a freedom in living in slavery, in a mental institution, in war, in peace, in agony or bliss, etc. A necessary relation between

[15] A. C. MacIntyre, *The Unconscious: A Conceptual Study* (London: Routledge, 1958), p. 51.
[16] James Collins, *God in Modern Philosophy* (London: Routledge, 1960), p. 371.

this sense of freedom and human action seems lacking. Aware of this fact, a sympathetic student of Sartre's philosophy, the English writer Iris Murdoch, in her book *Sartre: Romantic Rationalist,* argues that Sartre actually employs at least three different meanings when, in different contexts, he writes about "freedom." The original sense of "freedom," presented in Sartre's *Being and Nothingness* (a huge work), sees it "as if it were a sort of *scar* in the wholeness of the consciousness; a sort of fault in the universe." This sort of "freedom" is a spontaneity which characterizes each and every man. "Freedom" in a second sense is like "a sort of spiritual discipline; it is a *purging* of the emotions, a setting aside of *selfish* considerations, a respect for the autonomy of another's (the author's) creative power, which leads on to a respect for the autonomy of all other men (the 'taking of mankind as an absolute end')." Sartre's book *What Is Literature*—in which the author "sees" a writer as "committed" and not as disinterested—exemplifies this notion of "freedom." But there is also a third sense of "freedom" in Sartre's prolific writings, characterized by Miss Murdoch in the following manner:

> This freedom is an ideal state of society, the willing of which imposes practical commands of an anti-totalitarian nature upon its adherents. In this sense . . . the word readily picks up the flavour of that vague but powerful *liberte* in the name of which we fought fascism. It becomes a weapon to use against the soul-destroying ossifications of both capitalism and communism.[17]

Some Criticisms of Sartre's Existentialism

The popularity of the writings of men like Jaspers, Sartre, Heidegger and other existentialist thinkers is a fact of our contemporary world. These writers worry about the growing sense of directionlessness and estrangement which afflicts persons trying to "save" ancient values in a restless social universe of change. Obviously, their readers are hungry to understand "what the situation is" in which they must live out their lives, often without the clear and absolute guideposts known to men in earlier ages. Nonetheless, these writers also stimulate other

[17] Iris Murdoch, *Sartre: Romantic Rationalist* (New Haven: Yale University Press, 1959), p. 68. Used by permission of the publisher.

thinkers to the task of criticism, some of whom are suspicious of the *philosophical* arguments of existentialists. Some critics object to the unscientific bent of much existentialist philosophizing, others to its individualism and subjectivism, yet others to what they consider its carelessness with language. There are also sympathetic persons who, though willing to admit that existentialist writers hope to diagnose aspects of the contemporary human plight, are convinced that existentialism offers no positive "solutions" to the predicaments thus diagnosed. Only a few of these criticisms can be stated here, as samples rather than as definitive of the wide range of criticism. These will be done imaginatively, as if individuals were in the presence of Sartre or another existentialist and given an opportunity, though brief, to tell what troubles them.

Imagine, in the following statements, that a living philosopher is addressing his remarks to Sartre (or to some other existentialist thinker) in an informal setting. The content of the critics' remarks should indicate which ones are sympathetic, which ones hostile. These criticisms concern ideas held by men in differing philosophical "schools," yet are representative of important objections to one or another of the features of existentialist thinking.

The first critic represents those thinkers who, though aware of the diversity of cultures, believes all men share some basic traits and needs, and thus may be said to possess an underlying basic human nature (a fact questioned by Jean-Paul Sartre). Our critic, in this instance, shall be named Aristotelian Naturalist with the understanding that philosophers other than naturalists and Aristotelians might agree with some of the critic's comments.

> *Aristotelian Naturalist:* You maintain, Jean-Paul Sartre, there is no basic human nature. Yet you insist that all men share a basic human condition—one of despair, abandonment, anguish. Thus, they do possess something in common—a condition. Your position is a peculiar one. Even if, as you argue, there is no God— even that man is not the product of a planning creator—men may still have evolved as a specific species marked by common biological and physical characteristics which determine the needs they must meet in any number of differing cultures. They cannot "choose," as it were, to jump out of their very skins. Similarly, if

they are to make choices, they can seek to do so in the light of intelligent estimates of the consequences. Certainly men do not literally create themselves. Therefore, when you argue that men make themselves, I assume you mean that men are responsible for the kinds of values which exist or fail to exist. Intelligent men make decisions on the basis of their pressing wants and the nature of existing environments. Men's biological characteristics influence their *potentialities,* and in this sense, essence may be said to precede existence, contrary to your view of the matter. In your desire to emphasize men's need to assume responsibility for his decisions, you fail to give sufficient attention to regularities in biology and in aspects of man's physical universe. I would feel more satisfied with your brand of "existentialism" if it recognized that some classical writers who argued there's a basic human nature meant, in part, that men everywhere have some common biological characteristics. Frankly, I am at a loss to understand how men lacking any common nature can meaningfully be said to share a common condition, unless you want to say that dogs, cats, stones and women *also* share that same condition, though they obviously aren't men. Your conception of the enduring features of the natural processes in and around men is inadequate and unrealistic.

For a second criticism, let us turn to an imagined representative of those persons who think that human freedom is a capacity to act deliberately to achieve specific goals—a function of certain capacities exercised in specific environments, partly in terms of available human knowledge. Not the mere fact of decision but, rather, the *kind* of decision a man makes will be fundamental to this notion of freedom. Our second critic shall be named Pragmatist (after the philosophy which "sees" ideas as guides to action), although others—including Marxists—might also say some of the things that follow.

> *Pragmatist:* Existentialists moan and groan about human anxiety but say very little about how to act to improve the human condition. Of course, death is inevitable—men knew that long before existentialism came on the scene. Does the inevitability of death mean that philosophers should spend much of their time playing recital "organ music" to that fact? Life demands action, yes—but intelligent action differs from caprice or whim. Some existentialist analyses of freedom appear too exclusively to stress the need of men to make decisions as individuals. They disregard the rational aspect of deciding in the light of possible alternatives, and the best

available knowledge of circumstances and goals. Freedom is a capacity to choose influenced by existing conditions. A useful social philosophy should make men aware of how to relate their decisions to the existing regularities in the social and political environment. Existentialist thinkers fail to understand the *social* setting of human action, thus their individualistic position tends toward romanticism.

The third set of critics shall be named Linguist A and Linguist B, representing those contemporary philosophers who think that many philosophical writings are troublesome and often incomprehensible because philosophers abuse language in one way or another. Linguist A shall represent a critic who has some favorable views of aspects of existentialist thought, while Linguist B shall speak for more hard-headed critics from this side of the philosophical track. Language-oriented philosophers often view philosophy as being exclusively concerned with criticism. They are often suspicious of the speculations of philosophical system-builders and wary of those who philosophize from a personal vision of the "hang" of things.

> *Linguist A:* You existentialist philosophers say some important things about human values, but you also "get away with murder" in the way you lightly toss around terms like "being-in-itself" and "being-for-self" and the like. In your more technical writings I think you are much less clear about what you're doing than your admirers give you credit for. I suspect your writings appeal to persons who, having lost a more orthodox religious faith, are at loose ends in the contemporary world. But you are often deep-dyed metaphysicians even though most of you claim to be suspicious of this questionable old enterprise. For example, you, Sartre, make what sound to be psychological observations which sometimes turn out to be more like metaphysical and theological assertions—as such perhaps lacking any cognitive meaning, being neither true nor false. I shall give one illustration. In *Existentialism as a Humanism* (Sartre) the following peculiar argument occurs—and it is not an atypical one. "The existentialist frankly states that man is in anguish. His meaning is as follows: When a man commits himself to anything, fully realizing that he is not only choosing what he will be, but is thereby at the same time a legislator deciding for the whole of mankind—in such a moment a man cannot escape from the sense of complete and profound responsibility. There are many,

indeed, who show no such anxiety. But we affirm that they are merely disguising their anguish or are in flight from it." Now, this is either sheer nonsense or simply expressive writing. "Anguish" is a psychological word, such that—in normal circumstances—we could say that Harry's in anguish but Sam is not. Yet, Sartre, you are saying "All men are in anguish," which sounds more like "All men are sinners" than like "Harry has a headache" or "All men sometimes bare a few aches and pains." The statement applies as much to a man happily playing with his children as to a depressed person seriously contemplating suicide. There is thus no way in which either to verify or to falsify the assertion. Similarly, the assertion "God does not exist" cannot be meaningful unless the statement "God exists" is also meaningful, since the meaningfulness of a statement doesn't depend on its truthfulness. Other existentialists also make such hard-to-comprehend metaphysical assertions while often claiming to be opponents of metaphysics. We really can't know what "All men are in anguish" means, since it may be made to mean anything a writer says it does. This is a poor model for philosophizing.

Linguist B: My philosophical friend has been too easy on you existentialists! You are really charlatans in the philosophical world. You are vague, confused, fond of obfuscation and dramatic posing, so far as I can see. As writers of novels and drama you do very well, but the novel and the drama aren't substitutes for genuine philosophizing—whose real task is to achieve clarity and to help weed out some of the nonsense which all of us are too prone to speak. You like to emote in public! Your expressions possess only emotive significance—and say nothing universally true of all men. You would replace thinking and careful analysis by feelings. Now, feelings are important—but, as I said earlier, they can't solve our philosophical problems for us. Existentialism is a philosophical blind alley, incapable of bringing light to the genuine philosophical confusions into which even the man in the street is only too prone to fall because language is what it is. If you would get over your vain efforts to appear profound, you might try to show us the sense in which you use words like "freedom," "responsibility," "being," "abandonment" and the like. A generation which reads your philosophical works may end up incapable of a clear statement of a problem and careful consideration of it. Really, I'm very much against your emotional pontificating and vain soul-searching. What the world needs is rather clarity, clarity, clarity!

In spite of criticisms like these, existentialist writers continue to produce their analyses of human anxiety, finding a widespread acceptance by the reading publics of the world. Their concern to change men from passive spectators into active participants in the affairs of cultural and political life; their dogmatic insistence on each person's responsibility for his or her choices; and their search after a *personal* vision of the lived world, in an industrial age which seems ever increasingly to specialize human functions, have aided many in their efforts at self-understanding. Existentialism may be an unsound philosophy, as some of its severer critics maintain. Nonetheless, it appears as a powerful movement which will stimulate discussion and argument for the next decade. Among professional philosophers, it has gained wider attention in continental Europe than in England and America, but there are signs that even in the latter countries a growing interest is afoot. Of the contemporary modes of philosophizing, it appears to have had singular success in getting a hearing among nonprofessional thinkers, partly because of the broad human themes treated, partly as a result of its expressions in poetry, drama, and the novel. Existentialist philosophers write books with titles like *Being and Nothingness* (Sartre), *Being and Time* (Heidegger), *The Mystery of Being* (Marcel), and *The Perennial Scope of Philosophy* (Jaspers); while contemporary professional philosophers in England and America produce titles like *Logic and Language* (Flew), *The Vocabulary of Politics* (Weldon), *The Language of Morals* (Hare), *Word and Object* (Quine), *How to Do Things with Words* (Austin) —indicating something like a fundamental cleavage in philosophical subject matter and orientation. This gulf between two different philosophical approaches raises the question whether a dialogue, if not a synthesis between the approaches, might not be timely.

Conclusion

The current popularity of existentialist treatments of the nature of man and human anxiety is sufficient justification of the present chapter. Existentialists have rebelled against philosophical abstractions. They insist that the aim of human inquiry is to understand the *con-*

crete man in the specific circumstances in which he happens to find himself. Their aim is to describe as fully as they can the whole range of human emotions and action which occurs in the "lived world." There can be little doubt that existentialist writers, however romantic some of their themes, have sought to fasten sympathetic attention on the individual's plight in our century.

Yet, a serious question remains. Does existentialism as a philosophy *necessarily* say anything specific about pressing social and political issues? Is the individualism of a Jean-Paul Sartre compatible with the demands for cooperative social effort? If not directly, can existentialist analysis of the human predicament suggest ways in which to meet some of the national and international difficulties which are objectively there? This chapter has attempted to indicate how analyses of anxiety may indirectly have relevance to politics—especially to the contemporary threats of social conformity and even totalitarianism in its most barbarous forms. Existentialists "see" the modern predicament as involving the salvation of man's human individuality. The existentialist writers, however they differ in their technical positions, share a passionate regard for what it is that makes each man unique, a responsible person in his own right, in a mass age in which individuality is threatened on many fronts.

Even if the existentialists should be guilty, as sometimes charged, of lack of clarity and too great a stress on mood rather than on detailed analysis, they have managed to write about basic and enduring human problems. That is one reason why they are so widely read. In this sense, at the very minimum, they have earned a place in the forefront of contemporary thought. Even critics who suggest they are wrongheaded philosophically usually admit that the existentialists are right about matters of the heart. And as Blaise Pascal once pointed out, matters of the heart often count for more than matters of the head. A bothersome question remains: Do matters of the heart count for that much even in philosophy?

Some Questions and Problems

1. Can you think of ways in which a concern about types of human anxiety may be said to bear directly on political issues and movements?

2. On the basis of the preceding chapter, do you think existentialism, as a philosophy, offers any constructive program for the resolution of actual social or political problems and crises? If not, can you derive such a program from existentialist views?

3. If, as J-P. Sartre maintains, no basic human nature exists, does it make any sense to worry about a philosophical treatment of political affairs?

4. Discuss the following topic: *Resolved,* That existentialism helps individuals to face their personal problems but is inapplicable to the difficulties with which active politicians must deal.

5. Does belief in God play any fundamental role in the political life of nations? If so, in what ways? If not, should it?

6. Discuss the ways, if any, in which the notion of social alienation may help to reveal problems with which politicians and citizens must learn more adequately to concern themselves.

7. How far do you think that human happiness and welfare can be legislated? Are there any limits?

8. Can you think of any ways in which totalitarian movements may be viewed as responses to contemporary men's anxieties? Can you supply some historical examples?

9. To what extent do economic dislocations in a modern society tend to produce some of the conditions which influence men and women to give up the search for rational solutions to problems?

10. Does philosophical talk about politics have much chance of influencing what realists like to call "political reality"?

Some Suggested Readings

Blackham, H. J. *Six Existentialist Thinkers.* London: Routledge, 1952.

Copleston, F., S.J. *Contemporary Philosophy.* London: Burns, 1956.

Desan, W. *The Tragic Finale: An Essay on the Philosophy of Jean-Paul Sartre.* Cambridge: Harvard University Press, 1954.

Greene, N. N., *Jean-Paul Sartre: The Existentialist Ethic.* Ann Arbor: Michigan University Press, 1960.

Jaspers, K. *Man in the Modern Age,* trans. Eden and Cedar Paul. London: Routledge, 1933.

Kaufmann, W. (ed.) *Existentialism from Dostoevsky to Sartre.* New York: Meridian, 1956.

Marcel, G. *Man Against Mass Society,* trans. G. S. Fraser. Chicago: Regnery, 1962.

————. *The Existential Background of Human Dignity.* Cambridge: Harvard University Press, 1963.

Molina, F. *Existentialism as Philosophy.* Englewood Cliffs, N.J.: Prentice-Hall, 1962.

Murdoch, I. *Sartre: Romantic Rationalist.* New Haven: Yale University Press, 1959.

Olson, R. G. *An Introduction to Existentialism.* New York: Dover, 1962.

Sartre, J.-P. *What Is Literature?,* trans. B. Frechtman. New York: Philosophical Library, 1949.

————. *Being and Nothingness,* trans. H. E. Barnes. London: Methuen, 1957.

Stern, A. *Sartre: His Philosophy and Psychoanalysis.* Indianapolis: Liberal Arts, 1953.

Tillich, P. *The Courage to Be.* New Haven: Yale University Press, 1961.

Tucker, R. *Philosophy and Myth in Karl Marx.* London: Cambridge University Press, 1961.

Warnoch, M. "Existentialism: J.-P. Sartre" in *Ethics Since 1900.* London: Oxford University Press, 1960.

White, M. G. *Toward Reunion in Philosophy.* Cambridge: Harvard University Press, 1956.

Index of Names

Index of Topics

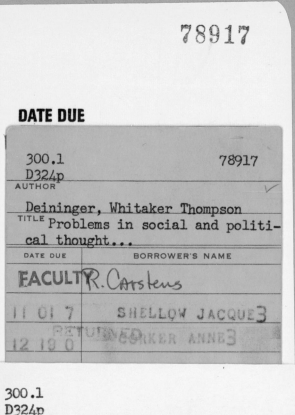